Strategic Media Decisions

by Marian Azzaro

with Dan Binder, Robb Clawson, Carla Lloyd,
Mary Alice Shaver, and Olaf Werder

First Edition • ©2004
ISBN# 1-887229-17-5

The Copy Workshop
2144 N. Hudson • Chicago, IL 60614
(773) 871-1179 FX: (773) 281-4643
www.adbuzz.com or thecopyworkshop@aol.com

To Dan and Adam

Introduction

YOU'VE GROWN UP WITH MEDIA. From your first favorite TV show and video, to the first music you liked on the radio, to reading your first comic strip; media has been in your life for as long as you can remember.

You know media as a consumer, but now we're going to take a look behind the screen – we'll look at the world of media from another perspective – a business perspective. Because most of the media you are familiar with is also part of another business – advertising.

This book is going to teach you about media in a whole new way.

What is Media?

Media is the business side of the advertising business – the business end of the stick, so to speak.

People say the advertising business is big, and they're right. Total 2003 advertising spending in the United States was almost $249 billion. In the U.S., the advertising business largely supports the media. Advertising support makes our favorite television programs, radio stations, magazines, and newspapers a real bargain.

Even though media is widely considered "part" of the ad business, it's also much bigger than just advertising.

In fact, it's a lot of businesses.

Media Means Business.
Media is the business side of the advertising business.

Media is Big Business.
It includes over $249 billion in ad revenue.

Media is a lot of businesses.

Media is the business of delivering content to an audience. Interesting content is what attracts audiences to the media.

These audiences then attract advertisers who want their ads to be part of that content. Advertisers spend money to buy access through media channels to communicate with consumers in the audience who might buy products.

And those ads help pay for the media you enjoy. Sometimes the ads pay for part of it, as with newspapers and magazines, and sometimes for all of it, like most TV and radio.

Media is a Delivery System.

Media serves as the conduit for a marketer's message; it's the delivery system. And effective delivery takes planning.

One key part of media is the business of strategic planning for the allocation of a client's advertising budget. In this sense, strategic media planning is the art of determining the optimum channel connecting a client with a specific target audience.

That client may be local, national or multi-national.

The strategic planning may be at an agency working on a client's business or at the client managing the agency-client interface. The media job could be almost anywhere because media jobs are almost everywhere in the world of marketing.

For example, media is also the business of program development, station management, and editorial content.

See, lots of jobs. It's the art of creating and managing interesting content, and for each job there is an art to doing it well.

The media may be print, broadcast, cable or even wireless. You may not think about it this way yet, but your phone, your mail box, and even your email address are, in very important ways, part of the media business.

The part of the media business we'll be focusing on is the business of buying and selling time and space for the advertiser's message. Here, making sure that a marketer's message makes the most effective connection is a critical job. Media buyers purchase time and space to provide the advertiser access to the desired target audience.

Media about Media.
This popular general interest magazine gives people information about their choices in another medium – television.

Media representatives are sellers who represent the media; they set and negotiate the pricing of time and space in large part depending on the size of the audience the media might expect to deliver.

Media is a Lot of Jobs.

But, the jobs don't stop there. Media is also the business of measuring and tracking audiences as they interact with the media. Media jobs in this area in particular demand discipline and skill.

Media researchers devise extensive systems for measuring the audience delivery of all kinds of different media.

Media research analysts support all areas of media including planning, buying, sales, and program development by providing data that informs decision-making. The critical task for each of these jobs is making sure that advertisers realize the full value of the media.

Media is About Strategy.

Whatever your job in the world of media, you'll be involved in making strategic decisions.

It's the best strategy for a marketer, the best strategy for the medium itself, and the best strategy for you.

This incredible, big business of media is chock-full of choices. And, making choices means making decisions.

The more choices we face, the more decisions we must make. Thinking it through to make the best decisions, that's what strategy is all about.

Media is Strategic Decision-making.

From the more traditional practice of media planning to the cutting-edge world of interactive media, professionals in the fast-paced, fast-changing media world are faced with more and more choices every day.

As advertising legend David Ogilvy once said, *"Strategy is about choice."* And, now you know why the title of this book is *Strategic Media Decisions*.

What this book is about...

The purpose of this book is to introduce you to the business side of the media business and all the jobs it takes to make that business work.

So, as we introduce you to the role of strategy and decision-making, we'll also try to introduce you to some of the jobs in each important part of the media world.

We'll look at this world in 5 parts. Here's a sneak preview:

Part I: The World of Media

In these first two chapters we'll take a broad overview and look at the significant and expansive changes in the world of media – there's a lot going on.

Chapter One, The World of Media

We'll start with a brief history of media and progress to today's generation of media conglomerates and the mega-entertainment brands of media.

Chapter Two, The Media Age

Next, we'll talk about the exciting changes happening in the media world and about opportunities born of growth and expansion and rapidly advancing new technologies.

Part II: Media Methods

In this section of the book, you'll learn how media people think. We'll describe in detail the more traditional business of analysis, planning, and implementing media for a client. We'll take four chapters to do it.

Chapter Three, Media & the Marketing of Messages

Here, we'll introduce the key terms and processes you'll need to know.

Chapter Four, Creative Media Analysis

This covers the role of creativity in analyzing and understanding media research data. We'll also use this chapter to go into some specific applications of media analysis.

Our First Media Mogul.
Benjamin Franklin, often called "The First American," *made his mark in media. His newspaper,* Pennsylvania Gazette *had the biggest circulation in the Colonies. Franklin made it a dynamic force for Revolutionary change! Media makes history.*

Local Media.

Each and every market has its own unique media environment. Part Three will focus on that part of the media world.

Niche Media.

Media fills every nook and cranny of the marketplace. That's the focus of Part Four.

Chapter Five, Modern Media Planning

This chapter presents the basics of the traditional media planning process; setting objectives and strategies, setting budgets, and planning media.

Chapter Six, Buying and Selling Media

Next we'll cover the implementation of that media plan including the buying and selling of media time and space.

Part III: Local and "Niche" Media

Here we're going to move to a world that may be closer to home – local and "niche" media – almost a world in itself.

Even though the media in your market may be part of a national (or international) company, every local market is a separate media market.

Every "niche" is also a separate media market.

For example, you may have a hobby or special interest. That "niche" has its own media. So does every major field of business – even the media itself.

For this part of the book, we'll first take an overview, and then look at unique applications in market-by-market and niche-by-niche planning, buying and sales of media.

Chapter Seven, The Local Media Mix

This chapter presents the range of media in every local market of any size and offers a discussion of the strengths and weaknesses of each of the local media.

Chapter Eight, Local Media Planning

Next, we'll put it all together on a smaller, local business scale. You'll see how local businesses and local media companies work together to develop marketing programs that work.

Chapter Nine, "Niche" and Specialty Media Markets

This chapter covers another kind of "local market," one that may have very broad boundaries.

New and Interactive Media.
Media is evolving into exciting new forms and new opportunities. Find out about the technology that's driving these changes and how the new media marketplace works. It's all in Part Four.

It's All Media!
Find out how to put together cross-platform programs. Learn to see the whole world as a media opportunity. It's all in Part Five.

This market may be hardware store owners, or guitar players. It might be members of your church, people who share a common hobby, or people in the same business.

These markets have their own special media world.

Part IV: New and Interactive Media Planning

In Part 4 we're going to discuss some exciting changes in the media world – the many technological advances and the impact of each on present and future media applications.

Chapter Ten, Media's Changing World

First, we'll look at the driving force of technology and how it's changing the media world – and your world.

Chapter Eleven, New Media Technology

Next, we'll look at some specific new technology; the Internet, personal video recording devices (TiVo) and the new world of interactive media.

Chapter Twelve, Media in Cyberspace

This chapter presents the details of planning and executing technology-based media.

Part V: Media in IMC

What happens when you put together different forms of media and different forms of marketing communication?

It's a whole new set of strategic media decisions – and a new area of growth in the world of media – IMC, Integrated Marketing Communications.

This part of the book will introduce you to more exciting changes and we'll take a look at the future of media in an integrated marketing world.

Chapter Thirteen, Media Across IMC Elements

We'll take a brief look at the "other" media of integrated marketing communications; direct media, promotional media, and PR media. Also in this chapter, we'll consider some of the specialized practices of IMC, like sports marketing and CRM.

Chapter Fourteen, Multi-Media and Cross-Platform Integration

In this final chapter, we'll explore applications of integration theory in today's IMC media environment. We'll talk about the marketers and the media companies leading this developing field.

What's in it for Us,
What's in it for You?

We love media. Each author associated with this book has an important and long-standing connection to the world of media. For each of us, the media world has been a source of professional growth and personal satisfaction.

And, it has been an exciting source of jobs for our students and other young people like you.

We know it because we see it; media is a growth field in advertising and marketing.

More so than any other area of advertising, new jobs are available in media for young, motivated people.

So, one of our goals with this book will be to introduce you to career opportunities in the world of media.

Just as ads try to sell you on products, we'll try to sell you on jobs in media. (And, of course, you can't choose every job any more than you can buy every attractive product.)

Throughout this book we will identify a broad range of career opportunities – some are already standard career options in media and some are expected for the future.

Some People You Will Meet.
Lisa Weidman works for Thrasher Magazine, *and Ryan Kirvida is a media planner at Fallon*

Sales and Management.
Julie Lonergan is a senior sales rep for Time magazine, *and Jim Pastor is President and General Manager of ESPN's WMVP radio.*

Career Capsules.

Now you understand why throughout this book you'll find career capsule insets. Each profiles a key professional representing one of the many facets of the media world.

For example, you'll find profiles of the more traditional positions of media; a media planning professional, a media buyer, a media sales representative, a media researcher, and even a client-side media services manager.

You'll also find profiles on some out-there media jobs like cross-platform sponsorship sales and entertainment media planning.

These career capsules are written to inform your career decision-making. Each presents a description of a real job in a different part of the media world. Along with the job description you'll find a summary of the job responsibilities and a brief discussion of the traditional career development path for professionals in the area.

And, of course, we've tried to show each job in a good light.

So we won't dwell on the long hours, the tough meetings, the challenging decisions, and not-so-great starting salaries. You'll have to factor those things in for yourself as you learn more about each of the many media career choices out there.

When you've finished this book and you are thinking about your own career, remember what the great man said – strategy, after all, is about choice.

About the Authors:

AS WE SAID, "WE LOVE MEDIA!" Each of the authors has two important qualifications. First, they've worked in and with the media. Second, they've taught the topic, so they know how to connect students like you with this interesting but complicated world. Here they are, in alphabetical order.

Marian Azzaro

Named a Media All Star early in her career by *MediaWeek* magazine, Professor Marian Azzaro is now Assistant Professor of Integrated Marketing Communications and head of IMC studies at Roosevelt University in Chicago, the largest IMC masters program in the US. Prior to joining Roosevelt, Marian worked in media planning at Foote Cone and Belding/Chicago and at Kraft-General Foods, where she evaluated media plans for all Kraft brands and agencies. Having taught media at the graduate and undergrad levels, this book represents Professor Azzaro's view of what you need to know to succeed in today's exciting media world. She is the editor and lead author of this book.

Dan Binder

Daniel Binder is the founder of Strategic Media Management, and is known for his innovative work in media, particularly in cross-platform and added value programs. He served as VP Client Media Director at the Foote Cone & Belding ad agency and as VP Media Director, Print Investment, at the StarCom media agency. Dan also teaches media. He shares his expertise and experience in Chapters 13 and 14, which focus on cross-platform programs. He is the lead author for these chapters.

Robb Clawson

Alexander "Robb" Clawson has been teaching new media classes for more than five years and led the development of this book's new media chapters and online support. He is the Marketing Communications Director for Experian Automotive. In addition to his professional responsibilities, Robb serves as a valued member of the adjunct faculty at Roosevelt University and area community colleges, where he teaches courses in new media and marketing communications.

He is the lead author of Chapters 10, 11, and 12 in this textbook and in charge of the online support for this book, which appears on www.adbuzz.com.

Carla Lloyd

Professor Carla Vaccaro Lloyd is an Associate Professor at Syracuse University's S.I. Newhouse School of Public Communications and Chair of the Advertising Department. Her students now work at leading agencies nationwide. Professor Lloyd has taught advertising media for 15 years and specializes in media topics.

She is the lead author of Chapters One and Three, which are based on her comprehensive treatment of this topic in *Advertising & The Business of Brands,* where she was also a key author.

Mary Alice Shaver

Professor Mary Alice Shaver is Director of the Communications Department at the University of Central Florida. She is former head of the Department of Journalism and Mass Communications at Michigan State University. Professor Shaver teaches classes in advertising media and media sales and actively consults with media organizations on issues related to media placement, sales, and revenue generation. She is the former President of the American Academy of Advertising (AAA) and the incoming head of AEJMC, the Association for Educators of Journalism and Mass Communications.

Professor Shaver is the lead author of Chapters Seven and Eight, which are based on her work in *Make the Sale: How to Sell Media with Marketing*. She knows her topic, having paid her way through grad school with jobs in media sales.

Olaf Werder

After a media career that included working on both local and national accounts and time spent at cutting-edge agency Fallon in Minneapolis, Olaf became Dr. Olaf Werder, joining the University of New Mexico Communication and Journalism faculty in 2002. He teaches courses in the advertising sequence and is the adviser for the UNM student chapter of the American Advertising Federation. His specialties include multicultural and International advertising.

Olaf is the lead author of Chapter Nine and has made other important contributions throughout the book.

Contents

This appendix presents several fictionalized media plan examples based on real brand planning situations. Three plans are included: a conventional plan, a niche plan, and a cross-platform plan.

The words you need to know in the world of media.

Media Today

PART ONE OF THIS BOOK provides a broad overview of the many and changing faces of the world of media. We'll take the time here to provide a general media education familiarizing the reader with all that is media.

One Huge Task. Two Chapters.

It's a huge task that we'll cover in just two chapters.

Chapter One looks at the world of media from three different perspectives – the media company, the consumer, and the advertiser. Within these perspectives we cover a lot of ground. This includes:

- A brief history of media; very brief.
- Today's media world and the very big business of media.
- Consumers and the media and your role as a consumer of the media.

You'll discover that the media itself is a fascinating and complex business of conglomerates and entertainment brands.

Chapter Two considers the Media Age; an exciting and burgeoning market full of opportunities and challenges.

This chapter considers each of the major media and the forces driving change throughout the industry.

Our goal with this section is to present the world of media for the dynamic, exciting and fast-paced business that it is.

After completing these first two chapters, you should have a new awareness of the media world and the role of media in your own world.

1 The World of Media

MEDIA IS A HUGE BUSINESS IN ITS OWN RIGHT. Advertising is a big part of that business. Most media depend on marketing and advertising dollars for their support.

Advertising Makes Media Happen.

Without advertising, there'd be no free "Must-See" TV. *Monday Night Football* would fail to hold the bottom-line.

Without advertising, *Friends* would have ended long ago. *Sports Illustrated* would cost a lot more than $3.50.

Super-Bowl Sunday, *The Simpsons,* and *Saturday Night Live* would be swallowed up by pay TV or wouldn't exist at all.

There'd probably be no sports strikes, either.

Because there'd be no big bucks to strike for.

From 50% to 100%.

Advertising is vital to the American media.

"Advertising is the financial heart of the newspaper," states former Associated Press vice president and author of Strategic Newspaper Management, Conrad Fink. It contributes about two-thirds of newspapers' total revenue.

"Advertising is the lifeblood of the magazine business, accounting for almost half of the industry's total revenue," notes the Magazine Publishers of America.

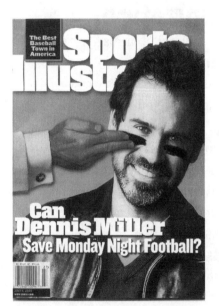

Advertising Makes Media Happen.
It helps pay for the magazines and newspapers we read, and the TV shows we watch.

Major Dates in Media History.

1455 Guttenberg develops printing with moveable type (Germany).

1609 First regularly published newspaper (Germany).

1631 First classified ads (France).

1650 First daily newspaper (Germany).

1704 Newspaper in Boston prints advertising (U.S.).

1798 Senefelder invents lithography (Germany).

1819 Napier develops first rotary printing press (France).

1833 First penny newspaper (U.S.).

1839 Jacobi invents electrotyping – allowing the duplication of printing plates (Russia).

1841 First advertising agency (U.S.).

1842 Illustrated London News (England).

1871 Halftone process – printing pictures.

1878 Full-page newspaper ads (U.S.).

1887 Montgomery Ward mails out 540-page catalog (U.S.).

1892 Four-color rotary press.

1897 GE creates publicity dept.

1903 London Daily Mirror illustrates only with photographs (England).

1904 Offset lithography.

Advertising, by and large, pays for media. With commercial radio and TV, advertising provides essentially 100% of total revenue.

A Monster Topic.

This is a monster topic for one chapter – it even covers monsters, like *Godzilla,* an entertainment brand (just like NBC is a brand, as is *Ally McBeal,* the *Super Bowl,* and *The Simpsons*).

But it's a great way to get started talking about media. So… let's.

Chapter Organization.

Here's how we'll cover the world of media.

A Brief History of Media.

From Egyptian graffiti to the Internet, we'll see how each new media development changed the business of advertising.

Today's Media World.

This is the longest section in the chapter.

We'll cover the business of media one medium at a time.

Consumers and the Media.

We'll look at how you and the media interact today.

Media Conglomerates and Entertainment Brands.

We'll see how today's growing, fast-changing media companies are changing the media world we live in.

And we'll see it all from the perspective of people who work for these fascinating companies. (We'll save new media forms, like the Web, for later in the book.)

First, let's look at how our world of media grew.

A Brief History of Media.

This section of the chapter will briefly review how the American media system evolved, how advertising became the force it is today, and how consumer brands, like Campbell's Soup, profited from each major media development.

Major Dates in Media History (Cont.)

1904 The comic book (U.S.).

1905 The Yellow Pages (U.S.).

1907 DeForest begins regular radio music broadcasts (U.S.).

1907 Rosing develops theory of television (Russia).

1911 Rotogravure aids magazine reproduction of photos (U.S.).

1915 Electric loudspeaker.

1916 Radios get tuners.

1917 Condensor microphone.

1920 First broadcasting stations (U.S.).

1922 First radio commercial (U.S.).

1923 Neon advertising signs (U.S.).

1926 NBC (U.S.).

1927 CBS (U.S.).

1927 Farnsworth assembles complete electronic TV system (U.S.).

1927 U.S. Radio Act.

1929 50% of U.S. homes own a radio.

1929 The car radio.

1932 Disney adopts Technicolor (U.S.).

1932 The Times of London uses its new Times Roman typeface (England).

1933 FM radio invented (U.S.).

1934 Communication Act creates FCC.

1936 Kodachrome.

1939 Regular TV broadcasts begin.

This background is important, but we'll be brief.

The Big Picture Begins...

Three thousand years ago, ancient Babylonians put up posters to make announcements to their local community.

Graffiti was splashed across the walls of Pompeii and the stone obelisks of ancient Egypt, delivering the earliest sales promotion messages.

The Word Goes Forth...

Just as much culture was in the oral tradition of folk tales and epic poems, most early advertising relied on sound, not images, to get the word out on goods and services.

Hawkers and their cries roamed the streets and markets of ancient towns promoting everything from medicinal "cure-alls" to hot cross buns.

Each of these forms of advertising had strong local appeal and was based on the available technology – painted signs and the human voice.

Your Message Here...

One of the earliest recorded forms of advertising with a wider reach and more of a mass audience was a silver coin.

More than two thousand years ago, in the North African city of Cyrene, silver coins or tokens were minted to carry the image of a local plant grown specifically in Cyrene.

This plant was a pain reliever and condiment, and the coins helped market this plant throughout the ancient world.

The Beginnings of Mass Media.

Newspapers made their debut in the early 17th century.

The first newspaper ad appeared around 1650.

Early advertising was more like our classified ads.

Even then, there was comment. Samuel Johnson said, in 1759, *"Advertisements are now so numerous that they are negligently perused, and it is therefore necessary to gain attention by magnificence of promise and by eloquence sometimes sublime and sometimes pathetic."* Sound familiar?

The Rise of American Mass Media.

Though newspapers and magazines were published virtually everywhere, for a variety of reasons, both economic and political, mass media and mass advertising grew more dynamically in the U.S..

It took the other basics of a modern economy to bring about the kinds of businesses that needed advertising.

In every major American city, newspaper publishers were big businesses. They helped inform. They helped shape opinions. They helped sell goods. And they grew.

Cities and Retailers.

The newspaper was the perfect vehicle for growing urban centers and urban advertisers.

It contained local and national news, and provided an efficient and inexpensive medium for local retailers – a relationship that continues to this day.

$45.4 Billion. Over 1,500 Newspapers.

In 2003, newspapers amassed $45.4 billion from advertising. The top seven newspaper companies have a daily circulation of over 20 million.

Daily newspapers reach 58.7% of all adults. Readers have 1,509 daily newspapers to choose from.

Useful News.

A recent study by the Newspaper Association of America and the American Society of Newspaper Editors shows readers find newspaper advertising useful – 78% rely on newspapers for employment ads; 69% use newspapers to find an apartment; and 64% read the newspapers when looking for grocery ads.

The Rise of National Magazines.

Around the turn of the century, with improved printing techniques and a literate middle class, magazines became a part of everyday American life.

Early Transit Advertising.
Cards like these helped heat up sales for
Campbell's Soups.

Publishing started to become big business. It was a magazine publisher, Cyrus H. Curtis, who firmly established the ad agency's role by promoting agency commissions with a magazine created by his wife – *The Ladies Home Journal*.

Meanwhile, exciting new consumer products – like soup in a can – began advertising.

While newspapers worked well for retailers, magazines were a far better medium for packaged goods.

Example: Campbell's

Campbell's Soup, a relatively new company, responded to the opportunities provided by the new technology.

They began with posters in transit advertising – and then moved on to newspapers. But magazines were a better way for Campbell's to reach the growing American market.

By 1914, Campbell's had dropped newspaper completely from its advertising schedule, throwing the bulk of its advertising dollars into mass-market magazines, like the *Saturday Evening Post* and *The Ladies Home Journal*.

Their ads in magazines served a growing group of educated consumers with money to spend.

Through the decades, Campbell's kept growing and the magazine industry kept growing.

Early Media Movement.
Campbell's moves from newspaper ads to magazine ads.

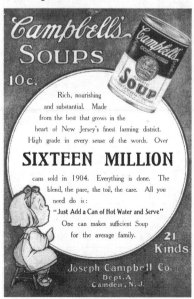

The Magazine Industry Today.

Today, Condé Nast, Hearst, and Time Warner are the largest U.S. magazine publishers.

They each publish 16 magazines.

Condé Nast publishes such recognizable titles as *Vogue, GQ,* and *Glamour.* Hearst titles include *Cosmopolitan, Esquire,* and *Good Housekeeping.*

Time Warner, a huge media conglomerate, publishes *Time, Sports Illustrated,* and *People* to name a few.

The three top-circulating magazines in the United States are the *AARP Bulletin* (20 million subscribers), *Reader's Digest* (11 million), and *TV Guide* (9 million).

Broadcast – Media Turns On.

In 1906, the first radio program of voice and music was broadcast in the United States. Advertisers grew increasingly interested in radio as more people tuned in.

In the beginning, direct selling was forbidden. Advertisers were not allowed to quote prices. They were only allowed to mention their company or brand name.

Early radio commercials were *"polite and unobtrusive,"* says mass communications professor, Joseph Dominick. Advertisers, as Dominick points out, were actually *"embarrassed to invade the privacy of the home with their sales messages."*

Known as indirect advertising, it was nothing more than product names incorporated into radio programs.

This ushered in the concept of sponsorship.

The Age of Radio.

But by 1930, audiences had grown. Radio was the undisputed king of the air waves, resembling network TV of not that many years ago – before the rise of cable.

Radio was big. As many as 88 million Americans followed the thrilling adventures of *The Lone Ranger* every week.

The Depression was also in full swing. Stations were ripe to sell their air time to companies. Direct advertising and 60-second spot announcements were born.

The beginnings of radio.
It began as a primitive luxury item.

Commercials became slicker and hard-selling. The singing commercial, later known as the jingle, was developed.

The Growth of Radio Networks.

Networks were a natural outgrowth of the technology.

The first network was born in 1923, when a radio station in Newark, New Jersey, linked itself together with a telegraph line to another station in Schenectady, New York, so that the two stations could simultaneously broadcast the *World Series*.

Linking local stations with one another had all sorts of commercial potential, and stations were quickly connected to one another all the way across the country.

Huge and diverse audiences tuned into comedy, drama and music – all broadcast by three major networks – NBC, CBS, and DuMont. It was big business. Look at all that went into *The Lucky Strike Hit Parade* broadcast on NBC.

Radio became a medium that got companies results.

For example, General Mills credits early radio for the success of its Wheaties cereal.

Great radio advertising then, like now, captures our imaginations – and builds brands.

Every year, the best radio advertising receives a Mercury Award for its creativity from the Radio Advertising Bureau.

You can listen to these Mercury Award winning radio commercials by going to the RAB website, www.rab.com.

Spend some time there; you'll enjoy it.

The Evolution of Radio after TV.

Let's skip ahead for a minute. When TV emerged, the big-budget prime-time show – the mainstay of network radio soon became a thing of the past. For a while radio was adrift.

But radio retained some strengths. You couldn't watch TV as you drove to work. A radio spot was a lot cheaper and quicker to produce than one for TV.

And, if you wanted to listen to your favorite music, there was usually a radio station eager to play it for you.

Radio grows into mass popularity.
Here, the Lucky Strike Hit Parade *broadcast on NBC. Radio then was as popular as TV is today.*

TOP 10 RADIO COMPANIES

RANK	MEDIA COMPANY	NET RADIO REVENUE	% CHANGE
1	Clear Channel Communications	$3,717	7.6
2	Viacom	1,859	4.5
3	Walt Disney Co.	579	5.9
4	Westwood One	551	6.8
5	Cox Enterprises	421	6.5
6	Entercom Communications Corp.	391	17.5
7	Citadel Broadcasting Corp.	310	16.3
8	Radio One	296	21.3
9	Hispanic Broadcasting (Univision)	257	6.5
10	Cumulus Media	253	25.0

Dominant Ownership. Clear Channel and Viacom at the top of the radio industry.

Philo Farnsworth.
He invented TV as a teenager in Idaho.

So, even as the focus shifted to television, radio evolved its own strong and unique role in the media mix.

Drive time became a key advantage for radio.

The ever-widening variety of music styles allowed radio to evolve into a uniquely powerful "niche" media.

Local retailers and national advertisers after "niche" targets, like teenagers, became heavy users of radio advertising.

The Radio Industry Today

Like all media, radio is going through dramatic ownership changes and consolidation. In the last few years, Clear Channel and CBS Viacom have become the two dominant ownership groups in radio, often owning multiple stations in each major market.

Television Turns on America.

In 1933, Philo Farnsworth, a 16-year-old high-school student in Rigby, Idaho, patented "an electronic image dissector tube." He thought of it while mowing his father's hay field. Five years later, at 21, he transmitted the first television picture.

Ten years later, Americans saw their first TV commercial – for Royal Crown Cola on Schenenctady, New York's, WRGB.

Early Television.

Early TV didn't have mass appeal. There wasn't much mass.

Television sets were expensive. Programs and commercials only reached an upscale urban audience.

Live drama and opera suddenly cropped up in homes.

This programming reflected the cultural tastes of those who could afford a set, as well as the taste of those early TV sponsors.

Percent of US Households with Television

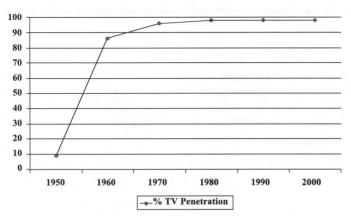

The Rapid Growth of TV Penetration.
As you can see from the chart above, less
than 10% of households had a TV in the
early 50s, but there was almost 90%
penetration by 1960.

From 10% to 90%.

In 1951, there were only 1.5 million television sets in the U.S. Soon, expanded production and department-store credit plans made purchasing a television set possible for more people.

By 1952, television had spread to 15 million households. Three years later, they were sitting in half the living rooms in America. Now advertisers were directing their messages to a larger and more diverse audience. By 1960 almost 90% of all U.S. households had at least one TV set.

Multiple Advertisers and "SPOT."

Television programs cost more to produce than radio.

Therefore, advertising changed. Instead of one advertiser sponsoring an entire program, several advertisers sponsored small segments of that program.

Local television stations benefit from network affiliation.

For starters, local stations receive high quality programming that they could not afford to produce on their own. With high quality network shows like NBC's *Friends* or FOX's *24*, local affiliates attract large audiences.

This means local affiliating stations can charge higher rates. Local stations reap other benefits, too.

For instance, networks pay each of their affiliates 30% of the local advertising rate when a national ad runs. Nearly 10% of a local station's income stems from the network.

Early Growth of Cable.

By the late '70s, network television was the reigning champ of the airwaves and advertising revenue, but a young and rambunctious newcomer – cable TV – was on the rise.

Actually, cable television had been around for quite some time. But nothing much happened for thirty years.

It started about 1950, just after broadcast television began. In the beginning, its role was simple: improve the television reception of people living in remote areas.

Then things changed dramatically.

Three Major Developments.

Three major developments allowed cable to gain strength:

- **Growth of domestic satellite relays**
- **Creation of TV superstations**
- **The introduction of pay cable services**

Again, technology reshaped the world of media, helping cable TV compete for audiences and advertisers.

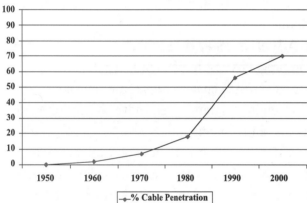

Percent US TV Homes with Cable TV

—●— % Cable Penetration

The Growth of Cable TV. Here, the penetration is later and slower, but still impressive. Particularly since cable represents the top 70% of the marketplace.

Growth of Cable in the '80s.

Until 1980, cable had recycled old TV shows and movies. But no sooner had this decade begun than cable started producing its own programming.

Suddenly, a host of channels bounded into cable subscribers' homes. The new channels offered specialized programming on many subjects: health, finance, sports, and cultural events.

Advertisers discovered a new kind of TV, one that delivered specialized audiences.

Advertisers with specialized products (such as fly rods) could now use television without wasting ad dollars on viewers not interested in their products.

Smaller local advertisers could now afford television – audiences weren't as big, but it was TV, and customers responded.

Today, cable is one of the fastest growing media.

In 1997, cable reached more than 70% of American television households. During the first month of the new 1998 television season, cable triumphed over broadcast television, securing a larger audience in two dayparts: late fringe and weekend day. In 2002, advertising revenue hit $10.2 billion.

Cable lets advertisers target specific groups of viewers.

Example: BET

For example, the Black Entertainment Network, which has 74 million subscribers, was the first cable network to appeal

 strictly to African-Americans.

Advertisers seeking to reach an urban audience can do so with the special programming BET offers – music videos, public affairs, jazz, gospel, sports.

An Interactive Future.

Now technology may change TV again. Television, long a passive medium, is now becoming interactive.

Most of today's television asks little of the viewer.

There are, of course, some exceptions.

Cable's shopping channels ask the viewers to call in to buy. That's not passive.

And, of course, the channel changer gives viewers more control over what they watch and hear.

Soon, viewers will program their TV to receive information and entertainment. They will be able to choose what they want to see when they want to see it – this is video on demand.

The shift from a passive to interactive medium has those in the TV industry reeling. But they aren't the only ones.

Telephone companies and computer manufacturers are also looking to get involved in the media world's next evolution.

Today's Media World.

Every year, every American consumes over $800 in media, spending about nine hours a day consuming it!

Our media world has grown into something pretty amazing – and pretty big.

First, think about how much media spends on you.

You receive $800 a year in advertising supported media (that's an average).

Now think about your own media budget. Think of how much you spend to purchase media.

Advertising Becomes Interactive.
Here, Nike lets you "vote" on the possible endings of one of their TV commercials.

TOP 25 U.S. MEDIA COMPANIES

From 100 Leading Media Cos. (AA. Aug. 19, 2002), this table ranks U.S. media companies by estimated total U.S. net revenue from media. Figures are from public documents or Ad Age estimates for calendar 2001. Dollars are in millions.

Rank	Company	Net U.S. media revenue	% change
1	AOL Time Warner	$27,205.3	9.0
2	Viacom	15,211.2	0.1
3	AT&T Broadband (AT&T Corp.)	10,329.0	16.6
4	Walt Disney Co.	10,228.0	-1.9
5	Cox Enterprises	6,266.2	7.7
6	NBC TV (General Electric Co.)	6,033.7	-13.1
7	News Corp.	5,914.7	3.2
8	Clear Channel Communications	5,703.2	-6.4
9	Gannett Co.	5,571.3	0.8
10	DirecTV (General Motors Corp.)	5,550.0	18.2
11	Comcast Corp.	5,130.7	21.9
12	Tribune Co.	5,104.4	-8.5
13	Advance Publications	4,000.0	-8.2
14	Hearst Corp.	3,986.0	-3.6
15	Charter Communications	3,953.0	21.7
16	EchoStar Communications Corp.	3,683.2	52.4
17	Cablevision Systems Corp.	3,064.4	2.2
18	Adelphia Communications Corp.	3,060.0	19.7
19	New York Times Co.	3,027.5	-10.6
20	Knight Ridder	2,900.2	-9.7
21	Bloomberg	2,108.8	20.3
22	Washington Post Co.	1,923.0	-6.6
23	Primedia	1,922.1	-9.7
24	Dow Jones & Co.	1,773.1	-19.5
25	Belo	1,364.6	-14.1

From $1 Billion to $27 Billion.

Media is big business. Here is a listing of the Top 25 Media companies. But it's a list that changes quickly – so it may be out of date already!

Media competes with Media in Media.
Here, a newspaper uses outdoor advertising to advertise its superiority to television.

Start with newspapers and magazines. Add entertainment brands like sports and movies (including the poster, T-shirt, and soundtrack album) and that number is even bigger.

Big Business!

The world of media includes some of the biggest companies in the world. While many media companies own more than one kind of media, it will be useful for you to first look at the media world by category.

Three Major Categories.

For our purposes, there are two major media categories – print and broadcast, plus a number of other important types of media, which we will call "other." It looks this way:

Print

Newspapers.

Our oldest major medium. And, until very recently, our largest revenue generator.

Magazines.

Print media aimed at specific audiences.

Out-of-Home.

This is the oldest media form of all – and one of the newest, with technology such as digital painting and electronic video signs.

It includes the other "place-based media" such as the posters in your student union, your laundry rooms, and maybe even the walls of your dorms. Kiosks at bus stops and posters in subways are also included in this out-of-home category.

Broadcast

Radio.

This was our first electronic medium, and the first one fully sponsored. It's gone from a major national medium to a local "niche" medium.

Television (network, local, and cable).

Television is the medium you probably know best. But you'll see there's a lot you don't know behind the scenes.

Other

This catch-all category contains some pretty big things you might not think of as media.

Your Mailbox.

Direct mail accounts for 23% of all advertising expenditures. And it's growing. Direct media channels like your mailbox are part of the growing world of database marketing.

Your Telephone.

It's called "telemarketing." Whether it's the toll-free number in the infomercial (inbound), or the call that interrupts your dinner (outbound), it's also a big part of marketing. Recent legislation has changed this industry dramatically.

Your Computer.

You're already receiving ad messages on your computer, and maybe you're beginning to buy things by computer as well. Your computer and its Internet connection is a brand new kind of medium.

And it's making its own huge impact.

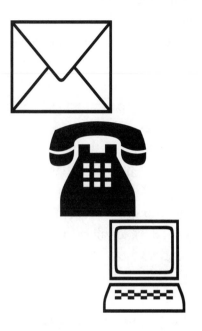

Your Mailbox, Telephone, and Computer.
These are media channels, too.

Big Changes!

Media today is changing with the daily headlines.

In the past two decades, these changes have been radical.

So significant in fact that we will devote the entire next chapter to a discussion of the changing world of media.

For now though, let's look briefly at some of the big changes in the business of media, one medium at a time.

Print Media.

The Scoop on Newspapers.

Until 1995, newspapers were the #1 U.S. ad medium.

From Number One to Number Two.

Now they're #2, having been surpassed by TV in total ad revenue. Even so, newspapers are still a big piece of the media business.

In 2003, newspapers garnered a total of $45.4 billion in advertising spending.

The Newspaper Association is using ads like this to encourage readership and to encourage parents to help their children develop the newspaper habit.

U.S. Newspaper Companies

Gannett, Inc.

80 dailies	5,984,526 circ.
70 on Sunday	6,000,609 circ.

Knight-Ridder, Inc.

33 dailies	3,893,639 circ.
31 on Sunday	5,512,197 circ.

Newhouse Newspapers

23 dailies	2,806,016 circ.
21 on Sunday	3,602,725 circ.

Dow Jones & Co.

20 dailies	2,349,419 circ.
14 on Sunday	549,745 circ.

Times Mirror Co.

9 dailies	2,348,407 circ.
7 on Sunday	3,040,125 circ.

Newspapers have local businesses to thank. More than 85% of newspaper revenue comes from local advertisers.

Advertising = 67% of Revenue.

Advertising is critical to newspapers. Historically, advertisers have contributed two-thirds of newspaper earnings.

60 Million Households.

In 2000 there were 1,480 daily newspapers, and 917 Sunday newspapers in the United States.

Daily newspapers reach 60 million households.

This is called circulation. Almost 60% of adults 18 and older still read a newspaper.

According to a national readership study done by the Newspaper Association of America, 58.8% of all people 18 and older read a daily newspaper and 68.5% of these folks read a Sunday paper.

Circulation Trends…

But the bad news is that the number of adults who read newspapers has declined sharply. In 1970, a significant 77.6% of all adults 18 and over read a daily newspaper and 72.3% of them read a Sunday paper. You can see the decline.

As you might guess, the big challenge facing newspapers today is trying to reverse this trend.

An example from a campaign for the Newspaper Association work featuring Meryl Streep (among others) appears here. Take a look. What do you think about it?

Newspaper Ownership.

As you can see from the list on the left, most newspapers are part of large chain newspaper companies.

Some publish their newspaper nationwide, such as *USA Today* (Gannett), *The Wall Street Journal* (Dow Jones), and *The New York Times* (Times Mirror).

Others specialize in media in their own market, such as the *Erie Daily Times* and *Morning News* published by Times Publishing located in Erie, Pennsylvania.

Some, like Gannett and Rupert Murdoch's News Corporation, are part of larger multimedia operations.

Newspapers Respond to the Marketplace.

Intense competition has forced all media outlets to become more aggressive. In an unprecedented move, Thomson Newspapers, the 8th largest American newspaper company, that publishes 65 daily newspapers in the U.S. and Canada, broke tradition and began selling ads on the front page. This had long been considered a taboo.

Patricia Gillies, of Thomson Newspapers, says this bold strategic move *"recognizes the changing environment in which newspaper operate."*

She's also quick to point out the tough realities of the media marketplace by saying: *"Our customers have access to an increasing variety of marketing and information resources, and the competitive edge will belong to the company that draws upon those options to most effectively meet customers' needs."*

Responding to Competition.

Severe competition has made media outlets more in tune with their audiences and more willing to adapt to their needs, wants, and interests.

The New York Times was recently forced to adapt to the demands of the aggressive and scrappy media marketplace. A supplement inserted in the September 11, 1997, issue explained the paper's bold strategic move – color!

"This fall, we will unveil the most substantial, dramatic enhancements The New York Times has seen in over 20 years. The world's most esteemed newspaper becomes even better.

Starting September 15, The New York Times will employ the most sophisticated production capabilities in the newspaper business. This enables us to offer you, our readers, later-breaking news and sports scores as well as new sections, new features, better printing quality and daily color."

"Reader" Readers

Here's a profile for the Chicago readers of the *Reader*.

Median age: 34

52% are 18-34

62% are 25-44

Median household income:$47,110

90% have attended college

47% professional/managerial

55% male; 45% female

73% are single

Alternative Newspapers.

Another niche has grown in the newspaper industry, one you're familiar with – "alternative newspapers."

These papers, often free, feature a focus on entertainment and arts-driven features with ads targeted at a younger audience. The first of these was *The Village Voice*.

America's First Alternative Weekly.

The Village Voice, America's largest weekly newspaper, founded by Dan Wolf, Ed Fancher, and Norman Mailer in 1955 is considered the founding father of alternative weeklies.

The "Voice" introduced a new type of journalism that brought a *"free-form, high-spirited and passionate journalism into the public discourse."*

A Growing Category.

Some alternative papers are quite large. Chicago's *Reader* has a weekly circulation of 136,957.

Readers of the *Reader* tend to be better educated, single, and young. The inset shows who reads this alternative paper.

The *Austin Chronicle* boasts a readership of 243,500.

It provides stories that address the political and environmental concerns unique to Austin, the capital of Texas.

The *Chronicle* also provides in-depth coverage of Austin's rich cultural scene.

The Onion, which began as a small humor paper in Madison, Wisconsin, now covers a number of markets, with ad sales offices in Madison, Milwaukee, Chicago, and Denver.

Their outrageous humor has helped them establish a unique niche in the marketplace.

Check it out at www.theonion.com.

Magazines.

You Can Judge These Books by Their Covers.

In 2003, there were 17,321 magazines in the United States.

They generated $22 billion in total sales and $11 billion in advertising revenue.

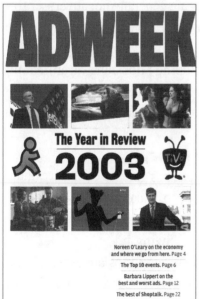

A magazine the size of a phone book. Lots of advertisers want to connect with brides – this is a great place to do it.

A Business Magazine for Every Business. AdWeek is just one of several advertising industry trade magazines.

Historically, magazines have realized 50% of their revenue from advertising. The rest comes from subscriptions (which, not surprisingly, are about half price) and newsstand sales.

Magazines can be broken down into various types:

- **Consumer**
- **Business or trade**
- **Newsletters and journals**

Consumer Magazines – General or Specialized.

Consumer magazines are divided into two groups:

- **General interest**
- **Specialized**

There are general-interest consumer magazines, such as *TV Guide* and *Reader's Digest.* These magazines carry editorial content that appeals to a broad variety of people.

Specialized magazines appeal to readers with specific interests, hobbies, and lifestyles.

For example: *Ceramic Magazine, Becket Baseball Card Monthly, Keyboard,* and *Opera News.*

THRASHER is an "extreme" example of this type of magazine – it appeals to skateboarders.

Though general-interest magazines, like *People* and *Newsweek,* have circulations that are quite large, you might be surprised at how large some specialized magazines, such as *PC Monthly* and *Bride,* are in terms of ad pages and ad revenue.

And as we told you, the largest circulation magazine is the *AARP Bulletin.*

A Business Magazine for Every Business.

Trade magazines usually focus on some type of business with a specialized audience and a specialized advertiser base.

Sometimes there's a grouping of magazines, sometimes two compete, sometimes there's only one.

Standard Rate and Data Service (SRDS).

You can find a complete breakdown of these magazines in Standard Rate and Data Service (SRDS).

How George Did It.

Here are some (not all) of the job titles that were on the masthead of *George* – the jobs that have to do with the advertising-based economics of running a magazine:

Publishing Staff:
Publisher
Associate Publisher
Beauty & Luxury Goods Director
Fashion & Retail Director
Account Managers (2)
Sales Assistants (2)
Interns (2)
Promotion Coordinator
Advertising Coordinator

Regional Sales Offices:
West Coast
Detroit
Chicago
Atlanta
New York
Europe

Business Office:
VP Eastern Region
Corporate Sales Director
VP Midwest Corporate Sales
Analysts (2)
Assistants (2)

This directory breaks consumer and business magazines into different classifications.

SRDS then lists a brief description of each of the magazines, circulation information, advertising rates, and other important information critical in scheduling and running a magazine ad.

You can usually find a copy of SRDS at your local library and probably your school library. And on the Internet at www.srds.com.

Newsletters and Journals: Controlled Circulation.

Newsletters are small publications that deal with the special interests of a particular group.

They may be sold by subscription, or they may be sent free of charge by the publishing group. Unlike magazines, you generally cannot buy a newsletter on newsstands.

Journals are supported by universities, grants, and institutions and circulate to small groups of specialized readers.

Many journals do not include advertising.

These types of magazines are generally not advertiser supported in the traditional sense. They are paid for by:

• Subscribers

• Dues-paying members of the publishing organization

• The company publishing the publication may fund it for promotional/marketing purposes or for some other reason, such as employee relations.

How Magazines Make Money.

Magazines come and magazines go.

But, most magazines want to make a profit – and to do that, they need a sales staff to help make it happen.

Example: What It Takes to "Swing It"

Advertising revenue and subscriptions are especially important to new magazines, like David Lauren's *SWING* magazine and John F. Kennedy, Jr.'s, *George*.

David Lauren, son of famed fashion designer Ralph Lauren, started *SWING* magazine while attending Duke University.

He wanted to create an intelligent publication that dealt with the interests and concerns of twenty-something culture – the people who have the ability to influence their generation.

He couldn't swing it. *SWING* folded.

John Kennedy, Jr., co-founded *George,* a guide to the people and the process of politics as they relate to popular culture.

The aim of this new magazine was to *"bring politics to life with insightful reporting and cutting-edge commentary."*

Advertisers quickly responded to the idea of *George*, and the magazine was packed with interesting articles and colorful ads. But the magazine was dependent on the Kennedy charisma.

Its life was cut short soon after the death of its founder.

The Importance of the Sales Staff.

Advertising sales staffs, like the one in the sidebar for *George*, are made up of account managers, sales managers, advertising coordinators, and regional sales offices directors.

They help service clients and get ad space sold. This keeps the magazines on newsstands and coming to your mailbox.

Rate Cards and "Added Value."

Heightened competition has made media outlets more flexible and service-minded. For the past ten years, magazines, with the exception of the Condé Nast periodicals, have been very flexible about their advertising rates, making the price of advertising now fully negotiable.

Prior to this, advertisers paid the rates on the rate card.

Rate cards include a detailed listing of the various ways advertising can be purchased.

To see some sample rate cards, check out the resources section for this book at www.adbuzz.com.

In *Glamour* magazine, for example, the rate card tells us that a four-color, full-page ad costs $122,000.

Three Free with Ten.

Some magazines will give advertisers three free pages of advertising if they purchase ten.

Condé Nast magazines, such as *Glamour* and *Vanity Fair,* are willing to kick in all sorts of free promotional programs to advertisers paying the full price of advertising.

Instead of discounting the cost of their advertising, the Condé Nast magazines provide "added-value" to their clients by *"organizing and subsidizing department store displays and mall fashion shows."*

Other added-value deals that publications offer advertisers include "data bases and marketing partnerships."

"The Big 3" Make a Big Change.

Even the biggest media respond to the marketplace.

Newsmagazines, like *Newsweek, Time,* and *U.S. News & World Report,* often referred to as "the Big 3," have had to adapt their editorial content to remain relevant to today's readers.

Facing fierce competition from broadcast sources and declining public interest in traditional news media, they were forced to reinvent themselves.

As reported in the *Chicago Tribune,* what the Big 3 did was to critically examine the way they had been doing business.

They shifted their emphasis from traditional coverage of national affairs of government to an editorial product that newspapers and TV news were not serving. The Big 3 now cover more stories on business, technology, and healthcare.

They also now concentrate on maintaining long-term relationships with their readers.

You'll notice throughout this chapter (and this book) that the marketplace is always changing, and many brands have to adjust to that change.

Next, another example of that change – newspapers.

**Newspapers Become Magazines
– The Domino Effect.**

With the rise of TV, newspapers were no longer the source of the latest "scoop" on late-breaking news. The scoops were now for local TV news and the all-news stations like *CNN.*

So, newspapers focused more on depth and breadth, something TV news couldn't do.

In short, they became more magazine-like.

At the same time, the Big 3 weekly newsmagazines turned to more long-term in-depth articles – they became more like the once-popular monthly newsmagazines that provided in-depth discussion of issues. These faded.

However, monthly magazines that focused on an area of great interest to a specific group could still do quite well.

For example, *Wired,* which features articles for the "online generation," has prospered, going in-depth in the area of new and emerging technology.

Inc. has connected with smaller companies and entrepreneurs. *Fast Company*, a hot new business monthly, features cutting-edge issues for today's new corporate warriors.

Out-of-Home & Outdoor.

Outdoor ad revenue has grown 7% annually since 1993, according to *American Demographics.* 2003 was the best year ever at $5.5 billion.

Place-based Media.

Traditional outdoor media include billboards and bus shelters, to name just two.

New money is coming from nontraditional locales – health clubs, bathrooms, airport baggage carousels, restaurants, and bars, to name a few.

Walk into any convenience store, fast food outlet, or neighborhood tavern and you will be surrounded by a dizzying array of promotional media.

Outdoor on the Move...

With new large-screen video technology, outdoor signs will start to provide more video images.

Advancement in traditional technology now has resulted in "wrap" advertising suitable for buses and trains locally and even regionally. The wrap is created with a light-weight but very strong material. The material is printed with quality, high-resolution graphics and then applied (or affixed) to the exterior of a bus or rail car, creating a moving billboard.

Place-based Media.
Bus kiosks provide advertisers with new venues (on the avenue), and municipalities sell their "space" and get income.

"Just Wrap It, I'll Drive It Home."
The entire bus was wrapped to deliver Godzilla's big message.

In addition, many companies are now putting more value on their own rolling stock, so you'll see more brand imagery on trucks and vans.

Technology is migrating everywhere.

There are major projects afoot to replace the old posters at McDonald's with computerized video screens that can change the offer quickly and flexibly – according to locality, time of day… almost anything you can imagine. Super-sized.

McTV – coming soon to a restaurant near you.

Broadcast Media.

Now let's look at the business of broadcast – radio and TV.

Television is now a bit bigger than newspapers (a fairly recent phenomenon), and radio, like magazines, is now more of a "niche" medium.

Radio.

Between 6 a.m. and 6 p.m., more people spend more time with radio than any other medium – even TV.

The numbers tell the story. Radio reaches 94% of all Americans over age 12. Every day.

The reason is simple. At least 95% of all cars have radios.

Drive Time Is Radio Time.

During morning drive time (6-10 a.m. weekdays), 50% of Americans 12 or older listen to the radio. And, 42.2% of these people listen from 3 to 7 p.m. on their way home from work.

The vast majority of those behind the wheel are also in the driver's seat at work. A recent study shows that 92% of professionals and managers tune into the car radio weekly.

Radio has become our companion medium.

It goes where we go, no matter where our lifestyles take us.

Among people 12 and older, 37.2% listen to their radios at home, 41.6% listen in their cars, and 21.2% tune in at work and other places.

At work, 65% of all adults have a radio nearby – though it's not always on.

Radio also accompanies people on their way shopping. It is the last medium people hear before making a purchase.

Radio reaches 63% of adults 25-54 within one hour of making their largest puchase of the day.

Some people even listen while browsing through stores.

A Local Medium.

As we mentioned, radio was once a national network medium. Now it's primarily a local medium.

From 1985 to 1996, advertising revenues nearly doubled.

Radio's real strength is now at the local level. It depends on local advertising for the bulk of its revenue.

In 2003 advertisers spent $19.6 billion in spot radio.

Only $1 billion was spent in network radio (4.4%).

Of that spot revenue, 78% comes from local sales. National spot accounted for about 17%.

More Radio Than Ever.

From 1983 to 1993, the number of stations grew by 22%.

Now, the number is at an all-time high – 13,898.

Growing Listenership

Radio listening has increased steadily. Americans now spend 20 hours listening to radio every week.

A 1996 study done by Arbitron, a radio ratings firm, found that 95% of all Americans 12 and older listen to their radio every day. Highly successful new programming like *Radio Disney* captures listeners' attention.

A recent launch in Boston connected with 70,000 kids the first two weeks on air.

Radio is everywhere.

Fully 99% of all households are equipped with radios. Nearly half of all rooms in a typical American home have a radio. The average home has six radios.

Radio not only offers advertisers a steady flow of listeners, it delivers loyal audiences.

Radio Disney Online.

Numerous Niches.

There are radio formats that fit almost every musical taste and political ideology.

The programming and on-air personalities speak directly to you. They tap into how you are thinking and feeling at a particular time in your life.

And you listen. We all listen to our favorite dee-jays, music and talk show celebrities – long and often.

Radio Networks.

Radio networks still exist, working much the same way as television networks, interconnecting local stations and providing affiliates with programming.

But, for the most part, it's a looser affiliation. They're a lot smaller and less important.

In 1991 there were 27 radio networks ranging in size from 41 to 4,450 affiliates.

Networks offer local affiliates news, weather, talk shows, and children's shows. Local stations might even affiliate with several networks to get a variety of different programming.

Radio Formats.

Radio stations are also categorized by various formats.

To appeal to specific segments, stations will select music, on-air personalities, and promotions to attract particular niches.

This is the radio station's program format.

The Most Popular Formats.

The four most popular radio formats are:

- **News/Talk – 16% of all U.S. radio stations**
- **Country – 13%**
- **Adult Contemporary – 13%**
- **Contemporary Hit radio – 10%**

Formats are constantly evolving. As Gary Fries, President of Radio Advertising Bureau (RAB), states, *"There's something out there for everyone. Wherever people develop a new taste, radio develops a new format."*

Radio Marketing Guide & Fact Book.
A great source for information about the radio industry. www.rab.com

Radio formats break listeners down into highly targeted, very small portions of the population.

According to the *Radio Marketing Guide & Fact Book,* progressive or alternative formats capture the restless and rebellious 18-to-29-year-olds.

The middle-aged crowd (35-to-54 years old), prefer listening to Golden Oldies (52%) and jazz (54.3%) formats. The 50 and older segment prefers nostalgia (63%) and full-service (57.2%).

You may find stations in different cities with essentially the same playlists, station identification packages, and sometimes, even the same advertising campaigns.

For example, Clear Channel owns, operates, or sells time for more than 1200 stations nationwide. Many of these stations program a similar playlist throughout the country.

Visit the RAB site at www.rab.com and you'll find out more.

Television.

In the U.S., television is the biggest medium, and for the most part, it is commercially supported. In the U.S., commercial TV depends almost entirely on advertising for revenue. Cable TV derives most of its earnings from subscriber fees.

In 2003, TV advertisers spent $57 billion.

Ad spending in cable television accounted for $14 billion of that total.

Advertisers Like Television.

TV stations and networks generate income by selling time. Television is prized by advertisers.

They consider it to be one of the most effective and persuasive of all advertising media.

Viewers Like Television.

American TV viewers have an ongoing love affair with TV. Over 98% of all U.S. households own one television set; 67% have two. And 85% of all American homes have at least one VCR or DVD player. (How many TVs in your home? And how many VCRs? How about DVD players and burners?)

Number of TV Sets in the Average US TV Home

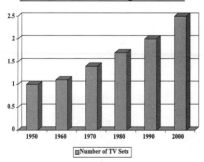

From a Luxury to a Necessity. As you can see from this chart, there is now an average of more than two TV sets in every home. How many do you have in your home?

For years, TV has brought the news, big sports events, and broad-based entertainment into America's homes.

And we watch it all. Social scientists report that the average high school graduate has spent more time watching TV (15,000 hours) than in school (11,000 hours).

They're watching the commercials, too.

Depending on which study you believe, researchers report that by the age of 18, the average American child has seen between 350,000 and 640,000 television commercials.

With More to Come...

In 1985 the average American family had 18 channels to choose from. By 1994, it had jumped to 38.

Now, the average American family has more than 80 channels – with more to come.

Cable viewers spent $35 million on cable services.

There are now six major broadcast networks. More than 70% of American homes are hooked up to cable. And digital technology is making even more programming possible.

For all these reasons, television is attractive to advertisers.

Four Kinds of TV. Six ways to Buy It.

Television can deliver a nation, a region, or a city.

Basically, there are four kinds of TV programming:

1. Network
2. National cable
3. Syndication
4. Local (mostly news)

When it comes to buying television, advertisers can buy from the network, the producer of the syndicated TV show.

Or the advertiser can make a "spot" purchase from any carrier – network, cable, local affiliate, or local cable carrier.

This results in these six options:

National

1. Network
2. National spot
3. National cable

First there were three. Then four…

Now we are six.

Local

4. **Local Spot**
5. **Syndication**
6. **Non-network Cable**

Let's start with the big guns….

Network Television.

Network television comes into our homes free of charge.

There are currently four major national broadcast television networks in the United States: the American Broadcasting Company (ABC), the Columbia Broadcasting Company (CBS), the National Broadcasting Company (NBC), and FOX Broadcasting Company.

Three have dominated broadcasting for 40 years. FOX is a relative newcomer, but, in less than a decade, it has established itself as a legitimate fourth network.

Two New Networks.

There are two new and growing networks – WB (Warner Brothers/Time Warner) and UPN (Paramount).

This is all part of the trend of media companies developing their brands across media forms.

This trend is also a result of the fact that there are now more TV stations broadcasting in virtually every major market.

Networks don't "rule the tube" anymore, but their prime-time hits – from *The O.C.* to *ER* – still draw the biggest crowds. Network ratings still dwarf the majority of top-rated cable programs.

Nonetheless, ABC, CBS, and NBC are all working hard to create distinct brand images for themselves in order to hold onto their diminishing audience share.

A Dramatically Decreasing Share.

As you can see from the chart on the following page, the older networks have seen their prime-time audience decrease drastically in recent years.

Major Network Ratings Erosion by Daypart
Average ABC/CBS/NBC Household Rating - Spring

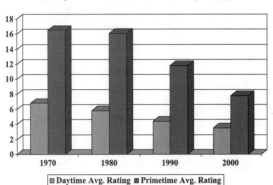

■ Daytime Avg. Rating ■ Primetime Avg. Rating

Declining State of Network TV. This chart shows the steady state of ratings declines in both daytime and primetime television for the three major networks.

TOP 25 CABLE NETWORKS BY AD REVENUE

From Cable TV (AA, June 10, 2002), this table ranks cable TV networks by ad revenue as measured by Taylor Nelson Sofres' CMR. CMR monitors 40-plus cable TV networks. Dollars are in millions for calendar 2001.

Rank	Network	Ad revenue	% change
1	ESPN	$1,007.3	-4.6
2	Nickelodeon	846.0	-4.8
3	MTV	670.1	6.3
4	Lifetime	648.2	12.1
5	TNT	591.1	5.3
6	TBS	546.8	-2.4
7	USA Network	491.3	-15.4
8	CNBC	472.9	10.2
9	Discovery Channel	437.5	7.5
10	A&E	390.1	-14.2
11	Comedy Central	299.6	5.4
12	VH-1	297.2	14.8
13	CNN	293.9	-23.8
14	TLC	279.7	2.8
15	E!	272.2	11.6
16	TNN	260.3	-20.6
17	Cartoon Network	225.4	19.2
18	FX	205.5	22.0
19	Sci Fi	198.8	-8.9
20	History Channel	193.0	3.2
21	The Weather Channel	179.3	-0.3
22	ABC Family (was Fox Family)	178.4	-3.9
23	MSNBC	174.9	11.5
24	HGTV	160.5	3.0
25	BET	151.0	-8.8

In 1980, three networks, ABC, CBS, and NBC, had a total audience share of 90%. In 1999, four networks, ABC, CBS, NBC, and FOX had a total audience share of 45.7%.

Why the big drop?

This is a big, important question for everyone. On judgment, network TV's audience continues to decline due to cable, the Internet, and computer/video games making claims on the time once devoted to watching network TV.

Cable – More New Networks.

Cable has eroded network television's audience share.

Cable now accounts for 43% of all TV viewing and claims 25% of the ad revenue, according to *Electronic Media* reporter, Lee Hall. And, it's all TV to kids.

A recent survey found that 275 children ages 6 to 11 "could discern little or no difference between broadcast TV and cable television channels."

When asked which TV network they turn to first, 31% picked Nickelodeon, 14% picked FOX, followed by the Disney Channel, and the Cartoon Network.

It appears as if future generations of TV viewers will not see much of a distinction between cable, pay, and broadcast.

To them, it will truly all be TV.

Network, "O&O," and Affiliate.

Network TV consists of a group of local TV stations that are joined together electronically. Today, most networks rely on satellites to link all their local stations.

Until recently, regulations have allowed networks to own and operate (O&O) only five stations.

So, unless you grew up in one of the biggest markets, chances are the network station you grew up with was an affiliate.

Here's how it stands today.

Each local station signs a contract with a network that makes the local station an affiliate.

Syndicated TV.

Syndicated television sells, licenses, and distributes programs to stations.

The process is worth reviewing.

First, Get a Program.

The first thing syndicators do is secure programming.

They can produce their own. Or, they can acquire programming from independent program producers.

Then, Get a Station.

After rights are secured, syndicators will offer the programs to stations.

The license lets stations use the programs for a fixed length of time. Once the license is signed, syndicators supply the station with a tape of the program.

Some Examples.

Original syndicated programming (called first-run syndication) includes talk shows (e.g., *Oprah*, *Jerry Springer*, etc.), original dramas (e.g., the new *Star Trek*), and game shows (e.g., *Jeopardy*).

Hit Shows – Old and New.

Off-network shows (e.g., *Happy Days*) are syndicated programs previously shown on network TV.

Baywatch is perhaps syndicated TV's biggest success story – the world's most-watched TV show.

Barter.

Local broadcast and cable TV stations and syndicators make their advertising revenue through a system called **advertising-supported syndication** or **barter syndication**.

In the 1980s, many stations were desperate for fresh programs but short on funds to pay licensing fees.

Continued on next page...

An affiliate agrees to air only that specific network's programming. Both parties benefit.

First, the network gets approximately 90% of the local station's commercial air time to sell to national advertisers.

Through this collaboration, the network extends coverage.

Local stations come out ahead, too. All TV stations have a lot of air time to fill. You will recall that programming is the backbone of all TV stations, and it's expensive to produce.

A Shift in Policy.

Recent developments may alter these long-standing network/affiliate payment arrangements.

First, Rupert Murdoch's FOX Network bought many more than five stations. A smaller, less-dominant network, they were essentially allowed to buy as many as they could afford – they ended up with 22. And, FOX was already in the programming business.

Growing Networks. Shrinking Audiences.

Meanwhile, audiences are shrinking at the same time the cost of producing shows is going up.

On average, it costs $1.2 million for an hour's worth of drama programming. Big shows like *ER* cost even more.

You may need 22 episodes to fill a broadcast year. As audiences shrink, programming gets even more expensive.

Obviously, one local station can't afford to produce enough of these shows to fill its weekly schedules.

Therefore, local stations turn to the network to do the job. The three largest networks, ABC, CBS, and NBC each have approximately 200 local affiliate stations. They can blanket close to 100% of the U.S. with their broadcast signals.

Changing Production Relationships.

When there were only three networks, there were restrictions on those networks producing their own shows – except for news and sports programs.

Now, with more network competition and a greater need to recapture production costs through syndication, networks

Syndicated TV (Cont.)

Syndicators devised an alternative payment method – barter syndication.

Under this system, a local station gives the syndicator a portion of its commercial air time – instead of cash.

Generally, barter syndication sells shows to local stations on a 50/50 basis.

Here's How it Works.

Let's say a syndicator sells *Home Improvement* to a local station with six minutes available on each episode.

The syndicator takes three minutes and the local station takes three.

Variable Time Slots...

Advertisers who purchase syndicated TV buy programming, not time slots.

Stations can broadcast the programs whenever they choose. In Dallas, *Baywatch* might run 8 to 9 on Monday.

In Denver, it might be 7 to 8 Sunday.

...Mean Variable Ratings.

This is a big difference. A 30-second spot on a network show will run in all U.S. TV markets at essentially the same time everywhere.

Syndicated TV doesn't deliver that same consistency.

But it's Profitable.

Even so, it tends to be win/win.

Let's say 20 local stations buy *Home Improvement* through barter syndication. This gives the syndicator 60 minutes of commercial air time.

The syndicator packages the time and markets for sale to national advertisers who want their ads on that program – usually at a very good rate.

Continued on next page...

are more deeply involved in producing shows and retaining syndication rights.

We'll be keeping you up to date on this on our adbuzz.com website – stay tuned.

Syndicated Television.

Syndicated TV supplies programming to stations and to some cable networks.

The demand for programming is always intense. In the '80s, however, competition really heated up – as many new broadcast and cable stations came into the market.

Demand for original programming exceeded supply.

That's when syndicated shows, like *Oprah, Jerry Springer,* and *Wheel of Fortune* really came into their own.

The Advertiser Syndicated Television Association (ASTA) reported that *"in a little over 10 years, syndicated television has grown from almost nothing into a $1.6 billion advertising medium."*

1993 was a breakout year as ad revenues grew 12%, which was twice the rate of broadcast network TV. And syndication continues to grow in ad dollars, to more than $3 billion in 2003.

Syndication is an interesting, but complicated arrangement. We've explained it more fully in the sidebar.

National Cable.

National cable television is currently in more than 75% of American TV households.

There are currently 11,385 cable systems in the United States servicing about 75 million TV households.

Unlike broadcast TV, where a local station airs only one channel and receives its programs from just one network, local cable systems offer subscribers multiple channels and get their programs from many cable networks – at least a dozen or more.

That's why cable is often referred to as multi-channel.

Syndicated TV (Cont.)

The local station sells its three minutes to local and regional advertisers.

Compared to network TV, syndication splits the inventory of commercial air time more evenly with local stations.

Consequently, syndicated shows are apt to be more profitable to a station.

Although, it's not problem-free.

Then again, what is?

Program Suppliers.

In order to fill all the available air time on their many channels, cable systems use a variety of program suppliers.

They include:

- **Cable networks**
- **Superstations**
- **Local original programming**

When each local cable system has filled most or all of its channels with programming, it becomes a basic cable package that is marketed and sold to cable subscribers for a monthly fee.

The lowest fee gets "basic cable." Higher fees add various sport and movie "premium" channels, such as Outdoor Life and HBO.

Cable Networks.

Local cable systems contract with many different cable networks. Cable networks consist of 24 hours of specialized programs appealing to practically every taste and interest.

Sports enthusiasts tune into ESPN; women watch Lifetime.

Superstations.

Cable systems usually include a few superstations in their basic package. A superstation is a local broadcast station that is distributed nationally to cable systems via satelite.

Superstations that have proven most popular with viewers are Atlanta's WTBS and Chicago's WGN. They offer two-tier pricing for local and national advertisers.

Local Programming.

Some cable systems originate their own local programming – generally created by community and/or educational organizations – and show it on local access channels.

Pay-cable Networks.

Pay-cable networks offer commercial-free programming: premium movies, special events, concerts, and original series for a monthly fee beyond their basic cable service charge.

Home Box Office (HBO), Showtime, and Cinemax are examples of pay-cable networks. Some of today's hottest pro-

gramming originates from these pay-cable, premium networks – for example, HBO's *Sex and the City* and *The Sopranos*.

Pay-cable networks are delivered to subscribers by the cable system in their local area. They do not carry advertising.

But now let's look at a few who do ...

Cable Case History: Subway – Smile & Bite.

Hal Riney staffers joke about two pictures on their office wall: one is a great big smile and the other is Mike Tyson biting Evander Holyfield's ear.

They represent the essence of "Smile and Bite" – a successful campaign that combined an upbeat image campaign with aggressive comparisons to Subway competitors.

Its unanticipated star, however, was cable TV.

As this was written, Subway was the fastest growing major fast food franchise – the only one experiencing real growth during the past few years.

(They followed the success of this program with the popular "Jared" testimonial campaign, featuring "the Subway diet.")

Two Campaigns in One.

"'Smile and Bite' is basically two campaigns that work together," explains Doug Seay, senior VP at Hal Riney.

"Smile" is a branding campaign designed to promote long-term sales and build Subway's image.

"Bite" is a short-term sales, or promotion-driven, campaign that's more aggressive. It often addresses the competition's vulnerabilities and offers Subway as the positive solution.

The Cable Connection.

What really made "Smile and Bite" work, however, was Riney's use of cable. Prior to this campaign, the agency had used cable more as a complimentary medium, rarely committing more than 20% of a TV budget to the medium.

"When the smile campaign rolled out on Nick-at-Nite, we were surprised at how the flow from show to commercial and back to show seemed so natural."

The "Smile" commercials worked with any Nick-at-Nite show or, for greater reach, with family shows on Turner and USA Network.

The "Bite" commercials are competitive 15- or 30-second spots – like "Runner," where a slightly rotund junior exec races out of an office building and sprints across town, passing marathon runners along the way, in order to burn up the fat calories he's about to consume with his burger.

As he runs, a voice-over compares the 30 grams of fat in a Big Mac or a Whopper with the six grams of fat available in seven of Subway's sandwiches. "Runner," and spots like it, aired on ESPN, Turner Sports, and Comedy Central.

"There's nothing better than running those grams-of-fat commercials in the middle of ESPN's triathlons," Seay says. *"The people watching know you have to be healthy. It's really synergistic with the message."*

Kevin Armstrong, Subway's marketing director at the time noted, the two-pronged campaign gave the chain a new level of flexibility.

"For example, if we need a more female audience, we can increase our frequency with VH1, or if we need more reach, either Smile or Bite will work with Turner and USA networks."

Smile. A Bigger Bite for Cable.

When Subway adopted its Smile and Bite strategy, it increased its cable budget by 8-10%.

Subway won't divulge results of the campaign except to say that awareness rose dramatically.

Case History: New Business at Old Navy.

Prior to 1997, Old Navy had focused its ad efforts on newspapers, magazines, spot TV, and radio.

However, the popular division of Gap, Inc., was growing so fast that it decided to include network cable in back-to-school and holiday campaigns.

Results so exceeded initial expectations that Old Navy now considers cable a very comfortable fit.

A Kick in the Cargo Pants.

The back-to-school campaign promoted a signature Old Navy product – cargo pants – in what was intended to have been a three-week flight. *"Toward the end of the second week, we were asked to turn off national cable, because cargo pants were no longer available in stores,"* says Pam Marcus, VP and Director of National Broadcast at Old Navy agency Deutsch, Inc.

Fleece for the Fall.

Old Navy spent approximately $10 million on its fall cable TV campaign and $15 million for the holidays highlighting fleece products.

It put nearly all its national TV firepower into cable because it could deliver on a number of fronts, according to Walter Coyle, VP and Associate Media Director at Deutsch, Inc.

It provided an opportunity to build brand image, drive traffic to local stores (now nearly 300), and enabled Old Navy to expand and support local marketing efforts, while reinforcing their vision that shopping is fun again.

Deutsch also worked to carry its messages beyond its spots. *"One of our critical missions was extending the brand essence through each cable network we selected,"* says Coyle.

"The outcome of this strategy included extensive product placement and ownership positioning." Model Marcus Schenkenburg wore Old Navy clothes hosting an MTV Jam episode, and MTV's Mike Davis wore Old Navy for appearances on Winter Lodge.

Comedy Central and More.

The company-sponsored programming marathons on Comedy Central, a top-ten countdown on VH1, and a block party and Christmas party on Nick-at-Nite.

It was also involved in a series of fashion question vignettes on E! Entertainment TV.

"The beauty of cable TV was that we could get younger target prospects to find us on MTV, males on Comedy Central, and moms on Lifetime," Coyle says. *"Cable let us zero in on individual target groups to an extraordinary degree."*

What are Friends for?
To deliver an audience for advertisers with content that consumers want.

When the dust and snowflakes had settled, cable had consumed 100% of the national television budget for the Old Navy fall campaign. Today, this is unusual, but it will become more common.

Both national TV campaigns also had support from local TV and local radio, newspaper, direct mail, and out-of-home advertising in key markets.

Deutsch anticipates another campaign in which cable will again take center stage. *"There's no other vehicle that allows you to separate your client's products from all its competitors in so many unique ways,"* Marcus says. *"The ability to gain added value product placement – achievable by pushing the proverbial envelope – means gaining serious advantages for one's client."*

A Desirable Marketing Partner.

Cable's target focus, flexibility, and willingness to work with advertisers makes it a desirable marketing partner. That, and a growing audience make it even more desirable.

Your Media World Keeps Growing.

Newspapers, magazines, outdoor, radio, and TV are the media forms with which we're most familiar.

But as media interacts with today's fast-moving marketplace, it keeps changing and evolving.

As we said before, we'll be covering this in greater detail in Chapter 2, but, for now, just remember that it's a big world and getting bigger – and more complicated.

Let's talk about what that means to us as individuals.

Consumers & the Media.

We have become a media-saturated culture. Professor James B. Twitchell notes in *AdCult USA, "the culture we live in is carried on the backs of advertising."*

He observes that *"much of what we share, and what we know, and even what we treasure,"* comes from ad messages created by advertising agencies and delivered by vast and sophisticated media outlets.

Got Media?

Media personalities help brands connect more meaningfully with consumers.

From Stickers to Spectaculars – Indoors and Out.

Advertising is everywhere. Take a look for yourself: oranges, apples, bananas, and grapefruits affixed with little stickers used to promote the *Liar Liar* video, Snapple fruit beverage, *Anastasia* animated-film premium offer, the "Got Milk" campaign, and the remake of *Mighty Joe Young*.

A new "Got Milk?" TV commercial makes fun of the campaign's ubiquity – and the relative ineffectiveness of advertising. A man comes home from work through a veritable gauntlet of Got Milk messages. And when he gets home he discovers he forgot milk.

New York Times reporter Carol Marie Cropper recently found that today's advertising gives consumers little privacy and even less room to escape.

Privacy? For $75 a month per site, Minneapolis-based AJ Indoor Advertising will plaster a page-size ad on 3,000 bathroom stall doors and urinal walls.

For $100 a month, Market Media of Massachusetts will place an ad in the form of a tile on the floors of grocery stores.

Escape? Ski Lift Media, Ltd., based in Banff, Alberta, mounts "advertising tubes" that include full-color ads on chair-lift safety bars to reach skiers and snowboarders.

From the fenders of a NASCAR racer to our favorite sports teams to toddler's T-shirts asking "Got Milk?", we now live in a media-saturated environment.

We're also media-saturated as individuals.

In 2002, advertisers spent almost $240 billion on advertising, an increase of more than $5 billion over the previous year.

3,000 Messages a Day – or More.

What this translates to is approximately 3,000 persuasive messages confronting every man, woman, and child in the United States every single day of the year.

City dwellers are bombarded with even more ads.

Recent studies show many urban dwellers pelted with an astonishing 13,000 ads per day.

And what does this media glut mean for consumers?

Well, the first thing it takes is time.

The Great American Time Crunch.

Today's consumers feel like they are busier than ever before. They probably are. For example, in 1995, 59% of all American women were actively involved in the labor force, compared to 37% in 1967.

Married women, who juggle jobs, family, and household responsibilities may find little to no time to watch soap operas, daytime talk shows, or even read the daily newspaper.

The time crunch is severe. *"Americans currently spend an average of 9 1/2 hours watching television, going to movies, renting videos, reading magazines, listening to music or surfing the Web,"* reports Veronis Shuler and Associates, Inc.

"There are just so many hours in the day, and it looks like we've reached the saturation point," says President John S. Shuler to Business Week.

Studies show that as new media like the Internet emerge, Americans merely shift the amount of time they spend with other media – like television or magazines – to the new media experience. The Internet now gets about 11% of the average adult's time spent with media.

Many consumers do not expand the time they spend with the media, they just cut back on one to give to another.

Served or Delivered?
Whose Media Are They?

They're our airwaves. Broadcast television, the driving force of our media age, comes to us over our airwaves.

We own them.

Our government grants the use of the airwaves to broadcast stations – this is the basis for groups like the FCC judging how stations use the public trust.

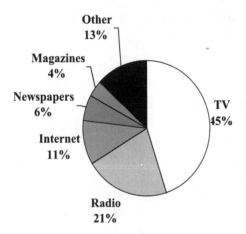

Time Spent Yesterday with Major Media

Average US Adults

Other 13%
Magazines 4%
Newspapers 6%
Internet 11%
Radio 21%
TV 45%

Pieces of the Pie. The Internet and other media are now carving out bigger slices.

Case History: Walt Disney's The Lion King.

Business Week reporters Elizabeth Lesly Stevens and Ronald Grover show how valuable an entertainment brand can be.

The Walt Disney Co. made *The Lion King* for $55 million in 1994.

Now look at the return on that initial $55 million investment.

$55 Million = $1.2 Billion ...

The animated movie took in $313 million in U.S. theaters and $454 million abroad, sold $520 million worth of videos, and was a main attraction on cable's Disney Channel.

That's just the beginning.

+ Merchandise ...

Fans spent $3 billion on *Lion King* merchandise. A percentage of that went back to Disney as licensing.

+ Records and Television ...

The Disney-produced soundtrack sold 11 million copies. Disney used the film again in September 1996 to boost ratings of its struggling ABC network.

+ A Broadway Show ...

The Lion King is still roaring.

In November, the Broadway musical debuted in a new Disney-run theater in Times Square.

Within days, tickets with a face value of $70 were going for $1,000 each.

Continued on next page...

It's the reason for those public service programs few of us watch. But whether we watch them or not, we should remember that these are our airwaves. They're our eyeballs.

As consumers, we can be selective – most of us are.

And, as media consumers we will continue to grow through an ever-expanding range of media options.

The Evolution of Media.

Media guru Marshall McLuhan notes that we evolve as our media evolves – from "ear-driven" oral cultures to the printed page – and now we're practically swimming in media.

"This new multi-media environment we live in is changing our consumption habits – greater amounts, greater variety, and greater sophistication. Today's viewer is not some passive victim.

"We exercise our options as easy as a turn of the page, a thumb twitch on the channel changer or a click of the mouse."

Today's Media Challenge.

This abundance of media has created a challenge.

How have media outlets themselves reacted to all of this change? By becoming brands – and creating new ones.

Media Conglomerates & Entertainment Brands.

Let's look at how the media compete in the marketplace.

Even in the early days, media companies were big.

Today, they're huge.

Big Stakes. Big Profits. Big Brands.

The media marketplace has always been one of high stakes and profit potential, where competition for consumers' attention and advertisers' dollars is fierce.

There's a lot of excitement in the world of media – there are a lot of interesting jobs and interesting brands.

Many of our most popular media outlets have become part of even larger media conglomerates like Viacom, Time Warner, General Electric, News Corporation, and Disney.

The Lion King (Cont.)

+ Future Revenues.

By now sales are almost pure profit.

Stevens and Grover sum it up, *"Just look at old movies such as* Casablanca *and* Star Wars, *TV shows such as* I Love Lucy, *books such as* Gone With the Wind, *or records such as Fleetwood Mac's* Rumours, *which continue to sell well and attract new audiences long after they were created."*

The goal isn't merely to create a hit, but a "cultural touch-stone" that will earn revenue for many tomorrows.

That's the long-term economic power of an entertainment brand.

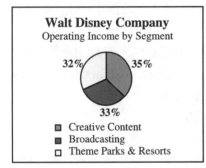

Walt Disney Company
Operating Income by Segment

32%   35%

33%

■ Creative Content
■ Broadcasting
□ Theme Parks & Resorts

RugRats.
An entertainment brand.

These are massive media organizations.

Rupert Murdoch's News Corporation includes newspapers, magazines, book publishing, 20th Century FOX film and video production, FOX television, cable/satellite, and new media.

But big as they are, it's not an easy business.

Media Challenges.

Audience fragmentation and media clutter have also forced entertainment media companies to adopt *"cost-cutting tactics, layoffs, more sophisticated market research and the formation of strategic joint ventures"* to survive in the overly crowded and competitive media world.

What this means to entertainment media organizations, like Disney and Time Warner, is the pressure to:

• Spend more to produce a product (like a movie, book, or television program) that exceeds the quality of other media producers, and

• Sell this product over and over again in different markets, venues, and formats to maximize profits.

Do it right, and your product becomes a long-lasting and profitable entertainment brand, like Disney's *Lion King*.

Note the balance of the Walt Disney Company earnings statement. A third of operating income comes from what they call "creative content."

Splintered Media Audiences.

Size doesn't always help. Although they're big, media companies are finding that they have to spend more to capture segments of a splintered media audience.

They've added new divisions like record labels, and to leverage their "entertainment brands," new movie studios, broadcast and cable networks, theme parks, and online ventures.

Splintered audiences mean that properties that can accumulate big audiences are worth even more in today's media marketplace. When they can generate profits in more than one division, so much the better.

Big Brands. Big Bucks.

Media organizations also are paying more on producing the content or securing the rights to run certain programs.

NBC agreed to pay approximately $900 million to renew *ER* for three years.

CBS, FOX, and ABC paid a staggering $17.6 billion for rights to broadcast NFL games for eight years.

These dynamic outlays translate to weakened profit margins. In 1987, Disney had operating margins of 25%; a decade later, this has dropped to 19%. Viacom, Inc.'s, 1987 operating margin was 13%; now it's half of that.

The Need for Branding Media.

Faced with intense competition, individual media outlets, like Viacom's MTV Networks, are finding that to connect with young viewers and attract ad dollars, they must handle their media property like a brand. In essence, to understand today's media environment is to understand branding.

FOX Builds Their Brands.

In its 1997 financial report, FOX Broadcasting credits a strong brand identity for part of its phenomenal success, stating: *"Broadcast television remains the primary medium to reach a mass audience in the U.S., and FOX Broadcasting has one of the strongest brand images and attracts the highly sought after audience of young viewers."*

Revenues hit record levels at FOX in 1997, thanks to the network's unique strategy to distinguish itself from the older more established networks (ABC, CBS, and NBC). They've continued to grow from there. FOX revenues today are over $2 billion.

FOX's strategy focuses on targeting a younger audience with distinct programming and promotions.

In 1997, shows like *The Simpsons*, *King of the Hill*, *The X Files*, and *Melrose Place* made FOX the #2 network among

2003 REVENUE: $2.24 billion
OWNER: News Corp.
TOP EXECUTIVE: Sandy Grushow, chairman, Fox Television Entertainment Group
PROGRAMMING: General entertainment
TYPE: Broadcast
TV HOMES REACHED: 106.0M
VIEWERSHIP: 9.7M

HOT PROPERTY:
Arrested Development

the hip 18-to-34-year-old crowd during the lucrative prime-time hours.

Strong brand identity and a focused strategy has won over even younger television audience members.

For example, after holding the number-one position among kids for the past four years, FOX continues to be extremely popular among youngsters. In May 1997, FOX secured the #2 ranking among the 2 to 11 set by averaging 1,385,000 kids with its FOX Children's Network.

Good Sports.

The accumulation of small regional cable sports channels resulted in FOX Sports Network, showing 70 of 76 pro baseball, basketball, and hockey teams.

Domination with local sport brands has made FOX Sports a strong player in TV sports almost overnight.

But the competition in sports is tough, too. In Chicago, the owners of the Cubs, White Sox, Bulls and Blackhawks are leaving FOX to start up their own sports channel – their partner is Comcast, one of the main local cable providers. That means FOX Sports Channel in Chicago is going to have a much tougher playing field.

They play hardball in the media business.

The Growth of Media Brands.

Media outlets, like MTV, have long understood the importance of branding when it comes to distinguishing a media vehicle in a competitive marketplace.

ESPN is another media brand on the move with everything from theme restaurants (ESPN Zone) to a radio network, retail stores, a newsmagazine, and some of the cleverest commercials on TV – done by Nike agency Wieden & Kennedy.

A Bigger Challenge for the Largest Media Companies.

An understanding of branding is helping some cable networks survive, even thrive, in a time of competitive chaos.

2003 REVENUE: $2.87 billion
OWNER: Disney and
The Hearst Corp.
TOP EXECUTIVE:
George Bodenheimer, president
PROGRAMMING: Sports
TYPE: Ad-supported cable
TV HOMES REACHED: 88.2M
VIEWERSHIP: 2.0M

HOT PROPERTY:
NFL Sunday Night Football

As ad agency Ogilvy and Mather describes, *"It is understanding the relationship between the product and its users."*

This is exactly what MTV is doing.

This takes keen consumer insight and a firm understanding that *"the brand's true owners are the loyal consumers who drive the bulk of profits."*

Ogilvy and Mather further suggests that it is essential to *"understand the relationship between the product and its users, searching for the full significance of the product in the user's life."*

But this is much clearer for specialized media brands like MTV, Nickelodeon, and ESPN – they each stand for something with a key target. If you're NBC or Time Warner, the problem can be a bit more complicated.

The largest media conglomerates must act like multi-brand marketers. And, again, it's entertainment brands that can be the organizing concept for marketing efforts.

Entertainment Brands in Action.

In the fields of media and entertainment, new brands are popping up every weekend and every TV season.

Some will be here and gone in an instant, and others will become a major part of our media culture.

Godzilla's Brand Manager.

Bob Levin worked on big brands in Chicago. Now his brands are blockbusters – *Jerry Maguire, My Best Friend's Wedding, Godzilla, Air Force One,* and *Men in Black.* Bob became President of Worldwide Marketing for Sony Pictures.

One of its more visible marketing and tie-in efforts was the *Godzilla* campaign. It was big! Size does matter.

Today's media world is big brands, big budgets, and a new appreciation for the value of a brand property. To make the most of that investment, Sony Marketing worked tie-ins with Taco Bell, toys, and an outdoor campaign that captured everyone's attention.

TOP 10 MOTION PICTURES

From 100 Leading National Advertisers (AA, June 24, 2002). Movies listed had to be released in 2001 except for "O Brother, Where Art Thou?" which had only $2.4 million in B.O. receipts in late 2000. Movies shown also had to have both VHS and DVD release in 2001. Movies were taken from Variety's top 250 by box office receipts, and VHS and DVD rentals were required to be among VSDA/VidTrac's top 50 by revenue in 2001. Ad spending figures are for calendar 2001, from *Ad Age* and Taylor Nelson Sofres' CMR. Dollars are in millions.

Rank	Movie/DVD/VHS	Box office, DVD, VHS sales in 2001	Measured media advertising In 2001	Per share point
1	Shrek	$318.9	$76.5	$4.2
2	Hannibal	228.2	34.1	6.7
3	Save the Last Dance	152.3	15.9	9.6
4	Legally Blonde	139.9	20.8	6.7
5	Along Came A Spider	125.7	24.9	5.0
6	Mexican	124.9	21.8	5.7
7	Wedding Planner	124.0	13.5	9.2
8	Swordfish	121.8	32.9	3.7
9	Down to Earth	112.8	21.2	5.3
10	O Brother, Where Art Thou?	106.9	8.0	13.4

A more comprehensive ranking is available in the DataCenter AdAge.com

Movies cost millions to make. To make the most of that investment, most big movies spend millions more in advertising. Here is a list of ad spending for the top 10 movies of 2001.

Big media for a big impact.

Size Matters.

Licensing, spin-offs, and merchandising can top $1 billion. To promote Godzilla, Sony spent an estimated $50 million. Marketing partners committed $150 million more.

A movie marketing blitz is sort of a mixed media work of art: publicity, movie trailers, advertising, and merchandising create a six- to eight-week cultural event.

"When the public only sees things in advertising, they're skeptical," says Levin. *"But if it's in all the forms where they expect to see things, then it lifts [the campaign] to another level."*

Godzilla is more than a movie. It's an entertainment brand that can be used to sell lots of products. 220 licensing partners signed up.

Size does matter. Here Lizard, Lizard…

Good job, Bob.

Summary.

This has been a quick tour through the media world and some of the things that make the world of media go round.

You've looked at it from three perspectives:
- **The Media Company**
- **The Consumer**
- **The Advertiser**

And we've covered a lot of territory:

- **Media History.** You should have a good sense of how media and marketing have evolved and interacted. Remember, every time media changed, advertising changed.

- **Today's Media World.** You've been introduced to the business of media – a very big business.

You now have a sense of each of our media channels, their size, their power, and their ownership.

- **Consumers and the Media.** You also have a bit more of a feel for your role as a "consumer" of media and some of the emerging issues as the media marketplace continues to evolve.

- **Media Conglomerates and Entertainment Brands.**

You've seen some of the evolution in the world of media.

Toby Trevarthen's is a story of energy and enthusiasm for all things new and exciting in media. He has enjoyed a successful career in media by eagerly embracing new media developments. Toby sees new media as new opportunity, and it is this powerful perspective that keeps him at the cutting edge of innovation and integration in the media world.

Career Capsule:

Toby Trevarthen, Regional Vice President, NW Region, Media Networks.

Toby Trevarthen is a regional VP for Media Networks, a division of AOL, a division of Time Warner. Toby actually started out in advertising as an account executive, not in media. He says it was his experience in school at Michigan State University that led him indirectly into the media path. And, he's never looked back.

That First Job.

Once he got out of school, Toby was primed for account management and looking for a job with a blue chip agency to launch his career. He sent out about 100 résumés and hotly pursued any lead until he landed that first job. That was Dentsu, Young & Rubicam in Los Angeles.

He was living the life when he joined the agency's new business team pitching a prospective computer/software client. He had some experience launching a new software company as part of his campaigns class at MSU. He says he *"fell into the media world"* at that point. He realized then that the media world was a better match for his entrepreneurial spirit.

A Mover on the Cutting Edge of Media.

Toby joined the advertising sales staff for USA Weekend in the Los Angeles market. He accepted a promotion to run the Chicago office in the Midwest region as the Chicago Sales Manager. From there Toby built his media career by aggressively pursuing media jobs on the cutting edge of media business development.

He worked in corporate sales at Meredith where his job was to create innovative, multi-media solutions for Fortune 500 clients. He was packaging and selling the Meredith home and family media properties before most marketers even thought they needed such packages.

The only other major media company doing this kind of work was Time, Inc. and soon enough, they came to hire

Toby away from Meredith. Toby started his career with Time, Inc. just over ten years ago. Except for a brief stint with a dot.com start-up, he's moved consistently up the organization.

He was there as Time, Inc. became Time Warner and then back again as the AOL/Time Warner merger began to fully integrate. What he likes the most about his work today is *"Building strategy, making sales calls and ideating solutions to business problems for both customers and AOL."*

Looking Ahead.

"As I look across the media landscape today, I see that it has become far more complex. There are more types of media and the blurring nature of 'who owns media, who delivers media, and who creates media' is still evolving." Toby Trevarthen sees media today as *"changing the social fabric of how people gather and communicate."*

Toby says, *"You (the student) are living with media all around you. You consume it. You use it. You create it. You publish it."* You are in control like never before.

Advice.

If you want a job in the media world, Toby suggests that you work the angles.

Be a creator of media. *"If you have a passion and or ambition about something – publish it."* Create the content. Build your own personal portfolio to showcase your talent, *"think multi-dimensional in terms of how to represent yourself."*

Sell media assets. Lots of people like him make a terrific living selling media to agencies and clients. He says it's a fascinating way to learn business because you can call on every conceivable business in any given day.

Or, start on the agency side. Learn by osmosis as he did. Most of the people in media sales today learned the business in an agency role.

However you do it, he says just do it. Find the angle that works for you. Do your homework, *"Use the Internet, Google the people you are going to meet."* Get the job, then figure out where to go.

Discussion Questions.

OK, let's take what we've learned and put on our "thinking caps." What do you think about these questions?

1. Media and Audiences.

If you were to start up a new magazine, who do you think would be the best audience for your magazine?

Why would this audience be attractive to advertisers?

What would your magazine offer readers and advertisers that current magazines do not?

What would be the name of your magazine?

2. Media History.

How did advertising media help build Campbell's Soup into a powerful brand? How does advertising media continue to make Campbell's Soup such a strong brand?

3. Media Brands.

Why must today's media brand themselves?

How would you create a brand for your campus radio station or newspaper?

4. Your Media Network.

What is one of your favorite ads? Where did it appear? Television? Magazine? Newspaper? Outdoor?

How did the medium enhance the ad's persuasive power?

5. Media and Society.

Do you think that ads should appear everywhere?

Why or why not?

6. Media Jobs.

Your roommate has asked for some career advice. He/she wants to know what kinds of jobs exist in ad media.

What do you tell him/her?

7. Entertainment Brands.

What is one of your favorite entertainment brands?

In what media does it appear?

How does the medium enhance the brand?

Entertainment Brand Exercise:

A sports team is an "entertainment brand."

Your college has one (if not, think about your high school sports team). Here's your assignment.

1. **Describe your school's "entertainment brand."** What do you think are some unique aspects of your school's brand equity?

2. **List some of the current ways that your school's "entertainment brand" is marketed.**

3. **Think up a few new ways to expand your brand.**

SRDS Exercise:

Let's get some practice with SRDS. Let's say you're a media planner and your job is to select and schedule media.

Your client, 20th Century FOX Home Entertainment, is rolling out the home video DVD for the popular feature film *Dodgeball*.

One of the magazines being considered for the DVD release advertising campaign is *People* magazine.

A current SRDS listing for *People* magazine is available online at www.adbuzz.com. When you get to the AdBuzz website, click through Strategic Media Decisions to find the *People* magazine listing. Study the information provided and answer the following questions.

1. 20th Century FOX is a frequent advertiser in *People* magazine, on average spending about $5 million per year. Is 20th Century FOX eligible for any high volume discount? If so, what percent discount will they earn?

2. What are the special issues of *People* magazine? Which one do you think would make the most sense for this DVD release? Why?

3. How much will it cost (including the dollar volume discount) to run one full page, 4-color advertisement in a regular issue of *People* magazine?

4. You know that a high percentage of *People* magazine sales come from single copy sales. Knowing this, the rate-base guarantee becomes more important. Look at the listing and find the information for the "Issue-by-Issue Tally (IBIT) Pricing System." From what you see here, if *People* falls short of the rate-base guarantee, can 20th Century FOX recoup advertising credits on another DVD home video release? Why or why not?

5. You are thinking about a heavy-up of advertising in the top ten metropolitan areas. Your supervisor wants to know:

   5a. Can you run an ad in *People* magazine in just the top ten metro areas?

   5b. What is the circulation rate base for *People* magazine in the top ten metro areas?

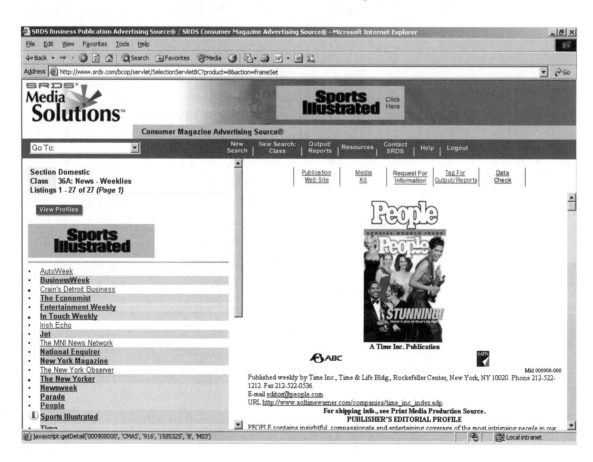

2 The Media Age.

WHILE YOU'VE BEEN BUSY GROWING UP and living with the media all around you, the media industry has been busy too.

Energy, Technology, and Change.

Today, we are all living in "The Media Age."

There's an energy we've never seen before. It's revolutionary technology creating unprecedented change.

In Chapter One, we gave you the brief history. There was the newspaper age, the magazine age, the radio age, and the television age. And every time media changed, advertising changed right along with it.

Right now, some think that we are in the Internet age, or maybe the age of technology, or even the multimedia age.

Certainly, technology is one engine fueling growth in the industry. But, this exponential expansion we see all around us is more than just technological advancement. It's a whole new world. And media is the common denominator.

Chapter Organization.

In this chapter, we're going to consider the driving forces and the tremendous opportunities of this media age.

Here's what we'll cover.

1. The Media Industry Comes of Age.

First, we'll look at the exponential growth of media options in our world. We will dazzle you with facts and figures. You will be the envy of your peers, the Master of Media Knowledge. Then, we'll consider the driving forces of growth.

2. The Technology Engine.

Technology is certainly a major force contributing to the expansion of media options.

Here we will reflect on major technological advances like the Internet, desktop publishing, cable, cellular, and wireless communication, and interactive technology.

Each technological advance has served to improve not only our access to the media, but also our ability to customize our own personal media network.

3. The Land of Opportunity.

Free speech is another big factor driving media.

Do you have something to say? So does the guy next to you. And, the gal next to him.

This is the land of opportunity and media is the new American Dream. Go ahead, say what you want to say.

Sometimes it seems that if you can dream it you can do it. You can broadcast your newsletter to the world on the World Wide Web. You can publish a 'zine and burn it onto a CD, or post it on the 'Net.

With a little money, you can run your own radio show. With a little more money and equipment, you can go on cable.

4. The Media Whirl.

Hold on. This might make your head spin. Marketers want consumers to see their messages. Consumers want entertainment and information. Media companies program content to attract both consumers and marketers.

But, the balance is very difficult.

Good content attracts a lot of consumers. That attracts a lot of marketers' messages. And that results in clutter.

Too much clutter detracts from the content – so consumers seek new content. They fast-forward or change the channel until they find content they like again.

And where media consumers go, marketers follow.

And, so on. And, so on. And, so on.

Media Comes of Age.

As we were writing this book, this was the shape of the American media industry. There were six broadcast television networks and 60-70 cable television networks programming media content for the 80 channels received in the average U.S. TV home.

There were 13,898 radio stations delivering more than 30 different kinds of radio program formats.

There were an estimated 1 billion different websites.

There were almost 1500 daily newspapers, 17,321 magazines, and countless newsletters.

There were more than 550,000 outdoor locations.

There were only a few big telemarketing services firms, but they kept millions of people busy placing calls every day.*

There were hundreds of direct marketing services sending out almost $45 billion in individually addressed advertising messages.

There were more than 36,000 movie theatre screens in the U.S., and about 75% were running pre-movie advertising.

All these media. All programming entertainment and information content for you!

Every imaginable segment of the media industry has exploded with options. Let's look at the trends for each segment.

Television.

Television really caught on in the '50s when mass production of TV sets began. By 1955, the demise of the DuMont network and the rise of ABC left just three networks, ABC, CBS, and NBC, in control of more than 90% of all American TV viewers.

Due to recent "no-call" legislation, this business is changing dramatically – just one more example of how fast things can change in the Media Age.

As recently as the early-1980s, a media planner could place an advertiser's message in primetime simultaneously on all three networks, and reach 90% of all American TV viewers.

Shortly thereafter, it all changed. Cable TV penetration reached critical mass with more than 40% of all U.S. TV households and Rupert Murdoch launched the new FBC network (now FOX).

With the growth of cable and Internet technology, the fragmentation and splintering of the media began in earnest.

For example, the average number of TV channels per U.S. home has grown from only 2.9 in 1950 to more than 70 in the year 2000. And today, more than 80 channels.

1000 Channels?

The next wave is digital television. With digital compression of television signals, we'll soon have more than a thousand channels to choose from. And digital brings with it interactivity.

Soon, we'll all have what they call a personal video recording device, capable of customizing programming and advertising for our own personal wants and needs. Some of you may already have such a device: TiVo or RePlay.

You may be using yours right now just to cut out commercials or maybe you're just recording your favorite shows. But soon, you'll be calling up programming content on demand. You'll be watching the show you want to watch, when you want to watch it, not when the network wants to show it to you.

And yes, you'll be watching advertising too. But, you'll see the ads you want to see, when you want to see them.

Radio.

Radio used to be like TV used to be. There were powerhouse radio networks and big signal, clear-channel radio stations in the big cities. Media planners could count on radio to deliver a broad and loyal audience for a marketer's message.

Average Number of Channels Receivable
Per US TV Home

Year	Number of Channels
1950	2.9
1960	5.7
1970	7.1
1980	10.2
1990	27.2
2000	71.5

TV Channel Mania.
Expansion of TV channels has exploded in recent years; even before digital TV, the average U.S. TV home receives more than 70 channels.

Tivo Mania.
Many predict that expansion of DVR technology will explode in the next few years, dramatically changing viewing habits of the most desirable demographics.

There were fewer radio stations – and virtually everybody listened.

Today, there are more than 13,898 U.S. radio stations.

And people still listen a lot.

The average adult in America listens to more than two hours of radio every day, across a selection of 3-4 favorite stations.

Radio used to be broadcast exclusively by Amplitude Modulation (AM) signals. AM radio signals bounce around off hard surfaces. At night, when the earth's ionosphere hardens, stronger AM signals bounce even farther.

For example, the Chicago sports talk radio station WSCR-670AM can be heard at night in 37 states across the U.S.

Oh, if only they had something good to say!

Everything changed when the FCC cleared the way in 1961 for Frequency Modulation (FM) radio signals. FM signals can travel through solids. For example, you can pick up an FM radio station on your car radio even when you are traveling through a tunnel, whether it's through the Rocky Mountains or under the Hudson River. But FM signals travel over a much more finite geographic range. As a result, we have many FM stations throughout the country broadcasting on the same frequency.

FM radio stations try to improve their geographic range by broadcasting from an antenna placed as high up as possible. Have you ever wondered why we see so many radio antennae on the tops of tall buildings? This is why.

Today we have XM and Sirius (pronounced like "serious") radio gaining in popularity and penetration. These new services bounce their radio signals off satellites so they can be heard anywhere within the range of the satellite.

And more and more of us are doing our radio listening on the Internet. Speaking of the Internet…

Satellite Subscription Radio.
One of the newest things in radio.

Top 10 Internet Destinations by Weekly Audience, December 2003	
Brand/Channel	Unique Audience (000)
1. MSN	44,407
2. Yahoo!	43,478
3. AOL	37,477
4. Google	20,659
5. eBay	17,947
6. Amazon	10,732
7. Lycos Network	8,341
8. AOL News	6,900
9. Weather Channel	6,289
10. About Network	6,217

Source: Nielsen/Net Ratings

Internet.

The figure, 50 million households, is widely accepted as the base audience needed for mass media status. It took radio 38 years to reach a U.S. audience of 50 million households. It took television 13 years and cable television just ten years to clear the 50 million households hurdle.

It took the Internet less than 5 years to reach that number.

Internet addresses come and go at a mind-boggling pace with an estimated 40,000 new websites added every day.

Despite the sheer quantity of sites out there, the average adult in America visits only a few sites on any given day. The most popular sites tend to be the larger Internet service providers like MSN and AOL and the bigger search engines like Yahoo! and Google.

As you probably know, there are many different kinds of Internet websites. From simple news and information to interactive gaming and commercial sites, consumers have a vast number of choices to incorporate into their lives.

Similarly, for every different kind of website available, there is a different kind of advertiser use available as well.

Advertisers can and will do everything on the Internet. They can place advertisements on an existing website, they can create their own informational website, or they can create their own interactive or commercial website.

From an advertiser's perspective, there are many advantages and uses of the Internet as an advertising media.

All at once, the Internet provides any advertiser with cost effective, worldwide message delivery to a precision-targeted base of consumers. Production costs can be very reasonable, messages can be updated or changed at a moment's notice, and consumers can spend as much or as little time as they want with the message.

Top 10 Blogs by Linking	
1. Instapundit	www.instapundit.com
2. Daily Dish	www.andrewsullivan.com
3. Scripting News	www.scripting.com
4. Girlwithagun	www.livejournal.com/ysers/girlwithagun
5. Wil Wheaton	www.wilwheaton.net
6. Where is G.	dear_raed.blogspot.com/
7. Faith@LiveJournal.com	www.livejournal.com/users/labile/
8. Eschaton	http://atrios.blogspot.com/
9. Kottke.org	www.kottke.org/
10. Little Green Footballs	www.littlegreenfootballs.com/weblog

Web Logs: To blog or not to blog.

Web Logs – or blogs – are one of the newer developments in the ever changing world of the Internet. Blogs are a hybrid – a kind of evolved version of a hosted chat room melded together into a sort of e-newsletter.

Blogs started as a voice in the wilderness; a place where people with strong opinions and perspectives could speak their mind. They've recently grown in popularity with several mainstream media now publishing material. Today, even the Wall Street Journal is host to a blog.

And, of course, as blogs have gained audience, they have also gained advertisers.

As of this writing, some of the most popular bogs were taking in as much as $5,000 per month in advertising revenue.

Newspapers.

Newspapers have long been a favorite local medium.

From the early 1700s in America, newspapers have been the perfect media vehicle for developing and growing communities. They can even do a pretty good job growing a revolution. Newspapers like Benjamin Franklin's *Pennsylvania Gazette* played a key role in the American Revolution. Newspapers have always delivered news, information, and entertainment content across a broad range of geography from local city-area to regional, national, and even international importance.

It used to be that every city in America had one or two newspapers. In the larger cities, there also used to be smaller suburban community papers that advertisers could buy together in a group in order to cover a city with a newspaper advertising campaign.

Niche Newspapers.
The Chicago Tribune's Red Eye *and the Chicago Sun-Times'* Red Streak *target a younger market.*

Not Just News.
Many Sunday papers come packed with special advertising inserts, such as this free product sample and discount offer.

The business dynamics of newspapers are changing dramatically. Costs and technology have combined to drive a consolidation in this field. From a high of more than 1,760 daily newspapers in the 1970s, daily publications have shrunk to just under 1,500 in 2000.

While daily newspapers have declined, Sunday papers and alternative and niche market papers are on the rise.

We already talked in Chapter One about alternative papers like the *Village Voice,* the *Chicago Reader*, and more recently the *Onion.*

Today we have some new, niche market papers like the *Red Eye* and the *Red Streak.* These papers were launched by traditional newspaper companies like the *Chicago Tribune* (parent of the *Red Eye*) in an attempt to attract a younger audience. They take the same news written for the traditional paper and rewrite it in a style more desirable among younger 18-25 year old adults.

Another new development in newspapers is neighborhood zoning. If you live in a bigger city, you may have noticed a change in how your paper is delivered, particularly your Sunday newspaper. You used to always have a bundle in the middle of the paper comprised of all of the special sections, magazines, comics, and advertiser inserts.

Today, that same bundle of extras comes sealed in a plastic bag. Working with that plastic bag, newspapers can now efficiently insert different materials – advertising and editorial – for people living in different neighborhoods.

And, of course, newspapers are on the net.

Today, if you are willing to take the time, you can set up a newspaper home page to greet you with your own customized presentation of news and information. Tomorrow, newspapers will provide all the news that's fit for YOU – no longer just "All the news that's fit to print."

Magazines.

Magazines are also part of rapid growth in the Media Age. Today, we have more than 17,000 magazines published in hard copy form. You know, the kind you can flip through, page by page.

Magazines come in all shapes and sizes.

No matter what your market, there seems to be a magazine that is just right for you.

If yours is a consumer product, there are magazines for kids, magazines for adults, magazines for older adults. Magazines for women, magazines for men. Magazines for boys, magazines for girls. Magazines for people who have cats, magazines for people who have dogs. Magazines for people who have ferrets or other unusual pets.

Magazines for people who like politics, and magazines for people who don't.

Magazines for people who like travel, and magazines for people who don't.

Magazines for skateboarders, magazines for snowboarders, magazines for surfers, and now there's even one for kiteboarders.

If yours is a business product, there is a magazine for virtually every standard industry classification (SIC) in the U.S. There are magazines for computer buyers, magazines for car manufacturers. Magazines for shoe makers, magazines for shoe stores, and even a magazine for people who design shoes. If you are selling aglets – the hard-tip covers for the ends of shoe laces, you need to know this stuff!

In fact, if you don't like the magazine choices you have available today, just wait a short while. The Magazine Publishers Association (MPA) says there is a new magazine launched every day in the U.S.

Actually, as many as 9 to 10 new magazines are launched every week. It's only a matter of time before you'll have a new selection of magazine titles from which to choose.

Custom Publications.
This is the Kraft Foods magazine. It's called Food and Family; *and it's filled with Kraft advertising and custom editorial content.*

Probably the biggest new development in magazines has been the birth of e-zines. These are magazines produced and distributed via the Internet. Even more so than the hard-copy magazines, e-zines provide editorial and advertising content for the smallest of the niche market segments.

Customized publication is the future of magazine publishing. More and more today we see magazine publishers and marketers collaborating on news, entertainment, and advertising content for marketer defined audience segments.

Newsletters.

Newsletters have been around for a long time, but they are a newer phenomenon as an advertising media. As e-zines and online newsletters gain popularity and audience, they attract advertisers.

The Newsletter Access Directory, an online listing of newsletters by topic, lists almost 10,000 newsletters from business, to culture, to health, and everything in between. It is interesting to note that they claim their list of newletters represent viewpoints, *"often untainted by the pressure of corporate sponsors."* Interesting, because this too is changing.

It's getting to the point now where it can be hard to tell the difference between an e-zine, a blog, and an online newsletter. But, that's OK. Think about television; do consumers really know or even care whether they are watching a cable network or a broadcast network? No.

Consumers want content and the only thing they really care about is that the content is delivered to them at their convenience.

Out-of-home.

Of all the media, out-of-home may be the most amazing.

Out-of-home advertising used to mean outdoor boards and other outdoor signage like bus shelters and transit advertising. Now, this media has exploded.

According to the Outdoor Advertising Association of America (OAAA), out-of-home advertising today includes:

billboards (large and small), street furniture like benches and shelters, mall signage, in-store advertising, transit signage and vehicle wraps, airport signage, and stadium/arena signage.

Altogether, the OAAA reports almost 550,000 out-of-home advertising locations throughout the country.

And, this isn't even counting the many recognized yet un-measured and unrated locations we see almost every day.

Sites like highway toll plazas, bar/restaurant restrooms, side-walk paintings, and beach/event airplane-trailer signs.

Creativity in Outdoor Advertising. *Like this award winning effort for Outhouse Springs bottled water. Are they kidding? Fortunately, yes.*

Think of some of the other places you've seen advertising lately. Where else do you think marketers might place an advertisement? If you were in the me-dia business, how might you capitalize on this unexploited oppor-tunity?

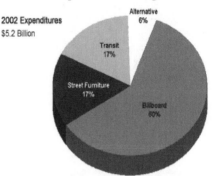

Out-of-Home Advertising. *Spending hit $5.2 billion in 2002 with 60% going to billboards.*

This will be a business opportunity for someone and it may as well be you.

And, it's not just about new places for advertising. There are new formats, too. We've seen taxi advertising for many years. Recently, we've started to see interactive touch screens installed inside taxis.

These screens are programmed to display informational content like restaurant reviews and movie show times as well as advertising content. As flat-screen technology keeps im-proving and prices keep going down, we'll see them in more and more places. Elevators and movie lobbies are just the beginning.

Telemarketing.

Telemarketing is probably the most intrusive of all the media options out there. As such, telemarketing is at once the most powerful and the most scorned of all media.

The Most Intrusive Media.

Let's consider this notion of intrusiveness. Television advertising is intrusive; it interrupts our favorite shows and almost always at the most inopportune moment of the story. Internet pop-up ads are intrusive and annoying.

While advertising is intrusive in other media, the intrusion was only an interruption of the media content, where we had already decided to participate with the media. With telemarketing on the other hand, the intrusion is an interruption of our lives. Telemarketing took a personal communication device, the telephone, and turned it into a medium. As consumers, this makes us angry.

The Most Powerful Media.

Now, let's consider that notion of power. Telemarketing is the most powerful of all the media because it is effectively personal selling. Ideally telemarketing is one person selling something to another person who actually wants to buy the product. Of course, nothing is perfect and sometimes the telemarketer reaches out to a consumer who they think will be interested in the product but, really isn't interested at all.

Actually, this happens a lot of times; most of the time. But, even so, when the marketer does reach the right consumer, the conversion to sale is very high. And so telemarketing is an incredibly powerful medium.

Millions of People Just Doing a Job.

Because telemarketing is so powerful, an ever increasing number of advertisers use telemarketing in one form or another. The Telemarketing Association tells us that this industry provides jobs for millions of people (2-6 million depending on the source) throughout the U.S. They're just trying to do their jobs, but these are the people we hang-up on when their calls interrupt our family dinner.

You may not realize it but, the very best thing you can do if you are not interested in the call is simply hang up. The people who work in telemarketing are expected to make a certain number of calls per hour. If you aren't interested and you hang up, you've freed them up to make the next call. From their perspective, the worst calls are consumers who listen politely and say no thank you at the end of the call.

New Technology Goes Both Ways.

Telemarketers have added new technology to improve their call productivity. Today, they use computer assisted dialing so their workers don't waste time on unanswered calls.

They've also started using pre-recorded introductions in an effort to get the consumer to self-select – indicating their interest in the product. These are the calls you have been getting lately where the recorded voice on the phone asks you to "press one" on your phone for more information about a product.

Just as telemarketers are using technology to limit wasted phone calls, consumers are using technology to help avoid unwanted phone calls.

Several years ago, phone companies introduced "Caller-ID" technology and consumers could use Caller-ID to ignore the "unknown caller." Shortly after that, we got "privacy manager" products. These are devices that stop the "unwanted caller" before the phone even rings.

Government Intervention.

But, even with all this new technology the phone call interruptions have become so pervasive that the government has stepped in. The government instituted "national do not call registry" took effect in the fall of 2003.

NATIONAL
DO NOT CALL
REGISTRY

At the time this book was being written, an estimated 55% of U.S. households had signed up for the do-not-call list.

We predict that even with a do not call registry, telemarketing will survive in the U.S. The unique, personal selling nature of the medium is simply too powerful. Where marketers have the will, they will find a way to succeed.

Do You Currently Subscribe To A Caller-ID Service?

YES 41%

NO 59%

Caller ID Technology.
New technology helps consumers avoid those annoying telemarketer calls.

Direct Marketing Examples.

Direct Marketing.

Direct marketing puts mail and e-mail in our mail boxes. It puts product samples in our newspapers and coupons and flyers on our doorsteps.

Like telemarketing, direct marketing is intrusive but in a much less irritating way. Because anything we don't want, we simply throw away.

There is no person at the other end; no one to yell at, and no one who might be offended by our indifference.

Also like telemarketing, direct marketing can be a highly effective way to sell a product. Direct marketing is as close as an advertiser can get to personal selling with out actually using people.

Increasingly Personalized.

Some direct marketers, like Val-Pak, send coupon savings to pretty much everyone in the zip-code area. Others are more targeted.

Zip-code zoning, printing, and addressing technology have advanced allowing advertisers to personalize direct marketing communications. Direct marketing materials used to come to our mail boxes addressed to "occupant" or "resident."

Today you get mail addressed to you by name on the envelope and most likely with a form letter inside that has been personalized for you. In fact, the actual packet of coupons inside the envelope might even be customized for you.

You might try this sometime. Open one of those direct mailer envelopes you get full of coupons and compare the coupons in your envelope with those in a friend's envelope. If your friend lives nearby, shops at the same stores, or buys many of the same things as you, then the coupons inside might be the same. But the coupons might just be different and you could have some fun trying to figure out why one of you got something the other didn't.

Top 10 Box Office Movies
Weekend: Jan 23 - 25, 2004

in millions

1. The Butterfly Effect $17.1
2. Along Came Polly $16.4
3. Win a Date w/ Tad Hamilton! $7.3
4. Big Fish $7.1
5. LOTR: Return of the King $6.8
6. Cheaper by the Dozen $6.4
7. Cold Mountain $5.0
8. Torque $4.5
9. Something's Gotta Give $4.0
10. Mystic River $3.

Big Business at the Box Office.
Advertisers targeting popcorn eaters at some of the most popular movies.

Movie Trivia.
Coca-Cola was one of the early sponsors of pre-movie slide advertainment.

Movie Theaters.

Movie theater advertising has been around for many years, but, for the most part, it was just slides for local area restaurants you might want to visit after the movie.

Today, cinema advertising has really taken off. Today we have advertisers producing commercials specially designed for the big screen.

The entertainment industry reports there are 36,000 theaters throughout the U.S. and almost 27,000 of them feature at least some form of pre-movie advertising.

In 2001, cinema advertising reached record-high levels with total advertising revenues of more than $250 million.

More importantly, advertising spending in movie theaters is projected to grow by more than 20% per year for the next several years.

In the Fall of 2003, Nielsen Media Research announced plans to collect audience data for cinema advertising clients.

Advertisers have found success in movie theaters for two big reasons. The first is a captive (and usually bored) audience and the second is relevance to a product tie-in.

The Early Arriver Gets the Ad.

Whether anticipating crowds or just their personal nature, consumers arrive early for movies and once they sit down, they wait impatiently for the feature film to begin.

Coca-Cola was one of the first major national advertisers to take advantage of this captive and bored audience. The soft-drink company created, and continually updates, a series of sponsored Coca-Cola Screen Play slides providing trivia and light information about movies and the movie business. This relationship between Coke and the theaters made tremendous sense, as Coca-Cola was the leading provider of soft-drink fountain service in theaters.

Other advertisers have caught on and as product placements in movies have expanded, so has the corresponding cinema advertising. One of the more recent high-profile ex-

Movie Tie-ins.
BMW has long been a partner with James Bond movies, featuring customized cars like this Z8 Roadster from The World is Not Enough.

amples of this was the BMW product placement in the James Bond film *The World is Not Enough*. For this film, the car manufacturer customized a BMW vehicle for the movie and then customized a commercial specifically to run in theaters prior to each showing of the movie.

We will certainly see more and more of this kind of movie tie-in advertising.

The Technology Engine.

This is the story of the little engine that could and did.

From the moveable press, to the telegraph, to radio, to television, to cable, to the Internet, to digital, and now wireless and interactive; the rush of technological advance has changed the American mediascape.

What the moveable press did for the printed media, the telegraph did for our broadcasting media. From the telegraph we learned that sound could be communicated over longer distances. From there, getting to where we are now was just a matter of time and resources.

Virtually all of our media today are the result of some form of technological advance. And, while it may be hard for some of us to imagine, there is still much more to come.

Think of some of the wildest things you've heard about lately; today's wild idea may turn into the media vehicle of the future.

Ad Messages from Above.

One of our favorite, recent wild ideas came up with some seriousness in 2002. An inventor of some merit suggested a new form of out-of-home advertising involving projecting messages in the night sky.

The idea is reasonably simple. We've all seen the bright beam of a search light panning through the sky for one reason or another. The point is that we can see the beam of light set off against the dark of night. And laser light technology has taken this even further to visibility. With all this in mind, we should be able to create and project a light or laser-light image that can be seen clearly by consumers below.

Interactive Technology.

Another big new idea that isn't so wild anymore is evident in the interactive nature of the new, personal digital-video-recording (DVR) devices like TiVo and RePlay.

These devices work off satellite or broadband technology and digitally compressed signals. The technology enables a vast capacity for recording and storage such that the television viewer can be watching a show and, in real time, skip forward through a commercial break or maybe even backward to replay a commercial they found interesting.

Ultimately, this amazing technology will allow consumers to interact with their television sets. Consumers will be able to program the TV to deliver desired media and advertising content on demand. Consumers will be able to call up a program that they want to see, when they want to see it, not when the media wants it to air. Likewise, consumers will be able to call up advertising they want to see. Yes, there is some advertising out there that consumers want to see.

And, of course, consumers will be able to eliminate advertising they don't want to see. It just won't be there anymore on their TV screen. This is not like fast-forwarding through a recorded commercial; the commercial will just be gone.

The important question facing most media innovations right now is whether we should do it, not whether we can.

We've reached a comfortable point of self-confidence about technology. We believe that we can overcome almost any technological barrier.

The bigger question is whether we should – and whether we can make any money at it.

Fragmentation and Segmentation.

The ultimate effect of all this technology so far has been an almost mind-numbing explosion of media fragmentation.

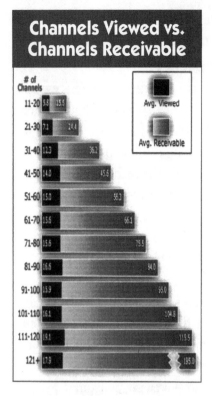

Channels Viewed vs. Channels Receivable

# of Channels	Avg. Viewed	Avg. Receivable
11-20	5.8	15.5
21-30	7.1	24.4
31-40	12.3	36.2
41-50	14.0	45.6
51-60	15.0	56.2
61-70	15.6	66.1
71-80	15.6	75.6
81-90	16.6	84.0
91-100	15.9	95.0
101-110	16.1	104.8
111-120	19.1	115.5
121+	17.9	195.0

Stable Channel Usage.

After a certain point, channel usage becomes fairly stable even when the number of channels receivable grows significantly. However, with more channels, there is obviously greater range and variety among individuals.

Consumers today have so many media content options that they are often times not even sure what to do.

For example, early research shows fairly stable channel usage in households with more television channel options.

Several researchers have confirmed this finding looking at television usage behaviors in households with recently installed satellite or digital cable television.

In both cases, the household's channel options increased dramatically, from around 100 channels to a high of more than 800 channels. Confronted with so many choices, the people who lived in these households defaulted to their favorites among the new set of choices – an average of between 15 and 19 channels.

Cable TV and satellite system providers found it necessary to add a "favorites" programming feature to help consumers more comfortably navigate the expanded content.

This kind of reaction is completely consistent with human behavior theory. When confronted with too many choices, it is a natural human reaction to either withdraw entirely from a decision, or, at minimum, to default to a comfort zone.

The result of this withdrawal has been a finer segmentation of the media audience. Every new fragmentation of the media has served to further drive consumers into their own naturally comfortable segments, making it even easier for marketers to address target market segments with greater accuracy.

This is good news for marketers who really know the right audience segment for their product.

The Age of Opportunity.

Another major factor driving the fragmentation of the U.S. media world is the American right to freedom of speech.

Anyone who has something to say can do so through media. There's opportunity for everybody.

Steve wanted to ask Jennifer to marry him. So he bought a billboard on the highway where Jennifer would see his message.

Dan has a lot of strong opinions about the professional sports teams in the Chicago area. Talking with his buddies at the bar was fun, but he wanted a bigger audience. So Dan went to a small, Chicago–area radio station where he paid a fee to rent a two-hour time slot on a weekly basis. Just like that, Dan had made himself a radio talk-show host! He went back to his favorite bar and convinced the manager to advertise on his show.

Mary and Susan started a neighborhood coffee club. They meet once a week for coffee and talk with friends and neighbors. One day Mary heard about a local cable access station where they could buy a time slot and produce a televised version of their coffee club.

Mary and Susan decided to invest the money and they started their own cable talk show. They still meet for coffee once a week, but now they take along a video camera.

Personal Interest Media Content.

Maybe you have something to say? With a little money you can run your own radio show or cable access show.

With access to a computer and little or no money, you can produce and distribute your own newsletter on the World Wide Web to anyone in the world who might be interested.

If you can show that you have an audience or following, you can even attract advertisers or sponsors to help you cover your costs.

Personal interest in media content is what built the U.S. media industry in the first place.

Several recent developments, however, have rejuvenated this particular kind of highly personalized media development.

Accessibility.

First, there's accessibility to the media, and in particular, access to media technology. We've already talked a lot about technology, but here we talking specifically about the technology of producing media content.

Access to Media Technology.
With a DV camera, a computer, and some editing software, you could develop your own content and be in the programming business.

Whether it is a digital video camera or a home studio sound system, quality is improving and prices are dropping almost every day.

Media technology today is available and increasingly affordable for anyone who may be interested.

Content.

Second, there is a vastly expanded need for media content. As each new media vehicle develops, success depends on developing media content that people want.

This need for content has led directly to a media industry that actively seeks new sources for content.

It's not that the media business has gotten easier to break into, it's just that there are more media than ever and the need for content is so vast. Media management today is more willing to take chances; they'll take a risk on new content if it helps them fill a time slot.

Syndicating Reruns.

Consider the content programming side of network TV. Networks used to be the exclusive outlet for first-run television programming. The networks would premiere original programming in the fall and then rerun episodes during the summer season when original programs were filming.

After the first couple seasons of original programming, the networks would sell previous seasons into syndication for rerun of dated episodes on independent stations or during local programming time on local market network affiliated stations.

Today, we have original programming created for first-run on syndication and cable networks.

We have networks releasing original programming almost immediately into syndication for some of the most popular shows like *"ER"* and *"Friends."*

And with media ownership today of multiple broadcast and cable outlets, we even have extreme examples of programming developed for networks going instead directly to cable.

Rerun Programming.
Syndication programming today still largely relies on reruns of network programming, like Frasier.

Showtime for *"Reagan."*

For example, the *"Reagan"* mini-series developed in 2003 for the CBS network. With just two weeks left before the scheduled air date for the *"Reagan"* mini-series, CBS announced it would shift the first-run programming to its cable "sister" Showtime.

Simple Math.

Just think about it this way. There are 24 hours in every day and 365 days in every year (not counting leap years). If the average TV household in the U.S. has access to 70 television channels, that would be 600,000 hours of programming content per year. And that's just the average household. Have you noticed how many programming hours are filled every day with "paid programming" or "infomercials?" Is it any wonder?

Growing Sponsorship Opportunities

Finally, we have advertisers today more willing than ever before to take a chance on sponsorship of new media content. Advertisers are looking for a better platform for their sales message. As media choices have expanded, media audiences have scattered. Attention has scattered as well.

Today, advertisers are more willing to take risks. As technological advances come faster and new media appear faster, audiences tend to move faster. Advertisers and their agencies must respond faster to this spinning market and often times this means taking a risk and not waiting for proof or measurement.

Advertisers will always follow the audience. In the past, advertisers would wait for some established measurement. Advertisers and their agencies generally wanted some third party validation of audience before committing budgets to any new media.

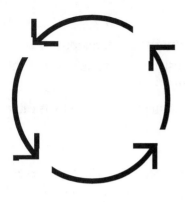

The Media Whirl.

Media management strategies are another force driving changes, challenges, and opportunities in the media business.

In the Media Age, the whole media business is spinning like a top. It has always been in a state of motion, but today that motion has picked up speed.

The spin goes something like this:

- Marketers want consumers to see their advertising and sales messages.
- Consumers want entertainment and information.
- Media management programs content to attract both consumers and marketers.
- Media content is a combination of entertainment, information, and advertising. But managing the balance is very difficult.
- Good content attracts a lot of consumers and a lot of marketers, so media managers sell more advertising time/space, resulting in clutter.
- Too much clutter detracts from program quality so consumers seek out new content.
- Where consumers go, marketers follow because… marketers want consumers to see their advertising and sales messages.

The good news about a spin is what goes around, comes around. The bad news is centrifugal force.

Let's consider each briefly.

What Goes Around Comes Around.

Technology may be driving a lot of change in this business, but the one constant will always be the audience. The audience will always be there, somewhere. And, marketers and media alike will always find a way to find the audience.

Any individual media vehicle may come or go, but no medium, once established, will ever go away. The media business will perpetually reinvent itself.

What was good once will be good once again.

Centrifugal Force.

Here's a metaphor that might help you understand the concept of media whirl.

When you were younger, did you ever take a spin on one of those kid-powered playground merry-go-rounds? You know the ones where some kids sit on the hard metal base while other kids make it spin? If you ever did take a spin, then you certainly know the feeling of centrifugal force.

Centrifugal force is the physical force that throws kids from a spinning merry-go-round. The kids who went flying were usually lighter weight or just the ones who didn't have a good grip.

It's the same thing in the spinning media whirl.

Media Grip.

Any medium that wants to stay on the merry-go-round must have a heavier audience weight and/or a very good grip.

Any individual medium or media vehicle can have more or less audience weight. As marketers and media go spinning around in pursuit of an audience, the media with less mass will fly off in an arc of trajectory.

Those media with heavier mass will keep up with the spin even as it gains speed.

And this holds for media with a good focus on its audience, even if the audience is small.

Got it?

If you are representing a marketer, it is best to balance the heavy-weight and lighter-weight media in order to get as much audience as possible. The real trick is knowing when to let go of the lighter-weight media; just before it flies off the base.

What makes this a driving force of change in the media business is simple survival. As the spin of the media whirl picks up speed, even the heavy-weight media can find themselves slipping on the hard metal base. As the heavy-weights slip toward the edge, they look for ways to add weight in order to keep their place in the business.

This is exactly what is happening right now. The media heavy-weights of today – the big media holding companies – are actively looking for new media acquisitions or partnership deals to maintain or gain mass.

Legally, however, the media in the U.S. can only go so far because we have laws regulating the amount of media any one company can control. At the time we are writing this media book, U.S. media are aggressively lobbying for changes in regulatory controls over their industry. They are arguing that they need such changes just to stay in business. Think about that merry-go-round spinning faster and faster, it is somewhat easier to understand their argument.

Summary.

So, this is it, the exciting world of the Media Age. We're in a time now that is booming with opportunities and challenges.

In this chapter, we've covered a lot of ground.

We spent time talking about each medium and the many important and exciting changes and opportunities facing each medium today.

We discussed the forces driving change in the media business. Technology is a major force driving changes in the media industry, but it's not the only factor. The other important factors we discussed here are increasing personal interest and involvement in media and even media management.

Anywhere you may go in this media world, you'll find these same challenges we've outlined here. The key is understanding the challenges and learning how to manage each.

The bottom line is this: in the U.S. the media exist for the audience. It takes an audience to make a medium and it takes a bigger audience to make a medium bigger.

Debbie Solomon has built an outstanding career in media research. Her academic studies in psychology and her early work in product research gave her an excellent foundation on which to build. When it comes to consumer psychology, Debbie Solomon is a lifetime learner.

Career Capsule:

Debbie Solomon, Senior Partner, Group Research Director, MindShare USA.

Debbie Solomon has built a terrific career in media, and in particular, media research. With a psychology undergraduate degree from the University of Chicago and a psychology master's degree from Duke University, media research has been the perfect place for Debbie.

A Psychological Advantage.

Debbie's studies in psychology gave her a big advantage getting into advertising. After all, advertising and advertising media is all about understanding the psychology of the consumer as it relates to the products they purchase and the media they choose to use.

In the beginning, Debbie parlayed her psych degree into a research profession starting as a toy tester for Milton Bradley. From there she continued her work in product research at both consumer products companies and industrial products companies. This work laid a solid foundation helping her understand the mind and motivations of the customer, all kinds of customers.

After her work on the product side, Debbie joined the media research department at Leo Burnett and then J. Walter Thompson (JWT). She was with JWT when the parent company, WPP, merged the JWT and Ogilvy & Mather media departments to create one large media agency, MindShare.

At MindShare, Debbie's work encompasses all media disciplines and she has worked on all of the agency's clients.

An Honorable Career.

Throughout her years in advertising, Debbie has earned many honors. Most recently, she was named by *Media* magazine as one of the ten most influential people *"navigating the waters of the magazine business."*

She received other awards before that.

She was named Top Kid Researcher by *KidScreen* magazine in 1998. In 1992, *Media Week* magazine elected her a Media Research All-Star largely for her work developing a system for measuring children's interest in and usage of the media.

Debbie serves as chair of the Advertising Research Foundation's (ARF) Youth Research Council and the American Association of Advertising Agencies (AAAA) Consumer Magazine Committee.

She has also participated as part of the Nielsen Kids Task Force and the prestigious conferences on Children and Television convened in Washington DC by the Annenberg Public Policy Center.

Advice for Students.

In her position Debbie meets a lot of students looking for a start in research. She says that what she looks for is *"insatiable curiosity, initiative, and the ability to find another way even when someone says 'no.'"*

But, it's more than just ability, you have to want it, and you have to have the drive and desire to make things happen.

Debbie goes on to say, *"It is also very important to be interested in people and what interests them; you need to have a good understanding."* It is that interest that first drew her to psychology in her academic studies. And, it certainly seems that advertising has been a great practical application for Debbie Solomon.

Discussion Questions.

1. The Media Industry.

Is there any such thing anymore as "mass" media?

Is the Internet a broadcast medium or a print medium?

Will newspapers continue to exist in printed form?

How small can a magazine's audience be?

How would you tell the difference between an e-zine, a weblog, and an online newsletter?

What is the next new place where you think you'll see an advertiser's message?

As a movie goer, how do you feel about seeing advertising before you see a movie?

How do you feel about product placements?

2. The Technology Engine.

From an advertiser's perspective, is continuing technological advancement a good thing?

3. The Land of Opportunity.

How would you convince an advertiser to support your new media idea?

4. The Media Whirl.

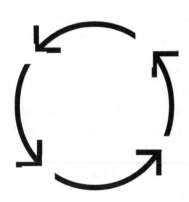

As an advertiser, what are the advantages and disadvantages of supporting a new media?

Why does the U.S. government regulate the media and company ownership of the media?

Should our government relax its regulation of media ownership?

Exercises.

1. **Go visit www.mediapost.com.**

Sign yourself up for this *free* service. Once you are registered and activated, go exploring. Take notes on what you find as far as media news and information, media jobs, and specific resources to support the many aspects of the advertising media business.

Prepare a short (2-3 minute) presentation on two features of the website that you feel would be most useful.

2. **Go find some media facts of your own.** This chapter is loaded with facts and figures. Now that you've read some of our highlights on the industry, go on the Internet to find some facts of your own.

   • Visit www.magazine.org and download a copy of the magazine marketers fact book.

   • Visit www.rab.com and download a copy of the radio marketers fact book.

   • Visit www.ncta.com, the National Cable and Telecommunications Association site, and search through the "industry overview" section, download the year-end overview.

   • Visit the Newspaper Association of America at www.naa.org and search "information for researchers."

   • Visit www.oaaa.org and search "marketing research" for free reports on the Outdoor industry.

   Write a short paper (1-2 pages typed) on what you see as the most significant changes in the business and how you expect these changes will impact the future of the business.

3. **Wanted: New Programming Ideas.**

   Focus on TV: survey your local TV Guide and record the hours of any one full week for which you find the listing "paid programming" or "infomercials."

   Do the math – what percentage of the week is paid-for commercial content?

Media Methods

PART TWO OF THIS BOOK is a big, meaty section. It contains a lot of detail specific to the planning and buying of advertising media.

Marketing, Math, and Planning.

We'll cover this material in four chapters.

Chapter Three will focus on the important relationship between media and marketing. It introduces some key media terms and concepts. Upon completion of this chapter, you'll be able to see why media planning has a bright future.

Chapter Four is probably the toughest chapter in this book.

Even though media is much more than just numbers, it is still very much a numbers game. Basic math skills are an absolute necessity. This chapter tackles the math question head-on in a creative and meaningful way.

Our goal here is to identify some of the key mathematical techniques all media professionals should know.

Then, we'll demonstrate media math in action.

If you do well in this chapter, you'll know you might have a bright future in media planning. If not, you'll know early on that this might not be a career option for you.

But look at it this way – you'll appreciate those number-crunchers you're going to work with even more.

Next...

Chapter Five is dedicated to media planning and the major steps of the media planning process.

You'll understand the importance of informed and strategic decision-making in media planning.

Chapter Six is about implementation of the media plan. We'll look at every step of the process – from the time the client approves the plan through the time the agency traffic department ships the creative materials. This chapter covers the planner's role, the buyer's role, and the seller's role.

You'll also see how others fit into the process.

By the time you're done with Part Two, you'll have a solid understanding of the process of media planning from the starting point of the marketing objectives to the end point of the post-buy analysis.

Ready? Let's go!

3 Media & The Marketing of Messages.

COMMUNICATING THE COMMUNICATION is the all-important job of any marketing communications plan. After the marketing plan is developed and after the ad message is created, it still has to get to the target audience.

This is where media comes in.

You're about to enter a world where big dollars are on the line. You may even have to learn a new language.

Chapter Organization.

In this chapter, we're going to roll up our sleeves and see what it takes to put marketing messages in front of a target.

This will be the big set-up chapter in this book. After this chapter, you'll be talking like a media pro and you'll be ready to tackle the rest of the book.

Media Speak.

First, we'll show you how to talk media. There are a lot of important terms. We'll put them in context. You'll have to learn them. They'll be on the test.

The Media Building Blocks.

This section will look at media from a professional's point of view – including the Strengths and Weaknesses of each major medium.

81

Many Terms, One Objective.
All of this chapter is focused on getting media messages to the target in the most efficient and effective way possible.

The Media Plan.

What it is. How to create one. Media strategies and objectives made simple.

The Media Planning Revolution.

Throughout, you'll see new ways planners are leveraging the explosion of new media opportunities.

From network TV, to cable, to out-of-home, to hanger tags at a local clothing store – you'll see how media planning is at the cutting edge of our Media Revolution.

When we're done, you'll know what it takes to take those first steps into the world of media.

Media Speak.

GRPs? CPMs? HUTs and PUTs and Double Trucks – Oh My! Wandering into the media department can be like crossing the border into a foreign land.

We'll cover these terms in much more detail in Chapters Four and Five, but for now let's take a moment to crack the code of the media world.

Commonly Used Media Terminology.

There are some key terms in media that you have to know and use correctly to avoid confusing yourself and others.

Let's review some basic, yet critical, media terminology.

You'll also find them in the Glossary at the back of this book. By the time you're done, you'll know what they mean.

Media and Medium.

Let's start with the term advertising media. It refers to all the channels of communication used to deliver advertising messages to consumers. It is also the plural of medium.

Primary Media, Mediums, and Vehicles.

Advertising media come in many forms, with the primary media including newspapers, magazines, television, radio, Internet, directory advertising (i.e., yellow pages), direct mail, business publications, outdoor, and point-of-purchase.

A single type of media, such as magazines, is called a medium; a single carrier, such as Sports Illustrated, is a vehicle.

These are the three major terms used to refer to the various categories of media delivery.

Media professionals use many other terms and acronyms. Some of these will be described in this chapter or later in the book. But, in case you need to know something right now, we've attached a whole glossary of media terms as Appendix 2 in the back of the book.

The Eyeball Business.

What media planning boils down to is that advertisers are investing in "eyeballs." They're striving to get their messages in front of the eyes (and ears) of the people most predisposed to buy their product or service.

In media speak, these pinnacle people with real purchasing power are called prospects.

As a matter of fact, media professionals have a variety of key terms to define the folks they want to reach with their messages.

Let's review a few of these important terms now, starting with the concept of audience.

Audience.

Audience refers to the number or percent of homes or people exposed to a media vehicle or advertising message.

Audience coverage is a term that tells us the number or percent of people or homes who are reached by a single exposure of a particular media vehicle in a specified area.

On Target.

Thanks to the ability of technology to give us detailed information on consumer attitudes, preferences and behaviors, specialized media, and databases, advertisers can be more precise in terms of defining, and ultimately reaching, their audience.

In their book *The New How to Advertise* Ken Roman and Jane Maas state that precision marketing is *"increasingly possible"* and describe this approach as *"marketing aimed at specific segments or even individuals."*

Got a Niche? Scratch It.

ABC/Disney leverages entertainment brands and media properties to focus on a small target – kids. With more media choices, niches are getting smaller. Here, a weekly audience of 1.6 million kids and 600,000 moms.

Rolling Stone:

Circulation: 1,271,000

Page Rate: $72,400

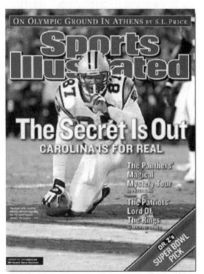

Sports Illustrated:

Circulation: 3,210,000

Page Rate: $146,310

As you can probably guess, the benefit to precision marketing is, according to Roman and Maas, *"less waste and a more personalized message."*

The terminology that matches this more exacting approach to marketing and advertising starts with target market.

This is the group who has been identified as having real sales potential for the brand and can be defined, not only in terms of demographics (i.e., age, education), but by other distinguishing characteristics such as psychographics (i.e., attitudes, behavior) and/or product usage (i.e., heavy users, light users).

A target consumer is a member of the target market.

Prospecting for Prospects.

Advertisers pay big bucks to reach prospects.

For instance, a 30-second spot, called a unit, on the 2002 Super Bowl cost over $2 million. The same spot on the Academy Awards had an $800,000 price tag.

Print can also be costly, with a full-page ad in *Rolling Stone* magazine costing $72,400, and the same insert in *Sports Illustrated* going for $146,310.

With those kinds of dollars involved, you can see why media companies are so concerned with both the quality and the quantity of the audience they deliver.

Because advertisers are spending so much money to reach these "pairs of eyeballs," they demand measurement statistics to both quantify and define the people they are reaching with the advertising media they're buying.

In other words, advertisers demand that the media be accountable for delivering a specified audience. In their quest for accountability, one of the first things that advertisers want to find out is who reads, listens, or tunes into a particular media vehicle.

Audience composition gives advertisers this statistical breakdown by spelling out the demographic classification of individuals within a media vehicle's total audience.

Reach and Ratings.

The next thing advertisers are concerned with is finding out just how many people are being reached by a particular media vehicle. This varies depending upon the type of media that is being measured.

Broadcast media use rating points to report the percent of the target audience reached by a media vehicle.

For instance, way back in 1997, *Seinfeld* was the top-rated television program, securing a 22% audience rating.

Print media, on the other hand, relay their target audience statistics through circulation figures that tell advertisers precisely the number of copies of a publication sold or distributed.

For example, *Spin* had a circulation of 488,000 in 1997.

Then again, some copies of *Spin* have more than one reader. That is computed as passalong, and it's quite controversial. Passalong readership is a measurement of the additional people that read or look at a copy of a magazine or newspaper. For example, according to the research *Spin* has an estimated 5.56 readers per copy, one of the highest in the business.

Advertising Spending.

In Chapter 2 we saw how marketers spend billions of dollars every year trying to coax people into buying their products and services.

Above-the-Line and Below-the-Line.

The revenue that is spent on paid advertising in mass media like broadcast network TV and newspapers, and specialized media like cable and magazines, is called above-the-line.

Below-the-line is all promotional expenditures that are not allocated in above-the-line media. It consists primarily of direct marketing, sales promotion, public relations, and event marketing.

$4,300 per Household. $1,600 per Person.

According to an *American Demographics* magazine article, private and public agencies spend almost $400 billion a year to bring above- and below-the-line messages to every man, woman, and child in the United States.

Consequently, these agencies spend $4,300 on every American household, or about $1,600 per person.

79% Consumer. 21% Business to Business.

U.S. advertisers spend their ad budgets trying to reach either consumers or businesses.

Typically, 79% of all money plowed into advertising is spent on media that is aimed at the consumer.

The remainder is appropriated to business-to-business advertising media, like specialized business periodicals that are geared toward professionals working in specific industries or businesses, such as Putman Publishing's *Chemical Processing*, which is aimed at chemical engineers.

Between 1% and 3%.

The investment that advertisers make in media is the largest chunk of their advertising dollar, far surpassing the money spent on advertising production.

On average, U.S. companies spend between 1% and 3% percent of their annual earnings on advertising.

The Largest Categories.

Companies that spend the most on advertising tend to be the largest manufacturers of food, soft drinks, automobiles, tobacco, and beer, as *Competitive Media Reporting* points out.

For example, in 2002, media giant, Time Warner, the second largest U.S. advertiser, spent $2.9 billion on media advertising. GM, the nation's largest advertiser, shelled out $3.7 billion for ad media.

Consumer-goods giant P&G was the nation's third largest advertiser in 2002 with spending reported at $2.7 billion.

As a rule, 60% of ad dollars are spent in local media.

Newspapers have historically been the largest medium for local advertisers and continue to be so today.

Traditional and Nontraditional.

Today, advertising media are often categorized as measured or unmeasured.

Measured media are more traditional, made up of newspaper, magazines, TV, and radio. These media still control the

Largest Advertisers:

Rank/Name - Ad $ (in billions)	
1. GM	$3.65
2. Time-Warner	2.92
3. P&G	2.67
4. Pfizer	2.57
5. Ford	2.25
6. Daimler/Chrysler	2.03
7. Walt Disney	1.80
8. Johnson & Johnson	1.80
9. Sears	1.66
10. Unilever	1.64
11. Sony	1.62
12. GlaxoSmithKline	1.55
13. Toyota	1.55
14. Verizon	1.53
15. McDonald's	1.34

Big Spenders. *The biggest advertisers spend billions of dollars each year on messages aimed at consumers.*

vast majority of advertising spending. And many industry experts don't see this changing until around 2005 when interactive technology should begin having a significant impact on how media budgets are appropriated.

Unmeasured media are more nontraditional and are often driven by technology. These can be any new media form that allows for commercial expression.

These unconventional media forms are far-reaching and include everything from truck advertising, where sides and backs of freight trailers or vans are leased to advertisers, to Internet advertising where destination sites, micro-sites, or banner campaigns can be used to interact with consumers.

Digital technologies are forcing marketers to re-think how they advertise to their consumers.

Traditional Media: about 50% of All Ad Dollars.

Traditional advertising media these days gather just under 50% of all advertising dollars.

In 1996, television inched out newspaper for the first time, receiving the largest share. In 2002, broadcast and cable TV combined for 25% of all U.S. media spending. In the same year, newspapers still accounted for almost 19% of spending.

The Growth of Direct.

Increasingly, direct marketing and one-to-one target marketing are becoming part of general advertising campaigns. It already receives 19% of advertising dollars.

There is more concern of accountability across the board.

That's why seasoned advertising practitioners project that most advertising in the future will include some type of direct response capability – such as a website address.

Follow the Money.

All media – whether traditional or nontraditional – have to be measured, priced, negotiated, and bought to stay afloat.

And advertisers only invest their dollars where there is opportunity to make sales.

---

www.mccann.com

These Numbers Change Every Year.

Find the latest update on U.S. media spending at www.mccann.com where Robert Coen tracks the latest in media spending patterns.

Here's the data for 2003:

Medium – U.S. Spending – ±%

(in billions)

Medium	U.S. Spending	±%
1. Direct Mail	$46.07	+3.0
2. Newspapers	44.03	-0.5
3. Broadcast TV	42.07	+8.2
4. Radio	18.88	+5.7
5. Cable TV	16.3	+3.6
6. Yellow Pages	13.78	+1.4
7. Magazines	11.0	-0.9
8. Out of Home	5.18	+0.8
9. Internet	4.88	-13.5
10. Business Pub	3.98	-11.0
Misc. Total	30.73	+2.4
Total	$236.88	+2.4

Direct Spending. *Looking at spending by media type, Direct Mail is the largest category with almost $46 billion in spending for 2003.*

When it comes to media, advertisers invest in audience members. For example, when purchasing prime-time TV's Dr. Quinn, advertisers put their money toward reaching a predominantly female audience.

According to advertising agency BBDO, the term audience refers to the persons (or homes) reading, listening to, viewing, or seeing a particular media vehicle.

With that general overview of media terms, let's move onto reviewing where the media world is heading and what exciting things are in store for those who use them.

Media Building Blocks.

We reviewed the world of media in Chapter One. Now we're going to look at it from a different perspective – the advertiser's.

It's a Whole Different Media World.

Thanks to new technologies, media mergers, media/audience fragmentation, and recent federal court decisions, media have been evolving and are continuing to evolve into a burgeoning and not yet clearly understood, complex communications system.

An Unprecedented Number of Choices.

Nowadays, there are an unprecedented number of media choices that advertisers can choose from.

See for yourself. Stop reading for a moment. Look around.

Come on now, be thorough. . . are you in your dorm room? Is the radio or TV on? Okay, that's easy. But keep going.

Did you count the Outkast poster above your desk? That favorite baseball cap?

Did you remember to include the T-shirt with your school's logo? Don't forget the phone in your room or that computer on your desk. How about the candy bar wrapper or soda can next to your notebook? Did you count these packages? You should.

Brand Contact Points.

Increasingly, product packaging and in-store advertising are brand contact points that are becoming extremely important as we consumers become less brand loyal.

Did you know we make more than two-thirds of our brand decisions right at the grocery shelf?

Throughout this chapter, we'll remind you that even cereal boxes can become an important media vehicle.

How about the pen or pencil you're taking notes with? Is there any specialty advertising on it?

And what about your roommate, besides being a friend and part-time pain in the neck, he or she is a living, breathing billboard – as well as a narrowcasting communications channel (remember word-of-mouth?).

Check out the logos on his shoes, jacket, sweatshirt, watch, cap, and jeans. Not to mention his notebook.

Okay, the break's over, let's get back to reading.

How many different advertising messages did you locate? What were some of the more unusual places?

The purpose of this little exercise is to help you understand what we mean by advertising media in today's media world.

Now, to get you started on your own course of action to understand media, let's begin with the fundamentals of where it all starts: media delivery and what it means.

Media: Everywhere a Brand Needs to Be.

As we showed you in Chapter Two, there's never been so much advertising media.

Advertisers are using them, sometimes abusing them, to splash their ads everywhere.

Consumer Reports recently reported, *"Advertisers are putting their messages in public lavatories, on the sleeves of pro athletes, on TV screens in kids' classrooms – even on clouds."*

The list of new media is growing at a startling rate.

A New Media Sampler.

In addition to the traditional mass media of television, magazines, radio, newspaper and out-of-home, a wealth of new or alternative media are emerging or becoming more prominent as advertisers seek new ways to avoid clutter or simply hit their target market without the waste associated with much of the mass media.

Here's a brief sampler:

Supermarkets.
Supermarket TV, carts, belt dividers, & receipts
Scanner-sensitive coupons
Grocery bags

The New Outdoor.
Mobile billboards
Flying signs, blimps, etc.
Inflatables
Outdoor video panels
Public restroom stalls

Traveling with the Target.
Airline ticket jackets
In-flight magazines
In-flight video

More New Video Opportunities.
Home shopping networks
Long-form commercials
      (infomercials)
Leaders on video rentals
Movie theater advertising
Product placements in movies & TV

Continued on next page…

Business Marketing points out: *"There's a proliferation of new-media options just waiting to be tapped,"* such as, *"CD-ROM catalogs and magazines.*

"Online commercial services. Interactive floppies. Electronic niche publications. E-zines [digital magazines delivered directly to the recipient via e-mail]. Internet newsgroups and real-time chat sessions. Electronic public relations. Kiosks. Interactive TV tests. The World Wide Web."

And this is just the interactive stuff. The media list continues to swell, sprawling to some pretty unlikely places, where advertising sprouts up on everything from shower stalls to sailboats.

Five Media.

Until recently, advertisers basically relied on five media to make their brands thrive: television, radio, newspaper, magazines, and outdoor.

Compared to some of the new media forms, using these five media isn't too complicated.

As Renetta McCann, Senior VP-Media Director at Leo Burnett USA, points out *"[They]… were sitting right there in front of you."*

Challenges.

With all of these new media opportunities come real challenges for the media professional in charge of selecting and scheduling the media.

Today's media professional is having to change to deal with the complex media world. They *"must become more flexible, have more tools and more placement options,"* says McCann.

Because today's advertising media are much more than magazine ads and television commercials.

Today's media have been expanded to refer to any opportunity that speaks on behalf of a brand to any consumer.

New Media (Cont.)

Other Brand Contact Points
Coupons on ATM receipts
Ads at the bottom of golf holes
(talk about tightly targeted!)
Stick-on ads on the front page of
newspapers
Directory advertising
Town crier

All the World's a Media Buy.

It's everything from a Fortune-500 corporation sponsoring a black-tie dinner to a local automotive parts store's sky writing. (These ideas come from Keith Reinhard, CEO of DDB, the sixth largest advertising agency in the world).

Arthur Anderson, Principal at the management consultancy Morgan, Anderson & Company, sums it up:

"Wherever the message is that's the medium: the Internet, event marketing. . . All of these things, if you look at it are media."

And as advertising continues to embrace integrated marketing strategies, the definition of media is stretched even more to include event marketing, product publicity stunts, and computer hookups, to name a few.

Debra Goldman in *Media Quarterly* supports this claim. *"Potentially everything can be an [ad] medium: schools, sport stadiums, calling circles, shopping malls."*

Ad messages placed in these unconventional media have the potential of making immediate, if not intimate, contact with consumers right when these consumers are most predisposed to think about purchasing and using the brand.

And that's powerful communication.

Perception or Reality – Your Media Aperture.

Are these professionals' perceptions our media reality?

Let's put their observations to the test. Suppose you're on a ski trip in Utah. While riding the ski lift, you see an advertisement that reminds you how nice a piping-hot cup of cocoa would taste.

This ad appears as a small billboard affixed to both the back of the chair in front of you as well as the ski-lift tower.

A company called Ski View posts these billboards for clients. What an imaginative and effective way to communicate to a group of consumers who have an immediate need for the product as soon as they whisk their way down the chilly ski slopes.

Bite-Size Media: Fragmentation and Clutter.

Advertising messages have generally appeared as commercial interruptions in electronic or print media.

There are two major reasons why some advertisers are turning away from traditional media to some pretty unconventional methods to deliver ad messages to consumers.

The first has to do with media and audience fragmentation. The second has to do with advertising clutter.

Let's take a look at both.

Audience and Media Fragmentation.

Yesterday's mass media once attracted large numbers of diverse audience members. These media have been blown to pieces – fragmented. And so have their audiences.

Take broadcast network TV and mass-circulation magazines, once the media darlings of nation's advertisers.

Years ago, if you wanted to be seen and heard, you bought network TV ads and printed big spreads in magazines.

Now, however, these media superstars have lost some of their shine as their audiences have shrunk and spun off to more specialized media.

Some Examples.

Take broadcast network television for example. Just ten years ago, the networks had a whopping 42 prime-time shows that delivered an average 15% household rating.

In 1996, the average rating for network primetime shows had dipped to 10%.

One year later, there were only five broadcast-network prime-time shows that delivered a 15 household rating or better.

And where have the numbers gone? They've been spread across cable TV, which in 1997, boasted 164 national services, 48 regional services, and 54 new networks in the works.

And what about mass-circulation magazines? Their large audiences have been eroded by the drastic growth of specialty magazines (2,318 in 1992, up from 759 in 1960).

The Magazine Publishers Association catalogued a list of 289 new specialty magazine titles launched in 2002.

As a result, the American media are fragmented as never before. Advertisers are no longer capturing mass audiences. They are chasing after small niches to secure enough target-audience members.

Clutter Clutter Clutter.

Another reason why advertising messages are cropping up in all sorts of noncommercial areas, like laundromats and health clubs, is because of advertising clutter.

Clutter refers to an overabundance of advertising within a particular advertising medium.

That means if the September issue of Vogue is overflowing with 800 ads, how is your ad going to stand out?

The reason clutter has advertisers concerned is it can lower overall consumer awareness levels. It can also get in the way of establishing favorable brand attitudes.

Clutter can even suffocate some pretty good ads.

Broadcast Clutter.

Relaxed codes in the broadcast industry and elsewhere have created more advertising in traditional commercial media.

At the end of 1999, commercials and promo spots on ABC and NBC took up over 15 minutes per hour of primetime.

Some of the nation's advertisers have found that their messages can no longer communicate effectively to consumers in these cluttered media. Their advertising messages get lost.

Advertising clutter in the traditional media have forced advertisers to search for new, more effective media vehicles.

They've started inserting their ads in some pretty unexpected places, too.

Blimps, Weinermobiles, and Other Vehicles.

For example, Goodyear hovers in the sky with a blimp. Oscar Mayer prowls the roads in a Wienermobile.

One of the most ubiquitous images in the latest Super Bowl was Budweiser One – a helium-filled logo hovering above the stadium.

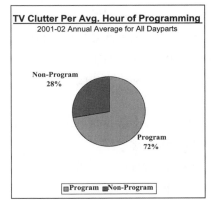

TV Clutter Per Avg. Hour of Programming
2001-02 Annual Average for All Dayparts

Non-Program 28%

Program 72%

▪Program ▪Non-Program

Broadcast Clutter.
On average, commercials of some sort take up 28% of every TV programming hour.

Not just hot air.
Branded objects like the Budweiser Blimp can be very effective – if you have the right media partnership for your airship.

This was the visual that the Fox Network cut to after virtually every group of commercials.

Consumer Reports magazine says that advertisers can now rent space on garbage cans, bicycle racks, and parking meters, even the bottom of golf holes.

Coca-Cola has even stamped its logo on eggs.

Bristol Myers Squibb has made it an annual tradition to dole out free samples of aspirin at post offices on April 15 to soothe the jangled nerves of late income-tax filers.

Absolut Vodka carved its bottle into a 20-acre crop field next to the Kansas City airport.

Carro-Sell, a revolving media company, sells ad space on the moving metal plates of airport baggage carousels.

RJR Nabisco, the makers of Camel cigarettes, hands out sandals with the word "Camel" embossed on the soles, so that beach goers can leave "camel tracks" in the sand.

Now if a blimp is too small and a billboard too stagnant, then the sky is truly the limit – CTA Lasers has beamed laser images for Doritos, Coors beer, American Airlines and other advertisers on the California clouds. The lasers can also generate ad images onto walls, buildings, bridges, and even mountains.

And, as you can see, the Weinermobile is no longer alone on the road to greater brand awareness.

In the new world of media there are no missed opportunities. Not even when you duck inside a restroom. WeeWee Advertising of Jackson, Mississippi, will place an ad in a strategic spot in public bathrooms. But no matter where advertising eventually crops up, its purpose will remain steadfast. Advertising, no matter if it's splashed on health-club shower curtains or beamed across LCD display units in urinal stalls, will continue to try and solicit positive attitudes.

Strengths & Weaknesses.

We've learned about media companies as businesses.

Now let's talk about them as advertising vehicles.

We'll save "other" for later in this book (see Part IV).

But we should be clear that these new media opportunities are an exciting and growing area that may provide the right extra impact in delivering the message for your brand.

We'll walk through the media forms in the same sequence, and what you'll see is that each medium is unique, offering advertisers a variety of strengths and weaknesses.

You'll discover that newspapers and radio are powerful local media. Magazines and cable are some of the best media around for delivering specialized audiences.

Outdoor advertising grabs consumers' attention right before they make a purchase. We'll be sure to point out the plusses, as well as the minuses, of each of these five media.

These are the sorts of considerations you will have to make if and when you create or evaluate a media plan.

Print - Strengths & Weaknesses.

This section of your text will also discuss how indoor print media, founded on journalistic principles, distinguish themselves from other media in a variety of ways.

Print advertising is an effective way to reach consumers both inside and outside of their homes.

As advertising vehicles, newspapers and magazines share some common strengths. First, we'll highlight common characteristics these print media share and why advertisers find them attractive.

Some Unique Characteristics.

Advertising media professionals and print sales representatives agree that newspapers and magazines possess some unique characteristics that can enhance advertising messages.

Of course, newspapers and magazines have their own individual strengths and weaknesses, which we will explore later. But let's begin by taking a look at the plusses these two print media share.

First, we'll look at the traditional print media that readers use indoors: newspapers and magazines. Then, we'll take a short look at the "other" print advertising – outdoor and out-of-home.

Newspapers and Magazines.

Newspapers and magazines contain different editorial content that make reading either very urgent, somewhat pressing, or downright unhurried.

It all depends on the timeliness of the subject matter.

Newspapers are usually read and gone in a day or so, while magazines tend to hang around awhile.

Newspapers and magazines are both members of the journalism family. They rely on advertisers for financial survival.

Through advertising, newspapers and magazines supply important consumer information that readers depend on.

Print editorial content affects:

1. how long readers hang onto a print medium, and

2. how advertisers use the print medium.

Newspapers and magazines share 11 characteristics that appeal to advertisers. Let's take a look at them.

Print Advantages – Eleven Shared Characteristics:

1. Print is portable.

Newspapers and magazines go where people go.

Let's put this statement to the test. What do you do with your school newspaper when it's time for class and you're not quite done reading the last few paragraphs of a good story? Don't you stuff it in your book bag and take it along to class?

What about when you head off to the gym? Does a magazine tag along? Does it help you pass the time while pounding away on the Stairmaster?

Shared Print Advantages

1. Print is portable.
2. Print is "time independent."
3. Print is not a fleeting medium.
4. Print accommodates complex copy.
5. Pictures can be better in print.
6. Print can feature more than one product.
7. Print media are versatile.
8. Print can be preserved and read.
9. Print is personable and intimate.
10. Journalistic content adds credibility and prestige.
11. Print can deliver coupons and other sales promotion devices.

A handful of reasons to give your dog a wormer he likes.

Target – Dog Owners. Print makes it easier to make more than one point.

Magazines and newspapers are portable. They're compact, bendable, and lightweight. They can go anywhere.

So you can find print both inside and outside your home.

Print can keep you company. And you don't have to turn it on.

When a magazine or newspaper is in a waiting room, or an airplane magazine bin, it can be read by many different people other than the subscriber. We call this passalong readership.

When this happens, advertisers get more than what they bargained for, although a passalong reader is generally not as committed to the publication as a subscriber.

2. Print is "time independent."

When you think about it, print is incredibly interactive. Unlike TV, print doesn't have a schedule. Readers choose the time and order of what they want to read.

Print is convenient. Advertising messages aren't bound by time, either. In print, advertising messages can be longer, more detailed, and tell an entire story.

3. Print is not a fleeting medium.

Reading is an active and involving mental process.

Print media engage people's minds. Consumers tend to glean more accurate information by reading than by viewing a rapidly changing image on a screen.

They can study the body copy, stare at the photography, or even reread the entire ad.

If a consumer needs to find an address, or phone number, or compare prices, print makes it easy.

4. Print media accommodates complex copy.

Products that are expensive, complex, or technical tend to require a more comprehensive sales message.

Print advertising is great for that.

For example, cheeseburgers are a low-involvement purchase. We know what they are, where to get them, and how to use them.

A Lot To Say. *This copy-heavy, two-page spread for the Nissan Pathfinder offers a great deal more information than could reasonably delivered in a :30 or :60 broadcast spot.*

Laser printers are an entirely different story. They're a high-involvement purchase – complicated and expensive.

Print advertising can deliver the whole sales message.

If you've got a lot to say, like Nissan does for their Pathfinder, print is the way to say it – and the place.

Newspapers and magazines deliver readers – people who like to read. They enjoy reading articles – long and short.

As Howard Gossage said, *"People read what interests them. Sometimes, it's an ad."*

Ads with complete sales messages help readers make informed buying decisions. Of course, whether that ad gets read or not depends to some extent on how involving it is.

It also depends on other things.

For example, think of tire and battery ads. Not terribly interesting. But when you suddenly need a tire or battery, they become fascinating literature.

5. Pictures can be better in print than broadcast.

Pictures are static in print media. They hold still. They can be held and studied. You can examine expressions on faces or focus on certain product features.

Pictures can sometimes look better in print than broadcast. Of course, a lot has to do with the press and one's television set, and we've all seen our fair share of bad newspaper photos.

But still, if newspaper photos are cropped just right, and the black-and-white tones are near perfect, the results can be pretty arresting, not to mention dramatic.

Think about the black-and-white photos that Calvin Klein uses in his magazine ads. Pretty attention-getting, aren't they?

6. It's easier to feature more than one product in print.

Broadcast's shorter ad units often limit advertising messages to saying just one thing. In print you're not as confined.

Of course, a lot depends on the advertising budget. If it's large, then advertisers can afford to buy a lot of space or pages. Small budgets limit advertisers to smaller print units.

Advertisers who command big budgets can feature their entire product line. Fashion designers can run ten to twelve pages of magazine spreads to announce their fall clothing line.

In specialty print, specialized advertisers have advantages. Capezzio can run four consecutive pages in a dance magazine.

On a local level, grocery stores can use four or five pages of the newspaper to advertise 50 to 60 of their products.

And, because you, the reader, are in control of what you decide to look at, it's very easy to scan the many items advertised until you find what interests you.

7. Print media are versatile.

Print media can be bought in a variety of sizes. And advertisers can choose from an enormous range of editorial content.

There's also geographic flexibility. Often, print can be bought on a local, regional, or national basis.

Print advertising media offer all sorts of creative and promotional opportunities as well. Flexible. Flexible. Flexible.

8. Print ads can be preserved and reread.

Print ads can have long lives. They can be saved for days, months, even years. They can be torn out, stored, and studied. Do you have any hanging on your walls? Plastered to your refrigerator? Stuck on your bulletin board? See?

9. Print advertising is personable and intimate.

Print advertising communicates on a one-on-one basis.

What do we mean by that? When you sit down to watch TV or listen to the radio, are there any other people in the room?

At school, you might watch TV in a big room along with a host of others or just a few friends.

When you sit down to read, it's a whole different matter because, as we've said, reading is a lot different from viewing.

This makes print advertising rather intimate and certainly personable. Advertising copywriters can take advantage of this.

Versatility. Print media can be bought in a variety of sizes.

Free rear end alignment.

If your rear end is starting to shimmy and shake, don't sit on it. Join the YMCA. We also do complete body work and fix spare tires.
Free trial membership during September.
YMCA

Print lends credibility and prestige.

10. Journalistic content lends credibility and prestige.

Advertisers prize print media for its fact-based content.

Good journalism and good writing tend to give advertising in newspapers and magazines an added dose of credibility.

Then again, you might not feel the same way about these ads if they appeared in a supermarket tabloid next to an article titled: "Aliens Ate My Head."

For example, AT&T might choose the *Wall Street Journal* to make a hard-hitting ad even more authoritative.

An over-the-counter drug manufacturer might run an ad in *Time* to give its product added credibility.

11. Print can deliver coupons and other sales promotion devices.

Print is a tangible medium. As such, it can often lend sales promotion endeavors a helping hand.

Coupons, samples, and premiums all take advantage of print. Coupons can be clipped, filled out, and sent in. They can all be delivered quite inexpensively through print media.

Example: Kellogg's

Kellogg's delivered two free samples plus coupons to Sunday newspaper subscribers in select markets. They placed a small box of cereal and a cereal bar, along with the Sunday newspaper in a plastic bag. Kellogg's supplied the bags.

The outside of the bag was printed with pictures of the samples and announcements of the offers inside.

What a creative media effort!

First, people have leisure time on Sunday. They spend it reading the paper. As a matter of fact, newspapers secure their highest readership on Sundays.

Second, people are not running to work, they have time for breakfast on Sunday. Kellogg's brought it to them.

Third, two samples were delivered right to people's doorsteps without any mailing lists or additional postage.

Newspaper Strengths & Weaknesses.

Wherever you live, the one media vehicle that ties a community together is still the newspaper.

Whether you're looking for a Friday night movie, weekend shopping bargains, complete sports scores, or more about an important news story, the newspaper is still the media vehicle that does the job.

Now let's take a look at some of the strengths and weaknesses of newspapers as an ad medium.

Newspaper Strengths:

1. They're considered a prestigious place to advertise.

Newspapers carry significant clout in local communities.

Many local business owners take this into consideration and believe newspapers add a certain degree of believability and prestige to their advertising.

2. Newspaper readers tend to be upscale.

Newspaper readers tend to be older, more educated, and have better jobs. They tend to be people advertisers want to reach – they have more money to spend.

Where else would you want to advertise for a "miserable wench" for an upcoming production of *Pirates of Penzance*?

3. Readers really use advertising.

A recent study showed that 60% of people said they look forward to newspaper advertising. This may seem high, but it's true. Think about newspaper ads like food ads for the grocery store or sales ads for the sporting goods store.

Only 28% of people said that they look forward to receiving direct mail, 20% mentioned magazine, 7% TV, and only 6% said radio.

Newspaper advertising spurs people to buy. Sixty percent of people reported that after seeing a newspaper ad, they went out and shopped for the item.

4. Newspapers require less lead time than other media.

Newspaper advertising doesn't require a lot of preplanning like some other media.

Upscale. Newspaper readers tend to be upscale, so this is the perfect place to advertise the theatre – for plays as well as for audiences.

It can be placed and canceled within a matter of days.
This allows advertisers all sorts of scheduling flexibility.

5. Newspapers have a strong local emphasis.

Newspapers' editorial content predominantly focuses on the local communities they service.

Regional and national advertisers who want to concentrate in certain local markets can effectively do so by using newspapers.

6. Newspapers have a strong sense of immediacy.

The editorial content contained in newspapers is perishable. It gives advertisers immediacy. This is particularly beneficial to advertisers who need an immediate response.

7. Newspapers have "cataloging value."

Newspapers' editorial content and advertising are neatly organized and categorized into different sections (e.g., sports, lifestyle, business, etc.).

This "cataloging value" helps advertisers reach specific demographic or lifestyle groups, and it does it when they are in the right frame of mind.

Newspaper Weaknesses:

It's not a perfect world. Here's some of the downside.

1. Newspaper print reproduction can vary.

When newspapers print on their own presses, it's called a run of the press (ROP).

Some newspapers have old presses, some have new, but the real issue is that when you're printing hundreds of thousands of pages every day, even the best newspaper presses may have variable reproduction quality.

2. Newspapers have small passalong readership.

Magazines reach larger audiences because they are passed along to other readers.

Newspapers publish perishable material; they have a very small passalong readership.

3. Newspapers can be costly.

This is particulary true for national advertisers, who are charged higher rates than local advertisers.

Additionally, national advertisers have to use numerous newspapers to build the kind of audience coverage they may need to effectively reach a certain region.

Newspaper advertising can be expensive for local advertisers, too. Newspapers publish frequently. The cost of buying ads on a continuous basis can mount up.

4. Newspapers may carry adverse editorial.

Newspapers report news that is tough, gritty, and unsettling. Some advertisers might not want their products associated with this type of editorial environment.

5. Newspapers are cluttered.

Newspapers carry a wealth of information.

Advertising competes with many other ads and articles.

It's sometimes difficult for a small ad to stand out.

6. Newspapers are not read thoroughly.

Americans have hectic and demanding schedules. They are pressed for time and often do not read the entire newspaper.

7. Newspapers have poor demographic selectivity.

Newspaper readers are older. Younger people don't get into the habit of reading a daily newspaper, although they may still read certain sections, such as the Entertainment section before the weekend, or the Sports section after the big game.

In general, a complete demographic cross-section of the population will not be available.

Rather, newspapers, along with other print media, are in the business of producing editorial content that engages, enriches, and educates specific and desired readers.

Magazine Strengths and Weaknesses.

Although they're both print media, magazines are usually used quite differently from newspapers.

Overall, magazines have some unique characteristics that advertisers view as both good and bad.

We'll examine these next.

Impact. Magazines can give your message extra impact and persuasion.

Whether you want to hook fisherman…

…or people with crabgrass, there's nothing like the right magazine.

Magazine Strengths:

1. Magazines deliver specialized audiences.

With more than 10,000 magazines to choose from, there's a magazine to suit practically everyone. Magazines break the population down into tiny niches based on lifestyles, hobbies, and interests. This lets advertisers target specialized groups with very little waste.

2. Magazines ads are long-lasting.

Magazine ads can hang around for months, even years. This means advertising has real staying power.

3. Repeat advertising exposure.

Magazine's audience coverage builds over time. Readers pick the magazine up over the course of the week, two weeks, or a month. As such, advertisers have the opportunity to have their ad seen multiple times.

4. Magazines have high passalong readership.

The articles found in magazines are interesting, thought-provoking, and not immediately perishable. They are read by multiple members of the household.

They make the rounds in waiting rooms, too.

Of course, the size of the passalong audience is different for each magazine. And numbers claimed are not consistently measured.

Example: Diamond Publishing.

Diamond Publishing, based in Gravette, Arizona, publishes printed materials exclusively for people who have to wait. The magazines offer readers two features: trivia and advertising.

Diamond says that the purpose of its magazines is to give readers "All the news you never knew that you never needed to know." Diamond circulates its materials at lunch counters, doctors offices, hospitals, lube shops, and pharmacies – practically any place where people have to wait for services or goods. The publications circulate in 29 states. And, as you might guess, these publications are passed along to more than one reader.

5. Magazines offer creative flexibility.

Advertisers can buy different sizes of ads and run them anywhere within the publication. The use of vivid color or stark black and white can enhance the effectiveness of ads – and magazines are a good medium for each.

Recent advances in production have made magazines more active and less passive.

Magazine ads can take on three-dimensional qualities with special die-cuts and assembly. These pop-up ads are dramatic and grab readers' attention.

Magazine ads can even include sound, by being equipped with special microchips that play a tune or have a voice-over read the advertising message.

Posters and "scratch & sniff" ads give ordinary magazine ads added value. Gate-folds make regular size ads extra-large.

A gate-fold is a magazine insert which is usually made up of an oversize page with extensions on both the left and right sides.

These extensions fold toward the center of the page – like a gate. Readers open the extensions to reveal portions of the ad.

Magazine ads can even fade in and out like TV.

Stoli Vodka ran a heat sensitive ad that only appeared after coming in contact with readers' body temperature. Readers had to hold their hand on the Stoli bottle to make the ad appear.

Magazine Weaknesses:

1. Audience accumulation takes time.

Magazines lack immediacy. Audience builds over time. Therefore, this medium is restricted to those advertisers who do not demand an immediate response from consumers.

2. Magazines can be cluttered.

Magazines can include significant amounts of advertising. Some advertisers may find themselves fighting against their main competitors within the same issue.

3. Early closing dates.

Advertising in most magazines does not allow for spontaneity. It requires significant preplanning.

For example, if advertisers want to include an ad in the January issue of *Architectural Digest*, they have to submit the ad and purchase order by October 20th of the previous year.

Out-of-Home Strengths & Weaknesses.

The Great Outdoors – and More.

"Outdoor advertising is a unique medium in that it communicates to an audience that's on the go – usually in transit, and always out of home," reports the Outdoor Advertising Association of America.

Outdoor advertising, or out-of-home, puts advertising right where consumers travel, gather, shop, and buy. As discussed previously, it is a growing and exciting area of the business.

According to Saatchi & Saatchi, *"out-of-home is a broad term referring to various forms of advertising that literally do not enter households, unlike print and broadcast. These include outdoor (billboards), transit, and place-based advertising."*

It's essentially all the advertising that can speak on behalf of a brand outside of the home.

Outdoor advertising offers some distinct advantages.

As you might guess, outdoor advertising that's plastered on everything from buses to railcars has some drawbacks, too.

Let's take a quick look at each.

Out-of-Home Strengths:

Marketing AD Ventures (MAV), a large outdoor advertising supplier, offers 5 reasons advertisers should use outdoor:

1. Outdoor can have great visual impact.

Outdoor advertising delivers a powerful visual message.

Advertisers can't buy a bigger print ad than a billboard.

Outdoor advertising provides bold, beautiful images printed on paper or vinyl using a computer printing process.

This means vivid color with all sorts of detail.

Outdoor ads that feature few words and compelling photos or art have real stopping power, even if we are driving down the freeway at 65 miles an hour.

Creativity at Work.

As the glue billboard on the left demonstrates, there are a number of very creative things you can only do with outdoor.

If you have one of those creative opportunities, an outdoor spectacular can be hard to beat.

2. Outdoor can give you blanket coverage of a market

Everyone who steps outside their door to work, shop, or play sees outdoor. According to MAV, *"Outdoor reaches a large percentage of the population between the ages of 18-45."*

Outdoor advertising can be placed in certain neighborhoods delivering upscale, ethnic, or professional markets.

3. Outdoor provides frequency and repetition.

Outdoor advertising is a medium that can't be turned off, these ads are *"on display 24 hours a day, 7 days a week, 30 days a month. It can't be shut off, tuned out, thrown in the trash, or used as a coaster on the coffee table,"* says MAV.

Outdoor is a high-frequency medium.

Some ads are seen over and over again by commuters driving to work, pedestrians walking to the office, and bus (and train) riders traveling in and out of the city.

Outdoor advertising serves as a constant reminder that can reinforce the advertising campaign's message.

4. Outdoor delivers large audiences at a low cost.

Reaching a thousand people with outdoor costs less than reaching that same group in television, radio, and newspaper.

Simply put, the CPM (cost per thousand) is far less expensive for outdoor than other types of advertising.

The numbers speak for themselves:

In 1998, a 50-showing of 30-sheets in the top 100 U.S. markets had a CPM of $3.50.

Compare this to a $9.90 CPM for a 30-second network TV spot; a $5.30 CPM for a 60-second drive-time radio spot; and a $21 CPM for a half-page newspaper ad in the same markets.

Godzilla Examples:

Remember these?

Outdoor made the idea work.

Large audiences for large ideas.

A Times Square Moment...

Outdoor is extremely cost efficient. Properly used, it can really stretch tight ad budgets.

5. Outdoor has versatility.

Outdoor advertising is versatile. It comes in many shapes, sizes, and formats.

Let's just use one example – buses.

An advertiser can buy vinyl posters in King-size (30"H X 144" W), Super King-size (30"H X 240"W), or Queen-size (30"H X 88"W). The advertiser can even wrap the entire bus – not to mention using the interior bus cards.

It Moves and Talks.

Thanks to technology, outdoor offers advertisers real flexibility. Outdoor can be equipped with moving parts, eye-catching devices, even video projection.

A two-story sized container of Cup of Noodles on Times Square spews a constant blast of welcome steam.

Planter's Mr. Peanut waves to bustling New Yorkers.

Outdoor ads don't have to stand silent. Some advertisers tie their outdoor messages to a toll-free cellular number or even ask listeners to tune into a low-band radio frequency being broadcast from that board!

It can be almost anywhere.

Outdoor ads also come in many formats that reach people in all sorts of places. An outdoor board may be the last message people see before they shop.

Out-of-home is unsurpassed at providing directional and location information.

An outdoor board can extend the borders of a retail location. A strong visual with directional information can be extremely effective in capturing an audience for a restaurant, gas station, or tourist destination.

Out-of-Home Weaknesses:

Outdoor advertising has the potential to be the ultimate "in your face" medium. It dares to be noticed.

Yet, outdoor advertising's unique characteristics pose distinct drawbacks to advertisers. Let's review them.

1. Poor demographic selectivity.

Outdoor advertising reaches just about everyone.

When a bus rumbles by with a big display on its side for Arrow dress shirts, everyone stuck in traffic sees the ad.

Arrow wants to reach businessmen.

This outdoor display may very well reach male commuters to and from work, but it may reach a lot of nonprospects, too.

That's one of outdoor's drawbacks. It isn't a specialized medium.

It doesn't deliver a specific niche like cable or magazines. Its reach is far-reaching.

Practically anyone who steps outside is part of the audience.

2. Limited time. Limited copy.

Outdoor is read as people pass by.

It doesn't get full attention.

As a result, most outdoor is easy to ignore.

The 7 word rule.

How much can an advertiser say on an 8-sheet poster?

Messages have to be kept to no more than 7 words if they want to be read and comprehended. No complex copy for these ads.

Outdoor only delivers simple messages with minimal copy.

3. Out-of-home has complicated logistics.

Getting those vinyl wraps up on the corner of 6th and Main requires a lot of money and lead time.

You can do it, but it's not like buying a newspaper ad.

Which side of the road are you on? The coming to work side or the going home side? That can make a big difference.

While it seems simple, an ad on a stick, it can be anything but – inexperienced people often have a bad experience.

4. Out-of-home can be expensive.

Over time, outdoor delivers a great CPM. But, on the front end, material preparation and scheduling isn't cheap.

5. It's subject to increased restrictions and availability.

Outdoor is often viewed as environmental clutter.

Simple Messages.
Complicated logistics. These kiosk posters reach the urban market of Daffy's.

If you have the wrong message at the wrong time, you could find yourself at the wrong end of a picket line.

Radio Strengths and Weaknesses.

Radio Is Alive and Well.

As we discussed a little earlier in the book, radio has taken some pretty big blows from emerging media – particularly TV.

On more than one occasion, media analysts have predicted radio's certain demise.

But radio is a resilient medium that has survived and even prospered by adapting to opportunities in the marketplace.

Some experts maintain that radio persists because of its personal, adaptable nature.

American Demographics magazine reported that radio is still with us today because *"it has a tenacious ability to adapt to changes in popular tastes and to mold itself to a listener's lifestyle."*

In the late 1940s, broadcast TV surfaced. It grew and stole most of the national advertisers away from radio.

TV was expected to consign radio to the dust heap.

Yet radio remade itself and rebounded.

Forced to search for new sources of revenue, radio went after the advertisers TV wasn't going after: local firms.

More recently, media competition has really heated up.

The emergence of cable TV and the boom of specialty magazines and newspapers were expected to contribute to radio's demise. But they didn't. Today, radio is a fast-growing, $12.2 billion industry – a favorite of advertisers and listeners alike.

Now let's tune into radio's strengths and weaknesses. Advertisers who use radio feel it offers some distinct advantages.

Radio Strengths:

1. Radio's various formats help advertisers reach special target audiences.

Radio's program formats help pinpoint specific groups of consumers that advertisers might want to target.

For example, Rush Limbaugh's program attracts the 35-55 crowd. Radio experts state that formatting does such a good job of targeting that advertisers don't have to worry about reaching the wrong audience.

Gary Fries from the Radio Advertising Bureau (RAB) explains, *"Radio is such a diverse targeting vehicle that you're able to be very successful by reaching a very small element of the population."*

Howard Stern's audience was key in the success of Snapple.

2. Radio can be inexpensive, making it a frequency medium.

Compared to television, radio advertising rates are less.

Even if cost per thousand rates are comparable (radio is usually lower), radio's smaller audiences mean that each spot costs less. This makes radio relatively inexpensive.

This lower cost per spot means advertisers can afford to advertise repeatedly (known as frequency). Most people feel that some frequency is needed for ads to be effective.

This low-cost frequency is also attractive to advertisers wanting to maintain brand name recognition.

3. Radio reaches the mobile market.

Radio sits in the dashboards of nearly 100% of the nation's cars and trucks. This can give radio real impact just before consumers make a purchase.

Consider these statistics taken from R.H. Bruskin's *Media Targeting for the '90s*. According to Bruskin, radio is the number-one medium adults listen to closest to the time of purchasing a product or service.

4. Radio is a flexible medium.

Radio's round-the-clock broadcasting allows advertisers to choose from a variety of different dayparts.

Formats can change throughout the day, as well.

Radio offers a variety of advertising opportunities. Sponsorship, live-remotes, and varied unit lengths are available.

Local firms can join with a national advertiser and share the expense of the radio commercial (co-op advertising).

Producing radio ads is not as involved (or as expensive) as television commercial production. Last-minute changes can

Big Radio.
You've heard and laughed at commercials done by Dick Orkin's Radio Ranch. They create and produce radio commercials for clients across the country – both local and national.

often be accommodated, and new creative can be done quickly.

5. Radio also offers creative flexibility.

Radio can put many other possibilities into the hands and minds of clever copywriters.

Radio is the "theater of the mind" medium. It is not restricted by visuals like TV.

Copywriters can conjure up all sorts of extraordinary scenarios through words, sound effects, and music.

Listeners use their imaginations to give characters and situations meaning.

In addition to its many vivid creative capabilities, radio also offers geographic flexibility in that it can be bought locally, regionally, or nationally.

6. Radio offers advertisers immediacy.

Radio plays current music and news that's up-to-date.

Consequently, this medium offers people immediate and fast-breaking entertainment and information all day long.

The radio dial is one of the first things people reach for in the morning. They flip the radio on to listen to the news. As a matter of fact, radio is often the first source of news. Forty-two percent of all Americans tune into radio in the morning to get their dose of news, compared to TV at 30%, and newspaper with 16%.

Local retailers who have a sale to announce benefit by placing advertising in radio's direct, instantaneous environment.

Radio Weaknesses:

As you've already seen, every medium also has weaknesses. Radio has a few, as well.

1. Radio is a background medium.

There is a possibility of radio commercials getting lost.

First, there are many radio stations in most markets.

Second, most people are doing something else while they're listening to their radio.

For example, at some time during morning drive time, 50.1% of adults listening to the radio are driving, 37% are eating breakfast, and 25% are cleaning up the house. (Some "multi-task.")

Only 23% of them are just listening to the radio.

2. Radio is a cluttered medium.

Radio carries a lot of advertising. Even the stations running what they call "commercial free hours" or "10 songs in a row" still manage to pack in the commercials.

3. Radio commercials are fleeting.

Radio commercials are short-lived.

And given the fact that this medium does not have visuals, it is sometimes limited to delivering simple messages.

Television Strengths and Weaknesses.

Television is the big gorilla of the media world.

You've grown up with it, so you probably think you know it pretty well, and you do – from your side of the screen.

But now let's see how TV looks to advertisers.

It's for Free!

For you, the consumer, broadcast TV is free and available everywhere.

What does this mean for advertisers?

With broadcast TV, advertisers have historically been able to reach just about every type of group in the United States – young and old, male and female, rich and poor.

This is often referred to as broadcasting.

Television also offers a wide range of programming.

Advertisers can schedule their commercials on news programs, talk shows, situation comedies, police dramas, game shows, soap operas, and sporting events.

It's for a Fee!

Cable TV travels into people's homes through a special copper wire (called a coaxial cable) that is as thick as a pencil.

The same signals may also be received by a dish. With smaller dish antennae, this type of service, once common only in rural areas, is now found throughout America.

Cable TV.

The dish is just another option for consumers who want more channel choices; satellite TV or digital cable, it's still the cable TV product.

Television connects with people.
Dave Thomas's personable style played a unique role building Wendy's brand personality in their TV advertising.

TV is the right thing to do.
It's a powerful visual medium that can reach a mass audience.

TV is our cultural reference frame.
Here's another older actor at work. Mr. Whipple is back! Everybody knows him and remembers "Please don't squeeze..." Classic campaigns become part of a brand's equity.

For simplicity's sake, we will refer to both cable and satellite delivery broadcast as "cable TV."

First, we'll discuss the major strengths television offers advertisers. Then, the various weaknesses.

Cable TV has some unique characteristics of its own. These will directly follow the general overview of television.

Television Strengths:

1. Television has impact.

Television is called the personal selling medium. To some extent, TV replaces a sales person at a store.

For years, Dave Thomas, the owner of Wendy's fast-food chain, really utilized the personal selling power of television. Amiable and persuasive, he simply told us about the merits of his menu.

There are other examples.

What about local car dealers? Celebrity endorsers?

Television also has impact because of its ability to combine sight and sound, motion, color, and graphics.

All these devices make TV an excellent medium to demonstrate, persuade, and create instant product identification.

How many times have you seen products effectively demonstrated on TV? What about all of the effective infomercials that crop up on late-night television?

Finally, TV is a great storytelling medium. In the hands of talented creative people you can tell an interesting and engaging story in just 30 seconds. Stories have impact.

2. Television covers the marketplace.

Network television has mass appeal and large market coverage. Cable has specific, narrowly defined targets which will be reviewed later.

Network television has traditionally been considered a mass medium. Its broad realm of programming - from sitcoms to the Olympics – tends to attract a wide range of viewers from all different age groups, occupations, and income levels.

Got a minute?

Well then, how about thirty seconds?
TV can tell a terrific short story. Here, a take-off on Michael Jordan Cologne featuring a less than appealing basketball player with a cologne that smells like cabbage – while you're waiting, enjoy a Snickers.

3. Television is intrusive.

Television reaches most people every day. It's part of the American landscape and certainly a part of our daily lives.

In 1950, the A.C. Nielsen Company reported people watch TV an average of 4 hours and 35 minutes each day.

By 1987, viewers were spending nearly as much time viewing TV (7 hours and 10 minutes) as they spent at work.

As cable TV, VCRs, videos, and video games entered, they helped keep Americans in front of their TV screens.

In 1996, the total daily viewing for all household members was 6 hours and 57 minutes.

With so much time spent in front of the tube, viewers have the opportunity to be repeatedly exposed to commercials.

This repetition helps build brand familiarity.

4. Television is flexible.

Television can be used in many different ways.

Television offers advertisers flexibility in how they buy and schedule commercials.

They can choose from 10, 15, 30, or 60-second units.

Even longer units of time can be negotiated.

In 1985, BBDO bought the first three-minute commercial on the Grammy Music Awards for their client, Pepsi. Pop music performer Lionel Richie performed in the commercial.

Television can be purchased nationally (network TV) or bought in only certain areas (national spot TV) or locally.

Dayparts. When it comes to scheduling ads on TV, advertisers have a number of options. The broadcast day is broken into a variety of different parts (called dayparts).

Particular programs are clustered into a number of time slots and are generally grouped during the morning, afternoon, early evening, night, and late night.

5. Television also offers a wide range of programming.

In terms of creating and producing the advertising message, television is also very flexible in this regard.

Advertisers can choose from a wide variety of production techniques to get their commercial message across to consumers: slice-of-life scenarios, extreme close-ups, voice overs, jingles, humor, animation, and the list goes on.

6. Television is a cost-efficient medium.

Television is considered cost efficient.

In other words, compared with other media, TV can deliver a thousand audience members at a relatively low cost.

Cost per thousand, or CPM, is a general standard used for media. It's a handy yardstick. To make media cost comparisons, advertisers calculate how much it costs to reach one thousand target audience members.

Network broadcast TV is expensive in absolute cost, but when you compare it to other media on the basis of audience delivery and cost, TV comes out a value.

Analyzed this way, broadcast television's big audiences tend to make this medium worth the investment.

However, the overall cost of producing and buying television commercials can require large advertising budgets.

7. Television is considered a prestigious medium.

The programs on television tend to lend this medium prestige, credibility, and authority.

Especially on a network broadcast TV level, large budgets are spent on production and celebrities. Consumer reaction to these lavish productions is powerful.

Viewers overwhelmingly think TV advertising is the most exciting. Compared to other media, 81% of people said that television advertising is the most exciting, compared to magazines at 6%, radio at 5%, and newspaper at 3%.

People also feel that TV advertising is more authoritative. Fifty-seven percent of people believe TV advertising is most authoritative. Twenty percent feel newspaper advertising is the most authoritative, followed by magazines at 9% and radio at 6%.

Television Weaknesses:

1. Television messages are fleeting.

Television commercials are not long lasting.

Fleeting Messages.
This TV commercial for Century 21 makes the point that your message is seldom the only one out there.

They normally last 10 to 60 seconds. This means that viewers do not have the luxury of analyzing the message.

2. Television advertising is expensive.

Network television is expensive.

A 30-second spot on NBC's *Law & Order* is $264,889.

If an advertiser buys three prime-time spots for four days on NBC's *Law & Order*, the bill quickly adds up to a hefty sum of nearly $3.2 million (of course this could be negotiated).

Television production is also costly, adding to the expense.

3. Popular TV programs can have limited time available.

Unlike newspapers or magazines, which sell pages, television sells time, which cannot be expanded to accommodate all advertising requests.

Television is confined to a 24-hour day with just so much time devoted to commercial air time.

Therefore, demand for commercial time on a highly rated show or daypart may exceed supply. Some advertisers may be closed out of the program, daypart, or season they'd like for their advertising.

4. Advertising on TV is intrusive and disruptive.

With newspapers or magazines, the audience can control its exposure to advertising by simply turning the page.

Advertising on television interrupts the program.

Advertising imposes itself and the viewer can either wait for the program to return, or take some action to avoid the advertising interruption.

Increasingly so, viewers are taking action or employing new technology to avoid television advertising. TiVo, anyone?

Not surprisingly, a study in 1998 found that TV is the worst of all media in terms of advertising avoidance behaviors. With this study, Michael Elliott and Paul Speck reported that television is the worst of all media for consumer ratings as well on issues of program disruption, hindrance of program search, and perceptions of a cluttered environment.

Cable TV Strengths and Weaknesses.

Remember, cable is narrowcasting. And many of the cable channels are niche media, with smaller audiences but higher concentrations of certain types of viewers.

Cable Strengths:

Today, advertisers consider cable television a strong and vital advertising medium for several different reasons.

1. Cable offers advertisers geographic flexibility.

When it comes to coverage, cable has any type of small, medium or large advertiser covered.

Local advertisers can buy commercial time from local cable systems and run them on a range of top cable channels.

Regional advertisers can take advantage of the more user-friendly buying that can be done with the larger cable carriers.

2. Cable is inexpensive.

Compared to broadcast TV, cable advertising is a bargain.

Although you should keep in mind that when advertisers buy cable, they are getting a lot less audience for their money.

First, while almost 100% of U.S. TV households can receive network broadcast TV, only about 70% of these homes have access to cable television. So far.

Therefore, cable has a smaller coverage area nationwide. Cable also costs less because its fragmented audience is spread across a variety of channels.

Remember that broadcast networks concentrate their programming on one channel. In doing so, broadcast networks are able to capture mass audiences.

Cable networks consist of multiple channels. Smaller audiences are dispersed across a variety of different cable networks. Consequently, cable costs less than broadcast TV.

3. Cable programming is varied. As a result it delivers specialized audiences.

Cable networks don't try to be everything to everybody.

Rather they concentrate on one particular group of people and strive to be absolutely everything to that one particular group.

TNT – NASCAR

Discovery Channel
American Chopper

Targeted Programming.
Cable networks focus their programming
on narrowly defined audiences.

Cable offers advertisers specialized programming and narrowly defined audiences. This allows advertisers to target specific markets without wasting ad dollars on nonprospects.

VH-1 delivers music-loving adults who are professionals.

Financial News Network (FNN) reaches investors and money managers.

CMT (Country Music TV) covers country and western fans.

In cable, if you've got a niche, you can scratch it.

4. Cable delivers upscale audiences.

Cable subscribers tend to be higher-educated and have a higher annual income than broadcast TV viewers.

These upscale consumers are attractive to advertisers because they have the disposable income to buy a variety of products and services.

5. Cable television allows a wider variety of ad formats.

Advertisers have many choices when it comes to buying commercials on cable television.

Cable offers advertisers the shorter advertising units found on broadcast TV and, at the same time, provides much longer commercial unit lengths called "infomercials," which can range from 2 to 30 minutes long.

Cable Weaknesses:

1. Cable has low audience ratings.

Compared to broadcast television, cable ratings are much lower. This is a drawback to some advertisers.

Often they have to buy multiple stations to obtain an acceptable reach level. There's small, and then there's invisible.

Some networks just don't deliver enough viewers.

But, this is beginning to change. As some of the bigger cable networks are starting to contract for big-time programming, cable ratings are on the rise. Consider for example, the 2003 NBA playoffs broadcast exclusively on the TNT cable network.

2. TV audience ratings reports are inadequate.

The current ratings system has some drawbacks to measuring cable audiences.

Small sample sizes and a system that was set up to measure broadcast instead of cable TV are called into question.

Agencies are sometimes reluctant to use the cable audience measurement statistics that are presented to them.

The Media Plan.

The advertising media world has changed, and it will continue to rapidly evolve. In this fragmented media world, branding becomes even more important.

To resonate with, and ultimately be remembered by consumers, a product or service needs to speak in a single message, a unified voice. It needs one theme to cut across today's fragmented media and be heard through the din and clutter of all the other competing messages.

To maneuver through this fragmented and tangled media world takes talent, smarts, strategic thinking, marketing savvy, and a tenacity to continue to learn.

Most of all, it takes a plan. And that takes a planner.

Do You Have a Plan?

Media planners are specialists who select and schedule the media that will carry messages to particular audience segments.

Most media planners work at advertising agencies or independent media buying services. And their job is being significantly affected by this media revolution.

New Expectations.

New expectations loom ahead for these professionals.

For instance, media planners will be expected to keep up on all of the hundreds of media possibilities and to know when it is appropriate to use them to help achieve client's marketing goals.

Planners won't be thinking just about TV, radio, or magazines. They'll have to select and schedule all types of media.

Jayne Spittler, Leo Burnett's Director of Media Research, offers this advice: *"It will be more challenging to work in adver-*

tising in new media. Do you, for instance, support a video menu or do you have a branded home-shopping store? It's a 'sky's the limit' type of thing. And advertisers have to know all of the possibilities. That's my job."

Yet media planners do not see traditional advertising media, such as network TV and magazines, going the way of typewriters and leisure suits.

Spittler echoed the sentiments shared by other media directors, stating in a recent *Mediaweek* article, *"There will always be a place for good old 30-second TV spots."*

So how do these media planners go about doing their jobs? How do they combine the conventional with the unconventional when it comes to scheduling media?

We'll cover this in great detail in Chapter 5 of this book. Here's a sneak peek.

Media Planning.

Making sense of the boundless new media world is the real challenge facing today's media planning.

Some experts contend it's a real balancing act between the old and new media.

In a *Business Marketing* editorial, today's media planning was described as: *"Getting a handle on emerging forms of media. That's what today's world of media planning is all about. Thinking out of the box. Pushing the envelope. Creating new standards."*

Where to Begin.

So where do media planners begin? What process do they follow to get advertising messages delivered to target consumers?

Successful media planning is the task of selecting and scheduling media that will reach as many of the target audience as frequently as possible for the least amount of cost.

After being assigned a client's product or service, media planners turn to devising a written course of action – a media plan.

A media plan strategically shows how an advertising budget will be used to buy media that will reach the maximum number of prospects for the brand with the greatest effectiveness at the lowest costs.

All media plans must work hard to help achieve the client's marketing objectives.

They are, in fact, a key part of the marketing plan.

Donald Evanson reported in *Mediaweek* that *"80% of media plans submitted for* Mediaweek's *Plan of the Year Award were anchored to a client's marketing situation."* He says, *"the media plan of today contains specific references to the marketing problem that the strategy of the media plan will attempt to address."*

Keep in mind that clients entrust their hard-earned money to media planners with the expectation that these dollars will be judiciously invested in media that will deliver target audiences who will react positively to the brand's message.

Media Planning Old & New.

Media planning is a hot topic. This wasn't always the case. Until recently, media selection and placement *"played second fiddle to... creative development,"* as Junu Bryan Kim noted in *Advertising Age*.

The Way it Used To Be...

For years, when it came to campaign development, the spotlight was really on what was said (ad message) not on how it was delivered (media plan).

Nor was advertising media planning considered all that exciting, or for that matter, creative.

Calling media planning creative was like saying Howard Stern is subtle. You get the point.

Sue Oriel, Media Director at Zenith Media, outlined the changes she has seen in the media planning process over the past ten years in a British publication, *Marketing*.

Oriel observed, *"Planners have finally shaken off the image of Neanderthals with calculators – not that there's anything wrong with the odd Neanderthal attitude when it comes to buying – and replaced it with that of the consumer-sensitive ideas merchant at the numbers end of the business."*

From Clerical to Creative.

Media planning in the old days was mostly a clerical task, with planners caught up in all sorts of numbers and forms.

They were the behind-the-scenes players in an advertising agency, and their job consisted mainly of filling out insertion orders and wrestling with reams of cost-per-thousand figures (which we'll talk about later) and audience delivery statistics.

Planners had little face-to-face contact with the client and the media plan tended to be sifted through the account executive to the client. Well, all that has changed.

The Way It Is Now...

As previously discussed, media fragmentation and the adoption of integrated marketing communications have, as Kim points out, *"Necessitated looking at advertising from the media standpoint sooner than was done before."*

The result has been a revolution in media planning.

Trends in Media Planning.

So what are the trends?

The big one is that media planning is, at times, actually driving the creative and has become an essential component of the client's marketing plan.

Today, it is not uncommon for media decisions to be made before a creative concept has even been born. And these decisions tend to fuel the entire creative ad development.

Another interesting development is that media planners are fast becoming more involved with the creative department's copywriters and art directors.

This is something pretty much unheard of years ago.

David Martin, CEO of Penta-Com, a BBDO division that does Chrysler's media planning, explains: *"The creative people and the media people must intertwine their work as much as possible. They have to understand the overall project is part of a targeting process."*

Moreover, the media planners are being pushed front and center into the spotlight that was once only shined on the account executives. Gone are the days when media planners were left back at the ad shop, giving their plans to account executives to present to the client.

Now, more than ever, planners are mixing it up with clients by going to important strategic planning meetings and making key presentations.

Zenith's Oriel describes this change, saying: *"Media planners now take for granted their ability to contribute above and beyond the targeted placement of spots and spaces.*

"They regularly enjoy the business confidences of their client in order to make sure their ideas are relevant and actionable."

Reasons for the Change.

Why the change? For starters, clients are more media savvy.

Second, media is a hefty expense and prices have been on the rise for years. Clients want that proverbial "biggest bang for their buck" and are fast realizing that a "smart" media plan can save them money.

Just ten years ago, the process of media planning was mostly driven by advertising costs and audience deliveries.

Traditional media planners had to think more about numbers than strategies. (Mind you, it is still important to find the best media prices for your client.)

But today's media planning demands that far more attention be given to media strategy and planning.

Andy Tilley of Zenith Media says, *"As media choice increases and the number of messages proliferates, then what will be required is media planning working hand in hand with account planning."*

He notes that the ad business needs *"people who understand communication from the consumer's viewpoint. And that means both the content of the creative work and the context in which it appears."*

He goes on to explain, *"If you do media planning correctly and account planning correctly, you answer the same questions – how is the communication going to work and how can we make it more effective?"*

Tilley says that it all boils down to having a keen understanding of the consumer, saying: *"And in a rapidly-changing media world, an understanding of the consumer/media relationship is of fundamental importance to the process."*

Have we convinced you?

Media planning is an exciting and demanding field.

Now, you're ready for the full details.

Summary.

You've learned basic "Media Speak." You understand the basic strengths and weaknesses of each medium.

The media have changed dramatically in recent years and likewise, the process of creating a media plan has changed as well. Some marketers, like UniLever, now consider media planning to be a driving force in their international marketing.

This "other agency service" has now become a key growth area, with agencies marketing their branded media capability – like Leo Burnett's Starcom.

There's more emphasis on strategy than ever before.

Media planners are now expected to develop total communications plans.

Media plans require concerted efforts that increasingly result from integrated teams made up of account planners, media planners, and creative personnel along with brand management groups.

The future of media planning is brighter than ever as our media universe grows.

Jim Pastor is a terrific example of how far you can go in a media career.

Jim started in media planning; then moved into media sales where he successfully advanced his career into media management. Editor's Note: Just as this book was going to press, Disney announced Jim's promotion to President and General Manager of WMVP-AM and WZZN-FM. WMVP is the Disney-owned ESPN Radio outlet in the Chicago market. Congratulations Jim!

Career Capsule:

James Pastor, Vice President of Sales and Marketing, Radio Disney.

Jim Pastor works for ABC Radio Networks. He's the VP over all sales and marketing for THE national kid's radio network, Radio Disney. Jim has come a very long way from his first media job working at a local market Dallas, Texas, television rental store.

A Whole Lot of Job.

As VP of Sales and Marketing, Jim has a big job and a lot of responsibility.

First, there's a VP of Advertising Sales reporting to Jim. There are a total of 22 people working on this side of the business. Jim oversees this staff in generating the network advertising revenue plan for Radio Disney, an important part of the vast Disney media portfolio.

Then, there's the Marketing side. This part of Jim's department is headed by a VP of Marketing with a staff of 17 people. Jim works with this team managing all aspects of consumer and trade advertising, website design and content management, audience research, brand management and research, affiliate station marketing, and public relations.

Finally, there's a part of his job focused on new business development. In this capacity Jim is working on development of new distribution platforms for the Radio Disney product and identification and development of alternative revenue sources.

How Do You Get to a Job Like This?

There are a couple of different ways to work your way into a position like this.

Jim did it by working his way up through the media side of the business. From his start in the business as "director" of advertising for Colortyme TV rental in Dallas, Jim learned about media from a local perspective.

From there, he worked his way north to an agency position at Foote Cone & Belding in Chicago. As a media supervisor at FCB, Jim ran several accounts including Kimberly-Clark, Cadbury Beverages, Zenith and Coors.

From the agency side of media planning, Jim made the move into advertising sales with ABC Radio Networks. His first assignments included sales for a variety of ABC network properties like ESPN Radio and Paul Harvey, among others.

Looking For Kids?

Think Outside The Box.

Outside the TV box, that is. With more than 1.6 million kids 6-11 and 600,000 moms tuning in weekly.*
Radio Disney is proving that the way to kids' hearts is through their ears, not their eyes.
Our listeners are loyal - listening nearly two hours a day!*
But, they're not on the couch, they're on the go - attending our events, participating
in our promotions and sampling our clients' products. They're Radio Active!
So tune in and discover what our listeners have…that there's life outside the box.

RADIO Disney
Radio Active!

For advertising information, contact Jim Pastor at 312-899-4076 or visit us at www.abc.com

After a short time, he took a risk and a promotion to Director of Sales for a fledgling ABC property they called Radio Disney. He started out as the only sales person with only 4 station outlets nationwide and virtually no advertisers. Jim says, *"In hindsight, this was without a doubt the best professional decision I've made in my career."*

Since then, Jim has been promoted multiple times in succession working his way up to where he is today, near the top of a major media property.

Looking to the Future.

Jim Pastor sees the media world changing every day. *"It's incredibly different today than even just five years ago."* And, it will keep on changing.

"Media fragmentation, new media technologies and the ability for audiences to have greater control over what they're exposed to and when, will continue to have a profound effect on how people experience media in the future and how marketers will attempt to reach them." This means a world of opportunity for the right person who wants a career in media.

Who Is the Right Person?

Media in the future is for people who are bright, creative, and strategic. Jim feels strongly that media is an art and not a formulaic science. Jim says, *"Remember, ultimately your objective is to utilize the media in ways that will drive sales or store traffic. You need to hold your suppliers accountable, be creative and thoughtful in your approach."* And, above all, *"Treat your client's money as if it were yours."*

Discussion Questions.

1. Radio.

What are the strengths and weaknesses of radio?

Why is this medium a good choice to advertise a second-level soft-drink brand, like Hires Root Beer? What are the drawbacks?

2. Magazines.

Magazines offer advertisers some real strengths and some real weaknesses. What are they?

How could Pop Tarts toaster pastries use magazines in a creative way to reach the college market?

3. Media Audiences.

Who are the most likely prospects for Welch's Grape Jelly?

Who is the audience for ESPN's Sports Center?

Which TV program has the largest audience coverage right now?

4. Below-the-Line.

What is the best example of below-the-line activity that you've seen recently? Why was it so good?

5. Brand Contact Points.

Can you recommend a brand contact point for Bic Razors that would happen sometime during the summer months?

6. Newspapers.

Pick up a copy of your local newspaper. How would you tell a local photo/film developer to use newspaper advertising throughout the year?

Exercises.

1. **Choose a magazine you normally don't read.** Look through the editorial content and the advertisements and make some educated guesses about the make-up of the magazine's audience. **Define the audience in terms of demographics, lifestyle, hobbies, and interests.**

2. Perform a media clutter experiment.

Do one or all three of the following.

a.) Television – watch one full hour of TV without changing the channel, not even once!

Record the exact time (in minutes or seconds) for programming versus advertising.

What percentage of the hour was advertising?

b.) Magazine – choose a magazine and flip through it page-by-page. Count the total pages of editorial versus total ad pages – remember to count partial pages too. What percentage was advertising?

c.) Radio – listen to one full hour of radio and record the exact time for programming versus advertising. What percentage was advertising?

4 Creative Media Analysis

NOW THAT YOU KNOW some of the basic media terminology, you're ready for the hard part. It's time for some basic media math.

This might not be your favorite chapter, but we guarantee that it's one of the most important chapters of this book. In fact, it might be…

THE most important chapter.

In media, you've got to do the math to do the job.

At least that's true for most media jobs. Most companies hiring media people today – media agencies, manufacturers, researchers, and advertising agencies – all say the same thing.

They are more likely to hire the job candidate who is able to do this work. In media, this means being able to do some basic math – and, something more, you must be able to be "creative" with it.

We'll try to keep this clean and interesting, but the fact is if you want to be in media, in any capacity, you have to know your way around numbers. And you have to be able to do the simple math that helps you deal with those numbers.

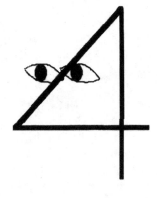

There's Creativity in Numbers
What do you see when you look at the number 4? Picasso saw a face.

You have to be able to look at data and know what you are seeing. You have to be able to analyze, manipulate, and interpret findings from data reports.

You have to be able to know whether or not you are looking at good numbers. So you have to be a bit of a detective.

There's a reason why we call it "creative" media analysis.

"Creative" Media Analysis.

The essence of "creative" media analysis is the fine art of telling a story with numbers.

Every research report, every data set, any set of numbers has a story to tell. And, it is often up to the media person to coax out the details.

Here are some examples:

- What is the most popular television show among young adults aged 18–25 years old?
- Are Budweiser beer buyers more likely to read the *Chicago Tribune* or the *Chicago Sun-Times*? And, are the people who buy the beer the same ones who drink the beer?
- What was the advertising value of that nifty Mini Cooper product placement in the movie *The Italian Job*?
- When is the best time of day to advertise breakfast sausages? And, what is the best day of the week?

This is media math. It's not statistics, and it's certainly not accounting or finance.

We're not talking about balancing the books or proving a correlation. And it's definitely not rocket science.

We're talking about digging up the numbers to support an important media decision. That's media math at work. Let's start with some basics.

Simple Math.

All you need to know to get started are the simple rules of math operations – add, subtract, multiply, and divide – that's it.

For example...

Here's a favorite question we'd ask students interviewing for media planning jobs at Foote, Cone & Belding.

"If you wanted to leave a 15% tip for a $30 lunch check, how much would you leave?"

Got it yet?

You can probably do this in your head, but you're free to use a calculator if you'd like. It's not about doing it fast. It's about knowing how to apply a simple percentage.

So, what's the answer?

And how did you get the answer?

An easy way to do this in your head is to think in tens. Ten percent of $30 is $3. And, 15% is one-and-a-half times ten. So, 15% of $30 is one-and-a-half times $3, or $4.50.

If you used a calculator, all you needed to know is how to rewrite a percent as a decimal.

In this case, 15% is rewritten as 0.15. Simply enter 30 times 0.15 to get the answer, $4.50.

However you did it, if you said the tip would be $4.50, then you were right and this chapter will be easy work for you to get through. If you said something else or had to work hard to get the right answer, then you'll have to work a little harder on this chapter.

Either way, we still promise to keep this as light and interesting as possible and practical. By the time you're through, you should feel comfortable about working with the kind of numbers you'll deal with in media and advertising.

More importantly, you'll know you can do this job.

Chapter Organization.

In this chapter we will cover some of the most common measurements used and the kinds of math and analyses media people do. We'll go step by step explaining each, why it's important to do, and how it is done.

We'll do this in sections starting with measurement techniques, then terms, and then some specific applications. There are four sections in total:

Step-by-Step Math

Calculating with Percentages

1) Remember that 15% can be rewritten as a decimal – 0.15.

2) Multiply the lunch bill times the 15% (0.15).

3) Solve for the answer:

$$
\begin{array}{r}
\$30.00 \\
\times\ .15 \\
\hline
15000 \\
+30000 \\
\hline
\$4.5000
\end{array}
$$

Media Measurements.

In this section we'll talk about some of the basic measurement techniques we use for analyzing the media.

We use different techniques to measure the effects of broadcast media, print media, and other media.

We'll talk you through the most frequently used techniques.

Audience Measurements.

Remember, marketers use the media to deliver a message to an audience. In this sense, any medium is only as useful as the audience it attracts.

Here we'll talk about how we measure audiences.

We'll use a little bit of math here, but mostly we'll be defining and describing some key terms we use in considering actual versus potential audience size, audience coverage and composition for any given media.

Then we'll cover some of the most basic calculations you'll need in media – gross rating points, gross impressions, reach, and frequency.

Efficiency Measurements.

Advertising can be incredibly expensive at times.

That's why media people need to know how to deliver a marketer's message in the most efficient manner possible.

This section will cover measures of cost efficiency like cost-per-thousand and cost-per-point.

Strategic Analyses.

This will be a big section describing some of the most common analyses used in media.

Here, we'll go step-by-step through some specific math applications in creative media analysis.

In this section we'll show you how to analyze measurement data for the purposes of determining:

- **Target Analyses – Who to advertise to**
- **Geographic Analyses – Where to advertise**
- **Scheduling Analyses – When to advertise**

So, let's get started.

Audience Measurement.
Any medium is only as useful as the audience it attracts.

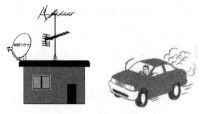

Every medium is different.
The TV audience is usually at home.
The radio audience is often in the car.

Media Measurements.

Every medium is different. And, every audience is different in how it interacts with each media form.

So, it makes sense that we have different ways of measuring different media.

First, we measure any medium for its ability to expose a message to an audience. Most, but not all, message exposures take place in the privacy of one's own home.

So, media researchers have devised techniques for sample groups so that this type of audience exposure can be projected for all of the major media.

While the technique may be different for each medium, in most cases, researchers measure media audiences with sample group surveys.

Broadcast Media – TV & Radio.

Broadcast media are measured through a combination of techniques involving meters and diaries.

TV Measurement by Nielsen.

Network television audiences are measured using an electronic device called a people meter. Nielsen Media Research runs this measurement service. A sample panel of about 5,000 homes across the country has these meters connected to their television sets. The meter automatically records the channel being viewed and the time and day when the set is on.

The people watching are measured when they push a button on their remote control identifying themselves as watching. The meter automatically prompts people with an on-screen message when it is time to push buttons.

Of course, the meter doesn't actually know who's watching. This measurement technique trusts that people are pushing the right buttons.

On a local market level, people meters in 53 major markets are supplemented with personal diary records of television watching. Another 157 mid-size and smaller markets are measured by personal diary only.

You can see that this is a big business – and this is just research for television.

Nielsen uses this meter/diary sample technique to project program ratings, audience size, and audience characteristics for all television shows.

Advertisers spend billions of dollars every year based on Nielsen television audience estimates. The stakes in this business are very high and the problems can be very significant. As we were writing this book, there were three big issues brewing.

First, Nielsen was making some changes in how they populate the household meter sample. Every minor change has a direct effect on the ratings results. And this is a major source of controversy.

Second, the Association of National Advertisers (ANA) issued a call for a major change in the ratings system. Specifically, the ANA is asking that Nielsen start rating *commercials* instead of programs. The point is sound, given that the primary function of ratings today is to measure audience for advertising and advertisers. The implications of this are huge – just think about it.

And third, even the U.S. government was getting into the act. The General Accounting Office (GAO) is considering an audit of AC Nielsen practices and procedures. As we said, the stakes (almost $50 billion in 2002) are very high.

Radio Measurement by Arbitron.

Radio is measured almost exclusively by personal diary.

A sample group of people in 270 radio markets are asked to keep a record of radio listening for one week.

The Arbitron Company uses this diary method to project ratings and average quarter-hour audience size for radio stations across the country.

Try this yourself, for just one day. Keep a record of your radio listening habits. Be sure to account for every radio station you listened to, the time of day you were listening, and the amount of time you spent listening to each station.

Don't forget to keep track of the times and different stations you listened to in the car.

Very soon you'll see how hard this is. You'll start to understand and appreciate some of the issues we face in getting good media measurement.

Print – Magazines & Newspapers.

Print audiences are measured by circulation and readership.

Circulation is a very simple measure, a count of how many printed copies of a publication are distributed.

Readership is somewhat more complex.

Magazine Readership by Mediamark.

The recent-reading technique is used to project readership for magazines. Mediamark Research Inc. is the company that conducts this research.

This survey is administered through in-person interviews.

Magazine readers in the sample group are shown a series of cards with the logo of different magazines. With each card, the respondent is asked whether he/she has read the magazine within the last month.

Respondents are counted as readers if they say they are "sure they have" read the magazine within the last six months.

Newspaper Circulation Measured by ABC.

Newspaper audiences are mostly measured according to circulation by the Audit Bureau of Circulation (ABC). But remember that circulation is just a simple count of the raw number of published copies distributed.

The yesterday-reading technique is used as a way to estimate readership for newspapers. In this technique, an interviewer asks each participant to identify which newspaper they read yesterday. As you might imagine, this tends to be a very brief interview as most Americans read only one daily newspaper.

Other – Out-of-Home & Internet.

Each medium has its own measuring service. And they do their measurement in a way that's appropriate to the media they're measuring. Now let's look at outdoor and the Internet.

Outdoor Measurement by the Traffic Audit Bureau.

Outdoor billboards are measured by "daily circulation." This is an estimate of the number of cars driving past each billboard each day. This measure is projected by the Traffic Audit Bureau.

Other out-of-home media are measured, but not consistently. Often times these media – transit signage, stadium signage, etc. – conduct their own survey research to estimate their audiences.

Internet Measurement by Neilsen/NetRatings.

Nielsen/NetRatings is the service used most often to measure Internet audiences. This is a newer service and because it is Internet based, it does not rely on surveys or diaries. Instead, this service uses special computer software to record the address of websites visited by panel members.

The panel is quite large at about 60,000 people. People in the panel have agreed to participate and allow the software installation on their computers.

The software works just like a "cookie," it reports automatically about websites visited, number of pages clicked, and length of time spent on each site.

All Audience Estimates.

No matter how the data is gathered, all media audience estimates can be reported as a percentage of audience exposed. The percentage is calculated off the sample and then projected to the full population of the area.

An Example.

In fall 2002, the Fox TV network was broadcasting the Major League Baseball World Series games between the San Francisco Giants and the Anaheim Angels, both California teams.

The Ratings Game.
The 2002 World Series matchup between the Giants and the Angels averaged a household rating of 11.9.

Step-by-Step Math
Calculating Ratings

1) How many households tuned in?
   595 viewing homes

2)   595 viewing homes
       ÷
   5000 total meter homes
       = 0.119

3) Expressed as a percent:
   11.9% household rating

Step-by-Step Math
Projecting Audience

1) Express rating % as a decimal:
   11.9% = 0.119

2) Multiply times total U.S. TV homes:
   105,500,000 TV HH
   x 0.119
   = 12,554,500 Total U.S.
   household audience

As an average across all World Series games, 595 of the 5,000 Nielsen meter homes were tuned in to the Fox network broadcasts.

That represents an average household rating of 11.9% – calculated as 595 divided by 5,000.

Quickly now, about how big is that audience?

There are just over 105 million TV households in the U.S. So, with rounding, you should get an estimated audience of about 12 or 13 million households. Now let's do the math.

First, we take that 11.9% rating expressed as a number 0.119 and multiply it times the number of U.S. TV households, 105,500,000. The result is a total U.S. audience projection of 12,554,500 TV households.

Audience Measurements.

From a marketer's perspective, any medium is only as good as the audience it delivers.

Media research companies, like those we named earlier, make their living measuring audiences so that media planners can evaluate each medium.

The media planner's goal is to match the media audience with the marketer's needs. To do this job effectively, media planners and everyone else in the media business use a set of common audience measurement statistics.

In the preceding section, we covered methodological differences in how the data is gathered for each medium.

While these differences are important, the resulting metrics are fairly consistently applied throughout the media industry.

This can sometimes lead to confusion.

Actual or Potential Audience?

The first key issue is whether the data reports an actual media audience or only a potential audience.

For example, in print media like magazines and newspapers, circulation represents only a potential audience.

Just because someone subscribes to a magazine doesn't mean that person will read every page or even every issue.

The better measures are actual audience metrics like magazine readership, but these are not always available.

As a rule, you have to work with what you have. The media planner needs to be able to distinguish between actual and potential audience measurements.

At best, circulation is a snapshot look at a medium – a frozen moment in time. Researchers know that media audiences build over time.

Think about your own media habits. What is your favorite magazine? Do you grab it as soon as it arrives in the mail? Do you read it immediately, cover to cover? Odds are that your answer would be no.

It's far more likely that after you receive the magazine you set it aside for later reading, like maybe on the weekend.

Then, once you have read the magazine, you pass it on to someone else. See? The magazine's audience builds over time.

Researchers also know that even the most loyal media audience will occasionally miss an episode of their favorite show or an issue of their favorite magazine. Actual audience measures work to capture this phenomenon.

Keep this in mind as you read through the remainder of this section.

What follows is a short selection of some of the audience measures most commonly used by media professionals.

Whether your job ultimately is media planning, media sales, media buying, media research, or even media management, you'll need to know these measures and, more importantly, how to make use of each of them.

Others need to understand these measurements as well. If you're planning to be in marketing or account management, you'll also need to be familiar with these basic concepts.

You may or may not have to do the math yourself, but it will be useful to know and understand these concepts.

Audience Coverage.

In media, the word "coverage" can mean a number of different things. Generally it's used to describe the percentage of population that might be exposed to a particular medium. This starts to become complicated when we consider actual versus potential audiences.

For our purposes here, coverage will mean *potential* audience exposure.

We have a different term for *actual* audience exposure; we'll describe that one shortly.

Right now, you just need to know that coverage is one of those words that might mean a couple of different things.

Audience Composition.

Composition is often used as a companion measure with coverage; as in, "the audience coverage and composition of a particular media vehicle."

Coverage describes a percentage of a target population that might be exposed to a media vehicle. Composition tells you the make-up of that audience. It describes the percentage of the media vehicle's audience that is comprised of the target population.

Here's how it works.

Example: Glamour and Cosmopolitan

Consider the example of young women and the magazines they like to read. The figure on the following page presents readership data for two popular magazines from Simmons Market Research Bureau (SMRB), a media research service like Mediamark Research, Inc. The data shows both audience coverage and audience composition for each magazine. Here's how each measure is calculated. Work through this along with us to see for yourself the difference between these two key figures.

Let's start with *Glamour* Magazine. The Figure on the next page shows that *Glamour's* coverage of young women 18-24 is 15.66% and composition is 29.49%.

Audience Coverage and Composition				
	Population (000)			
	Adults	**W18-24**	**Coverage%**	**Composition%**
Totals	194,341	12,404		
Glamour	6,588	1,943	15.66	29.49
Cosmopolitan	8,982	2,390		

Coverage is calculated by dividing the W18-24 who read *Glamour*, 1,943 by the total population of W18-24, 12404. $1,943 \div 12,404 = 15.66\%$

Composition is calculated by dividing the W18-24 who read *Glamour*, 1,943 by the total Adults who read *Glamour*, 6588. $1,943 \div 6,588 = 29.49\%$

Coverage means that *Glamour* has the potential to reach 15.66% of the total U.S. population of young women aged 18-24. Composition means that of all adults who read *Glamour* Magazine, 29.49% are young women aged 18-24.

Now, can you fill in the blanks for *Cosmopolitan*? Use the workbox to the left.

Coverage and composition are audience measures we can apply across any medium. In media, we use both of these measures to help us identify the best media for any given communication effort.

Coverage helps us to determine the total size of the audience we might expose to our message.

Composition helps us to understand that audience better and measure any wasted coverage in our exposure. Wasted coverage is unintended exposure. It's an added cost that we don't need for our communication effort.

While coverage and composition can work to measure any media vehicle, remember that both measures really only describe potential audiences. There are many times when we need better measures of the actual audience.

Step-by-Step Math

Coverage & Composition

Cosmopolitan Coverage

2,390 W18-24 Cosmo Readers

÷

12,404 Total W18-24

=

_____% Coverage

Cosmopolitan Composition

2,390 W18-24 Cosmo Readers

÷

8,982 Cosmo Adult Readers

=

_____% Composition

In television, coverage measures the size of a target population that lives in the geographic area covered by a TV station's broadcast signal.

For example, you may live in Minneapolis. Here, you would be in the signal coverage area for KSTP-TV, an affiliate station of the ABC broadcast network. As such, you would be reported as part of the potential audience coverage of the popular ABC drama, *NYPD Blue*.

See, you would be reported in the coverage for *NYPD Blue*, even if your TV wasn't turned on. You can see that coverage is not a good way to measure TV.

Fortunately, we have better measures we can use for TV.

Households Using Television (HUT).

One important basic measure is Households Using Television (HUT). HUT is a measure of the percentage of homes in a market that are actually using their television at particular point in time. HUT still only measures a potential audience but it is far better than just coverage.

HUT data helps media professionals to study the television usage behaviors of a target audience population.

HUTs are measured off a household base, but this statistic can also be measured off any other population base.

When we use a base target of people, we refer to the statistic as Persons Using Television, or PUTs.

Broadcast Ratings.

For broadcast media, like television and radio, we use ratings to estimate or project an actual audience for a program or a time period.

Because of how it is measured, a rating is an estimate of the size of the audience that actually watched a TV show or tuned in a radio station at a particular point in time.

Ratings are measured through set meters, people meters, and diaries as we discussed earlier in this chapter. Whether a meter or a diary, ratings are measured after the broadcast.

Top 10 Broadcast Shows

Total Households (in millions)

			WEEK
1. CSI		CBS	18.0
2. ER		NBC	16.8
3. Friends		NBC	14.5
4. Friends 8:30p		NBC	13.9
5. The Bachelor		ABC	13.4
6. CSI: Miami		CBS	13.3
7. 60 Minutes		CBS	13.0
8. Everybody Loves Raymond		CBS	12.9
9. Survivor: Pearl Islands		CBS	12.5
10. CBS Sunday Movie		CBS	12.4
10. Law & Order		NBC	12.4

Adults 18–49 (in millions)

			WEEK
1. ER		NBC	14.8
2. CSI		CBS	12.2
3. Friends		NBC	12.1
4. Friends 8:30p		NBC	11.8
5. The Bachelor		ABC	11.3
6. Will & Grace		NBC	11.0
7. Scrubs		NBC	9.1
8. Survivor: Pearl Islands		CBS	9.0
9. CSI: Miami		CBS	8.8
10. Monday Night Football		ABC	8.4

Source: Nielsen Media Research

HUTs and PUTs.

Ratings can be measured for households or people as shown here.

TV Ratings and Shares Tuesday 9pm CST

	HH Rating	Share
NYPD Blue	6.7	11
CSI: Miami	7.2	12
Law & Order: SVU	9.6	16
Diagnosis Murder	0.7	1
Other Shows	35.8	60
Total HUT	60%	100

Source: ACNielsen 11/17-23/2003

A rating is a percentage of an audience that reported, electronically or manually, to be tuned in at the particular time measured.

Like HUTs and PUTs, ratings can be measured for any population base, either total households or total people in a target group.

Ratings are calculated as a percentage of a total population base. As long as you are working off the same population base, you can add up total ratings for all programs broadcast in a certain time period.

The total ratings added up for any given population base and any given time period, by definition, is the HUT/PUT for that time period.

Audience Share.

Another common broadcast media measure is share.

Audience share is a companion statistic of ratings.

Share represents the percentage of households using television that were tuned in to a particular program. In this sense, share is like ratings only it is recalculated to a HUT/PUT base instead of a total population.

The point here is that share is a percentage of an actual, tuned-in audience, whereas rating is a percentage of a total possible population base.

Let's go back to our *NYPD Blue* example. *NYPD Blue* airs on ABC on Tuesdays at 9 p.m. in Minneapolis. So do a lot of other shows. The table in the figure to the left shows a listing of several television programs that are broadcast on Tuesdays at 9 p.m. central time. For each show listed, the first column indicates the household audience rating and the corresponding audience share is in the second column.

Look at the math. Play with the numbers for a little while.

You should be able to see that the audience ratings add up to a total HUT of 60% for the time period.

Then, if you take the *NYPD Blue* rating of 6.7 divided by the HUT of 60, you see that the audience share tuned in to *NYPD Blue* was 11%.

Gross Rating Points (GRP).

From the previous example, you see that we can add up rating points across television programs as long as we do so using the same population base.

In fact, we can add up rating points across multiple media and different time periods, as long as we do so using the same population base.

We call this sum of ratings, gross rating points.

Gross rating points (GRPs) represent an accumulation of an actual audience over time and across multiple media. As such, GRPs are a consolidated measure indicating the expected audience weight of a combination of media.

This is a basic principle of math that when you express statistics as a percentage of a certain base, you can add, subtract, multiply, or divide those percentages relative to the same base and the relative proportions stay the same.

This basic principle of math allows us to make media comparisons beyond just one particular program or one particular magazine. This is important in media because we often have to use more than just one media vehicle to deliver the audience we need for a marketer's message.

Just like program ratings, GRPs can be expressed in both household and people terms.

In media, we generally use the word "gross" to mean households, one of the broadest measures we use.

Target Rating Points (TRP).

When we are talking about a particular population of people, we use the word "target" and the corresponding measure, target rating points or TRPs.

TRPs are measured and projected in exactly the same way as GRPs.

As long as we are working with the same "target" base, we can add, subtract, multiply, or divide TRPs just as we do GRPs. We can use TRPs to make media comparisons beyond

Never. Never Ever.
One thing we can never ever do is combine GRPs and TRPs in any way.

just one particular program or one particular magazine; just as we can with GRPs.

In fact, the only difference between the two measures is the base we use to calculate the percentage. And because the base is different, the only thing we can't ever do is combine GRPs with TRPs in any way – any math operation.

For that matter, you must know that we can never combine TRPs across different "target" bases.

GRPs and TRPs for a General Interest Media Schedule

General Interest Media	GRPs (HH)	TRPs (M18-34)	TRPs (W18-34)
Media 1: TV – 6 Spots	60	35	45
Media 2: Radio – 36 Spots	40	25	30
Totals	100	60	75

This is mathematically important, so let's consider a brief example. Notice in the figure above that our general interest media schedule uses two different media and yet we can add up the GRPs combining both media. Notice too that each media delivers men and women differently. Still, as long as we are adding the same TRPs, men with men or women with women, we can combine the two media.

Gross Impressions.

In comparing multiple media, or possible combinations of media, we can also revert back to the common population base.

As long as we go back to the same base, we can add up the raw numbers the same way we added up the percentages.

We call this audience size in raw numbers, impressions. Gross impressions means total household impressions while target impressions means total people impressions.

Combining Ratings and Impressions.

If we know ratings, we can calculate impressions. And, likewise, if we know impressions we can calculate ratings. This is important because, as we've told you, some media are measured by ratings and some by raw audience (like readership). If you know how to go back and forth, then you can estimate the audience impact of any combination of media.

To make this work, you must know the raw number total possible audience for your target market.

Let's say your target audience is adults aged 18-34. From MRI we see that there is a U.S. base population of 65,815,000 adults aged 18-34. This is the raw number total possible audience for adults 18-34.

Now let's say that we have a television plan that delivers 200 adult 18-34 target rating points and a magazine plan that delivers a total adult 18-34 readership of 80,000,000. What would be the total audience impact of television and magazines together?

Here's how to answer that question. Remembering that rating points are a percentage, we can calculate that 80,000,000 magazine plan as a percentage of adults 18-34. 80,000,000 divided by 65,815,000 equals 122% or 122 rating points.

Now all we have to do is add 200 TV rating points to our 122 magazine rating points to equal 322 total plan rating points.

The box to the left shows this step-by-step. Remember, the important thing here is working from a common population base.

Audience Duplication.

It is also important to know that by adding statistics across time and media this way; we may be double counting a household or a person.

This is true for both ratings and impressions.

We call this audience duplication. It refers to the fact that people expose themselves to more than one media.

Step-by-Step Math

Combining Media

1) Express the magazine readership as a percentage of the Adult 18-34 base.

  80,000,000 Adult 18-34 readers
  ÷ 65,815,000 total 18-34 adults
  = 122%
    or 122 Adult 18-34 rating points

2) Combine TV and magazine ratings.
    200 TV rating points
  + 122 magazine rating points
  = 322 total media plan Adult
      18-34 rating points

This is easy to understand. Think about your own media habits. You might have a favorite TV program that you watch whenever you can, one day a week. You might have a favorite radio station you listen to in the morning.

You probably have a favorite magazine you like to read when you're taking a study break. Each of these is a different media and each one is an exposure opportunity.

If a clever marketer really wanted you to see her message, she would place her ad on your favorite TV program, your favorite radio station, and in your favorite magazine all at the same time.

Each exposure would be measured as a rating indicating that you saw the ad message each time. You would have been duplicated!

It's true that you saw the ad message each time, and we do want to count you in the audience.

But, is it right to count you three times?

The answer is yes and no. And it's one of the most important sets of measurements in media.

Reach & Frequency
What We Need Is a Way to Un-Duplicate You.

What we really want to do is count you in the audience only one time but then credit you as exposed three times. **We call this concept Reach and Frequency.**

This is our way of un-duplicating an audience and starting to get a feel for the impact our message is making with you and others in the target.

Reach.

We want to count our audience as the people in our target population who were exposed one time or more to our advertising message. We call this reach.

Reach is a measure of the percentage of a target population exposed at least one time to a message. Reach is an unduplicated measure. It counts each audience member only one time. In this sense, reach can never be higher than 100%.

In fact, most of the time, the best possible reach you can hope for is something much less than 100%.

Generally speaking, the only way to achieve any kind of high-level reach is to combine multiple media.

Frequency.

We also want to credit the media for delivering certain people in the population more than one time.

We measure this as frequency.

This measure is literally a count of the number of times each audience member is exposed.

Frequency is an important communications concept. Most advertising works best when the message is repeated. Frequency is our measure of message repetition.

So, how many times does a message have to be repeated to be successfully communicated?

If you think you know the answer to this question, write it down and go see the world's leading advertisers.

They'd really like to know the answer to this one. Skip this class and go directly into consulting.

You'll make millions!

But, the fact is, we really don't know how much frequency is enough. And we're pretty sure it varies based on the interest level of the category in general and the individual consumer in particular. We'll come back to this concept in Chapter 5, where we'll cover it in better context.

For now, just know that communication always works best when the message is repeated.

Would you like us to repeat that?

Efficiency Measurements.

It costs a lot of money to advertise a message.

Whether your client is a major national company paying more than $2 million for a 30-second TV ad placement in the Super Bowl, or a local market owner of a neighborhood bar/restaurant, the cost of advertising is a big deal.

Media people need measures to help them know if they are getting their clients the most for their advertising investment.

There are two specific measures used frequently by media people; cost-per-point (CPP) and cost-per-thousand (CPM).

In this section, we'll explain how each measure is calculated and how the two measures are related.

Cost-per-point (CPP).

Earlier in this chapter we showed you how rating points could be added up across time and multiple media vehicles to calculate a figure we called gross rating points.

Well, cost-per-point means simply the advertising cost of buying each one of those gross rating points. It's a simple rate calculation.

Add up the total cost of any combination of media and divide it by the total GRPs. The product is the rate we call cost-per-point.

This is a terrific measure of cost efficiency that we can use any time we can add up total rating points. This is particularly appropriate for measuring the cost efficiency of broadcast media.

For example, think about our World Series example from page 137. We showed you that the average household rating for one World Series game was 11.9. Let's assume one 30-second commercial cost $300,000. We divide that cost by 11.9 rating points to get a CPP of $25,210.

Remember that rating points are an actual audience measure. And, we don't always have the luxury of knowing an actual audience.

Print media audiences, and audiences for other media, are more commonly reported in raw numbers representing the potential audience. Because of this, sometimes we need a measure that is not tied directly to rating points.

Step-by-Step Math

Calculating CPP

1) Take the cost of the ad: $300,000

2) Divide the number of rating points: 11.9

3) $300,000 ÷ 11.9 = $25,210 CPP

Cost-Per-Thousand (CPM).

Cost-per-thousand is another simple rate calculation, but it is based on the raw numbers size of the audience, impressions, instead of rating points.

Cost-per-thousand can be calculated using any raw number measure of an audience – HUTs or PUTs converted to audience, circulation, or readership.

It's called cost-per-thousand because it literally means the cost we incur to buy exposure to every one thousand audience members.

Why do we look at this per thousand? Because it just makes more sense to us this way. Sometimes the numbers are just too big or too small to understand. Using the thousands metric helps us to better understand the numbers.

Think about that World Series example again. There we told you that the average national audience for one World Series game was 12,554,500 households.

If we had paid $300,000 for one 30-second commercial, then we paid 2.4 cents per household.

That's such a small number that it's hard to read and compare to other numbers.

It almost makes the considerable investment of $300,000 seem trivial!

On a thousands basis, our same investment would be calculated as $300,000 divided by 12,554.5 thousand households – that would be $23.90 per thousand households. That CPM, $23.90, is a more meaningful number than just ¢2.4 per household.

Comparative Measures.

Both cost-per-point and cost-per-thousand are comparative measures. Media professionals use either CPP or CPM to compare the relative cost efficiency of media options.

These comparisons can be done within a medium, like comparing different TV programs or different radio stations in a market.

Step-by-Step Math

Calculating CPM

1) Express the audience as a thousands figure:
$12,554,500 \div 1000 = 12,554.5$

2) Divide the ad cost by the audience in thousands:
$$\$300,000 \div 12,554.5$$
$$= \$23.90 \text{ CPM}$$

These comparisons can also be done across combinations of media, like comparing the efficiency of a media plan using newspaper relative to a media plan using radio.

Common Comparison Mistakes.

It is important to know, though, that the comparison is only valid as long as the comparative base is applied consistently. Households should be compared to households and target groups should be compared to the same target group.

For example, it would be wrong to consider the television cost-per-thousand TV homes relative to a magazine cost-per-thousand men aged 18-24.

It would also be wrong to compare cost efficiencies for a potential audience measures relative to actual audience measures. Media professionals need to be careful about this, a potential audience measure, like circulation, should not be compared directly with an actual audience measure such as one calculated from ratings.

The only way to make such cross-media comparisons is to restate the figures as a common audience measure, as we showed you on page 146.

It is also important to remember that there is more to media than just cost efficiencies. Media is all about getting the most effect for the least cost. We use many other techniques and measures to determine and compare the relative effectiveness media options.

Strategic Analyses.

Now we are going to consider some very specific applications of the effectiveness measures and techniques we just discussed.

The most common strategic analyses used in media deal with the specific questions of who, where, and when.

In particular:

- **Who to advertise to – target analyses**
- **Where to advertise – geographic analyses**
- **When to advertise – scheduling analyses**

In this section we'll go step-by-step through detailed examples of analyses commonly used to answer each of these three questions.

We'll use the measures we described earlier in the chapter, but there is another math tool you'll need to know.

The Index.

In order to do each analysis, you'll need to use a particular math technique called an index. An index is a calculated expression of a relationship between two numbers, either two percentages or two raw numbers.

As such, the index is a very important mathematical tool used to analyze and understand numerical data.

It is very easy to calculate an index. But it gets a little tricky when you have to express the result of the calculation and then state the meaning of the index.

Good media people do this well. It's part of telling the story of the marketplace.

The root calculation is simple division; one number divided by another number. But, an index is typically expressed as a whole number even though the calculated division will always result in a decimal number. To make this simple division into an index we use a conversion factor of 100.

The conversion is made by multiplying by 100 in every index calculation. So, the basic formula for an index calculation looks like this:

$$\text{Index AB} = (\text{Number A} / \text{Number B}) * 100$$

After this calculation, you simply round the number to the nearest one's place and you have an index.

The mathematical magic of an index is that it standardizes numbers so you can more easily interpret a finding. An index is a standardization or normalized relation of two numbers such that an index exactly equal to 100 means average.

Because of this, an index equal to 110 means 10% above average while an index equal to 90 means literally 10% below average. And, so on.

A Few Words of Caution.

While index analysis is a great way to interpret numbers, you do have to be careful about how you use an index.

First, it is a standardized number, so we want to be sure to draw conclusions on meaningful differences. An index of 101 means a finding is 1% above average; in most cases 1% is not a meaningful and significant difference.

As a rule of thumb, most media people will use a 10% significance test. This means that indexes are only considered significant when they are above 110, 10% or more above average, or below 90, 10% or more below average.

Second, remember that an index is only one number and we never want to make an important decision on only one number. When comparing multiple media options, a media professional will often times use the index as a screen, and then look at one or both parts of the index calculation (Number A or Number B from the index formula) to further prioritize the options.

Specific Applications.

Now that we know how to calculate an index, let's look at a couple of specific analytical applications commonly used by media professionals. In this section, we'll look at three specific examples used to answer the questions of who to advertise to, where to advertise, and when to advertise.

Who to Advertise to – Target Analysis.

For this example, let's look at the soft drink category. In particular, let's say that we are working on the Coca-Cola Classic product for the Coca-Cola Company.

Shown on the next page is a reprint of data from Mediamark Research Inc. (MRI). As we mentioned earlier in this chapter, MRI is a resource for data on both product user and media user characteristics.

Here we are focusing on the demographic characteristics of adults who use(buy) the Coca-Cola Classic soft drink brand. Using this data we can determine the characteristics of the best target prospect for Classic Coke advertising, thus answering the question, "To whom should we advertise the Coca-Cola Classic product?"

REGULAR COLA DRINKS, NOT DIET 171

BASE: ADULTS	TOTAL U.S. '000	CAFFEINE FREE COKE A '000	B % DOWN	C % ACROSS	D INDEX	CHERRY COKE A '000	B % DOWN	C % ACROSS	D INDEX	COCA COLA CLASSIC A '000	B % DOWN	C % ACROSS	D INDEX	COKE II A '000	B % DOWN	C % ACROSS	D INDEX
All Adults	195192	5009	100.0	2.6	100	11578	100.0	5.9	100	59745	100.0	30.6	100	2330	100.0	1.2	100
Men	93553	2190	43.7	2.3	91	6186	53.4	6.6	111	32157	53.8	34.4	112	1175	50.4	1.3	105
Women	101639	2819	56.3	2.8	108	5392	46.6	5.3	89	27588	46.2	27.1	89	1155	49.6	1.1	95
Household Heads	118644	2855	57.0	2.4	94	6897	59.6	5.8	98	36705	61.4	30.9	101	1213	52.1	1.0	86
Homemakers	121504	3127	62.4	2.6	100	6680	57.7	5.5	93	34038	57.0	28.0	92	1159	49.7	1.0	80
Graduated College	42453	1151	23.0	2.7	106	2392	20.7	5.6	95	13534	22.7	31.9	104	375	16.1	0.9	74
Attended College	51498	1215	24.2	2.4	92	3681	31.8	7.1	120	16861	28.2	32.7	107	498	21.4	1.0	81
Graduated High School	64868	1691	33.8	2.6	102	3365	29.1	5.2	87	18920	31.7	29.2	95	674	28.9	1.0	87
Did not Graduate High School	36372	953	19.0	2.6	102	2141	18.5	5.9	99	10430	17.5	28.7	94	784	33.6	2.2	181
18-24	24842	781	15.6	3.1	123	2905	25.1	11.7	197	10103	16.9	40.7	133	*421	18.0	1.7	142
25-34	40972	928	18.5	2.3	88	2623	22.7	6.4	108	13907	23.3	33.9	111	696	29.8	1.7	142
35-44	43561	1204	24.0	2.8	108	2453	21.2	5.6	95	13834	23.2	31.8	104	453	19.4	1.0	87
45-54	32521	808	16.1	2.5	97	1926	16.6	5.9	100	9525	15.9	29.3	96	*240	10.3	0.7	62
55-64	21227	551	11.0	2.6	101	772	6.7	3.6	61	5735	9.6	27.0	88	*182	7.8	0.9	72
65 or over	32069	736	14.7	2.3	89	899	7.8	2.8	47	6641	11.1	20.7	68	*339	14.6	1.1	99
18-34	65815	1709	34.1	2.6	101	5528	47.7	8.4	142	24010	40.2	36.5	119	1116	47.9	1.7	142
18-49	127841	3376	67.4	2.6	103	9106	78.6	7.1	120	43536	72.9	34.1	111	1649	70.8	1.3	108
25-54	117054	2940	58.7	2.5	98	7002	60.5	6.0	101	37265	62.4	31.8	104	1388	59.6	1.2	99
Employed Full Time	107605	2582	51.5	2.4	93	6629	57.3	6.2	104	34893	58.4	32.4	106	1131	48.5	1.1	88
Part-time	19881	659	13.1	3.3	129	1412	12.2	7.1	120	6314	10.6	31.8	104	*194	8.3	1.0	82
Sole Wage Earner	35254	704	14.1	2.0	78	2094	18.1	5.9	100	11262	18.9	31.9	104	406	17.4	1.2	96
Not Employed	67705	1769	35.3	2.6	102	3538	30.6	5.2	88	18539	31.0	27.4	89	1005	43.1	1.5	124
Professional	19522	467	9.3	2.4	93	1095	9.5	5.6	95	6165	10.3	31.6	103	*192	8.3	1.0	83
Executive/Admin./Managerial	18220	562	11.2	3.1	120	1090	9.4	6.0	101	6032	10.1	33.1	108	*88	3.8	0.5	40
Clerical/Sales/Technical	37144	906	18.1	2.4	95	2286	19.7	6.2	104	11971	20.0	32.2	105	340	14.6	0.9	77
Precision/Crafts/Repair	14111	*362	7.2	2.6	100	973	8.4	6.9	116	4989	8.4	35.4	116	*204	8.8	1.4	121
Other Employed	38490	943	18.8	2.5	95	2597	22.4	6.7	114	12050	20.2	31.3	102	*501	21.5	1.3	109
H/D Income $75,000 or More	38349	1320	26.3	3.4	134	2526	21.8	6.6	111	12703	21.3	33.1	108	436	18.7	1.1	95
$60,000 - 74,999	20921	390	7.8	1.9	73	1255	10.8	6.0	101	6627	11.1	31.7	103	*250	10.7	1.2	100
$50,000 - 59,999	18782	458	9.1	2.4	95	1180	10.2	6.3	106	5586	9.3	29.7	97	*156	6.7	0.8	70
$40,000 - 49,999	22135	449	9.0	2.0	79	1020	8.8	4.6	78	6385	10.7	28.8	94	*219	9.4	1.0	83
$30,000 - 39,999	25204	603	12.0	2.4	93	1428	12.3	5.7	95	7964	13.3	31.6	103	*231	9.9	0.9	77
$20,000 - 29,999	27129	561	11.2	2.1	81	1490	12.9	5.5	93	8274	13.8	30.5	100	*295	12.6	1.1	91
$10,000 - 19,999	26824	853	17.0	3.2	124	1729	14.9	6.4	109	7573	12.7	28.2	92	*432	18.5	1.6	135
Less than $10,000	15846	*375	7.5	2.4	92	950	8.2	6.0	101	4632	7.8	29.2	96	*311	13.3	2.0	164
Census Region: North East	39302	1166	23.3	3.0	116	2554	22.1	6.5	110	10532	17.6	26.8	88	544	23.4	1.4	116
North Central	45475	1120	22.4	2.5	96	3263	28.2	7.2	121	12625	21.1	27.8	91	552	23.7	1.2	102
South	68341	1996	39.9	2.9	114	3384	29.2	5.0	83	24538	41.1	35.9	117	805	34.5	1.2	99
West	42074	727	14.5	1.7	67	2378	20.5	5.7	95	12050	20.2	28.6	94	*429	18.4	1.0	85
Marketing Reg.: New England	10432	*277	5.5	2.7	104	520	4.5	5.0	84	3105	5.2	29.8	97	*134	5.7	1.3	107
Middle Atlantic	33414	1031	20.6	3.1	120	2357	20.4	7.1	119	8888	14.9	26.6	87	536	23.0	1.6	134
East Central	25623	919	18.3	3.6	140	1758	15.2	6.9	116	7967	13.3	31.1	102	*171	7.4	0.7	56
West Central	29279	478	9.5	1.6	64	2144	18.5	7.3	123	7886	13.2	26.9	88	420	18.0	1.4	120
South East	38021	1054	21.0	2.8	108	1837	15.9	4.8	81	13698	22.9	36.0	118	*353	15.1	0.9	78
South West	21996	579	11.6	2.6	103	868	7.5	3.9	67	7833	13.1	35.6	116	*287	12.3	1.3	109
Pacific	36427	671	13.4	1.8	72	2094	18.1	5.7	97	10368	17.4	28.5	93	*429	18.4	1.2	99
County Size A	79981	2228	44.5	2.8	109	5475	47.3	6.8	115	23779	39.8	29.7	97	1367	58.7	1.7	143
County Size B	58438	1620	32.3	2.8	108	3331	28.8	5.7	96	19289	32.3	33.0	108	390	16.8	0.7	56
County Size C	27978	*622	12.4	2.2	87	1178	10.2	4.2	71	7875	13.2	28.1	92	*143	6.2	0.5	43
County Size D	28795	*540	10.8	1.9	73	1594	13.8	5.5	93	8803	14.7	30.6	100	*429	18.4	1.5	125
MSA Central City	64706	1666	33.3	2.6	100	4266	36.8	6.6	111	20871	34.9	32.3	105	848	36.4	1.3	110
MSA Suburban	92438	2628	52.5	2.8	110	5457	47.1	5.9	100	27899	46.7	30.2	99	995	42.7	1.1	90
Non-MSA	38047	*716	14.3	1.9	73	1856	16.0	4.9	82	10975	18.4	28.8	94	*487	20.9	1.3	107
Single	45144	1076	21.5	2.4	93	4184	36.1	9.3	156	16429	27.5	36.4	119	859	36.9	1.9	159
Married	112383	3230	64.5	2.9	112	5699	49.2	5.1	85	33724	56.4	30.0	98	1017	43.7	0.9	76
Other	37664	704	14.0	1.9	73	1696	14.6	4.5	76	9592	16.1	25.5	83	454	19.5	1.2	101
Parents	68208	1965	39.2	2.9	112	4223	36.5	6.2	104	22891	38.3	33.6	110	685	29.4	1.0	84
Working Parents	53687	1481	29.6	2.8	107	3240	28.0	6.0	102	17894	30.0	33.3	109	444	19.1	0.8	69
Household Size: 1 Person	25014	389	7.8	1.6	61	1028	8.9	4.1	69	6374	10.7	25.5	83	*192	8.2	0.8	64
2 Persons	63398	1713	34.2	2.7	105	2971	25.7	4.7	79	17761	29.7	28.0	92	751	32.2	1.2	99
3 or More	106780	2907	58.0	2.7	106	7580	65.5	7.1	120	35610	59.6	33.3	109	1387	59.5	1.3	109
Any Child in Household	81339	2275	45.4	2.8	109	5516	47.6	6.8	114	27536	46.1	33.9	111	961	41.2	1.2	99
Under 2 Years	14305	*349	7.0	2.4	95	1034	8.9	7.2	122	5141	8.6	35.9	117	*217	9.3	1.5	127
2-5 Years	29745	886	17.7	3.0	116	2094	18.1	7.0	119	9860	16.5	33.1	108	*450	19.3	1.5	127
6-11 Years	38480	1053	21.0	2.7	107	2428	21.0	6.3	106	12846	21.5	33.4	109	*333	14.3	0.9	73
12-17 Years	37713	998	19.9	2.6	103	2635	22.8	7.0	118	12337	20.6	32.7	107	*351	15.1	0.9	78
White	164831	4032	80.5	2.4	95	8702	75.2	5.3	89	49887	83.5	30.3	99	1564	67.1	0.9	79
Black	22686	753	15.0	3.3	129	2308	19.9	10.2	172	7042	11.8	31.0	101	610	26.2	2.7	225
Spanish Speaking	19624	*459	9.2	2.3	91	1179	10.2	6.0	101	7050	11.8	35.9	117	*392	16.8	2.0	167
Home Owned	133858	3403	67.9	2.5	99	7199	62.2	5.4	91	40476	67.7	30.2	99	1368	58.7	1.0	86

According to the MRI data, 31% of all adults buy Coca-Cola Classic. Adult Classic Coke drinkers are more likely to be males between the ages of 18-49 who live in the South.

So why did we focus on these particular characteristics? Because, we observe that these are the characteristics for which we see both a high index and a large percentage of Classic Coke users. Some of these are easy to see because MRI actually calculates the index for us. Here's how we did it and what each means.

Classic Coke drinkers are more likely to be men.

The MRI data shows 53.8% of Classic Coke drinkers are male. This represents an index of 112 when compared to the total U.S. population. This means men are 12% more likely to be observed as Classic Coke drinkers than they are to be observed in the general U.S. population. This implies our target of Classic Coke drinkers skews more male than female.

Look closely at the data on the MRI page to see where we pulled these numbers. Look at the row labeled "Men" and follow that row over to the column labeled "Coca Cola Classic, B, % Down" and you'll find the percentage 53.8. Look next at the column labeled "Coca Cola Classic, D, Index" and you'll see the index number 112.

The index is calculated for us in the MRI report.

Classic Coke drinkers are between the ages of 18 and 49.

The MRI data shows a huge group of 72.9% of Classic Coke drinkers are 18-49. The index in the MRI report is 111.

Once again, the index is calculated for us.

But, you need to know how the index is calculated because you never know when you might need to do it for yourself. So, let's break it down.

To calculate the index on your own, you need only look at the raw numbers in the report, the column labeled "Total U.S. '000." Look at this column and find the numbers for the rows labeled "Total Adults" and "18-49" – you should have found the numbers 195,192 for "Total Adults" and 127,841 for "18-49."

Step-by-Step Math

Target Audience Analysis

1) What percent of U.S. adults are aged 18-49?

      127,841 Adults 18-49

      ÷ 195,192 Total U.S. Adults

      = 0.655 or 65.5%

2) What percent of Classic Coke drinkers are Adults 18-49?

      43,536 A18-49 drink Coke

      ÷ 59,745 Adults drink Coke

      = .729 or 72.9%

3) Are Classic Coke drinkers more or less likely to be Adults 18-49?

      72.9% of Classic Coke Drinkers

      ÷ 65.5% of Total U.S. Adults

      = 1.113

      x 100 and rounded to nearest 1

      = 111 Index

Now using those two numbers, you can calculate what percent of the total U.S. adult population is between the ages of 18 and 49 years old. Take 127,841 divided by 195,192, you'll get the decimal number 0.655. Expressing this decimal number as a percentage, we see that 65.5% of U.S. adults are between the ages of 18 and 49.

Using our formula, the index for Classic Coke drinkers is calculated to compare Classic Coke drinkers to the general U.S. population. We take 72.9 divided by 65.5 times 100, to get 111 (rounded to the nearest whole number). This means that adults aged 18 to 49 years old are 11% more likely to appear among Classic Coke drinkers than they are to appear in the general population. So, we see that our target of Classic Coke drinkers skews younger rather than older.

Classic Coke drinkers live in the South.

Considering geography, look at the group of rows labeled "census region." Find the data for the row labeled "South."

You'll see that people in the South are 17% more likely to be Classic Coke Drinkers.

Do you see that?

So, here we have shown you how to do a target audience analysis using a standard MRI report. If you were indeed working on the Classic Coke business, you might reasonably recommend a demographic audience profile of men aged 18-49 who live in the South.

But, before we leave this section, let's look at one more thing. At the bottom of the MRI page look at the row labeled "Spanish speaking" and follow it across to Coca Cola Classic column D Index. Here you see an index of 117. This means that we are 17% more likely to find Spanish-speaking adults among Classic Coke drinkers than we are to see Spanish-speaking adults in the general population. That's a pretty significant skew to the Classic Coke business.

Does this mean that we should target Spanish-speaking adults? The answer is yes and no.

Yes, that is a significant index, but look at the percentage down, column B. The percentage here is only 11.8 meaning that only 11.8% of Classic Coke drinkers are spanish speaking adults.

While the index is significant, the percentage is low. So, no, we really shouldn't specifically target Spanish-speaking adults. To do so would mean ignoring a vast majority (almost 90%) of Classic Coke drinkers.

What we should do instead is mix in some added media coverage of Spanish-speaking adults. This way, we recognize the strong skew without ignoring such a large group of consumers.

We'll move on now to the next application, answering the question of "where to advertise."

Where to Advertise – Geographic Analysis.

For this analysis, let's switch to a new product category, yogurt. Let's say that we are working for an advertising agency on the Colombo Yogurt business.

We've been asked to recommend a geographic advertising strategy for the Colombo Yogurt client.

There are two ways to do this, a defensive approach and an offensive approach.

This is an important concept. We'll cover both ways here and then later in the book we'll talk more about this offensive versus defensive decision in media.

The Defensive Approach.

In taking the defensive approach we are saying that defending our product's business is our most important criteria for decisions. This is the right thing to do in cases where our client has a strong business skew to a particular geography.

This is exactly the case with our client, Colombo Yogurt. Reprinted on the next page is a partial listing of an MRI report on Colombo Yogurt buyers geographically, by U.S. Marketing Region.

BDI

One of the more useful indexes is known as the BDI – the Brand Development Index.

For example, there may be some regions or target groups more important to a certain brand.

These groups or regions have a higher BDI. It helps a media person to "go fishing where the fish are."

Demographic Report for Colombo Yogurt Users

	Total U.S. (x 1000)	A (x 1000)	B % Down	C % Across	D Index
All Female Homemakers	89789	2749	100.0	3.1	100
Marketing Region:					
New England	4705	554	20.2	11.8	388
Mid-Atlantic	15444	970	35.3	6.3	205
East Central	11580	207	7.5	1.8	58
West Central	13616	411	14.9	3.0	98
South East	18271	135	4.9	0.7	24
South West	10224	94	3.4	0.9	30
Pacific	15950	378	13.8	2.4	77

Source: MRI, Spring 1998

Step-by-Step Math

Geographic Analysis

1) What percent of Colombo users live in the Mid-Atlantic and New England regions?

1520 (970 + 554)

÷ 2,749

= 55.5% of Colombo users

2) What percent of U.S. female homemakers live in the Mid-Atlantic and New England regions?

20,149 (15,444 + 4,705)

÷ 89,789

= 22.4% of U.S. female homemakers

3) Are Colombo users more or less likely to live in the Mid-Atlantic and New England regions?

55.5% of Colombo users

÷ 22.4% of U.S. female homemakers

= 248 Index

(2.48 x 100 and rounded)

From this data we see a very strong business development skew to the Mid-Atlantic and New England regions of the U.S. Together these two regions represent a total of 55.5% (20.2 + 35.3) of the Colombo Yogurt business as compared to only 22.4% of the Total U.S. base of female homemakers [(4705 + 15444) ÷ 89789]. That is an incredibly high index of 248 [(55.5 ÷ 22.4) *100].

This index means that residents of the Mid-Atlantic and New England regions are 148% more likely to be Colombo Yogurt buyers than they are to be observed in the general population.

That's more than twice as likely, and that's a very significant skew to the business.

Back to Business Development.

Getting back to business development, let's talk a little more about that index and what it means.

We have another term to describe this index as applied in a geographic analysis. This is the *Brand Development Index*, which we mentioned in the earlier sidebar. It tells us how well-developed a brand's business is (or isn't) in any given geography.

A Short Side-Bar Note

Notice the base for this analysis is female homemakers, not total U.S. adults. "Female homemakers" is a base the research companies typically use for grocery store products that are generally purchased by women who do most of the grocery shopping in the U.S.

The Classic Coke product we looked at earlier was reported against a general adult population base because it is as likely (even more likely, as we saw in our analysis) to be purchased by men.

To understand this, you need to remember that an index is a standardized number and that 100 means average.

So, any time we are looking at mutually exclusive parts of a particular sphere of analysis, we will see that where one part is high, another part will be low.

Colombo U.S. Brand Development.

Looking back at the Colombo Yogurt business we see this very clearly. That incredibly high index of 248 must be offset by a lower index in the rest of the country. Let's test this.

The whole of the U.S. is 100% of the female homemaker base, right. So if we saw 55.5% of the Colombo Yogurt business in the Mid-Atlantic and New England, then we should find only 44.5% (100 – 55.5) in the rest of the country. Because of rounding, we can't just add up the percentages so we add up the raw numbers instead and recalculate a new percentage the same way we did before.

We add up the numbers in Column A for all the regions other than Mid-Atlantic and New England to get a total of 1,225. Then we divide 1,225 by the total at the top of Column A – 2,749 – to get the number 0.4456.

Rounded and expressed as a percentage we see exactly what we expected – 44.5%.

Next we look at the general population of the female homemaker base. This too should be a whole that is equal to 100% of the U.S. So we can see that if 22.4% of the base lives in the Mid-Atlantic and New England, then 77.6% (100 minus 22.4) of the base lives in other regions of the U.S.

Finally, we calculate the index for the remainder of the U.S. as 44.5 divided by the base 77.6, then multiply by 100 and round to the nearest whole number.

This gives us an index of only 57.

Looking then at the Colombo Yogurt business, we see a very strong business skew. This kind of skew might be an appropriate situation for a defensive approach to advertising the business. It kind of depends on why the skew exists.

Defending the Colombo Business.

In our case, we know that the Colombo Yogurt business skew exists because Colombo started as a regional brand in the northeast. They have long since expanded their business nationally but, the Colombo brand name is not as well known in other regions as other competing brands of yogurt.

If we take the defensive approach, we would make the recommendation that Colombo Yogurt advertise heaviest in the Mid-Atlantic and New England regions of the U.S.

Of course, we would still advertise in the rest of the country because we want to support our whole business but, we want heavier emphasis in our two strongest regions.

To make such a recommendation we would use a geographic allocation model such as the one presented in the following figure.

Geographic Allocation Model						
	%U.S.	% Colombo	Colombo Index	Budget Factor	Allocated Budget	Budget Index
New England	5.2	20.2	388	.202	$2,020	388
Mid-Atlantic	17.2	35.3	205	.353	3,530	205
East Central	12.9	7.5	58	.075	750	58
West Central	15.2	14.9	98	.149	1,490	98
South East	20.3	4.9	24	.049	490	24
South West	11.4	3.4	30	.034	340	30
Pacific	17.8	13.8	77	.138	1,380	77
Total	100.0	100.0	100	1.000	$10,000	100

In this model, because the Brand Development Index is so strong, we can use the %Colombo Sales in each region to determine an appropriate allocation of our budget.

We did this by using the percent of Colombo business for each region as a budget factor, just re-writing each percentage as a decimal then multiplying the decimal times the total budget.

Step-by-Step Math

Defensive Budget Allocation

1) Use Colombo % of business as the Budget Factor by converting the percentage back to a decimal:
    20.2% is .202
2) Multiply the Budget Factor by the Total Budget:
    $10,000 x .202 = $2,020

For example look at the Allocated budget for New England. You'll see that the budget allocated equals the total budget $10,000 times the factor .202, $2,020.

In this way, we recommend a heavy spending emphasis on our most highly developed geography while we maintain a base level of spending in other areas of the country.

This is the definition of a defensive geographic strategy in that we are spending our money to support and defend our business strengths.

This is a defensive geographic budget allocation model that you can apply to any client for which you can calculate a regional or market level Brand Development Index.

The Offensive Approach.

The offensive approach is more aggressive.

With this strategy we will recommend advertising spending to support our greatest opportunity markets, not just our big business markets. So as you can see, one of the first things we need to do is identify and then somehow quantify our opportunities. This is where media math gets creative.

Thinking again about the Colombo Yogurt business, let's say that the client has told us that they have done a taste test of Colombo Yogurt versus a key competitor, Yoplait Yogurt. The results of the taste test suggest a terrific advantage for Colombo where 8 out of every 10 participants said they preferred the taste of Colombo versus Yoplait.

Since the advantage is so great, the client and the agency have agreed the advertising will directly target Yoplait in a head-to-head comparison.

Well, this changes everything. Now we are thinking about our business more aggressively. So now we want to translate that aggressiveness into our geographic strategy.

What we need to do is look for a way to define our strategy so that it fits with the advertising strategy. What makes the most sense here is to consider the Yoplait business. So, let's look at the Yoplait business compared to Colombo.

Geographic Comparison: Colombo vs. Yoplait

All Female Homemakers	Total U.S. (x 1000)	Colombo				Yoplait			
		A (x 1000)	B % Down	C % Across	D Index	A (x 1000)	B % Down	C % Across	D Index
	89789	2749	100.0	3.1	100	4310	100.0	4.8	100
Marketing Region:									
New England	4705	554	20.1	11.8	385	246	5.7	5.2	109
Mid-Atlantic	15444	970	35.3	6.3	205	599	13.9	3.9	81
East Central	11580	207	7.5	1.8	58	440	10.2	3.8	79
West Central	13616	411	14.9	3.0	99	857	19.9	6.3	131
South East	18271	135	4.9	0.7	24	593	13.8	3.2	68
South West	10224	94	3.4	0.9	30	419	9.7	4.1	85
Pacific	15950	378	13.8	2.4	77	1157	26.8	7.3	151

Source: MRI, Spring 1998

Step-by-Step Math

Offensive Budget Allocation

1) First you need to think creatively about how to quantify an opportunity. Here, we can use the Yoplait development index as an Opportunity Factor.

2) Calculate the Budget Factor:
   20.2% Colombo business (.202)
   x 1.09 Yoplait Index
   = .220 Budget Factor for New England

3) Adjust the Budget Factor to compensate for rounding errors in factoring:
   .220 New England Factor
   ÷ 1.030 Total Budget Factor
   = .214 Adjusted Factor for New England

4) Repeat step 3 for each region so that the Adusted Factor column adds up to 1.000 exactly.

5) Complete the model:
   .214 Adusted Factor
   x $10,000 Total Budget
   = $2,140 Budget Allocated to New England

Just as MRI gave us Colombo data, they provide the same information for the Yoplait business. We can look at Yoplait side-by-side with Colombo as shown in the figure above.

Here we see that where Colombo is strongly developed in the northeast, Yoplait does its best business in the West Central and Pacific regions of the U.S. The good news for Colombo is that although the West Central and Pacific regions are not strongholds, at least our business is better there than in some other regions. This then is something we can take as a sign of opportunity – that Colombo's business is respectable even where the Yoplait business is at its strongest.

So, this can work as the basis for our more aggressive geographic approach. We certainly don't want to overlook our own strengths but, we do want to take advantage of the fact that we have a great opportunity versus Yoplait.

What we need to do now is figure out how to quantify this opportunity and allocate the budget accordingly.

Remembering that an index is a standardized number, one way to do this would be to use the Yoplait index (from MRI) as a factor. The following figure shows how we would do this.

Yoplait Indices as a Factor on Colombo

	%U.S.	% Colombo	Yoplait Index	Budget Factor	Adjusted Factor	Allocated Budget
New England	5.2	20.2	109	.220	.214	$2,140
Mid-Atlantic	17.2	35.3	81	.286	.278	2,780
East Central	12.9	7.5	79	.059	.057	570
West Central	15.2	14.9	131	.195	.189	1,890
South East	20.3	4.9	68	.033	.032	320
South West	11.4	3.4	85	.029	.028	280
Pacific	17.8	13.8	151	.208	.202	2,020
Total	100.0	100.0	100	1.030	1.000	$10,000

Note that the total budget is still the same as we used in the previous allocation, but the spending allocation for each region has changed to reflect the Yoplait regional strengths.

In this new model, we are still spending a lot of our budget in New England and the Mid-Atlantic, but we are now spending more in the West Central and Pacific regions.

Factor With Care.

Let's take a brief moment here to caution the use of factors on top of indexes.

From the preceding figures you'll see that the bottom line total in the "budget factor" column equals 1.000. Sometimes this happens naturally.

But, more often, this is a forced calculation that becomes necessary when we apply a factor on top of a rounded number.

It is generally true that rounding will produce errors that will typically be nominal. However, when we apply a rounded number index as a factor on another rounded number index (as in the previous figure) the rounding error can become exaggerated.

To repair such errors, we need to create what we call an "Adjusted Factor." The adjustment is a simple restatement of a factor to a base of 1.000.

This is demonstrated in the step-by-step box, step 3, on the previous page. The base of 1.000 is important because that controls our budget allocation.

We have to be certain that our allocated budget does not exceed our available budget total.

The Geographic Game Summary.

In this short example of the Yogurt category, we have demonstrated a geographic analysis to answer the question of where to advertise. We also introduced you to the idea of a defensive or offensive approach to the analysis. We can think of this as a kind of game as long as we remember that the numbers have to add up at the end.

In the defensive approach, we would have advertised throughout the country but with a significantly heavier emphasis in the northeastern regions of New England and the Mid-Atlantic states.

For the offensive approach, we showed you how to incorporate an additional factor considering a more aggressive and opportunistic allocation of the same dollar budget amount. In considering the opportunities available to grow the Colombo business, we would still have spent some modest level of advertising nationally but, this time would have incorporated a heavier emphasis of spending in the Northeast and the West and West Central.

We'll move on now to the last of the most common applications – answering the question of "when to advertise."

When to Advertise – Scheduling Analyses.

To answer this question, we will once again use an index calculation but, this time it will be a little different.

This time we need to analyze specific periods of time within a broader period of time. So, this time the "whole" that we need to use as a base for our index is a period of time, not some predefined population base.

This means we will need a different process but, it doesn't necessarily mean it is going to be any harder to do.

The Seasonal Development Index.

In order to answer the question of when to advertise, we must consider a number of important factors. But, the most important factor is that of sales seasonality.

Annual U.S. Travel 2002 Monthly (% of person-trips)	
January	6%
February	6%
March	8%
April	7%
May	9%
June	10%
July	12%
August	10%
September	8%
October	7%
November	8%
December	9%

Source: Travel Industry Association of America

The idea here is that we would prefer to schedule our advertising to coincide with the times when sales are most likely to occur. To help us determine this, we will calculate a Seasonality Development Index, very much like the Brand Development Index we used in the geographic analysis.

Let's work through an example using the travel category – domestic travel in the U.S.

For this analysis we tracked down a great source for information, the U.S. Travel Industry Association. Each year they report a consolidated analysis of domestic travel in the U.S., by month. The data for 2002 are presented to the left.

Just looking at this data we can see that the biggest travel period in the U.S. is in the summer months.

You probably would have guessed that much on your own. But, you can't really tell by looking just how significant the summer months are. Remember that significant means 10% or more, higher or lower than average.

The better way to do this is to use an index analysis comparing each month's actual share to the average share we might expect for any month. This average is an easy calculation, just take the total 100% divided by the number of months, 12 – for an expected monthly share of 8.33%.

U.S. Domestic Travel Index by Month

Month:	Actual %	Expected %	Index	
January	6%	8.33%	72	Below
February	6%	8.33%	72	Below
March	8%	8.33%	96	Average
April	7%	8.33%	84	Below
May	9%	8.33%	108	Average
June	10%	8.33%	120	Above
July	12%	8.33%	144	Above
August	10%	8.33%	120	Above
September	8%	8.33%	96	Average
October	7%	8.33%	84	Below
November	8%	8.33%	96	Average
December	9%	8.33%	108	Average

Once we know the expected average for each month, we can compare each actual month to know if business that month was significantly better or worse than average.

The figure to the left shows this calculation and the resulting index for each month. Here we see that U.S. domestic travel is average in March and May and then again in the Fall and that domestic travel is significantly above average in the summer months of June, July and August.

Where Do You Find this Data?

We've mentioned some standard sources here for this great data.

As a rule, industry associations are a great source for data. Such associations are in the business of supporting their membership. Often this means they conduct and store research on the industry and trends that impact business.

If you are trying to find an association for your industry, search online for an Encyclopedia of Associations. You'll find an interactive online guide to associations for every American industry sector, complete with links to available websites.

With this analysis we can know when trips are taken in the U.S., but that may not be the very best time to advertise. It depends on the kind of business we might be working on relative to the travel industry.

If our client's business is a chain of highway restaurants where travelers decide to stop for food while they are en route to their destination, then this analysis of actual travel by month might be very useful.

If on the other hand our client's business is a very expensive line of cruise ships for which travelers make their travel arrangements many months in advance, then it might be better to know the details of when U.S. travel plans are decided and travel arrangements made. We would need a different set of data to determine significant times when travel plans are decided.

Either way, this is a fairly easy way to look at the raw data and figure out what we most need to know in order to decide when to advertise.

When we are looking at seasonality we can look at this by month of the year, by week of the month, by day of the week – a lot of different ways.

And just as we did with geography, we can use seasonality to set a budget allocation and we can do this either defensively or offensively.

As we said earlier in this book – a lot of choices to make.

Summary.

In this chapter we've covered a lot of ground and done a lot of math. We hope this has been enlightening but not too challenging. And that maybe you'll leave this chapter with a better understanding of math in general and, in particular, some of the simple principles of math you'll need for a career in media.

First we covered the basic tools and techniques we use in measuring media and media audiences.

We learned that each medium is different in how it delivers an audience and so each medium is measured in a different way.

Next we covered the definitions of the most common measures we use in media. We described the difference between actual audience measures and potential measures. And, we defined key terms like reach and frequency, ratings, share, impressions and circulation.

In the third section of this chapter, we very briefly covered the two most commonly used measures of media efficiency – cost-per-point and cost-per-thousand.

We talked through how to calculate each measure and when to use one versus the other.

Finally, in our last section, we went through specific examples of three of the most commonly used analyses in media, target analyses, geographic analyses, and scheduling analyses. We introduced the index analysis technique and defined the basic process for calculating and using an index to interpret a key finding.

Overall this chapter has been loaded with a lot of basic math and important media techniques you'll find immediately useful on the job in media.

Susan Arl doesn't mess with success.
She's spent her entire career in media research. She feels that media research is a job she does well and it's work that she loves, so why mess with success. Why indeed! Susan made only one major career move when she switched from agency-based media research to the media-side perspective.

Career Capsule:

Susan Arl, Research Director, CLTV.

Susan Arl is the Research Director for CLTV, a division of the Tribune Company. She is truly a media research maven, having spent most of her long career in the practice of media research.

Research, Then Planning.

Susan started her career at Foote Cone & Belding as an analytical assistant in the research department. After a short time, she moved into the media training program as a print coordinator. Susan was excited about the opportunity to be part of the strategic process for developing media plans. She sensed *"an extraordinary energy in the media department and a team spirit that was second to none."*

Media Planning.

Ultimately, Susan worked her way up through the media ranks to a position as Media Director for FCB Direct, a direct marketing division of Foote Cone & Belding. Her responsibilities in this position included general advertising, retail, and direct marketing clients ranging from Kraft Foods to Zenith Data Systems to the Royal Bank of Canada.

Susan spent her entire agency career at FCB. She says that *"FCB believed in providing junior staff with a wealth of opportunities."* And she took full advantage of this. She learned from exposure to all types of media and understanding how each media element worked to support the client's marketing focus.

Then Media Research.

Then Susan moved back to her research origins, but this time with a media bent. She took a position as Research Director working for the cable television station CLTV, Chicago's only 24-hour local news channel. In this position, Susan is responsible for the development of all sales research, sales presentations, and overall analysis of ratings trends. These responsibilities include the development of all questionnaires for research studies measuring CLTV viewership, working with moderators to develop and implement discussion guides for qualitative research, and traveling with sales representatives as needed to support sales calls with agency media buyers and other key personnel.

Susan admits that she enjoys this work. She's good with numbers and she likes being able to work with numbers to tell a story. In her case at CLTV, it is a story of success. She likes working with the sales staff in developing an approach and an appropriate sales pitch for clients.

The Future of Media.

Susan sees broadcast continuing as the leading edge of the media landscape. *"The growth and expansion of personal video recorders over the next few years will dramatically impact the way media is measured and how advertisers and agencies develop their communications strategies."* Susan predicts that local people meters, new technology from television ratings research giant Nielsen, will *"change the currency of the local broadcast marketplace."*

Advice for Newcomers.

Susan feels this is a very exciting time to join the field of media and media research. She sees the industry as a whole *"on the cusp of a dramatic change."* The particular challenge of the future will be the rapid expansion of alternative media choices and a lack of proven research to support and defend client use of these new media choices.

Discussion Questions.

1. Creative Media Analysis.

Review those questions we asked at the start of this chapter. Thinking about those questions, what resources would you use and what steps would you take to answer each of the questions listed below?

What is the most popular television show among young adults aged 18-25?

What was the advertising value of that nifty Mini-Cooper product placement in the movie *The Italian Job*?

What is the best time of day to advertise breakfast sausages? And, what is the best day of the week?

2. Media Measurements.

Most media measurements are based on sample group responses to some kind of survey. What are some of the common problems with sampling in research?

How do media research companies ensure valid respondent participation in their surveys?

3. Audience Measurements.

What is the difference between audience coverage and audience composition?

What is the difference between broadcast ratings and audience share?

In media, what does "gross" mean?

Explain the relationship between Reach and Frequency.

4. Efficiency Measurements.

What is the difference between cost-per-point and cost-per-thousand?

Describe a situation where cost-per-point would be the best efficiency measure.

Describe a situation where cost-per-thousand would be the best efficiency measure.

5. Strategic Analyses.

Why is an index a helpful tool for understanding numerical data?

What is a Brand Development Index?

How do you calculate BDI?

What is the best way to use an Index Analysis?

Exercises.

Use creative media analysis to answer the following questions about Budweiser beer buyers and drinkers.

For sources, start with the MRI or SMRB in your school library. You'll find a lot of information there, but you'll also need to get creative about some other sources.

Be sure to support your answers with data from your analyses.

1. What is the audience profile (demographics, lifestyle, and psychographic characteristics) of Budweiser beer buyers?

How about Budweiser beer drinkers? What do you think, are buyers and drinkers the same people? Why is it important to know this information?

2. Are Budweiser beer buyers in the Chicago market area more likely to read the Chicago Tribune or the Chicago Sun-Times?

3. Which of these two newspapers will be the most efficient way to reach Budweiser beer buyers?

Did you answer this question using CPP or CPM? Why?

4. Which of these two newspapers would be best overall for Budweiser beer advertising in Chicago?

5 Modern Media Planning

MEDIA PLANNING IS HOW the business end of the advertising business gets organized. Media planning is responsible for the allocation of billions of client ad dollars.

And make no mistake, there are lots of client advertising dollars out there to allocate.

According to *Advertising Age*, total U.S. ad spending in 2003 was almost $249 billion. That's about $825 for each U.S. citizen.

The Media Planner's Job.

It is the job of the media planner to consider the many media alternatives and recommend placement of an advertiser's message.

Media planning professionals can make a big difference in the effective delivery of a client's message.

In fact, a good media planner can sometimes make even bad advertising work for a client.

Conversely, a media planner who makes bad or uninformed decisions can bury even the best advertising campaign. In media, planning is a process of making informed decisions.

Chapter Organization.

This chapter is organized according to the media planning process, which consists of four major steps:

- **Setting Media Objectives,**
- **Deciding Media Strategies,**
- **Choosing the Media Mix, and**
- **Charting the Tactical Plan.**

The primary purpose of the media planning process is to identify the one, best combination of many media alternatives that will most effectively and efficiently deliver the client's communication to the right target audience.

This process demands critical decisions at each major step.

Let's consider each step one-by-one.

Setting Media Objectives.

Every media plan must first express an objective that will establish goals for coverage and delivery of exposures to an appropriate target audience.

These must be specific and measurable, quantitative goals.

Note the use of the word "must" not "should."

This is very important.

While much in media may be negotiable, this is not.

In order to gauge effectiveness and efficiency, the media planning process requires a specific and measurable, quantitative objective. Other, qualitative objectives can be incorporated, but a proper media plan starts with a quantitative goal.

The details of this quantitative objective statement suggest the focus of a media planner's decision-making.

First, the focus is on identification of "an appropriate target audience." Then, the focus shifts to coverage and delivery of exposures to that target audience.

The Media Target.

The media planning process is most often initiated as a sub-process of the advertising or marketing plan, with the target audience for a client's communication already established.

If this is the case, then the media planner's role will be to restate the marketing target audience in terms that match up to the typical measures reported by media research services.

Planning Targets and Measurement Targets.

Media planners restate the marketing target audience in two different ways, one for planning purposes and one for measurement purposes.

The **"Planning Target"** requires a media target definition that allows planners to analyze and evaluate multiple media options relative to the target audience. This is the heart of the target market – the bullseye.

The **"Measurement Target"** requires a simple, demographic target definition that allows planners to measure and compare the relative effectiveness and performance of alternative media plans. The Velveeta example below shows how a media planner might restate a brand positioning target audience for each purpose.

In some cases, media planners may be called upon earlier in the marketing process to help identify the best target audience for all marketing efforts. For example, this might happen when the client assignment is to launch a new product.

Media planners can be very creative in finding ways to use the syndicated research services.

Bullseye Targeting.
The planning target is a subsegment of a broader measurement target.

The Media Target for Planning and Measurement

The brand communication strategy for Kraft's Velveeta brand cheese product may state the target audience is "women who cook family meals with cheese." However, the media research and measurement services do not report media measures for "women who cook family meals with cheese."

The media planner for the Velveeta business uses syndicated secondary research services like Simmons or MRI to create a customized target definition by combining the profiles of women who buy cheeses commonly used for cooking; cheeses like shredded cheddar or mozzarella, and cheese products like Velveeta or Cheez Whiz.

The media planner then designates this newly created profile as the "Planning Target."

Next, the media planner studies the demographic characteristics of the customized target (women who buy cooking cheeses) to identify the principle demographic, probably something like women aged 35-64.

Finally the planner designates this principle characteristic as the "Measurement Target."

A media planner can do this by using other products currently in a category, or looking at research on competitive products that will be replaced by the new product.

Media planners use syndicated research resources to perform the target matching part of the planning process. Simmons and MRI are prominent examples of such research. These are competitive research services, each providing statistical detail on the demographic, socio-economic, lifestyle, and psychographic characteristics of consumers based on the products they buy and the media they use. Refer back to Chapter 4 to remind yourself about how media planners use Simmons and MRI to match-up media and marketing targets.

Media Coverage and Delivery.

Once the target audience has been defined, the media planner next considers the question of coverage and delivery of exposures to that target audience.

Media planners use several quantitative measures for this purpose. The most important measures are Reach and Frequency, Impressions and Rating Points.

You may recall that we defined these terms earlier in the book (Chapter 4). Even so, we will re-visit each term here to demonstrate context and applications in media planning.

Reach and Frequency.

Reach is the number of different people exposed, at least one time, to a message within a specified time period. Reach is usually expressed as a percentage of a total target audience such that Reach would never be greater than 100%.

Frequency is the number of times a person is exposed to a message, usually linked to the same time period as used for the Reach goal.

In media planning we use the words Reach and Frequency to mean coverage and exposures respectively.

Together, these two words represent a core concept of media planning – trade-offs.

Key Media Trade-offs: Reach or Frequency

Media planning is about making choices. We can't have it all because we'll never have an unlimited budget. So we make trade-offs to work within a fixed budget. One of the biggest trade-offs in media planning is the trade-off between Reach and Frequency.

If you want higher Reach, then you have to use the broad coverage media. Since the budget is a fixed number this means you'll have fewer exposures each for more people in the audience.

If you want higher Frequency, then you have to use more targeted media with a narrower audience focus. This way you'll buy more exposures each for fewer people in the audience.

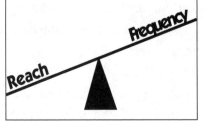

A Typical Frequency Distribution

Frequency	Net Reach	Cume
1	22%	61%
2	16%	39%
3	11%	23%
4	7%	12%
5+	5%	5%

Frequency Distribution.
This shows the relationship between reach and frequency.

Third Time is the Charm

Advertising works through repeated exposures to a marketer's message.

The general rule-of-thumb is that it takes three exposures to ensure effective communication. To understand this rule, consider the fleeting nature of a 30-second television advertisement. Most would agree that it would be lucky if the target audience actually noticed even part of an advertisement on the very first exposure to it.

Maybe the consumer saw something that first time that piqued her interest and so she paid attention the next time (the second time) she saw the advertisement.

This would be a lucky coincidence. Even so, the consumer, having noticed and paid attention to the ad, still needs to understand and agree with the message before being convinced.

Such understanding and agreement might be reached on a third exposure to the message if the message is compelling and clear.

Optimization or Balance.

Media planners can put together media choices to optimize Reach or optimize Frequency, or they can work within a budget constraint to balance Reach and Frequency. The media planner must decide which is best for the client's needs.

Media planners make this decision based on the advertising plan, matching the Reach/Frequency goal of the media plan to the corresponding advertising objective overall.

If the advertising objective is to increase top-of-mind awareness in order to remind consumers that Brand X is out there, then the corresponding media objective might be to achieve the broadest possible coverage (Reach) of the designated target audience.

However, if the advertising objective is to convince consumers that Brand X is better than Brand Y, then the corresponding media objective might be more exposure (Frequency) oriented.

As a rule it takes more exposure to convince a prospect than to simply remind a prospect.

How Much Exposure Is Enough?

Next, the media planner considers how much exposure is enough. We joked about this in chapter 4, but this is a subject of continuing debate in media planning circles.

Some say once is enough; some say three, four, or more.

The generally accepted rule-of-thumb is that it takes three exposures to be effective. The discussion inset above shows how it might take three exposures to make sure the advertising works.

Impressions.

Impressions are another important and often used quantitative measure of a media plan. Impressions are a summary figure representing the total exposures of an advertising message in a given period of time.

The phrase "Total exposures" is the key to this measure. With Impressions we count each person reached with our

HOT PROPERTY:
The Fairly OddParents

Rating Point:
As a top-rated cable show, Fairly Odd-parents *draws a household rating of 3.2.*

Choosing between Media Plan Options

	Media Plan A	Media Plan B
Total TRPs	1,000	1,000
Reach	80%	50%
Frequency	12.5	20

Consider a case of two media plans, A and B. Each plan delivers a total of 1,000 Target Rating Points in one calendar quarter. The media planner must look at the component statistics of the two plans to determine which is best. Plan A delivers 1,000 TRPs with a Reach of 80% and average Frequency of 12.5 (80 times 12.5 equals 1,000). Plan B, on the other hand, delivers 1,000 TRPs with a Reach of 50% and an average Frequency of 20 times (50 times 20 equals 1,000). If the goal was to optimize Reach, then Plan A would be the better choice.

message, for every time that person is reached. As such, some people are counted multiple times.

In most media plans this is a big number that can be stated either in "gross" terms, meaning a broad measure statistic like TV households, or in "target" terms, meaning a narrow measure statistic like Women 35-64.

Rating Points.

Rating Points are probably the most widely familiar form of media measurement. Most people in the U.S. have heard of the Nielsen ratings for TV shows.

The Rating of a TV show tells us the percent of a total audience tuned in to that show. We use ratings to compare TV programs across a common audience base and rank programs according to the relative size of the audience tuned in.

Rating Points are another measure that can be expressed in either "gross" or "target" terms, such as Gross Rating Points (GRPs) meaning household level ratings or Target Rating Points (TRPs) which means Rating Points among a specific target audience segment.

Rating Points are calculated as a function of percent Reach times average Frequency and knowing this is very important. The example to the left shows how a media planner would use this knowledge to choose the better of two similar media plans.

Any one of these measures, Reach and Frequency, Impressions, or Rating Points can be used as an effective, quantitative measure of media plan performance. The media planner uses one or all three to compare alternative media plans.

The best media plan objective defines a specific target audience, a specific percentage of Reach and a certain level of Frequency to be accomplished within a specific time frame. Depending on the circumstances, it might be appropriate to use an additional statistic like Impressions or Rating Points together with Reach and Frequency. The inset at the top of the following page shows several examples that would be appropriate media plan objectives.

Examples of Media Plan Objectives

Each of the following objectives provides a quantitative performance standard. The media planner considers alternative media plans against such a standard to choose the best plan for the client's assignment.
- Reach 80% of women 35-64 an average of 4 times every 4 weeks.
- Reach 50% of men 25-49 an average of 3 times each week before a home football game.
- Reach 70% of the primary target audience 5 times each quarter of the year.

Deciding Media Strategies.

Before we move into this discussion of deciding media strategies, we should talk briefly about strategic approach.

Basically, your strategy defines your priorities.

Planners will consider and recommend an approach early in the process because budget is always a media planning issue. Many planning decisions are based on working within a budget constraint.

A media planner has to make trade-offs, like Reach versus Frequency discussed earlier, throughout the plan.

The strategic approach defines priorities that guide the media planner's decisions in making such trade-offs.

Offensive or Defensive.

The recommended strategic approach to the media plan can be either defensive or offensive. We talked in Chapter Four about specific applications of this decision. This is the point in the planning process where the decision is made.

The Defensive Approach.

This leads the media planner to identify strategies and allocate the budget in such a way as to defend and support the existing strengths of the client's business.

The media planner uses research to prioritize the geographic and seasonal emphasis of the plan based on where and when the client's sales are greatest.

The Offensive Approach.

In the offensive case, the planner sets budget priorities in an aggressive, competitive manner. Message delivery is directed offensively and opportunistically towards the areas of greatest business potential, rather than existing sales.

The media planner uses research on the client's product and other factors to prioritize and focus on opportunities for growth of the client's business.

With focus and priorities established, the planner moves on to setting the budget.

Setting a Media Budget.

At this stage of the media planning process, the planner sets a budget that will guide the selection of media for the recommended plan.

Sometimes the client will clearly define a budget at the outset of the planning process.

However, this is not always the case.

There will come a time in your media career – more likely sooner than later – where you will be asked to develop and recommend a budget. So let's take some time here to talk about how to set a media budget. There are many ways to do this; we'll briefly cover the four most commonly used approaches.

- **The Objective Task Method**
- **Affordability Method**
- **Percentage of Sales Method**
- **Competitive Spending Method**

Each has its own logic. And you should become familiar will all four. Let's examine them one by one.

Objective-Task Method.

The objective-task method of budgeting is sometimes called "zero-based" or "ideal" budgeting.

This method builds your budget from the bottom-up.

It starts with the objectives of the plan and then matches the tactics that will be needed to accomplish the objectives. The total budget is determined by adding up the total cost of all of the tactics needed.

For this method, the planner relies on experience and supporting research to know how much media will be needed to accomplish the objectives of the plan.

This is the primary problem with this method.

It is extremely difficult in media to "know" and to subsequently prove that the recommended tactics are in fact what will be needed to accomplish the objectives.

How much message exposure will it really take to make the sale? That's the multimillion dollar question. Nonetheless, the objective-task method has long been a preferred budgeting technique. As research techniques have continued to improve and some traditional approaches deliver less than satisfactory results, this method is still gaining in popularity. Better research and more media options means better information on which to base planning and budgeting decisions.

Affordability Method.

This method of budgeting is top-down and simplistic.

Looking at the profit margins of the advertised product, the client and agency team simply decide how much margin they can afford to allocate to advertising media.

As simple as it is, this method is tied back to one important thing – the profitability of the product.

In this sense, we know that a company in business might actually hope to stay in business.

The dot.com advertisers of the late 90's might well have benefited from this approach.

The Pay-Out Point.

An important requirement for this budgeting approach is calculation of a pay-out point. A pay-out point is defined as the volume of product sales needed to pay for the advertising investment committed.

This is a necessary step given that most companies advertise their products in anticipation of generating future sales.

A pay-out point is a fairly simple calculation in which we take the total cost of the media investment divided by the

Step-by-Step Math

Calculating a Pay-out Point

1) Client has decided to spend $5 million on advertising this year.

2) Client earns $1 of profit for each unit sold and they currently sell 15 million units.

3) How many units do they need to sell incrementally to pay out $5 million in advertising?

$5,000,000 \div \$1 = 5$ million units

4) Is this a reasonable increase in sales?

$5,000,000 \div 15,000,000 = .33$ or 33%

A 33% increase in Sales

dollar profit contribution expected per-unit of incremental sales. The resulting figure tells us the number of incremental product units we need to sell in order to completely cover the cost of the advertising media investment.

Let's consider an example of the Affordability method.

Company A produces Brand X Widgets and they want to advertise to increase sales. Company A sells Brand X widgets at a wholesale price of $10 per unit. The Brand X brand manager has told the agency that they currently earn a 10% profit margin on $150 million in sales volume. The brand manager has asked the media planner to recommend a budget.

From the detail provided, the media planner knows that the client currently has a profit of $15 million (10% of the current $150 million in sales volume) from which a media budget might be allocated. The planner also knows that the company sells a total of 15 million units earning $1 of profit for each unit sold. Try this for yourself, how did we arrive at the total unit sales and per-unit profit figure?

With this basic information, the planner can meet with the brand manager to make an informed decision on a media budget. If they decide to spend $5 million on advertising, they know that they will need to generate sales of 5 million incremental units in order to fully recoup the profit allocated to advertising.

That would be a 33% increase in sales.

Together they can decide if this is a reasonable expectation for the business.

Percentage of Sales Method.

The percentage of sales method involves multiplying the total sales volume by a fixed percentage to arrive at a budget.

The sales volume figure used might be last year's sales or an estimate of projected sales. The fixed percentage used might be based on company experience or industry averages.

Either way, this method produces an informed budget recommendation based more on solid data rather than on subjective judgment.

A Good Source.

Advertising trade magazine Advertising Age *publishes an annual report on leading advertisers and spending by industry.*

Step-by-Step Math

Percentage of Sales Method

1) Brand X Widgets Total Sales:
   $150,000,000

2) Industry Ad to Sales Ratio:
   3%

3) Recommended Budget:
   $150,000,000
   x   .03
   $4,500,000

A to S Ratios.

One of the more interesting statistics in marketing is the A-to-S Ratio.

This stands for Advertising to Sales. It measures the relative proportion of the advertising budget as part of the overall sales volume.

It can be high, as in cosmetics, or low, as in cold-rolled steel.

Here are some examples:

Product Category	Ad $ as % of sales	Ad $ as % of margin
Ag chemicals	3.0	7.4
Amusement parks	10.7	20.9
Apparel	4.7	11.4
Beverages	9.2	14.3
Cosmetics	7.4	16.1
Detergent	11.3	21.8
Distilled liquor	14.9	43.7
Eating places	3.2	14.5
Grocery stores	1.0	4.2
Loan Brokers	38.4	43.2
Retail stores	4.9	11.2
Steel works	.3	1.2
Sugar & confections	11.7	23.3
Watches	7.4	11.3
Wine, brandy	3.9	12.4

2003 data from adage.com

To illustrate, let's look again at the Company A, Brand X Widgets example. We know that Company A sold $150 million of Brand X Widgets last year. From our research of the widget industry, let's say that we know that widget companies, on average, spend 3% of sales dollars on advertising. (There are many sources for this kind of information at an industry level; a good place to start is looking for special industry reports in trade magazines at your library. Other good sources for larger companies and industries are www.hoovers.com and the trade magazine *Advertising Age*.)

Putting these two figures together, we might reasonably recommend a budget of $4.5 million ($150 million times 0.03 equals $4.5 million).

Using this figure, you might still want to calculate a payout point for the recommended budget amount to test for reasonableness.

This kind of support and rationale can be very helpful in securing approval of the plan and recommended budget.

Competitive Spending Method.

Finally, there is the competitive spending method.

This method of budgeting looks at the spending history of competitive companies for the purpose of determining your own budget recommendation.

In order to use this method effectively, we need a good and consistent source for tracking competitive media spending and we need general agreement regarding identification of appropriate competitors.

Tracking competitive spending is the easy part. There are two good sources available for this information; CMR Taylor Nelson Sofres (CMR) and Nielsen's Monitor-Plus service. Both companies measure advertising activity by company in 11 major media categories.

Of course there are issues that you should be aware of.

First, neither service actually tracks 100% of media activity. That level of tracking would be cost prohibitive.

Instead, each company samples the 11 major media on several levels and then projects an estimate of media activity based on the sample results.

So, there is always a margin of error in the projection.

There is nothing you can do about this. You just need to know that the reports are not 100% accurate, but they are generally consistent.

The second big issue with both sources is that each uses standard media pricing to project an estimate of the dollars spent on media advertising activity. Standard prices are generally the published rate-card rates for each media.

The problem is that most, if not all, advertising is purchased at some discounted rate, below the published rate-card price.

Again, there is nothing you can do about this.

You have no official way of knowing whether a competitor has made a media buy at a reduced rate or not. You just need to know about this issue and keep it in mind as you consider how you might set your budget relative to how much your competitor is reported as spending.

Identifying the right competitor or competitive industry to use as a model for your budget estimate can sometimes be a difficult aspect of this method. Your client's product may be one of several close competitors in a particular industry. This would make it easier, but, again, that isn't always the case.

You may find yourself someday working on a product without any easily identified competitors. When this happens, you'll need to be creative about defining and then tracking the right competitor.

That is, if you hope to use this method.

The actual competitive spending method is a fairly simple way to set a budget. There are a couple of ways to do it.

First, you can determine how much money competitors are spending and decide your budget relative to that figure.

Step-by-Step Math

Share-of-Voice Budgeting

1) Here are the facts you know:

	%Share of Market	Ad Spending Last Year
Brand A	40%	_____
Brand B	30%	$5 mil
Brand C	20%	$3 mil
Other Brands	10%	$2 mil
Total	100%	_____

2) How much are competitors spending in total?
$5 mil + $3 mil + $2 mil = $10 mil

3) How much market share do these competitors have?
30% + 20% + 10% = 60%

4) If the competitors' share of spending matched their share of market, how much should total category spending equal?

$$\frac{60\%}{100\%} \text{ as } \frac{\$10 \text{ mil}}{X}$$

X = $10 mil ÷ .60
X = $16.7 million

5) How much should Brand A spend?
$16.7 mil – $10 mil = $6.7 mil for 40% Share of Voice

Second, you might go so far as to compare the competitor's spending to its total sales in order to get a competitive spending rate or A to S ratio. If you do this, remember that the competitive reports are not 100% accurate (so don't ever bet your job on this).

You would then apply the competitor's rate to your own client's sales. In this way, you can take into consideration how much larger or smaller your client's business is relative to the competitor.

Share of Voice.

Another way to do this is known as "share of voice."

This version of the competitive spending method is a little more complex and would be appropriate to use in cases where your client is up against several close competitors.

Then, you might want to set your budget relative to your client's market share.

For example, if your client holds a 40% share of the market, then you may recommend spending at 40% "share of voice" in order to maintain position in the category.

An Example.

Here's an example of how you might work through this.

Let's say your category is made up of three major brands, your Brand A and two other brands B and C.

There are several other brands out there, but all together they only make up about 10% of the market, while your client has a 40% share. Clearly your client, Brand A, is the category leader and you want to see them stay in that position. So you recommend that they invest a media budget that will equal 40% of the combined category advertising "voice."

To put a number to this recommendation, you perform an analysis of competitive spending and you find that Brand B is spending $5 million, Brand C is spending $3 million and all other brands in the category are spending a total of $2 million. That adds up to a total of $10 million in spending

"Grossing Up"

In this example, we tell you to Divide $10 million by 0.6. Wy did we Divide? The answer is clear if you think about it like a pie chart.

We know the $10 million is a piece of the pie, not the whole.

Further, we know the $10 million is 60% of the pie.

What we need to know is this: If $10 million is 60% of the pie, then how big is the whole pie? We need to Divide the $10 million by 60% to make it bigger.

In media speak, we call this "Grossing Up."

without counting your budget. How much spending should you add to that total such that your share of the total spending will be 40%?

Here's that simple math thing again. If your client will represent 40% then that $10 million must be 60%. So, you take $10 million divided by 0.6 to get a new widget category total of $16.7 million. If you subtract the $10 million from the new total $16.7 million, you'll see that you should recommend that your client invest a total of $6.7 million in media spending.

Now, check the math. If you take $6.7 divided by $16.7 you should get the answer 0.40 meaning 40%. This means that, if all things hold and your client spends $6.7 million, then the client's share of advertising voice will be 40%, consistent with its share of the category market.

That's the competitive spending, "share-of-voice" method.

Any Method Works.

Each method explained here is an acceptable method for setting a media budget. Each has strengths and weaknesses, and each will lead you through the process to a concrete, data-based statement of rationale you'll need to support your budget recommendation.

Once the budget is decided, the planner can turn to the important business of deciding the specific strategies that will accomplish the objectives of the plan.

Strategies to Accomplish Objectives.

Strategies represent the means by which we expect to accomplish the objectives of the media plan.

We define strategies in specific areas of planning relating to media scheduling, specific geography, and mix of media by class/type and by specific vehicle within each class.

Scheduling Strategies.

Scheduling refers to how advertising is scheduled over the time period of the media plan.

Media planners have three main choices in this decision:
- **Continuous scheduling**
- **Flighting**
- **Pulsing**

Of course there are combinations, but these are the three most common scheduling patterns.

Continuous Scheduling.

Continuous scheduling is a pattern that delivers an almost constant level of media support throughout the whole of the media plan period. For example, your favorite local grocery store probably runs a constant level of media support every week. This makes sense because we know that consumers shop for groceries every week. Sometimes even several times each week.

Flighting and Pulsing.

Flighting and Pulsing are patterns of media support delivered in peaks and valleys throughout the time period of the plan. In both cases, the media planner bundles media for heavier delivery in certain periods relative to others.

The key distinction between these two patterns is that a flighted schedule will leave certain periods blank with no media support at all.

Example: Matching Schedules to Peaks and Valleys.

Media planners will decide to use a flighted or pulsed schedule in cases where a client's business runs in peaks and valleys. For example, if the client is an expensive neighborhood steakhouse, it has likely been observed that business is much better after the 15th of each month.

This would be consistent with research indicating the importance of the 15th of each month as a common payday in the U.S. The media planner in this case would schedule advertising messages heavier around the 15th each month to build awareness when potential customers are more likely to have money to go out for dinner.

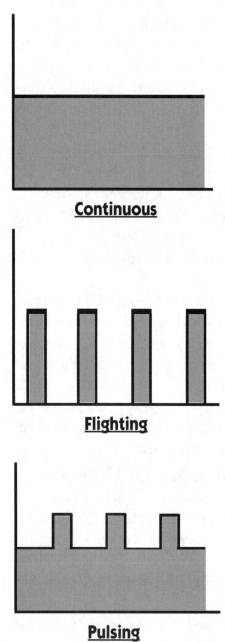

Continuous

Flighting

Pulsing

Regional Coverage of the U.S.

Many food products manufacturers started as Midwestern companies located close to raw material supplies like grain. These businesses grew and distribution expanded effectively to the East – but less so to the West.

Western expansion was an issue because of the extra time and cost required to move goods through the Rocky Mountains.

As a result, new companies started on the West Coast to serve Western customers. Many Midwestern-based food products companies still suffer weaker sales in the western U.S. Media planners for these national companies may choose to sell-off the western region of national media buys.

Regional Business Development.

In the U.S., the Rocky Mountains were a significant influence on the regional development for many food products manufacturers.

Specific Geography.

In identifying strategies media planners make decisions about the specific geography the media must cover.

If the budget was large enough, the media plan might cover all geography where the client's product is sold.

However, it isn't always possible or even correct to cover all geography equally. Often, a client's business or business potential is better in a particular geography.

The media planner will reflect such differences in the media plan. The general example of major national food products manufacturers is presented in the above inset.

The Media Mix.

The last area of media strategies is to decide media mix by general class/type and specific media vehicles.

The term "media class" defines different general types of media; network television, cable television, magazines, radio, and newspapers, are each a class of media.

The term "media vehicle" refers to specific media choices like television programs, cable TV networks and shows, radio station formats, and magazine titles.

This is a broad area of media decision-making that encompasses thousands of possible combinations. Not only that, but the choices are expanding every day as new media alternatives emerge.

The media planner first narrows the options by media class and then identifies specific choices of media vehicles. Media planners narrow the possibilities by considering each class of media relative to a list of criteria. Some of the more important considerations are: the audience/media relationship; the availability of resources (time and money); and the geographic emphasis of the product relative to the media.

Each class of media works in a different way, engaging different senses of its audience and because of this, consumers may feel more or less involved with the media.

The Audience/Media Relationship.

The media planner is expected to know the facts of the audience/media relationship.

A radio listener hears an advertisement but doesn't see it.

A magazine reader sees an ad but doesn't hear it.

A television viewer might actually hear and see an advertisement but can't interact with it; not yet.

This doesn't mean that any one media is better than another but one media might not be right for a particular client or marketing objective.

Consider the example again of cheese, any cheese.

If it is important to show rich, creamy cheese, then radio might not be the best media to use.

Instead, it might be better to use a beautiful photograph with 4-color reproduction to show that rich, gooey, melted cheese in a magazine advertisement.

Another relationship factor to consider is the active/passive nature of each media and the corresponding longevity of an advertisement.

Print media like magazines and newspapers allow readers a more active involvement with the content. The magazine reader can refer back to an interesting advertisement at his leisure. As such, a print advertisement has some longevity as long as the consumer keeps the magazine around.

Broadcast media are more likely to be passive and fleeting in nature; consumers are simply exposed to the advertising message. If the client's message is complex, then the media planner might recommend print media where the reader can take time and refer back to the message.

Mouth Watering.
Even in black and white, you can still see the beautiful melted cheese in this magazine photograph.

Availability of Resources.

The availability of resources can also be a big factor in media decision-making. For example, media planners know that production of advertisements require more or less time and money depending on the different media.

If the client has a message that needs to be delivered to consumers tomorrow, then the media plan won't use long lead time media like television, magazines or outdoor.

Instead, the planner might recommend radio knowing that a live announcer could read from a script thus getting the message out quickly.

Planners also know that the absolute cost of buying advertising time or space can vary dramatically from one media to another. At one extreme, the cost of a 30-second television ad to run during the Super Bowl is more than $2 million.

In contrast, a national advertisement in the Super Bowl edition of *Sports Illustrated* magazine would cost about one tenth of that.

Geographic Emphasis.

In considering geographic emphasis, the planner evaluates each media class for its effective coverage of the product's distribution geography.

If a product is only available for sale in the Midwest, then the media planner eliminates media with coverage outside the region.

On a more complex level, planners will consider that even the national media delivers its audience differently across the country.

For example, the audience for late night television is much better in the central and southern U.S. than on either coast.

Knowing this, a planner might recommend the use of late night TV for a national client needing a Midwestern emphasis.

Choosing the Media Mix.

After narrowing the possible media alternatives by class, planners must evaluate and identify specific media vehicles.

Adult TV Viewing Index	
	Late Night (EST) **11:30PM-1:00AM**
Northeast	94
East Central	100
West Central	114
South	116
Pacific	78

Early Late Night.
Late night television is stronger in the central and southern U.S. where shows air at 10:30PM instead of 11:30PM.

Magazine Coverage of a Target Audience

If your client is marketing a product for young, college-age women 18-24 years old, which magazine would you choose, *Cosmopolitan* or *Glamour*? Consider the following audience facts (data summarized from Simmons NCS Part 1, Spring 1999):

• The total audience for *Cosmopolitan* at 9 million is about 30% larger than the *Glamour* audience of 6.5 million.

• *Cosmopolitan*'s coverage of women 18-24 is about 2.4 million, while *Glamour*'s coverage is about 1.9 million.

• The wasted coverage of people who are NOT the target audience is just over 6.5 million for *Cosmopolitan* and only 4.5 million for *Glamour*.

• While you get a bigger audience with *Cosmopolitan*, you are also paying for more wasted coverage, not just for the coverage you want, women 18-24.

We call this Choosing the Media Mix.

Even after eliminating whole classes of media, there are still many alternative media vehicles among which to discriminate. The idea here is to choose the specific media vehicles that will most effectively and efficiently accomplish the media plan objectives.

In gauging effectiveness, we analyze data for two important criteria – audience use of the media and audience coverage of the media.

In considering these factors, the planner turns once again to syndicated research services such as Simmons and MRI.

As we showed you in Chapter 4, these services report vast tables of data detailing the demographic, lifestyle, and psychosocial characteristics of the people who use various media.

For example, for television alone these services report data on people who watch different program types, cable networks, times of day, and even specific TV shows.

Media planners use Simmons and MRI reports, cross-tabulating product use and media use, to help them choose the right kind of magazine or the right time of day for an advertiser's message.

These services help media planners to know the media use habits of the advertiser's audience.

To learn about a target audience's use of media, the media planner creates and studies a cross-tab report on the media class(es) of interest. This helps the media planner to identify the specific media vehicles that are most likely used by the target audience.

We call this composition – the percent of a media vehicle's audience that is within an advertiser's target.

Media planners will try to select media vehicles with a higher percentage composition compared to the base of the general population.

Higher composition means that the advertiser's target is more likely to be found engaged with that media vehicle.

Looking at this same report in a slightly different way can also help planners to see that different media vehicles are more or less focused in their coverage of different audience segments. In addition to composition (above), media planners will also look at coverage as a proxy for the reach of a media vehicle. The magazine example presents a discussion of audience coverage and composition among comparable media choices.

Efficiency – Getting Bang for the Client's Buck.

Efficiency is another important part of media planning overall and choosing the media mix in particular.

Efficiency is where the media planner factors in the costs we have alluded to so far. Efficiency is most often expressed as a rate of some sort – a cost per something. In this sense, efficiency is a measure of bang-for-the-buck.

The most commonly used measure of media efficiency is cost per thousand or CPM. As we showed you in chapter 4, CPM is calculated by dividing the target audience coverage of a media vehicle into the total cost of that vehicle.

Consider again the *Cosmopolitan* and *Glamour* example. From SRDS we know that the cost of a one page 4-color advertisement in *Cosmopolitan* is $156,000 and the cost of the same advertisement in *Glamour* is $122,000.

From our earlier example we see that the number of women 18-24 years old covered by *Cosmopolitan* is 2,400,000 and *Glamour* is 1,900,000.

The sidebar to the left shows the calculation of the CPM for each magazine's coverage of the target audience.

By studying each media vehicle and comparing vehicles across measures like composition, coverage and CPM efficiency, a media planner is able to confidently choose the best media vehicles for any client situation.

Once the objectives are set, the strategies are defined and the media mix is selected, the rest of media planning is simply layout and presentation.

Step-by-Step Math

Calculating a CPM

Cosmopolitan: $156,000 divided by 2,400 thousands equals **$65.00**.

Glamour: $122,000 divided by 1,900 thousands equals **$64.21**.

Charting the Tactical Plan.

This is where media planners draw pretty pictures.

OK, not really, but this step does result in a picture of sorts.

This is where we lay out all the media recommendations on a one-page flowchart.

The Flowchart.

The flowchart is a graphic illustration of all plan recommendations. The flowchart shows the media that is recommended for use and the recommended scheduling of the media over time.

Further, the flowchart shows the budget allocated by medium and by month and the estimated weight of message delivery also by medium and month.

Sometimes the flowchart is drawn to include even more detail such as the specific media vehicles to be used, number of messages or insertions to be delivered by medium, or sizes for the planned advertisements.

Study the flowchart example below.

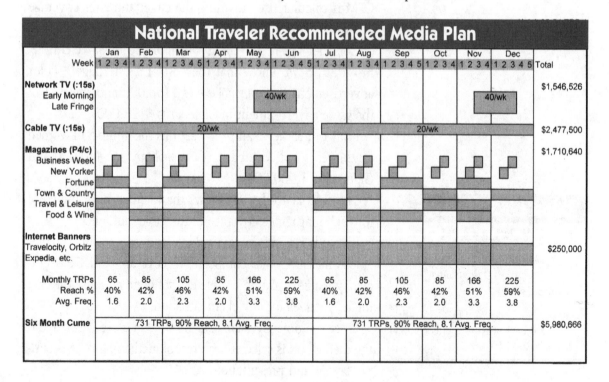

Notice that the flowchart shows the insertions scheduled for each magazine, the radio scheduling, the Internet schedules by type, and all other media including promotion activity.

The flowchart also shows the budget allocation for each media. On just one page, this flowchart shows the complete detail of the recommended marketing campaign for the client.

Flowcharts like this can be created a couple of different ways depending on your available resources.

Most major advertising agencies have media planning software for this purpose.

As a student, you could create such a chart using the MPlanner function available at www.mediapost.com. Or you can visit www.adbuzz.com, where you'll find a simple spreadsheet template like the one we used on the previous page.

You could also do the same thing with an Excel spreadsheet or any other kind of project planning software.

You might want to play around with a couple of different tools to find one that works for you.

So what does a Media Plan look like? Well, this is a big question, and there are a lot of different, correct answers. To see for yourself, look in the back of this book for Appendix 1, where we've provided a short selection of example media plans.

We find that the best media plans, no matter what they look like, are the ones where every choice is clearly identified and supported with detailed data and rationale.

Summary.

This chapter presented a framework for media planning. The media planning process consists of four major steps:
• **Setting media objectives**
• **Deciding media strategies**
• **Choosing the media mix**
• **Charting the tactical plan**
At each major step of the process the media planner is expected to make decisions and recommendations.

In setting media objectives, media planners use resources to establish goals for the media plan that will help the advertiser successfully achieve its marketing goals.

First media planners match media targets to the advertiser's designated marketing target. The media planner does this two different ways – the planning target and the measurement target.

Then, the media planner focuses on coverage and delivery of message exposures by considering the question of reach versus frequency and using measurement statistics like impressions and rating points.

In deciding media strategies, the media planner considers media scheduling and whether the scheduling pattern should be continuous or flighted/pulsed. The planner considers the geographic emphasis of the advertiser's product/service.

Finally, the media planner looks at the whole wide world of available media choices and decides which media would best serve the advertiser.

The planner does this best by narrowing media options according to the criteria of:

- **The audience/media relationship**
- **The overall availability of resources**
- **The geographic emphasis of each media class**

After narrowing the choices of media by class, the media planner moves on to choose the media mix. This is done by considering the target audience and its use of the media, considering the media for its coverage of the target audience and finally, considering the overall cost efficiency of each medium.

From this chapter we see that media planners have to know a lot – but they don't have to know it all.

Minimally, a planner needs to know where to find the facts. Planners use the facts that they learn from media research services to make big decisions and to explain their reasons for each decision.

To do this, media planners have to be comfortable reading, interpreting, presenting, and explaining numbers, percentages and indexes and what each means for the client. (That's why we spent time on this in Chapter 4.)

For a good media planner this work is enjoyable – part puzzle, part mystery, and part psychology.

It's a whole new land of knowledge and understanding what kind of audience reads a certain kind of magazine or watches a given TV show.

Once you get started, you'll want to learn everything you can about the existing media and emerging, new media developments.

The best media planners are important marketing partners. They are consulted as experts for their knowledge of audiences and specific media usage behavior.

Career Capsule:

Ryan Kirvida, Media Planner, Fallon.

Ryan majored in Journalism/Advertising at the University of St. Thomas in St. Paul, Minnesota. Ryan knew that he wanted to work in advertising but it wasn't until his senior year in college, when taking the media planning course, that he decided on a career in media.

A Great Start in Media Research.

Ryan got his start in the business as a research analyst with Haworth Marketing & Media in Minneapolis. Some of his college friends were interning at Haworth. They introduced him to the company, where he started as an intern. After looking around, checking out a couple of other agencies, he took a full time job at Haworth because it seemed to fit him best. He realized that the research side would be a great way to start. Ryan says, *"This job gave me the basic media knowledge I knew I would need for a career in media planning."*

In this first position, Ryan learned the media business from the ground up. He spent his time tracking industry and consumer trends in support of the media planning team. He had to work his way through quantitative and qualitative research. His job was to analyze and translate research data into useful

Ryan Kirvida is a media planner. He had a good start at it, took a short break to try something else, and now he's right back at it. Ryan's story shows how taking risks sometimes can help you to find what's best for your career.

information supporting plan recommendations for the agency's clients.

After about a year as a research analyst, Ryan had an opportunity to move into media planning at a hot, full-service agency in Minneapolis. He jumped at the chance. He started as an assistant media planner and was quickly promoted to media planner at Fallon. He was most impressed with Fallon's strong creative reputation and progressive media department.

An Adventurous Career Path.

Today Ryan works as a media planner at Fallon responsible for major clients including Citibank, Holiday Inn and the Bahamas. But, he hasn't been at Fallon all this time. Ryan took an adventurous and circuitous route to where he is today. And, he's probably a stronger planner and decision-maker because of the choices he made along the way.

After his first move to Fallon from Haworth, Ryan had an exciting opportunity to join a start-up agency group and so he did. Working with the start-up partners, Ryan helped to set up the media department and ran planning and buying for the agency's clients.

After the start-up partners sold the agency and the new owners folded the shop, Ryan decided to join his family's business. There he spent about a year developing and executing plans to brand and promote his father's fire truck manufacturing business in new international markets.

After only two years of being away from Fallon, Ryan got a call one day. They invited him back. And that brings us full circle. Ryan is thrilled to be back at Fallon.

On the Future of Media.

Like so many in the business today, Ryan sees the media business evolving and changing at a blazing pace. He feels that traditional media is not always the answer and that new forms are the norm. *"We have to be fully integrated with creative and work hand-in-hand with the creative team to determine the best media for a client situation. Sometimes we have to invent new media forms."*

Ryan says, *"Media is about ideas; it's about engaging a target audience; it's about surrounding the target and making your brand play an important role in their lives."* It's still true that you have to know the numbers, but media is so much more than numbers today.

Career Advice.

Ryan feels that media planners today, more than ever before, need to be *"driven by the desire to reach people in new, exciting, meaningful, and engaging ways."* According to Ryan, media people need to be change agents; leading change and thinking creatively all the time. This is a fast-paced career for high energy people who want to make a mark.

Discussion Questions.

1. Media Planning Process.

Media planning follows a process. What are the advantages and disadvantages of following a process?

What are the major steps of the media planning process? Briefly describe each step.

2. Setting Media Objectives.

Why is it important that we set objectives?

Why must objectives be written specific and measurable?

What are the component parts of a properly written media objective?

What are some of the specific measures we can use in a media objective?

3. Setting Media Budgets.

What are the four common methods used to set budgets?

For each of the four budget methods, write two to three pros and two to three cons.

Which is the best of the four budget methods?

4. Media Strategies.

What are the three specific areas for which we must decide a media strategy?

What is the difference between Flighting and Pulsing a media schedule?

Which scheduling strategy is better, continuity or flighting/pulsing?

What are the three important considerations relative to media mix strategies?

Exercises.

1. Target Audience.

Using SMRB or MRI (whichever source is available to you), **define a "planning target" and a "measurement target" for each of the following products.** Be sure to note the expected size of each target group.

    a.) Cherry Coke

    b.) Southwest Airlines

    c.) Philadelphia Cream Cheese

2. Setting Objectives.

Using the same three products and the targets you defined for each in the above exercise, **write a specific and measurable media objective for each product.**

3. Deciding Media Strategies.

Choose one of the three products from the above exercises. **Write and defend specific media strategies for this product in the areas of:**

    a.) Media scheduling

    b.) Media geography

    c.) Media mix

Be firm in your recommendations and back-up your decisions with facts and data from the resources you used.

6 Buying & Selling Media

THIS CHAPTER TAKES US to another side of the media business – implementation. Now we will describe and discuss the business of turning a media plan into a marketing reality.

Three Primary Job Functions.

To see how this all gets implemented, we will focus on three primary job functions and how they work together.

These three functions are:
- **Media planning**
- **Media buying**
- **Media sales**

Each of these primary job functions has a key role to play. In addition, media research and sometimes even media management have important supporting roles to play.

Chapter Five ended with what we called a pretty picture – the media flowchart. This flowchart is what the media planner sells to the client as a media plan.

That is, of course, the flowchart and all of the supporting analyses and rationales for each decision represented on that flowchart.

Once the client has agreed with and approved the media plan, things really start jumping in the media world.

Because virtually everyone in media has an important role to play in the implementation of a media plan.

Chapter Organization.

This chapter is organized into three main sections – matching up with those three main job functions:

- Media Planning
- Media Buying
- Media Sales

At various times, each will play a starring role in the process of implementing the media plan.

The Role of Planning.

First, don't think for a moment that the media planner's job is done when the client approves the plan. It isn't.

Once the client has approved the recommended media plan, the planner now has to translate the plan into relevant parameters that will direct the implementation of the plan details.

Such parameters will spell out the specific details of the implementation strategy. And they'll adjust from the ideal world to the much messier world of putting together the media buy.

For example, planners will specify the details of the budget by week/month/quarter, by media class, and by media vehicle. Then, working with their buying partners, planners will define a market strategy to guide buying actions.

The Role of Buying.

After the parameters are defined, then the job of implementing the plan is turned over to the media buyer.

The media buyer's job is to buy specific media that will efficiently and effectively deliver the objectives and strategies of the approved media plan.

Absolutely critical skills in the buying job function are analysis and negotiation. Media buyers work with any and all available media research to help them decide the best media in which to invest the clients' money.

And, since they are the ones actually spending the money, media buyers are the frontline negotiators working for the best buy for every client dollar.

Aside from analysis and negotiation, media buyers must also understand the dynamics of the media market.

This is a lot like playing the stock market; media buyers look for opportunities to buy at better prices. Sometimes this means committing early to buy in bulk in order to secure lower prices. In television, we call this an "upfront" market, and we'll discuss this in detail later.

The Role of Media Sales.

The function of media sales is to represent the media to the media buyers. Media sales representatives call on media buyers to present the costs and benefits of the media they represent for any and every client situation.

Even after the sale is made, the media sales job continues as the sales representative role turns to one of service representative. In this capacity, media sales representatives are expected to be watching out for their buyers.

Depending on the media, they may be working to secure better positioning for an advertisement. Or, maybe they are watching out for competitive ad placements.

And with more and more media company cosolidation, they may be representing a growing variety of media vehicles.

In this section, we'll review the details of media service for each specific type of media.

Other Media Roles.

Throughout each section of this chapter we'll also cover the supporting roles of media management and media research.

By the time we're through, you'll have a thorough understanding of the overall media business model, how the various jobs work together, and how the whole process works to deliver advertising messages to consumers.

So let's take them one by one. As we go you'll get a feel for how they work together.

The Role of Planning.

Let's say that you're a media planner. You've been working for a couple of months preparing that media plan for recommendation to the client. Finally, the big day is here.

It's 9 a.m. and you're settling into the big conference room at client headquarters. It's time to present your recommendations, and after a short introduction from the agency account team leader, you move to the front of the room and start talking.

You've got everything here. You've really done your homework and the client is nodding his head along with everything you're saying about the objectives and strategies.

By the time you get to the flowchart, you can feel they're already agreeing with you and you know the plan is sold.

So it's no surprise when the client says, "All right then, let's make it happen."

Congratulations! You've just sold a media plan!

Enjoy the moment, but don't go running off yet for that vacation; you've still got a lot of work to do.

Now your job is to translate that media plan into a detailed action plan for implementation. The way the business typically works these days, you'll be handing off your plan to a media buying group who will implement the buy.

This may be a different department in your agency or it may be a completely different agency – one that specializes in media buying.

More and more these days, it's a different agency, as clients are increasingly realizing the efficiencies and buying power of consolidated buying through specialty agencies.

Whatever the case, it most likely will be someone else, not the planner, who is making the buy.

Now the focus has to be on providing directions so that a buyer can bring the plan to life.

TOP 25 MEDIA SPECIALIST COMPANIES

From the Agency Report (AA, April 22, 2002), this table ranks media specialist companies by U.S. media billings. Figures are for calendar 2001. Dollars are in millions.

Rank	Media specialist company	U.S. billings	% change
1	Initiative Media Worldwide	$10,087.0	-19.0
2	MindShare Worldwide	8,500.0	3.7
3	OMD Worldwide	7,640.0	0.9
4	Universal McCann	6,108.1	4.6
5	Starcom	5,360.0	-5.9
6	Zenith Media Services	5,300.0	31.8
7	MediaVest	4,922.4	15.1
8	PHD	4,423.0	34.1
9	Mediaedge:CIA	4,050.8	-13.0
10	Carat	3,730.0	42.4
11	MediaCom	3,617.0	30.5
12	Media Planning Group	3,226.0	-5.3
13	Optimedia International U.S.	2,057.0	37.4
14	Newspaper Services of America	1,600.0	0.0
15	Horizon Media	800.0	1.9
16	Empower MediaMarketing	600.0	-7.7
17	R.J. Palmer	553.0	5.3
18	J.L. Media	514.3	26.3
19	Media Kitchen	450.0	NA
20	Camelot Communications	421.7	1.7
21	ICON International	400.0	NA
22	Haworth Marketing & Media	375.0	7.1
23	Media First International	320.0	7.0
24	Pro Media	244.0	-15.0
25	Cash Plus	230.0	-4.2

Media Agencies.

These are the top 25 agencies specializing in media. Most do media planning and buying, but some just specialize in media buying.

Directions must be specific and detailed, but not dictatorial. As with everything in advertising, media buying is both art and science. You'll need to leave room in the directions to allow the buyer to exercise judgment in a dynamic media environment.

As you're coming to realize, the world of media is constantly changing. Media buyers have to stay aware and alert to changes in the media such as magazine circulation and price changes, television programming changes, and emerging new media vehicles. Media buyers also have to stay attuned to changes in media measurements. But, we'll come back to this later.

So, how do you write directions like this; directions that are specific and detailed but not dictatorial?

The best way we know is to follow a format.

We call it the "Buying Brief."

The Buying Brief.

Just as agency account managers or account planners may write a "creative brief" to initiate the creative development process, agency media planners write a "buying brief."

Most advertising agencies use a form of some kind that serves as this "buying brief." The media planning group is responsible for writing the brief which translates the approved plan into detailed specifications.

While every agency's form may be slightly different, they all cover the same basic areas of:

- **Designated Buying Target**
- **Summary of Plan Objectives**
- **Summary of Key Plan Strategies and Rationale**
- **Detailed Media Requirements**
- **Budget Breakdown and Media Cost Parameters**
- **Media Market and Merchandising Strategy**

Let's look at each area in detail.

The Buying Brief

While every agency's form may be slightly different, they all cover the same basic areas of:

- **Designated buying target**
- **Summary of plan objectives**
- **Summary of key plan strategies and rationale**
- **Detailed media requirements**
- **Budget breakdown and media cost parameters**
- **Media market and merchandising strategy.**

Designated Buying Target.

At the start of the media planning process, the client would likely have provided the agency team with a designated marketing target for the product. The media planning team would have translated that marketing target into a media planning target for purposes of analyzing and planning the media to best fit the marketing plan.

Well, at this level, the media planner redefines the target once more, translating the planning target into a buying target.

The description of the designated marketing target was probably some richly worded statement about who buys, or is most likely to buy, the client's product.

This statement would have talked about the target as a person; who she is, what she likes to do, what products she buys and how much of the client's (or other) product she buys.

The planning target was a restatement that redefined the marketing target in terms of demographic and lifestyle variables. As discussed in Chapter 5, demographic variables are those characteristics we can actually know about people – like gender and age.

Lifestyle variables are other general characteristics that make a difference in lifestyle – household income, level of education, marital status or family status.

The buying target is a further distillation of the planning target generally stated only in demographic terms; gender and age. In Chapter 5 we talked about a "measurement target" as a simplified demographic target audience statement.

If the media planner did, in fact, define a "measurement target" for planning purposes, then this will likely be the same target used for buying purposes. We take this step for planning and for buying simply because this is how media ratings are measured.

Ultimately, this is how media buys must be made.

Throughout this whole process, the media planner must take great care to ensure that each successive redefinition of the target audience effectively captures the largest possible subgroup of the original marketing target.

From designated marketing target to media planning target to buying target.

Summary of Plan Objectives.

Beyond the target audience statement, the media plan will have also defined specific and measurable goals for Reach, Frequency, and the total "weight" of the plan.

In this section of the buying brief, the planner works to insure that the specific and measurable goals of the plan become the specific and measurable goals of the buy.

Do you get the point here? These goals must be specific and measurable.

When it actually comes to making the buy, the balance of Reach and Frequency will make a big difference.

An Example.

Consider a simple example of television primetime.

Let's say the planner sold a media plan using the primetime day-part of network television. The buyer will decide what specific primetime programs to buy.

If the media plan goal was high Reach, then the buyer will choose a variety of primetime programs across several networks so as to place the client's commercial in front of as many different people as possible.

For example, the buyer might place one ad each on nine different shows: *Everybody Loves Raymond, Frasier, According to Jim, Ed, 7th Heaven, Smallville, Friends, Will & Grace,* and *The Simpsons.* These shows all run on different networks and different days of the week and each delivers a part of a general audience of families – so reach is extended.

If, on the other hand, the plan goal is to emphasize Frequency, then the buyer may choose to focus more placements on a smaller selection of programs delivering the same basic

Frequency.

These three Primetime shows have a high overlap of a particular adult audience that loyally follows each show.

audience so as to build up more exposures on that core group of people – so frequency builds with that part of the audience.

For example, the buyer might place three ads each on ABC's *NYPD Blue* and NBC's *Law & Order* and *ER*.

In this case, notice the focus on only two networks and the choice of programs with a high overlap of a particular adult audience that loyally follows each show.

From each example above, you should be able to see that while the buyer placed the same total of nine ads, the Reach and Frequency would be quite different.

Summary of Key Plan Strategies and Rationale.

Recall from Chapter 5 the areas of media strategy are;

- **media scheduling**
- **specific geography**
- **mix of media by class/type and specific media vehicle**

In this section of the buying brief, the planner will summarize the approved plan details and important reasons for each area.

It is important for the buyer to know and understand the reasons behind the planning decisions. When it comes to actually executing the media buy, the informed buyer will be better equipped to negotiate a more effective media buy.

Media Scheduling.

In media scheduling, the planner identifies any and all specific strategies such as particular days, weeks or months for advertising. Maybe the advertising is meant to support another marketing plan activity, like a special promotion.

In this case the buyer needs to know that advertising *must* coincide with the promotional timing and that anything else will not be acceptable.

Specific Geography.

With specific geography, the planner tells the buyer where to focus the buy, nationally, regionally, on a specific market level, or any possible combination.

Remember, there is often wide variance in brand popularity from region to region.

Media Mix.

In the case of media mix by class/type, the planner might be writing one buying brief that covers all media, or she may be writing a separate buying brief for each specific media.

This will depend on how the buying team is organized.

Some agencies have buyers for each media housed together in one overall buying unit. In this case, the planner will write just one brief that provides specific breakdown details by media in this section.

Other agencies though may have designated buying teams housed separately; one for newspaper, one for magazines, one for radio, one for local television, one for national television, one for out-of-home.

If this is the case, or if the buying will be done by separate agencies specializing in each media, then the planner will need to do several versions of the buying brief based on the particular mix of media approved by type/class.

Finally, this section of the buying brief will summarize the plan details as to any specific media vehicles that were recommended to and approved by the client.

With television for example, the plan will usually specify the TV day-parts that will be used and in what combination.

The planner provides such detail here so that the buyer can focus on specific groups of programs for analysis and negotiation.

With magazines though, the plan might specify magazines by type or it may go so far as to specify actual magazines by title. The planner communicates this here, again so the buyer will be able to focus efforts.

Other major media types are generally planned only based on market, timing and weight. For these media, buyers have a lot of work to do determining the specific media vehicles

Media Requirements			
	Weekly GRPs		
	12/8	12/15	12/22
Atlanta			
Spot TV Day		100	
Spot TV Prime		50	
Spot Radio		50	
Baltimore			
Spot TV Day	100		
Spot TV Prime	50		
Spot Radio	50		
Chicago			
Spot TV Day			100
Spot TV Prime			50
Spot Radio			50

used to deliver the plan. We'll cover this is greater detail in the next section of this chapter.

Detailed Media Requirements.

This section of the buying brief will often be presented as a spreadsheet because of the great detail required. This one spreadsheet shows the buyer any and all requirements of the approved plan in one place.

The spreadsheet is typically laid out with timing across the columns, specific media vehicles down the rows and grouped by market and then planned weight levels in each cell. A small example is shown to the left.

When many markets need to be bought, these spreadsheets can be quite formidable.

With requirements laid out in this way, the buyer can see at a glance the exact specifications of the buy. For example, here the television buyer knows that he needs to buy 100 target rating points of daytime television during the week of December 15th in the market of Atlanta.

Check this for yourself, find the "Spot TV Day" listing under the heading of Atlanta and follow the spreadsheet over to the column headed "12/15." Now, find one for yourself. How much radio is needed during the week of December 8th in Baltimore?

Budget Breakdown and Media Cost Parameters.

Media costs money, a lot of it.

In order to create a media plan, the planner uses cost guidelines to determine how much media weight can be accomplished within a total budget. Some times the cost guidelines are very accurate, other times they are only a close approximation.

Either way, once the media plan and resulting budget has been approved by the client, the cost guidelines become cost parameters for the buyers.

Media buyers must work within the budget and cost parameters to effectively accomplish the plan as presented by the planner and approved by the client.

Based on the plan, clients are expecting their budget to be allocated and spent in a particular way and they build up their own internal financial reports reflecting the plan. In almost every case, clients are spending media dollars in anticipation of product sales; everything is projecting forward and there is little if any margin for error.

The planner has to be very specific in this section of the brief. In this section, the planner breaks out the total budget into separate pieces for each media, each market, and each quarter/month/week.

As you'd expect, this is another section generally presented as a spreadsheet.

The lay-out for this spreadsheet is similar to the requirements spreadsheet in that timing is shown across columns and media vehicles are presented in rows grouped by market. The only difference is that now dollars are shown in the cells rather than media weight.

From the example presented to the left you'll see that the buyer knows that his budget for daytime television in Atlanta during the week of December 15th is $12,500. How much is budgeted for radio in Baltimore during the week of December 8th?

There's not much wiggle room in this. In fact, in rare cases where the buyer's actual media costs turn out to be significantly higher (or lower) than the planner's cost/budget guidelines, a re-plan may even be necessary.

Media Market and Merchandising Strategy.

In this final section of the buying brief, the planner frames the client's desired approach to the media market.

Three important points are covered in this section:

• whether the client has agreed to commit dollars to buy media early, or wants to release dollars on a shorter-term schedule

• whether the client has agreed to a "pooled" buy

• how the client wants to allocate any earned merchandising credits

Budget Parameters			
	Weekly Budget		
	12/8	12/15	12/22
Atlanta			
Spot TV Day		12,500	
Spot TV Prime		30,550	
Spot Radio		10,000	
Baltimore			
Spot TV Day	7,800		
Spot TV Prime	20,150		
Spot Radio	7,500		
Chicago			
Spot TV Day			25,000
Spot TV Prime			55,000
Spot Radio			20,000

We'll explain each point here and then go into more detail in the buyer's section of this chapter.

The Early Bird Gets the Cheaper Worm.

As with any other product or service market, the early buyer can often get a better price.

Think about the airline industry. You probably know from personal experience that you can save some money on your airfares when you plan ahead for a trip and buy your ticket early. Airfares can be twice as high (or even more) for those poor passengers who wait to buy their tickets in the last day or so before the flight.

Media can work the same way.

Advertisers who are willing to commit their media budget early can take advantage of lower costs.

The media costs are lower mainly because the media managers don't yet know how high demand might go for their particular media vehicle. As the actual air time or issue date gets closer, if demand has been strong then the media manager will have raised prices to realize higher revenue.

Our common terminology for this economic model in media is "the upfront market" for long-term advance commitments, and "the scatter market" for shorter-term buys executed closer to the actual timing desired.

This question of media market strategy is important for any buy, but it tends to be even more of an issue for planning and buying national media. This is particularly true for national television where we have a well-established "upfront" and "scatter" market system for buying.

Other media, national and local, have a less formalized approach that results in the same outcome.

While they may or may not offer lower rates for early buyers, they do generally command higher rates from advertisers buying on short notice.

"Upfront" and "Scatter" Buys

National TV avails, both network and cable, are bought and sold two different ways:

"Upfront" and "Scatter."

As we mention in the text to the right, "upfront" refers to longer lead-time buy commitments made well before the scheduled airdate for the advertising.

"Scatter" on the other hand refers to short-term, short-lead-time buying executed closer to the scheduled airdate.

In the national TV market, the "upfront" buys all take place in the Spring buying season. Virtually everything else is considered a "scatter" buy.

Quantity Discounts – Cheaper by the Dozen.

When you go to the grocery store, you can buy a product for less if you buy it in a larger quantity.

For example, you can buy a four-pack of bathroom tissue for about $5; that's about $1.25 per roll. Or, you can buy a 12-pack for about $1 per roll. Sure you spent more money, but you saved $3 and you know that you will eventually need and use the extra rolls.

This is also true in the media market place where advertisers are given rate breaks for buying in larger quantities.

This is a simple matter of economies of scale.

It costs the media companies less money to service the business of one big client than it does to service the same amount of business sold through five smaller clients.

Most, if not all, media offer advertisers lower rate deals for bulk buying.

"Pooling."

Realizing this, many advertisers these days will agree to "pool" their media dollars in order to buy larger quantities and get the rate break.

This "pooling" is generally done within companies.

Large companies like Kraft Foods or Procter & Gamble will consolidate their media dollars for multiple products in order to buy in bulk. This works best when the products share a similar target audience.

The buying group will buy a large block of commercial time that will later be allocated to the products that joined the "pool." Allocation in this case is generally managed by someone on the client company staff.

Despite the advantages of "pooled" buys, there can also be disadvantages. One of the most significant disadvantages is commitment. Pooling requires a higher order of commitment from the client.

Think about that earlier example of bathroom tissue; to get the deal, you would have paid more upfront to get the bulk-buy discount. Not every client can afford to do this.

"Pooled" Buying at a Big Company

For a big company like Kraft Foods, "pooled" buying is a logistical nightmare but well worth the effort.

When I worked at Kraft, we had 26 advertised brands, most of which shared a common buying target of women 25-54.

In order to "pool" our national TV buys, we collected plan parameters from every brand using national TV into one massive spreadsheet.

We would then place the consolidated buy as one Kraft buy.

When it came time to run commercials, we would allocate the buy to the brands according to the original parameters for each brand.

The networks were instructed to run commercials according to a rotation schedule that reflected each brand's allocated portion of the buy.

It makes my head hurt just thinking about this again.

In this section, the planner tells the buyer whether the client wants to be "pooled" or not.

Earned Merchandising Credits.

Finally, in this last section of the buying brief, media market and merchandising strategy, the planner tells the buyer what the client wants done with any earned media merchandising credits.

This is another way that the media market is like any other market for goods or services. Good, consistent and loyal customers can earn bonuses.

In media, the bonuses tend to take the form of additional advertising time – or some other form of promotional merchandising. Depending on the media, this merchandising will come in many different forms. Here are common examples:

Television.

Television buys might earn bonus advertising time in other shows or on sister stations or networks. For example, a client sponsoring a network program might be offered the opportunity to run a logo with a sponsorship mention at different points during the program broadcast.

We see this frequently on big broadcast events like the Super Bowl or the Academy Awards.

Magazines.

Magazine buys might earn merchandising in the form of reader surveys for lead generation.

Major magazines often conduct research through surveys of their readers. Such magazines might offer advertisers the opportunity to ask questions in a survey. Other magazines like *Good Housekeeping*, shown left, will include reader-service cards to generate sales leads for advertisers.

Radio.

Radio buys can lead to merchandising such as a station promotion or a remote broadcast. Radio stations are always running contests, trying to boost listenership particularly during ratings periods.

Sales Leads.

This is a reader-service card insert from Good Housekeeping *magazine. Readers who reply are provided as sales leads to advertisers.*

Frequent and loyal radio advertisers are often asked to participate in such contests. In agreeing to participate, the advertiser generally contributes product in exchange for additional on-air product mentions in conjunction with the contest.

Knowing that this happens, good media planners will use this section of the buying brief to direct a media merchandising strategy.

For example, if the client doesn't want to participate in any contests, the planner might instruct the buyer to negotiate merchandising offers into additional commercial time instead. Here we've covered just a couple of short examples.

Later in this chapter and later in the book we'll talk more about media merchandising.

The Planner's Job Is Done.

Well, it's never really done, but this is about as close as it ever gets. Once the planner has prepared and presented the completed buying brief, the job of executing the approved media plan can be handed off to the buying team – this is their specialty.

At larger agencies, with clear delineation between planning and buying teams, the remaining involvement of the planner would be merely advisory.

In other cases, the planner might sometimes be designated as a participating member of the buying team.

Either way, though, it is time to move on to the buyer's role in the process.

The Hand Off.
Just like runners in a relay race, the planner hands off the job of buying.

The Role of Buying.

With a completed buying brief in hand, the media buying team takes over responsibility for bringing the approved media plan to life.

Remember, as we mentioned earlier, that the buying team might be a separate person or group within the agency – or it may be a different agency all together.

Remember, too, that the organization of the buying group might differ from one agency to the next.

Some agencies may have buying groups organized by client where the buyer has responsibility for all of the media a given client might need in its plan.

Other agencies will be organized by media. In this case, the agency will split up the client's buy requirements sending magazine buying to the magazine buyer, television to the network or local market buyer, and radio to the radio buyer.

Smaller agencies may or may not have a buying department. If there is a buying department, it may be only one or two staffers who buy all media. Where there is no buying department, smaller agency media buying may be the responsibility of the media planner.

The Basic Buying Process.

Regardless of how the agency or buying group is organized, the basic buying process is generally the same.

While this basic process may seem fairly simple in concept, it can in fact be quite complex.

The major steps of the media buying process are:
- **Identify the Alternatives**
- **Evaluate the Alternatives**
- **Negotiate the Details**
- **Execute the Buy**
- **Manage the Buy**

This all seems pretty straightforward. But complexity enters this process at each and every step. So, let's consider this step-by-step and see what we're dealing with.

Identify the Alternatives.

No matter how the media buying group is organized, and no matter how specific the media planner may be in making the buying assignment, there are many alternatives to consider for any specified media requirement.

Even a straightforward request like daytime network television carries an almost infinite number of possibilities.

For example the broadcast networks – like ABC or CBS – air many popular soap operas during the day but they also broadcast talk/variety programs and game shows.

The buyer's job is to identify the media content alternatives that best meet the complete set of parameters detailed in the buying brief.

To do this well, buyers use media research, meet regularly with media sales representatives, and read and follow the trades and other industry news sources in order to stay abreast of changes in media content and the movement of audiences among the media.

Whether a buy is currently assigned or not, this is a constant responsibility for media buyers and no easy task.

If you need a reminder, flip back to Chapter 2 for a quick refresher course on the ever-changing dynamics of today's media world.

The core skills needed here are both data analysis and intellectual curiosity. Buyers use data analysis to identify acceptable media alternatives based on matching media audiences to the specifications provided in the buying brief.

Buyers rely on their intellectual curiosity to help them see new media alternatives that might someday fit the buying specifications.

Evaluate the Alternatives.

This is a major math step where buyers consolidate cost and audience data in order to sort and prioritize the list of identified media alternatives. Accordingly, math is the core skill needed for this part of the buying process.

It's common at this step for a buyer to create a spreadsheet layout of all alternatives ranked according to each important criterion. The example presented on the following page shows a short listing of weekly news and entertainment magazines being considered for a buy.

The buyer's work at this step lays the groundwork necessary for the next step – negotiation.

Weekly News and Entertainment Magazines					
	Circulation (000)	P4C Cost	CPM	Positioning Surcharge	Subscription % of Circ.
Entertainment Weekly	1,647	$103,060	$62.57	+15%	97%
Newsweek	3,125	191,500	61.28	+10%	95%
People	3,633	226,000	62.21	+15%	65%
Time	4,110	212,000	51.58	+15%	98%
U.S. News & World Report	2,032	123,364	60.71	+13%	99%

Here we see each of five possible magazines with corresponding facts of circulation, cost, and a series of intangible variables like, preferred positioning cost, and percentage of circulation based on subscriptions.

Based on the requirements of the buy, the buyer ranks each magazine on each listed variable and then an overall rank is determined.

Negotiate the Details.

The next step is negotiation.

This is a particular skill unto itself. We won't go into the "how to" of the fine art of negotiation here; we don't have enough space to do justice to this topic.

Let's just say that a good media buyer knows that variables such as cost, positioning and merchandising are all subject to negotiation.

The buyer will use the spreadsheet detail, like the example above, together with knowledge of the client's budget and timing requirements as he or she meets the sales representative for each alternative magazine.

As negotiations are completed with each magazine, the buyer will then revise the spreadsheet and adjust the rankings accordingly.

Execute the Buy.

The next step in the process is the actual execution of the purchase contract. A separate contract is drawn up for each individual media company identifying the number and cost of each ad placement purchased.

Details of the contract must be provided to several other agency departments.

First, there's the agency billing services department where the agency generates media invoices to be sent to the client.

Also, there's the agency's media traffic department.

This department has responsibility for shipping the appropriate commercial materials to the right media place in time to run as ordered per the contract.

This department ships out video tapes to TV stations, camera-ready art or computer files to magazines or newspapers, and audio materials to radio stations.

At one time, communication between agency departments was literally handled by hard copy of the actual contract.

Today, this is a fully automated system of data management and communication among agency departments and even between the agency and the media.

Manage the Buy.

Finally, even after the buy is contracted, the media buyer continues to work with the media sales representative in order to track and optimize the client's advertising and media investment.

Most media contracts are written with clauses mandating certain conditions. Media buyers stay involved with the buy in order to track the ad placement relative to these conditional clauses.

Three of the most common contractual conditions are:

- **Proof of Run**
- **Proof of Audience**
- **Competitive Separation**

Each of these is important. Let's cover them one by one.

Proof of Run.

The "proof of run" condition requires that the media company must provide hard proof of the fact that the advertisement was run according to the contract specifications.

In the case of print media, such proof is commonly provided in the form of publication tear-sheets. These are literally advertising pages torn from the publication and provided to the agency.

Preferred Postitioning.
Good Housekeeping *magazine ran this Campbell's soup ad facing a page of editorial with soup recipes.*

In cases where the buy contract specifies preferred positioning, the magazine will provide proof of the positioning as well as the ad – perhaps sending a copy of the whole magazine.

In the case of broadcast media, proof of run is often provided in the form of air-checks – these are recorded broadcast segments that include the client's advertisement.

Proof of Audience.

The "proof of audience" condition is increasingly required as both media and media buyers are negotiating for ad pricing tied to audience delivery.

Consider, for example, a grossly simplified case of a primetime commercial purchased for a cost of $20 per thousand delivered TV households.

Let's say that the primetime program was expected to deliver an audience of 5 million so our agreed upon price was contracted at $20 times 5,000, or $100,000 (remember that 5,000,000 is the same as 5,000 thousands).

If instead, the audience came in at only 4 million TV households, then our cost would be only $80,000. The difference of $20,000 would either be credited back to the client or, more likely, accumulated and applied to additional advertising.

The handling of such a discrepancy is typically decided as part of the negotiated contract so the media company knows exactly what to do for the client in case such an issue arises.

Competitive Separation.

The last of the three common conditions we're discussing here is competitive separation.

This condition refers generally to a requirement that ads for a competitor's product must be separated from our client's advertising by some negotiated minimum spacing.

In magazines, the common unit of spacing is 6 pages.

In broadcast television, the common unit of separation is often within a commercial break.

This means no competitive ad placements should run within the 4–6 minute pod of commercials where the client's ad is placed.

The buyer and rep stay in touch throughout the execution of the buy in order to catch and manage any contractual issues as they may arise.

Upfront – The Other Buying Process.

From the preceding discussion, you can see for yourself that the basic buying process is fraught with opportunities for complicating issues. Now let's throw in a new wrinkle to which we referred earlier in this chapter.

Here we will consider the other process of buying media in an upfront market.

Recall from the previous section on the planner's role in implementation that we defined the upfront market as a specific situation of national television buying where the client commits advertising dollars on a longer-term basis in order to realize potentially lower prices.

From the buyer's perspective, the upfront buying process is similar in concept but quite different in application.

The key difference is that the upfront buy for all parties is more speculative in nature. In this sense, this particular media market is kind of like a future's market in commodity trading. Here's how it works.

The National TV Upfront Market.

The upfront market for national television advertising takes place every year in the spring as networks begin planning their programming for the fall premier season.

At the beginning of it, the major broadcast networks host large industry events to announce and premiere their new programming planned for the upcoming fall season.

Upfront Debate

Keep track of the Upfront Debate. As this book was being written, discussion and dissatisfaction with the current upfront process was growing.

Almost every week, you can read some comments in the advertising and media trade magazines.

You might want to go online and see what they're saying this week.

In conjunction with the big events, the networks will release projections for programming audiences and expected costs for advertising based on the audience projections.

After the big season premiere events, national TV buyers throughout the country go back to their offices and crunch their own audience and cost projections.

Based on both sets of projections, media planners and buyers work with the clients to decide how much if any budget should be committed to the upfront market.

This commitment is not to be taken lightly.

This is all taking place in March and April of one year for advertising that will be committed to run beginning six months later and continuing into the first three quarters of the next year.

Clients are not actually paying the money this far in advance. Instead, they are promising to buy at certain levels in each quarter. Each quarterly commitment is usually "locked in" at a certain level of firmness.

Degrees of Firmness.

The firmness levels are usually set on a sliding scale over time where the highest level is committed for the near-in fall quarter while the lowest level of commitment is locked in for the last quarter of the upfront buy. Firmness levels by quarter might be: 90% firm for fall, 75% firm for winter, 50% firm for spring, and 25% firm for summer.

This sliding scale of diminishing firmness builds in a necessary level of freedom for both the client and the media company. In the case of the client, the lower levels of firmness allow flexibility to back out of some part of an upfront commitment. For the media company, this can be okay as long as advertising demand is strong.

In some cases, where media management may have originally underestimated the advertising demand or the attractiveness of a particular program, the networks may even be happy to get back some of their advertising inventory.

They might then sell it at an even higher price.

From this discussion, it should be clear that the national television upfront market is quite different for a buyer.

It is much more complex in terms of the sheer quantity of dollars committed, the speculative nature of the audience projections and the need for commitments at varying levels of firmness.

A Look to the Future.

The role of the media buyer in advertising is changing. "Corporate procurement" is becoming a larger factor.

The Way It Was.

In the past, media buyers were never considered to be part of the corporate purchasing department.

For years, media buying was seen as a highly specialized procurement function. It was widely believed that the job of buying media time and space was best left to the service agencies that specialized in the field.

Even as corporate procurement departments grew in size, with growing responsibility for other large corporate purchasing needs, advertising was still considered different.

This was the case because the market for advertising is not typical.

It's not the same thing as buying computers for the marketing department or buying raw materials for production.

In the advertising business, advertisers buy time and space in the media only to gain access to an audience. So, while advertisers are really buying the audience, the only way to get the audience is through an intermediary – the media.

As such, the business market for advertising has an added level of complexity relative to other procurement activities.

The Way It Is.

Now, however, for several good reasons, corporate procurement is becoming increasingly and more deeply involved in the media buying process.

These corporate professionals were previously involved with purchasing supplies and raw materials, not media.

The most important reason for this change is the significant size of ad budgets. There's a lot of money at stake and corporations want to know that money is spent wisely.

As advertising costs have increased dramatically over recent years – significantly more than just average inflation – advertiser budgets have also increased.

Higher and higher advertising budgets have led to increasing scrutiny from senior corporate financial managers.

As these advertising budgets increase, it becomes even more important to show justification for the spending in the form of return on investment.

Corporate finance and procurement staffs are the people to whom senior corporate management will turn for justification and validation of expenses.

So it's not surprising that they are now becoming more deeply involved in the media buying process.

Learn as an Intern.

This has been a very brief discussion of the overall media buying process as it relates to implementing an approved media plan. For anyone interested in learning more about media buying we recommend a summer internship in a media buying group.

We can almost guarantee you'll have a fascinating and fast-paced learning experience. It will be an internship unlike anything you've done before.

The Role of Media Sales.

Finally, we come to the role of the media sales representative in this process of implementing an approved media plan.

Throughout our discussions so far in this chapter, you've read of the media sales representative in many places.

The media sales representative, or "rep," can be a valued and integral partner in the implementation process.

In the past, media sales had the job of selling media time and space; a unique and often intangible product. The best media sales reps today understand that advertising today isn't just about time or space but rather the audience exposed in that time or space.

Many Varied Responsibilities.

The job of media sales rep is a challenging and rewarding one with many varied responsibilities.

And the role can go from selling local radio time to running one of the largest media companies.

That really happened. Mel Karamazin, president and COO of Viacom, began as a radio sales person.

In many instances, the managers of media properties come from media sales. But before you take over the company, it's time to learn the basics.

For our purposes here, we'll focus on the three major responsibilities of the job:
- **Research and Analysis**
- **Sales and Negotiation**
- **Post-buy Tracking and Evaluation**

Let's take them one by one.

Research and Analysis.

The media sales representative relies heavily on media research to do his job. Whether working for a large media company or a small one, the media sales representative has the challenging job of analyzing research data so as to position his or her media in a most favorable way.

What makes this job particularly challenging is knowing that others out there, competitive media companies and agency media buyers, are in many cases looking at the same research data in their own way.

Despite this challenge, and in some cases even because of this challenge, the media sales rep goes out every day to present his perspective on the data.

This healthy exchange of views becomes the basis for further discussion and maybe negotiation later on in the process.

In this sense, the media sales representative must be comfortable working with numbers and facts in data.

Partners.

The media sales representative is a valued and integral partner in the process of executing a media plan.

Sales and Negotiation.

The job function of research and analysis described in the preceding section requires a certain level of skill in the science of numbers.

On the other hand, the job function of sales and negotiation requires skills of a more artistic nature.

Specifically, this job requires skill in the arts of problem solving and negotiation.

Sales, in general, is all about problem-solving and media sales is no exception. A good sales representative goes into a sales presentation anticipating the problem that his product can solve.

And, it takes a certain skill to be able to imagine or envision the important problems a prospective client may face.

This is the art of problem solving. It isn't so much about finding the right solution as it is about imagining or envisioning the right problem to be solved.

Problem solving is a critical skill at all levels of media sales – whether you're just starting out helping local clients solve their problems with the local medium you're representing or helping put together a big, cross-platform program working with a major retail advertiser.

It's all about problem solving.

If you can do this, if you can imagine the right problem – the one that your media company can best solve – then you will succeed and even excel in media sales.

Negotiation is another art form. It's the delicate balance of giving something to get something.

Two Players at the Table.

In the game of media negotiations there are only two players; each representing a broader constituency. The media sales representative sits on one side of the table while the media buyer sits on the other. In the background sits your management and the competition. Each side wants something and each side has something to give up in this process.

Player #1 – Sales.

The sales representative represents his media company.

He wants to get as many advertising dollars as possible for every minute or page of advertising inventory that's given up. While much of the negotiation will be on price, the media sales rep has other (non-price) options that can be used in negotiations.

For example, the sales rep might prefer to offer media merchandising, such as bonus spots or bonus pages, as an alternative to lower prices.

Player #2 – Buying.

The media buyer represents her agency and the client.

She wants to get as much advertising inventory as possible for every client dollar that's given up. In order to secure more advertising for less money, she will offer as much as possible in terms of firm, longer-term commitments to advertising spending.

The art of negotiation is finding the point of equilibrium where the scales are balanced between both sides.

Post-Buy Tracking and Evaluation.

In the preceding section we stressed the need for buyer involvement continuing even after the buy is executed; the same is true for media sales representatives.

A good media sales representative stays involved before, during, and after the buy, watching out for the needs of both the media company and the buying client.

A good sales rep knows that you build a career with satisfied repeat customers and positive relationships. Even problems can be a way of delivering extra service and demonstrating your value.

Any contractual or conditional issues that may arise during or after the execution of the buy are communicated back to the media buyer through the media sales representative.

It is the job of the sales representative to negotiate a resolution to any outstanding issue whenever it may arise.

As you can see, just like buyers and planners, the media sales job is continuously active. Today's sales call turns into tomorrow's sale. Then, the sale you make tomorrow will carry with it post-buy responsibilities.

And, your next sale will depend on how well you do your job from the sales call through the post-buy.

Sales careers are built on longterm relationships and repeat business. In sales, the whole process of implementation is one continuous loop.

Other Important Players.

In this chapter we've focused on three key roles in the implementation process – planners, buyers and sellers.

Throughout, we've mentioned other important players – media research, media management, media traffic, and agency billing.

Each represents another important job function in the wide world of media. We'll touch briefly on the role of each.

Media Research.

In each section of this chapter, media research plays an important part.

Planners use media research to inform the translation of the approved plan into an effective buying brief.

Buyers use media research to identify and evaluate alternative media choices.

Sellers use media research to help them position their product in a most favorable light.

Buyers and sellers both use the data provided by media research to inform their negotiation strategy.

You get the idea, don't you?

Whether it's product-based data like Simmons or MRI, or media-based data from sources like Nielsen or Arbitron, or even media-owned data from proprietary research, this process can't work without media research support.

Media Management.

We also mentioned media management in a number of places. Media managers decide the strategic and philosophical direction of the media company; they control the programming of media content.

Content is programmed by media managers so as to attract the best possible audience. It is the audience that then attracts advertiser support.

Advertising too becomes part of programmed content. Whether it's on TV or radio or in a magazine, too much advertising can hurt a media property.

Media managers have to balance editorial and advertising content to make and keep the media attractive to both advertisers and audiences.

Media managers control pricing of their product. This is less of a factor in broadcast television but a big issue in magazines and newspapers. If the media costs too much, the audience won't subscribe.

Media managers also control pricing for their advertising inventory. They set prices upfront, and they directly control any negotiated variations.

When media managers do their jobs well, they bring both ratings and financial success to their company.

Even when they get the balance right, the job can still be challenging.

Some audiences, while highly desired by advertisers, are very hard to reach through the media.

One of the most elusive audience segments today is the target group of young, 18–24-year-old men.

In cases like this, where the audience is particularly hard to reach, some advertisers will even go so far as to offer their financial support to promising start-up media ventures with the potential to reach the segment.

227

Media Traffic.

Media traffic is the agency department responsible for shipping advertising materials to the media companies indicated on the purchase contract.

This is a small but very important job in the process.

The primary, if not only, purpose of this department is implementation of the media plan.

Specific skills needed for this job include organization, time management, and attention to detail.

Agency Billing.

This is where the agency pays bills and collects pay for its services. Agency management at all levels will pay particular attention to this job function in the implementation process.

In the world of media, most agencies pay the media for the time and space they purchase. The agency then bills the client to cover costs and, in many cases, media commissions. Media commissions are a significant source of income for most advertising agencies.

Summary.

The topic of this chapter has been the implementation of an approved media plan.

We've tried here to introduce sufficient detail to explain the process but, in truth, this one topic could be (and has been) handled as a whole textbook of its own.

We've covered the roles and responsibilities of each major player, and the many other players, involved in executing a media buy.

From Media Plan to Buying Brief.

The media planner's job does not stop with the media plan. In implementation the planner's primary role is preparation of the buying brief.

The buying brief is a detailed document specifying the media requirements of the plan as well as the supporting reasons for the key plan strategies.

From the Brief to the Buy.

The media buyer's role is a big one.

The buyer remains continuously involved before, during, and after the buy is executed.

Negotiating the Buy and Managing the Relationship.

The media sales representative is a partner working with the media buyer. Like his buyer counterpart, the sales rep remains continuously involved before, during, and after the execution of the media buy.

This partnership is important and works best when the buyer and seller collaborate and cooperate.

Though the relationship might occasionally become adversarial, this should be the exception, not the rule.

The Objective – Client Success.

Both buyer and seller are in this to win success for the client.

The client is ultimately the one spending the money that keeps this business model working.

The other players in this model – media research, media management, media traffic, and agency billing – each play an important if somewhat peripheral role.

From this chapter, you should have gained a good sense of the inner workings of the advertising media market.

This market is at once both simple and complex.

This business is at once both challenging and rewarding.

Julie Lonergan built her media career in two major fields of the media world. From a solid start and growth on the media planning side, Julie then moved to media sales working for a major consumer magazine at the largest media company in the world.

Career Capsule:

Julie Lonergan, Senior Sales Representative, *Time* Magazine.

Julie majored in marketing/communications at Iowa State University in Ames, Iowa. She knew since she was in junior high school that advertising was the career for her.

A First Job in Advertising.

After completing her degree and in a tight job market, Julie networked through family friends to land a job at NW Ayer. She calls it her foot-in-the-door, NW Ayer called the position "group assistant." Here she learned about the business and departmental structure of an advertising agency. She had the chance to work with people in all departments – account management, media, production, creative, even human resources.

Although the pay seemed pretty low, Julie felt the perks were good (lunches, parties, premiums, etc.) and her skills seemed best suited to the media department. So, she approached the media director and after a couple of months worked her way into a position as an assistant media planner.

Of her first year in media, Julie says, *"I was basically a sponge – learning the very basics – media definitions, media math, syndicated research and research tools, how to write a letter/memo"* among other things. Julie says that she also learned here in her first media job that *"media was both an art and a science; that there were a lot of right answers and you had to choose the best option given the situation."*

Career Advancement.

From the first job as assistant media planner, Julie moved on to a new agency, Foote, Cone and Belding, and increased responsibility as a media planner, then supervisor. And, after more than 10 years in media planning, Julie moved to the media side as a sales representative for *Parade* Magazine before settling into her current job as senior sales representative for *Time* Magazine.

In advertising sales, Julie calls on advertising agencies and clients to identify opportunities and promote the most appropriate use of the magazine – that which best benefits the client. In her current position, Julie and her sales assistant sell national space as well as local/regional ad pages for *TIME* Magazine and all Time line extensions including special interest publications like *Time Style & Design*, Time.com and *Time For Kids*. And, whenever it is appropriate, Julie promotes and sells integrated packages across multiple Time Warner divisions including Turner Broadcasting, AOL, Time Inc., Southern Progress, and Time 4 Media.

It's a Great Job.

Julie says that she likes being a resource for her clients – *"my clients and coworkers respect me as an authoritative source for information and creative ideas."* Her favorite part of the job is putting together smart advertising programs that help advertisers meet their communication goals.

On the Future of Media.

Julie sees the line between traditional and non-traditional media blurring as the marketplace becomes more fragmented. She noticed early in her career that media was all about making choices and she sees this as even more challenging today.

She sees research as a key to the future. Not just more and better research but even more importantly, more and better information. This means more than just data. From Julie's perspective, media planners already have *"instant access to a lot of data which isn't always the best information."*

Career Advice.

"When you land a job in media, it is just as much your responsibility to learn as it your supervisor's responsibility to teach." Julie Lonergan suggests that anyone new in media should *"put time and energy into learning the basics and, if you've been assigned to someone who is not a good teacher, then you should take responsibility, go out there and find a better teacher to work with."*

Discussion Questions.

1. The Role of Media Planning.

What is the "buying brief" and why is it important?

What do we mean when we say *"directions must be specific and detailed but not dictatorial"*?

Why is this important?

Name and describe each section of the standard "buying brief" outlined in this book.

2. The Role of Media Buying.

What is the basic buying process?

What happens at each step?

What is the national TV upfront market?

How does it work?

What is the "scatter market?"

3. The Role of Media Sales.

List and describe a media sales representative's major job responsibilities.

What do you think is a typical day for a media sales rep? Be specific.

4. Other Players.

Name and describe the other media players named in this chapter who have a role in implementing the media plan.

Exercises.

1. The Buying Brief.

Use the National Traveler media plan presented in Appendix 1 of this book. Working with this media plan, **write a complete buying brief and be prepared to present it to the class.**

2. Media Buying.

Imagine that you are a magazine buyer working at a major advertising agency. You've received the following directions regarding a buy for the agency's client, Coca Cola Classic.

Use SMRB or MRI, the SRDS, and any other resources you can find to **recommend a magazine buy that would be best for the client**. Your final report should indicate the magazine titles you would buy and the number of insertions in each magazine you recommend in order to spend the full budget allocated.

> **Client:** Coca Cola Classic
>
> **Buying target:** Adults aged 18-49, with a 60/40 skew towards men
>
> **Plan Objective:** Achieve 70% reach of the target audience in each quarter of the plan year
>
> **Budget:** $5,000,000 for the full year to be fairly evenly allocated to each quarter of the year.

3. Media Sales.

Imagine that you are a media sales representative working for the Nickelodeon cable TV network. You'll be making a sales call to a media buyer working on the Milton-Bradley family board games business.

Using any sources you can find (hint: check out www.mediapost.com and you might also want to look in your library for an SRDS for Cable TV – there is one), **prepare a sales presentation**.

Your time will be very short, the buyer has agreed to give you a 5-minute appointment. At minimum your presentation should propose the costs and benefits of Nickelodeon. It might also be a good idea to propose a merchandising strategy.

Be prepared to make your presentation to the class.

III Local & "Niche" Media Markets

THIS PART OF THE BOOK will hit closer to home because it is closer to home.

In this section, we'll cover the markets we all live in – and some of the special markets that are a media and marketing world all their own.

Searching for Match-Ups.

You see the media all around you.

Some of it is broad, national, or maybe even international media. Someof it is small and local.

But, one way or another, each medium and every vehicle, local or global, is targeted to some specific market capability.

And, in fact, you will find a fascinating match-up between markets and the media that serve them.

"Market."

Now there's a big word. How many different ways can you think of to define the word "market?"

We've already used that simple but important word a couple of different ways in this book, so let's take a minute now to agree on a good definition.

We've been using "market" to mean a homogeneous grouping of people. Simple, right?

Well, here's the tricky part. The homogeneity of the grouping might be established a couple of different ways.

Geographically. In this sense, the word "market" means some common location or geography shared by a group of people. According to the media rating services A.C. Nielsen and Arbitron, there are just over 200 specific, geographically defined media markets in the U.S.

Demographically. In this sense, the word "market" refers to some common physical characteristic shared by a group of people. For example, we might talk about media specifically targeted to young adults between the ages of 18 and 24 years old.

Behaviorally. Here the word "market" refers to some common purchase or lifestyle behavior shared among a group of people.

For example, we might talk about young adult college students. This would be a grouping distinctly different from a whole group of all young adults.

Hobbyists or car enthusiasts or people who want to build a log cabin are each a market with media just for them.

Culturally. As in cultural heritage, race, or ethnic origin. For example, we might consider culture-specific media, such as Telemundo, the Spanish-language television network.

Commercially. As in commerce or business. Here the word "market" refers to some common business or commercial activity. For example, the business of retail clothing stores.

Or hobby shops. Or computer programmers. Or even the worlds of advertising and media.

Niche Is Another Great Word.

"Niche" can mean the same thing as "market." Typically it means a smaller part of some bigger grouping of people. But it can also mean a small coherent market group.

Each of the above terms – geographic, demographic, behavioral, cultural, and commercial – can be used to identify a niche market. And a niche market is a bit different from a mass market.

More importantly, as far as we are concerned, there is a media option of some kind for virtually every conceivable niche market.

This is the subject of this section of the book. We couldn't possibly cover all media options available out there. So, here we will start with the geographic.

In Chapter 7, we will discuss the specific characteristics of the local geographic aspects of each media. We'll hint here about some of the other, niche aspects of the media, but we'll save the full details for Chapter 9.

In Chapter 8, we will cover the media planning process again, but from a local, geographic perspective.

Finally, in Chapter 9, we'll go over some specific applications of niche marketing and the media that serve specific niches. In this chapter, we'll focus on applications among demographic, behavioral, cultural, and commercial niches.

7 The Local Media Mix

E VEN AS THE MEDIA UNIVERSE EVOLVES and expands, it is still fairly stable on the local level. Dynamic, but relatively stable.

"Think Global. Act Local."

Everywhere you go, our media world is much the same. We do similar things in different places.

Let's take a look at the primary local media options.

Chapter Organization.

In virtually every market, the primary local media are:

* **Newspapers**
* **Radio**
* **Television**
* **City and Regional Magazines**
* **Out of Home**
* **Directory Advertising**
* **Direct**
* **"New Media"**

These options exist in virtually every local market .

Advantages and Disadvantages.

We'll take another look at the advantages and disadvantages of each medium – only this time with a local focus.

As you read through this chapter, try to connect what we're talking about in general with the specifics of your market.

Newspapers.

The traditional metropolitan daily newspaper reaches a large and diverse audience with large and diverse content that ranges from national and international to local news and features.

It covers politics, crime, schools, opinion, reader letters, sports of all kinds, entertainment, comics, features on subjects from local people to child rearing to food, arts, travel, decorating, homes, and more.

Two Products.

In reality, a newspaper is selling two products:

1. News and information to readers

2. Audience access to advertisers

And newspapers make money both ways – from selling newspapers to readers and by selling ads to advertisers.

Local news and information is a primary reason for readership. Advertising is also an important component to readers – it's product news, the type of commercial information that can help people know about special shopping opportunities or where to go see that new movie.

Two Types of Advertising.

Newspapers offer both display and classified advertising.

Display advertising gives advertisers a chance to tell a message in detail, provides both text and illustrations, and may even distribute coupons.

Classified advertising is another fascinating example of the marketplace at work. In this case, the audience seeks out the item.

Those interested in a new puppy, a used car, or an apartment near campus will wade through the listings to find what they're looking for.

Circulation – Who Reads the Paper?

While newspapers are read by many differing kinds of audiences, the typical newspaper reader is slightly older (over

Newspaper Reader Profile

	% of Readers	Index
By Age:		
18-24	6	67
25-34	11	75
35-44	20	96
45-54	21	109
55-64	16	121
65 or older	27	133
By Education:		
Graduated College	27	124
Some College	17	100
Graduated HS	32	99
Some HS	11	69
By Home Ownership:		
Home Owners	87	109
Renters	13	78

Typical Readers.

The typical newspaper reader is older, more educated, and more likely to own his or her own home or condo.

Red Eye.

An offering for the younger market from the Chicago Tribune.

35), more educated, with more income, and more likely to own his or her own house or condo than a non-reader.

While newspaper circulation is up in many regions of the country, penetration (the percentage of households getting the paper) is down.

Penetration has dropped from about 100% after WWII – when many households received two papers – to an average well below 60% today.

Naturally, individual markets vary. In some markets, newspapers still enjoy a 90% penetration rate.

Other markets have a penetration rate of only around 40%.

While direct metropolitan daily competition exists in only a few markets today, there are many other kinds of media that have cut into newspaper readership and market penetration.

This is a problem for papers, as advertisers have traditionally bought papers for the large, mass audience.

Today, the mass market is dwindling while the niche market is growing.

Newspapers have responded to this challenge.

Two Kinds of Audiences.

Today, newspapers try to offer two kinds of audiences for advertisers:

- **the traditional large audience; and**
- **more narrowly defined audiences reached by niche market publications.**

For example, young people (18-35) are a low-reader group. Newspapers are working continually to attract more readers in this demographic category. A special program for school-age children, Newspapers in Education, puts newspapers into classrooms and provides instructional materials in an effort to make reading a habit for this future audience.

Some publishers are developing new newspaper products. For example, the *Chicago Tribune* has developed a five-day-a-week tabloid called *Red Eye* which is aimed at a younger demographic.

Newspapers are also working to get more women readers, as research shows they are less likely to read than men. Many papers conduct research to find out the interests of their female readers – and try to provide content that will attract them.

Lack of time is a major reason many women give for not reading – or for not reading regularly. Working women with children find it particularly hard to find time to read.

Newspapers on the World Wide Web.

Today, most daily newspapers have an online presence of some type.

Many offer some or all of the text of the main paper.

A few have a separate Web edition of the paper with a separate staff. The ability to provide links from a current story to related archived material gives readers more information as they need it.

At present, many online newspapers are free. Others, such as *The Wall Street Journal*, charge for access to the paper; subscribers receive a password. Some newspapers attempt to use the online edition to promote the regular daily paper.

Advertising in the online paper varies. Some papers provide the online advertising to clients as a value-added part of the regular newspaper ad package. Some will create banner or other ads for clients that are only for the online edition.

Home Delivery and Street Sales.

Many readers receive home delivery of the newspaper.

Advertising sales reps use the fact that readers choose to have the paper in their homes every day as a strong selling point.

Most of the rest of the circulation comes from "single copy sales." The papers are sold from locations in town such as stores, gas stations, news stands, dedicated vending machines, and other locations.

This type of selling is also called "street sales."

Chicago Tribune
—ONLINE EDITION—

Detroit Free Press
www.freep.com

THE PLAIN DEALER

On the Web.
Many newpapers offer limited or full text of the paper on the web where their advertisers can extend local newspaper coverage.

Single copy sales are very strong in large cities where there is a lot of activity in the downtown area as well as a lot of commuter traffic. This kind of sales means people see the ads when they are in shopping areas – also a selling point for advertising reps.

Beyond the regular readers (both subscribers and single copy buyers), there are "at-risk" readers who are only marginally loyal.

These people may be single copy buyers or subscribers. What distinguishes them from regular readers is their lower involvement with the paper. They may only buy a few days of the week or, if they subscribe, they read only a few days of the week.

Some readers subscribe only to the Sunday edition.

Placement – Selling the Whole Paper.

In a newspaper, placement can be a major issue.

One common problem that sales reps have to overcome is that Section A (the front page and its section) is generally perceived as the most desirable placement in the newspaper.

While it is true that most readers do look at the front page and through the entire front section, other sections of the paper are read as frequently and – depending on the target audience – with more time and more care.

Research figures from the paper will show both frequency and type of audience for the different sections.

The "A" section is most valuable for the largest and most general advertisers, such as department stores.

For smaller or specialized product advertisers, other sections may be a better placement and return more readership for the dollars spent.

Recurring Placement.

Fox Sports Net, for example, runs a recurring ad-strip placement on the sports page with box scores.

Advertisers may ask for placement within sections.

Some of the largest advertisers have the same placement day after day. For department stores, this is often facing pages or the back page in the "A" section; for some other kinds of stores, it may be the back page of other sections.

One "perk" that larger advertisers may request is this kind of special and consistent positioning.

Daily Newspaper Adults

Newspaper Sections Read	Adults	Men	Women
	%	%	%
Business/Finance	40	46	33
Classified	37	37	37
Comics	37	36	38
Editorial Page	42	40	45
Fashion	20	8	31
Food/Cooking	33	19	46
General News	70	67	73
Home/Furnishings/Gardening	27	18	37
Movie Listings and Reviews	30	25	36
Science & Technology	23	27	19
Sports	43	58	28
Travel	25	22	27
TV/Radio Listings	32	29	35
Average Weekday Audience (000)	100,544	50,193	50,351

Placement.

Newpapers offer different information in different sections of the paper. Advertisers can ask for placement within certain sections.

Sectionalization.

Placing the same kind of material in individual sections daily, weekly, or whenever it appears makes finding the information easier. Readers like to find the same kinds of news and features in the same place every day. It also provides a special content section for advertisers whose target audience is likely to be interested in the subject.

Some of the more typical newspaper sections are shown in the table to the left.

Zoned Editions.

Zoned editions offer special geographically based content for different local areas of the newspaper market.

Certain pages – or a section – offer readers an opportunity to find material of real local interest to them while offering advertisers a chance to reach a market close to their businesses.

Since the market areas are only a portion of the entire circulation, ad rates in zoned editions are less expensive, allowing small advertisers to reach their own neighborhood markets.

Some papers zone the city itself into four or five zones; others zone both the city and other areas within their retail trading zone.

Some newspapers will publish a special tabloid section one or more times a week to accomplish this zoning option.

Special Sections.
Many papers offer special sections from time to time, like this one on the Auto Show in Chicago. Compatible advertisers often seek out special sections like this one.

Preprints.
An increasingly popular marketing strategy. Disney has begun to insert preprints of full-size (folded) posters for new movie releases. Like this one for Finding Nemo.

This tabloid section concentrates on neighborhood news, enabling papers to print school and club news, cover neighborhood sports, and promote local events. Advertisers in these sections can target their copy to tie in directly with news of interest to these area readers.

Special Sections.

Newspapers also have special sections several times a year.

Topics may include gardening, house, back-to-school, high school sports, travel, special festivals, and so on.

Ads in these sections enable advertisers to place ads alongside content that interests their customers.

Nearly all daily newspapers have at least some special sections – advertising rates are generally favorable and offer a good opportunity to target readers with interests in specialized products or services.

Subsidiary or Niche Publications.

Many newspapers today publish subsidiary or "extra" publications targeted toward niche markets. These publications – which may look either like newspapers or magazines or can be in some other format – target special audiences.

These may be separated demographically, such as seniors or teens; by special interests, such as sports, auto, entertainment or gardening; or by some other category, such as real estate, brides, or jobs. Some are geographically based and either supplement or replace geographic zoning.

Newspapers are generally a paid reader medium. Subsidiary publications are more likely to be free.

Preprints.

Another type of advertising carried by newspapers is the preprint. These four-color slick ads are inserted into the newspaper as additional advertising.

The poster format and quality paper allows advertisers to use sharper color, to print the same ad pieces for a number of markets, and to be certain that these ad pieces are delivered to their target customers in all their markets on the same day. Preprints may be for local, regional, or national advertisers. Sundays are a heavy day for preprints.

The rate structure for preprints differs from other ads; preprint rates are discussed in a later chapter.

By keeping the cost of preprints at less than direct mail, newspapers are able to compete with this kind of delivery.

Advantages & Disadvantages.
Advantages.

Newspapers offer a good advertising opportunity for local advertisers because they can accommodate detailed copy, drawings, photographs, attention-getting headlines, and innovative layout and design.

Lead time is minimized by deadlines that are a day or two (sometimes less) before publication time. Ad space in papers can be purchased for the full circulation run or for specific zones or zip code areas.

Because the product is paid for by the customer, it is possible to track consumers by where they live.

Paid circulation also indicates that the customer wants the paper and indicates a likelihood of use of the newspaper product, ensuring exposure to the ads.

Disadvantages.

News and information content can't be updated as frequently as broadcast or web information. Newspapers lack immediacy.

Color is not up to magazine standards in run-of-the-paper ads. (Preprints are better.)

Fewer niches to target than with radio or magazines.

Readership Studies and Measurements.

Newspapers conduct readership studies to find out who their readers are, which sections of the papers are read most frequently, how readers use the paper for advertising information, how much time readers spend with the paper, and the characteristics of non-readers.

A frequently asked question is "Did you read the paper yesterday?" This is a very conservative measure that gives advertisers assurance that the numbers and preferences of respondents are indicative of actual reader behavior.

Weeklies.

Many smaller communities have weekly newspapers. They are similar to larger dailies that concentrate on a smaller geographic area.

Traditionally, they will feature more in-depth coverage of local events and activities, and advertising will be predominantly from smaller local merchants.

"Shoppers" & Others.

This newspaper-like medium is becoming a growing force in many areas.

Originally, "Shoppers" were free newspapers which consisted largely of advertising, developed to provide additional low-cost opportunities for retailers.

Since they have little in the way of an editorial staff and a fairly long shelf life, they can be fairly profitable and can provide a stiff competitive challenge to traditional papers.

Another form of free newspaper developed out of the alternative press of the '60s. These local newspapers often feature interesting editorial and graphics emphasizing local arts, particularly music and entertainment.

They are often distributed in local retail establishments, ranging from bars and record stores to local supermarkets.

They come out weekly or monthly, are usually free, and have circulations that range from a few thousand to over 100,000 for papers like the *Chicago Reader.*

They are generally targeted at a specific geographic and "lifestyle" demographic and offer another viable advertising opportunity for certain retailers.

The existence of a relatively large group in a youthful demographic is key to making these papers viable. On many

The **Chicago Reader.**
This free weekly has an average circulation of over 133,000 copies. It features contemporary entertainment news and articles and is packed with ads.
Is there a paper like this in your market?

large campuses, for example, there may be one or two "alternative" papers in addition to the on-campus student paper.

The growth of desktop publishing software has made these small special interest newspapers a new and vital force in the media world, both substituting for and reinforcing the traditional daily newspaper.

Radio.

Grabbing the audience on the go is radio's strength – people often listen to the radio when they're in the car. It's a medium that travels well.

Radio also provides background music and news highlights throughout the day in many homes and businesses.

Since the audience can listen to the radio while they're doing something else – typically driving or working – radio ads reach audiences at times and places other media cannot. This is a strength.

A Background Medium.

The fact that radio does not have the complete attention of its audience can be a weakness as well.

Advertisers need to overcome that with involving, attention-grabbing advertising and with frequency – repeating the commercial a number of times.

Formats & Fragmentation.

Listeners choose radio stations for the format – music and other programming – that appeals to them.

While listeners may scan across stations looking for music that appeals, most listeners develop their own "network" of two to four stations – usually established as preset buttons on their car radio. In addition to music format, individual stations can also build audience loyalty through on-air personalities.

Some radio stations may buy standard or customized formats from syndicated agencies or consultants to enable them to compete for a specific audience segment within their local market. With increasing concentration in radio station own-

Personalities.

Some radio stations build audience loyalty with popular on-air personalities. This is a publicity photo of the morning team for a popular country music station.

Who are the big personalities in your market?

ership, these formats are becoming more consistent from market to market.

Some stations may style themselves as country and western, as young adult, or as oldie stations. These formats are dictated by the desire to appeal to the particular age or demographic group the station considers its primary audience.

Every market has several radio stations, each one trying to appeal to a certain kind of audience. The result is a special kind of demographic fragmentation.

So, while radio is a mass medium in one sense, it is also a very selective medium with well-defined demographic targets.

Advertisers choose their radio "buys" based on their need to reach these specific and carefully defined audiences.

For example, one station may have the highest listenership among adults 18-34, another with teens, with women, or with the age 35-54 audience.

However, since there are so many stations in most markets, it is likely that there will be several formats that appeal to the same age groups.

Competition for ad dollars among stations with "reach" into the same demographic audience profile can be extremely intense.

Advertisers buy time based on the viability of a station with the desired target audience – they use radio to select the market segment or niche that their store or business identifies as key.

Drive Time.

Drive time – the time people spend going to and from work – is a valuable time for radio advertising. Audiences are high at these times as commuters listen while they are in city traffic or driving down the highway.

Roughly the time between 6:30 and 9:00 AM and between 4:30 and 7:00 PM, it is the most expensive radio ad time and it delivers the greatest audience.

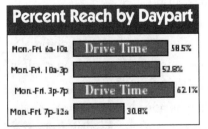

Percent Reach by Daypart

Mon.-Fri. 6a-10a	Drive Time	58.5%
Mon.-Fri. 10a-3p		52.8%
Mon.-Fri. 3p-7p	Drive Time	62.1%
Mon.-Fri. 7p-12a		30.8%

Travelling Music.
Peak time for reach of adults is when they are driving to and from work.

TOP 10 RADIO COMPANIES			
RANK	MEDIA COMPANY	NET RADIO REVENUE	% CHANGE
1	Clear Channel Communications	$3,717	7.6
2	Viacom	1,859	4.5
3	Walt Disney Co.	579	5.9
4	Westwood One	551	6.8
5	Cox Enterprises	421	6.5
6	Entercom Communications Corp.	391	17.5
7	Citadel Broadcasting Corp.	310	16.3
8	Radio One	296	21.3
9	Hispanic Broadcasting (Univision)	257	6.5
10	Cumulus Media	253	25.0

The Big Get Bigger.

The top radio companies in the U.S. just keep getting bigger. Every one of the top 10 U.S. radio companies saw revenue growth in 2002.

Actual drive time boundaries vary with the size of the local market, since commuting hours are longer in larger cities and more compressed in smaller ones.

Local & National.

While radio is largely a local medium, revenue for national and regional advertisers is beginning to grow as radio positions its programming for specific local audiences as a cost efficient way of hitting carefully defined niche audiences within a local target market area.

Radio is an ideal medium for niche marketing because it can deliver a defined demographic and geographic audience to an advertiser.

While no one station can reach teens, adults, and seniors with equal effectiveness, specific stations within a market will have one of these audiences as their primary listeners.

This selective appeal is an important advantage, and stations can position their more narrow demographic focus in a very positive way in selling themselves to potential advertisers.

For example, the teen audience is growing in importance.

This group has a high level of discretionary income, and teens are heavy radio users.

So if the target is teenagers, chances are, radio should be part of the media plan.

Flexibility & Frequency.

Flexibility is a strong selling point for radio – and so is frequency, the number of times your audience will hear your commercial in a certain time period.

Adequate frequency is key for effective radio scheduling.

Since the radio audience is usually doing something else while the radio is on, some amount of repetition is often necessary for the message to "sink in."

And, since much radio time is non-drive time, many messages reach a smaller audience. Naturally, smaller audiences mean lower rates. That's why the price of non-drive time spots is less. These smaller audiences also mean that more frequency is needed so that a large enough cumulative audience is exposed to the message.

Flexibility is another radio advantage. With the ability to place many ads in a schedule at differing times of the day, to custom produce ads within a short time frame, and to place ads on short notice, radio gives the advertiser an opportunity to respond quickly to changes in business and to competitive challenges.

Here are some examples of that flexibility:

Promotions.

Radio is an excellent medium for promotions.

Announcements and reminder ads can draw an audience for a special event, and the radio format can get attention at times and in ways other media cannot.

Remotes.

Radio can go on-site as well.

One common type of promotional event is called a "remote." The station brings an announcer or DJ to a store or business and broadcasts from that location.

The station provides refreshments and, often, games and small prizes, drawing a crowd to the store or mall for entertainment and a chance to see the radio personalities live.

The increased store traffic – often on a weekend – results in increased sales and inquiries from potential buyers, not only that day but for days to follow.

The remote is often part of an incentive package offered with an advertising schedule and contract.

Precise Planning vs. "Spray and Pray."

As we noted, because there are so many radio stations, the audience is necessarily fragmented, with many of the individual stations garnering only a small market share.

Some advertisers may feel they have to spread their advertising dollars over a number of stations to reach as much of the audience in the area as possible.

February 20, 2004
Join 93XRT at the Grand Opening of Lowe's Lake In The Hills!

Celebrate the Grand Opening of Chicagoland's newest Lowe's with 93XRT on Friday, February 20th from 6-8pm. XRT's Ken Sumka be at Lowe's of Lake In The Hills (300 North Randall Road) with plenty of fun and prizes, just look for the XRT Van!

Live on Remote.
An effective way to use radio in building local retail foot traffic.

Station reps call that kind of placement a "spray and pray" technique that dilutes the frequency and makes the advertising ineffective. Used this way, radio can be very expensive for the buying audience reached.

Getting good results from radio advertising takes precise and careful planning.

The most effective radio advertising is usually a result of identifying a carefully designated target audience segment and placing a schedule on one or two stations in the market that have high listenership within that segment.

Radio ads placed with serious consideration of the desired target audience and an understanding of the appeal and specific audience reach of the available stations can be very cost-efficient.

Sponsored Events.

Many radio stations sponsor separate events targeted to a specific niche audience. For example, one station sponsors an event for brides-to-be every spring. With co-sponsors such as caterers, photographers, and bridal shops, the event is both popular and profitable.

Another radio station sponsors an all-day investment seminar targeted to those listeners 50 years of age or more. By bringing in a well-known on-air personality (from a syndicated program) and by co-sponsoring with financial planners and area banks, the event is both informative and entertaining.

Larger radio stations in urban markets often have a sales rep whose sole job is to seek out, plan, and run events and promotions for the station.

Radio in a Combination Buy.

Radio can also be an excellent supporting medium for those advertisers who may use print as a primary medium.

Used in this way, radio advertising can provide specific focus for a key demographic target even for those advertisers who can utilize print as a broad-reach medium.

Surfin' for Sponsors.
Many radio stations sponsor events in order to build audience. The station brings in sponsors to cover costs of special events like the B96 (Chicago) annual Summer Bash.

Radio plus outdoor is occasionally referred to as "poor man's TV." One medium provides the visual, the other provides audio. Each has relatively low production costs (compared to TV).

Even their environments compliment each other.

Naturally, the perfect combination is when someone drives by your outdoor board while your commercial is playing.

Radio can also be used effectively with online advertising.

Using a combination of radio, print, outdoor, and online can be a dynamic way to introduce a new product.

There is some research to indicate that playing the audio track of your TV commercial on the radio offers some synergies. Assuming that a person has seen your TV commercial a few times, the TV commercial will be remembered just by replaying the audio track.

Radio Audience Measurement.

A new alliance of long-time measurement firms, Nielsen and Arbitron, has introduced the portable people meter system.

People being measured wear a lightweight device (similar to a pager) during the day and evening. This sophisticated technology can measure what consumers listen to on the radio and what they watch on broadcast, cable, and satellite television.

The audience profile will be available to advertisers daily so that they can easily track the reach/exposure of their advertising in the broadcast area.

Radio use is reported by average audience over 15-minute segments throughout a 24-hour period.

The demographics of users are reported so that both advertisers and stations know their reach and impact within demographic categories. This is particularly important with the demographics of most radio stations.

Thus, a station that claims it provides advertisers with "Results with Adults" can use age and use figures to back up this claim.

It's National. It's Local.
The TV stations in your market offer opportunities for both national and local advertisers.

MGM-NBC MEDIA SALES

Programming.
Syndicators like Universal and MGM-NBC provide the bulk of programming for local-market independent stations.

Television.

Television is the ideal medium for capturing the at-home audience. While many advertisers are national or regional in scope, network affiliates, independents, and local cable offer many opportunities for local advertising placement.

Types of TV.

Though there may be many stations in your market, they basically fall into three categories:

- **Network Affiliates**
- **Independents**
- **Cable Systems**

Let's review them one by one.

Network Affiliates.

Network affiliates are local television stations with a contracted affiliation to a particular network.

Such stations carry national advertising embedded in the programming content they pick up from the network, but there is local option time available as well.

As part of network affiliation agreements, local television stations are granted a certain amount of advertising time specifically allocated for sale to local advertisers.

This advertising time is available throughout the day.

Aside from the in-program time allotted by the networks, the local news broadcast is a particularly high profile time for local advertising.

And, the station wholly owns this local news time.

Independents.

Many markets have independent stations. These stations run their own operations independent of any affiliation with a network. They negotiate their own contracts for programming content and as a result, they have control of more advertising time for sales to local advertisers.

Independents, though, are not necessarily completely independent. Through the growth of "fourth" and "fifth" networks, such as Fox and WB, many now deliver some degree of "network" programming – including NFL football.

The bulk of independent programming consists of movies and syndicated shows – like game shows and sitcom or drama reruns. Some of these programs are quite popular, drawing significant local audiences.

Top 10 Cable Systems		
System Location	Operator	Basic Cable Customers
1. New York, NY	Time Warner	1,235,984
2. Long Island, NY	Cablevision Systems	683,718
3. Phoenix, AZ	Cox Communications	581,526
4. Orlando, FL	Bright House Networks	543,049
5. San Diego, CA	Cox Communications	530,000
6. Bronx/Brooklyn, NY	Cablevision Systems	502,205
7. Puget Sound, WA	Comcast	424,500
8. Pittsburgh, PA	Comcast	415,720
9. Chicago suburbs, IL	Comcast	390,602
10. Denver, CO	Comcast	369,844

Buying Cable.
More and more advertisers are buying into cable on a local-market basis.

Cable Systems.

Cable advertising provides a viable option for local advertisers. Audiences are more segmented, the costs are less, and advertisers can reach audiences with particular interests as well.

Many local advertisers are now using local cable and taking advantage of low-cost production offered by the providers.

For example, teenagers have been hard to reach on TV in a cost-effective manner. Special cable channels, such as MTV, offer new opportunities for local advertisers seeking a teen market.

As cable providers merge and consolidate, this will become an even more important area for both local and national media sales.

Interactive cable gives the viewer a way to respond to programming and provides a new level of involvement.

Advantages & Disadvantages.
Advantage: Sight & Sound.

Television, whether it's cable or broadcast, provides advertisers with the message potential of sight and sound. This can be a tremendous advantage, but it can also be detrimental if poorly conceived and executed.

It's easy to say "audio-visual integration" or "the words should match the pictures," but making a TV commercial that sells in a clear and entertaining fashion is always a challenge.

Disadavantage: Cost & Competition.

Television is also a challenge to many local advertisers because of high cost, production time, and competition with national advertising. While television production in a few large cities may be equal to that produced for national ads, most local television ads do not compare favorably.

It's easy to understand. It can be hard to compete with fewer resources overall and a production budget of a few thousand dollars. Developing creative ideas and execution at the local level is a challenge.

Yet, while locally produced advertising may not have the budget of a national campaign, it is still possible to produce creative and effective advertising on the local level.

Disadvantage: Longer Lead Time.

Producing television usually takes time as well as money.

Some local advertisers, particularly retailers, find this longer lead time to be an additional problem.

Resources for shooting and editing are usually much more limited (and much more expensive) than those needed for radio and newspaper.

It is also true that most local television stations require a greater lead time than newspapers or radio.

Another concern – advertisers need to remember that viewers will compare their ads to the more expensively produced ads for national advertisers that run in the same commercial break.

Many local advertisers, such as car dealers, or local "co-ops" of fast food franchises, benefit from television ads (or "stock footage") provided by manufacturers or national ad resources.

These ads only require a few seconds of local identification which can reduce costs substantially.

Disadvantage: Clutter & "Zapping."

Local ads can suffer from the same viewer inattention as national ads – audiences who leave the room when the advertising comes on and audiences who zap commercials and graze among channels.

And, as we mentioned previously, locally produced television advertising often compares poorly with the national ads surrounding it.

Still, it is a powerful medium.

Types of Local TV Usage.

Here are some of the reasons and some of the ways that local advertisers can use TV effectively:

• Some advertisers use television selectively as a supporting medium.

• Some advertisers find ad placement on the local news provides both coverage and impact.

• Local television is effective in promoting recognition.

• If showing the product in use is critical, television should be considered – it's great for demonstration.

• You can reach a lot of people. The large captive local audience can generate great reach in the marketplace.

• Institutional advertising on television allows a local store to get its name across to the viewing public without having to buy enough advertising to sell specific items. Many local stores and banks use television for this purpose around major holidays.

For these reasons, smart tactical thinking, in addition to strategic thinking, is essential when a local advertiser decides to use television.

For these reasons, many advertisers find local television too expensive for their ad budgets.

Television Audience Measurement.

Television use is measured by the quantity and demographics of viewers watching quarter hour segments.

Viewership is reported by time, viewer profile, and show.

Advertisers can match up the show itself with the viewers to make decisions about ad placement.

Geographic Selectivity.
City magazines offer local advertisers the advantages of national magazines without the excessive coverage.

Magazines, Part II.
Regional magazines offer advertisers an opportunity to focus coverage on a larger regional basis.

As noted in the radio section, the Portable People Meters allow detailed measurement of all television viewing.

Local stations use rating points to sell their advertising time to advertisers.

The most popular times with local advertisers are generally the local news hours and local sports, both of which draw high viewership. These local programs are rated separately from the network and syndicated programming, allowing advertisers to know which local programs and personalities have the largest audiences.

Magazines.
City Magazines.

This type of local magazine option offers an opportunity for certain kinds of local businesses to reach an upscale or geographically specific market.

Virtually every major city in America has at least one major city magazine – like Dallas and Chicago.

They deliver a high quality audience. Readers are generally in the upper economic levels with a higher-than-city-average discretionary income. Often, these magazines are also distributed at better hotels.

The quality audience and four-color reproduction in these magazines offers a good advertising option for specialty stores and restaurants.

Most local advertisers who include city magazines in their advertising programs use this as supplementary advertising.

Regional Magazines.

Many areas of the country have specific magazines that carry feature articles, commentary, and advertising related to that region.

For example, *Sunset*, based in Menlo Park, California, targets nine Western states and has sub-regional customization for Northern and Southern California, the mountains, and the desert. Other great examples include *Southern Living* and

Midwest Living – both of which are appropriately named for their specific regional coverage.

Magazine Advantages and Disadvantages.

City and regional magazines provide location-specific advertising for local, regional, and even national advertisers – all businesses with local outlets of some kind.

Since the content is of great interest to those living in the coverage area, city and regional magazines are ideal advertising vehicles for tourism, restaurants, area attractions, and specialty businesses of all kinds.

With glossy pages and excellent full color reproduction, these print vehicles are ideal for showing off high-end and niche specialty businesses.

The downside is similar to the downside of all magazines – a long lead time from when the ad is planned to when it appears. While some city magazines have a shorter-than-usual magazine turnaround, the time is still longer than for newspapers, television, radio, outdoor, and other local media.

Because of this, advertisers must plan ahead. Quick response to a market situation is not an option. Due to these factors, such magazines are often used as supplementary media.

Newest on the block are 'zines. These short, often for fun or personal info, mini-magazines are published online (could also in a few cases refer to desktop 'zines of similar content). Although becoming more and more popular, they are definitely niche publications and quite often are irreverent or esoteric in some way. These magazines typically carry very little advertising – although quite recently, some have been seeking advertising support. For their specific audience, they are well targeted and specific advertising could work. Definitely not mainstream, however.

Another 'zine approach is for a single sponsor or event – used as a supplemental media vehicle. Whether a major marketer, like Apple, or a small local band or business group, you can create a 'zine that combines audio (both music and narrative), photos, articles, and videos into an exciting multimedia product. Another approach is to put your website onto a disc.

Out-of-Home.

Unlike any other media, out-of-home is almost exclusively local in nature. This is one very place-based media class. While you may sometimes see a national product advertised on an outdoor location, such placement was most likely done for the purpose of local emphasis.

Outdoor advertising billboards and posters provide large-scale messages for continuous exposure to consumers outside of their homes.

Other types of outdoor – kiosks, transit signs, bus benches, balloons, taxi tops, airport signs, airplane trailer signs, stadium signs, building walls, and mall signs – make up the larger category called "out-of-home." A new method of transport advertising is cards with messages that hang down from the ceilings of subway and train cars. These put the messages very close to eye level for those commuters standing in the aisle.

Although the message is necessarily short, this kind of advertising can be effective in positioning a business in the audience mind and as reminder advertising.

Out-of-home advertising can provide such things as store or brand name awareness and location information (this type of message is often called a "directional").

Since the message has to be short, the combination of message and visual is crucial to success, as is frequency of exposure.

Simple messages can have a strong effect.

Some outdoor boards incorporate movement to draw further attention – particularly with new large-screen video technology.

Landmark Placements.
Certain high-traffic outdoor locations are known as "Landmark Placements" for their high-profile, high-priced, and highly demanded space, like this "stack" in Times Square.

Visuals Are Crucial.
Bright colors or surprising visual images are an important part of out-of-home advertising.

Local Advertisers Can Look Big.
Outdoor is one medium where small advertisers can have a fairly even playing field.

However, the speed at which the message is seen and the distractions inherent in traffic mean that the audience needs to have relatively long-term exposure to retain the message.

The driving audience is exposed to outdoor ads on a regular basis on well-traveled routes. This kind of high intensity can provide good supporting advertising for certain kinds of businesses.

This also allows for other tactical approaches.

For example, a directional – providing location information – can be very effective, essentially providing a store with an extension of their location.

Exposure vs. Recall.

Short, powerful messages are most likely to be effective.

As with all advertising, exposure does not necessarily mean recall of the message.

Recent research also indicates that audience involvement can further increase the effectiveness of outdoor messages.

And, since outdoor can build up very heavy frequencies (it is not uncommon for your audience to pass the board once or twice a day), additional involvement – ranging from humor to the time and temperature – can provide additional effectiveness for your message.

Outdoor Audience Measurement.

Outdoor is measured in terms of a "showing" or the number of people exposed to the advertisement over a given period of time.

This measurement indicates the level of exposure to an outdoor board in one day – a showing of 100 means that the number of people exposed to the advertisement in one day was equal to the number of people in the market.

This makes no distinction between reach and frequency.

Advantages and Disadvantages.

Out-of-home advertising is ideal for reaching customers on the go. Ad messages can be changed frequently. Often, the messages reach people who are driving, walking, or riding

Short and Sweet.
Brevity doesn't have to be a disadvantage.

Drawing More Attention.
Many advertisers use display ads to attract attention to their business.

on public transportation. Many times, these are captive audiences.

For example, on a bus or subway, people are exposed to the messages for a long time. A message on all public transportation for a period of time or on many outdoor boards along a busy city route gives an advertisement both reach and frequency.

Such ads can be attention-getting and compelling. A notable example is the California billboard for a weight-loss company. The message, which reached a million people, stated, "When the aliens come, they'll eat the fat people first." It was controversial, arguably in terrible taste, offensive, but drew much attention. The owner of the outdoor company reported the controversy led to increased business for the weight-loss firm and for his media firm as well. Obviously, one does not have to go to that extreme.

The necessary brevity of the messages can be a disadvantage.

For this reason, out-of-home advertising is most often used for reminder ads and as a supplement to other local advertising.

Directory Advertising.

The Yellow Pages – and similar directories – provide sales information that is always at hand.

While the basic directory listing provides only the name, address, and phone number of businesses by category, many local advertisers use display ads in the directory for the following reasons:

• To attract attention
• To state the range of services provided
• To position the business as a category leader

Position within the listings, clever headlines, and color make some ads stand out more than others.

Even position in the alphabet can have an effect – which you may see where someone has named their company AAAccurate – or something similar.

PLUMBERS

A-AAAA Plumbing
Romvl
Chicago Tel No 773 282-2878
A-AAAA Plumbing & Sewer 773 282-2878
A Aaba Bathrooms & Kitchens AABA
Cicero..773 296-4090
A Aardvark Plumbing Cicero...............773 395-9000
A-Ability Plumbing & Sewerage Co
Toll Free Dial '1'......................................800 654-6080
A Active Plumbing & Sewer
4651 N Elston Ave Chgo.........................773 583-0075
A Best One Plumbing & Sewer
2944 N Narragansett Ave Chgo 773 804-0101
Or..773 539-5868
A Better Man Plumbing & Sewer
Chgo Tel No...773 286-9351
A Bob Egan Plumbing & Sewer
830 W 89th St Chgo 773 723-9418
A Bob Egan Plumbing & Sewer Chgo.773 581-8091
A-Buds Plumbing & Sewer
Chgo Tel No...773 568-2348

AAAlphabet.

Directory listings are alphabetized, and an early or even first listing can be very important.

There are some restrictions and industry policies that work to prevent abuse in this area.

Listing vs. Display.

Advertisers must balance the expense of the additional size and color in a display ad with:

- The size of the audience using the directory
- The ability of the ad to attract that key target audience
- Place of directory advertising in the available ad budget

This will vary for different advertisers – even those in the same category.

Location Issues.

For some advertisers, a convenient location may be the primary reason customers shop there. In that case, a simple listing may be all that is needed to let potential customers know the store is nearby.

For advertisers in more distant locations, increased directory advertising may be necessary to compensate for the less desirable location.

For example, a key determinant of choosing a branch bank or drugstore may be convenience to work or home.

Then, as long as the service is satisfactory, customers are unlikely to look for other options.

Purchase Patterns.

For less frequent and higher risk purchases – like building a fence, remodeling a kitchen, or having carpets cleaned – buyers will often choose among a number of local companies.

The company that provides the best information about itself may be the one that gets the first inquiry.

Annual Decisions.

Directory advertising is a once-a-year decision. The influence on attracting buyers must be balanced with the limitations on spending in other media.

Virtually all businesses need some kind of listing. But, just as with all media choices, the place of each type of advertising in the overall media mix requires careful consideration.

Enhanced Visuals.

Competitive directories may even compete on points like printing process and color reproduction.

The selection of categories and cross listings with similar businesses is another choice that should be made with the entire year advertising plan in mind.

Many cities have several directories beyond the Yellow Pages – so advertisers must think of these options as well.

For most advertisers, directory advertising is a supplement to other local advertising.

Most local advertisers feel that basic information listings are essential, but that newspaper, radio, and direct mail are needed to reach out to the audience with different messages throughout the year.

Advantages & Disadvantages.

Here are some additional considerations.

A Directional Medium.

The Yellow Pages generally is not a medium that creates awareness or demand for products or services.

People don't pick up the Yellow Pages to look for a car. They do, however, pick up the Yellow Pages to look for a car dealer that carries a specific model after they've been influenced by advertising in other media.

Yellow Pages is a "directional" medium: its major strength is that it points willing consumers in a direction where their purchase can be made.

Yellow Pages, then, can be said to be the final link in the buying cycle.

After seeing ads in other media urging them to buy certain products, consumers turn to Yellow Pages to help them decide where to buy.

A Voluntary Medium.

The Yellow Pages is "willingly consulted." Yellow Pages advertising does not intrude on editorial content.

When a consumer opens a Yellow Pages directory it is for the purpose of viewing advertisements and collecting information for a possible purchase – a critical difference from turning on the radio or TV or opening up a newspaper.

People voluntarily seek Yellow Pages information when they're ready to buy.

Wide Availability.

Yellow Pages directories are just about everywhere.

They are distributed to every home and business with a phone and to many public phones, as well. Over 350 million Yellow Pages directories are distributed annually.

Long Life Span – Long Lead Time.

Yellow Pages' main strength – long life span – can also be a problem. Directories are generally published once a year, therefore, a business's Yellow Pages ad cannot feature price or other sales information that can change before the life of the directory is over.

Accuracy is even more important. A typo or phone number error in a newspaper ad is troubling, but minor.

In a Yellow Pages ad, it can be a disaster.

Sales representatives often call on advertisers six to eight months prior to directory distribution, due to production and printing requirements.

Audience Measurement.

There are two measures of Yellow Pages' audience size: circulation and usage.

Circulation.

Similar to other print media, Yellow Pages' audience size is measured in terms of circulation, which is either the number of households or individuals possessing a directory.

Circulation data is an important indicator of a directory's potential in a marketplace. After all, an ad cannot be seen if a directory is not in an individual's home.

Usage.

Given the fact that many individuals have more than one directory in their home and use them differently, a method for distinguishing directory usage from directory possession was developed by National Yellow Pages Monitor (NYPM), a division of NFO Research.

Yellow Pages directory "ratings" are compiled by tabulating Yellow Pages usage data recorded in diaries over a one-week period by a representative sample of consumers in a market area. Data collected from the weekly diaries are accumulated over a calendar year, after which share ratings are calculated and reported.

These ratings are important because they allow advertisers to distinguish between two directories on more than the basis of gross circulation.

Direct Marketing.

Direct mail has been the fastest growing advertising medium and has gained share of advertising dollars steadily over the past ten years.

It provides an opportunity for local advertisers to reach the target audience in their homes with messages designed specifically for them.

It provides a self-contained sales message that can be targeted to specific demographics or buying history.

When direct mail incorporates couponing, or some other form of direct response, it also provides a built-in measurement device.

Because it is measurable, direct mail, more than any other medium, is judged by specific results.

"DataBase Marketing."

"Database marketing" is the name for the approach which is becoming increasingly popular with local advertisers who are now able to develop databases of current and potential customers.

Direct mail is currently the major type of database marketing – but not the only one. The field also includes telemarketing and will probably include other forms of direct contact – such as computer e-mail.

Direct mail provides the retailer with a great deal of control. Messages can be customized for certain types of cus-

Database Marketing.

This mailing is from a local restaurant. They noticed from their database a customer who hadn't ordered in a while. So, they sent a coupon reminder.

Frequency and Different Messages.
More mailings from Philly's Best. Notice
that each offer is different and each card
says "Please mention when ordering." This
way, offer responses can be measured.

tomers, and the customer's name can even be integrated into the printed piece.

Direct mail is relatively easy to measure. It is possible to provide the advertiser with information about what kinds of ad messages and approaches work in different situations.

For example, advertisers can try different types of messages and test which draws the most store traffic or sales.

Database formation is relatively easy for any advertiser who has a computer. Lists can be purchased or developed from a customer base of checks, charges, and mail response. Some local retailers share database information.

Lists can be segmented by neighborhood, by buying history, by location, or other categories. Commercial lists are also useful for some kinds of local businesses.

For example, suppose a local car dealer decides to target all owners of the types of cars he sells and particularly wants to reach owners of cars three or four years old – people who may be ready to trade in their older cars. The dealer can buy a list of all such owners in his market area from the state Division of Motor Vehicles.

Costs & Problems.

One problem with database use is the continual need to update. Local advertisers who develop their own lists may find that many names are no longer useful, particularly in areas where there is high mobility.

Another issue is cost. Even with slightly reduced postal rates, your message, including postage, printing, envelopes, and tasks such as folding, stuffing, and sorting, can result in a piece that costs 25-50¢ a customer – or more.

On a per impression basis, this is far more expensive than other forms of advertising. Of course, you can do much more with that single impression.

Other cost-reduction options, such as group mailing with other marketers, accomplish the reduction of costs, but they

Money Mailer.
This national service offers zip code-by-zip code advertising in bulk packs to save postage costs for individual advertisers

also reduce the impact. Card decks, for example, have a notoriously low response rate.

The customization capability of direct mail makes it attractive to local advertisers. Other local media find it to be a challenge to their own advertising sales success.

Computer-based technology is enabling the small advertiser to use direct mail to target specifically with the same tools used by large companies.

From mailings to your customer base, group mailing to nearby zip codes, or mailing to special lists, every marketer should examine some sort of direct marketing program.

Many direct mail providers feature a sales force where the sales representative plays a key role formulating the program.

Other programs, such as Val-Pak, feature a local franchise arrangement where each franchisee will focus on retailers in a specific area.

"New Media."

New media development is rapid in today's technologically advanced world.

A convergence of technological capability provides new means of reaching audiences with information of all types.

Now messages can be targeted more exactly and transmitted almost instantly to all parts of the world.

Much of this new technologically driven media offers opportunities for advertising as well.

Here are some of the most important new areas for local marketers – in alphabetical order:

Audiotext.

Audiotext uses a combination of phone and computer capability to provide users with instant online connections to advertisers and information.

It's voice mail for advertisers.

Daily newspapers are rapidly developing audiotext capability that allows readers to call in for additional information – sports scores, stock market prices, updates on developing stories – and allows advertisers to provide a voice message as an additional service to their other advertising.

For example, with audiotext, an employer can list a phone number in a classified ad. When interested applicants call the number, they may be asked a series of screening questions designed to sort out eligible applicants. Employers can then review the taped interviews and call back selected applicants.

A similar technique can be used for other kinds of sales, including real estate. Advertisers may receive a certain number of free call-ins and reviews for the price of the ad.

Audiotext capability may be offered at a special rate with regular advertising, or it may be sold separately depending upon the policies of the provider.

Advertisers can provide "800" numbers (which are free of charge) or "900" numbers (which have a per-minute charge). These calls provide respondents with additional information.

Many papers are initiating voice personal services – allowing readers to respond to personal ads in the paper. Responses are recorded for the person placing the ad to review.

Again, these calls may be free or there may be a charge.

Alternate Delivery Systems.

These systems provide home delivery of advertising, magazines, and other information as a substitute to using the mail.

Some newspapers provide alternate delivery utilizing their regular carrier service; there are also separate companies that provide this kind of delivery.

The charge to advertisers is calculated by the type of piece and by the length of the route. This kind of service provides advertisers with control over both content and delivery time.

In-store Couponing and Tracking.

The introduction of scanners for bar codes now allows tracking of purchases as well as inventory control.

Many stores have also added coupon generating capability at the cash register. With this, scanning of one product may

Valued Customers.
Preferred shopper cards offer the store the opportunity to track customers and, as a result, customize offers.

produce a coupon for a discount at the time, a special offer for a next visit, or a coupon for a competitive brand.

Some stores have developed a database of regular customers who receive a "preferred customer card." When the card is scanned, all purchases are recorded in the database, giving the store a complete shopping profile of that customer – who is then sent special offers and information in the mail and provided with coupons and recipes from a dispenser at the check out counter.

VisionValue is one of the leaders in this area, with initial funding from Procter & Gamble and RR Donnelly.

Kiosks and "Interactive."

More stores and malls will have kiosks with interactive computer programs for locating items within the store and distributing material like coupons, product information, and recipes.

Online and CD-ROM.

Media and messages can now be delivered via broadband through a variety of different online services.

Most of these interactive systems are programmed to carry advertising as well as information and often offer the opportunity of buying directly through the program – or at least receiving more information.

You can literally have your own custom newspaper, magazine, or information delivered to your computer.

In addition, several media companies are developing publications that will be delivered via CD-ROM and feature music, moving pictures, and interactive features.

Although some of these systems are in the fledgling stage at present, they do offer the potential for advertising messages as a means of reaching customers.

Catalogs are already being offered in a CD-ROM format, where the computer can even transmit your order over the phone lines.

As we get up to speed on the information superhighway, there will be more and more activity in this area.

Newsletters for Niches.

Another result of the computer has been the increased ease of creating and producing quality newsletters.

Many marketers use newsletters to reach their niche markets. While these are similar in some respects to direct mail and database marketing, they have an additional function.

The integration of information and selling messages directed at an identified and segmented target market make these newsletters – which may be delivered by traditional methods or via the Internet – a key medium for not only selling very specialized products and services, but for building a relationship with the target group.

"Relationship Marketing."

For many years, advertising's job ended when the sale was made – and advertising, quite properly, focused on recruiting new customers.

Today, advertisers and marketers also need to be more concerned with maintaining and building a relationship with current customers.

In addition to starting the initial dialogue with a new customer, marketing programs are working to develop a deeper dialogue and relationship with their current customers.

Each of the media forms we've discussed can play this relationship-building role as well – strengthening the relationships between marketers and their customers.

Cross-selling and Synergies.

One of the newest opportunities is the increased use of cross-selling among media and the synergies that provides for advertising. Examples are: combinations of radio with print, with TV, with outdoor, and with Internet. All of these work well together.

Niche Newsletters.

Newsletters are gaining ground as an advertiser-sponsored media. Like this media newsletter from MediaPost.com; sponsored, as you can see, by Forbes Online.

Radio, Outdoor, Concerts

Cross-Selling.

Clear Channel is a major media company cross-selling advertisers seeking multimedia message delivery.

All media has the opportunity to not only cross-promote for synergy, but also to sponsor events, concerts, and sports.

How many media-sponsored events can you find in your city or region? How many are cross-sponsored?

Summary.

This chapter has been largely focused on the geographic definition of the word "market."

We've reviewed each of the major media for specific aspects of its geographic coverage of markets. While we have hinted at other aspects, we'll really cover these in detail in Chapter 9.

For now, we've covered newspapers, radio, television, and magazines. All are media with both national and local geographic possibilities. We've tried to show here how a local advertiser in your own city might try to promote his business using each media.

In this chapter, we've also covered some other important media options available for local advertisers. We discussed out-of-home advertising options. Out-of-home included such possibilities as outdoor boards, transit shelters, bus benches, stadium signage etc. Remember that out-of-home is a uniquely local media. If used at all by a national advertiser, its purpose is strictly to provide local emphasis.

Yellow Pages and Directory advertising was much the same, another very local and even directional media.

Finally, we covered a wide range of direct and "new," alternative media increasingly available for the use of local advertisers. Each of these media options affords a level of precision marketing that is most needed by local advertisers.

Discussion Questions.
1. Newspapers.

Explain how newspapers are really selling two products.

Which section of the newspaper is best for advertisers? Explain your answer.

From a reader's point of view, what are the differences between a daily newspaper and a Sunday newspaper?

2. Radio.

What is a radio station format?

Is radio a local medium or a national medium?

How should local advertisers use radio?

3. Television.

What are the differences between a local network affiliate station and a local independent station?

How do local TV stations manage programming?

How do local TV stations make money?

4. Magazines.

What makes city or regional magazines a good choice for local advertisers?

What kind of advertisers are more likely to use city or regional magazines?

5. Out-of-Home.

What makes out-of-home advertising so popular these days?

Exercises.

1. Consider each section of the newspaper listed below and describe an example of a *local* advertiser situation for each section. Name and describe the business and explain why the business is well suited for that section of the paper. Choose a different business for each section.

    a. Business

    b. Local News

    c. Sports

    d. Travel

    e. Arts and Entertainment

2. **Get a consumer magazine SRDS** from your school or local library and find a listing for your local city magazine or a regional magazine that covers your area. Name the magazine and answer the following questions.

    a. **Circulation.** What is the total circulation of the magazine, and what percent of the total circulation is subscription circulation versus single copy sales?

    b. **Cost.** What is the cost of advertising for a full-page, four-color ad? Is there a discount for multiple insertions? What is the discount structure?

    c. **Special Issues.** Does this magazine offer any special issues? Does advertising in the special issues cost more than in the regular magazine?

    d. **Sales Positions.** Does this magazine list any advertising sales representatives and contact information?

3. **Visit a major grocery store and take note of ALL of the many forms of advertising you see there**. You'll see ads on shopping carts, ads on the shelves, coupons by the packages, ads on the floor, ads on the windows and on the doors of the refrigerated-cases. You might even see TV screens and kiosks. Take note of all forms you see and notice if any shoppers are pay attention or not.

Write a short paper (1-2 pages typed) describing the advertising you see and the effect it seems to have (or not have) on shoppers. Do you think the advertisers got effective and valuable exposure for their messages?

8 Local Media Planning

Local Talent.
Local companies depend on ad messages to connect with their market.

Y OUR MARKET – EVERY MARKET – contains a dynamic combination of media choices.

They compete with each other.

They reinforce each other.

They can work individually or in combination.

Let's see how marketers and media work together.

Three Keys to Success.

Each is a key section in this chapter.

- **Matching Media with Markets**
- **The Local Market Profile**
- **Research on a Local Level**

They add up to success in working in local media.

Chapter Organization.

This chapter will cover media planning on a local level.

Many of the same principles apply, but we're not going to rehash everything we just went through in Part Two.

In the three sections mentioned above, we'll demonstrate how to put the media together for local client businesses.

Matching Media with Markets.

We'll talk about the decisions a media planner must make.

The planner's goal as a marketing partner is to find the perfect media match.

Neighborhood Connection.

National companies, like franchised restaurant chains, need to connect with their local markets.

The Local Market Profile.

In this section, we'll show you a format for developing a fairly complete Local Market Profile.

We'll give you data and lots of questions to answer.

Finding answers for your own market will take a lot of time and effort. But, it will be worth it.

Research on a Local Level.

Here, we'll cover some research tools you can use to fill in the blanks in your Local Market Profile.

And then, finally, we'll show you local market research in action – we'll show a few examples of how you can pull together state-of-the-art information and "street smart" judgment into a plan that will result in more business for your client.

The overriding theme of this chapter is application, so we'll throw in a lot of examples along the way.

An Overview.

We covered this in the previous chapter, but let's remind ourselves briefly by taking a quick "snapshot" of the overall media mix in a local market.

Again, as we review the mix, think of the specific examples in your market.

The Local Media Mix.

Newspaper and radio remain top local media choices.

Direct mail is strong and increasing in share every year.

Television – network affiliates, cable, and independents – provides a growing array of options.

Other traditional forms, such as outdoor, transit, and specialty advertising, may all be used by local merchants depending upon budget and strategy.

Local listings – Yellow Pages and other directories – are a necessity for every business, and today there are new electronic options for the listings as well.

New technology adds opportunities for retailers and service businesses on an almost daily basis.

With electronic options, like online computer services and audio text, a phone call can put would-be customers in touch with stores and businesses in virtually every category.

Increasing choice (and expense) makes it harder for retailers to choose where to place messages.

Matching Media with Markets.

Some businesses need to focus their messages and media on narrow target markets. Other businesses want to reach as broad a market as possible.

The right media match will make it easier and more efficient for retailers to get in touch with the right kind of would-be customers.

To do your job in a local market you need to understand the market overall, and then understand the best ways to match this wide range of media options with specific marketer needs.

This is a decision process that demands good information on the media options in your market.

Important Decisions.

Some key factors in making those media choices are the "breadth" of the audience and, particularly with local businesses, geographic considerations.

Broad or Narrow Audiences.

Local media can reach broad or narrow audiences.

Depending on client needs and strategy, one medium or a combination may be used. A single client may vary the media mix throughout the year according to differing goals.

Some Examples.

For example, a local restaurant in a resort town, where summer tourists add to both the population and business, may use the Thursday or Friday newspaper on a regular year-round basis. They may also run radio and television ads throughout the year as reminders for weekends, holidays, or special occasions.

During the busiest time of the year, additional radio and television may be used.

Ads may also be placed in a local magazine highlighting weekly events during the busy season.

A toy store may rely on radio, some newspaper, and direct mail with special offers, coupons, and special birthday offers to a database of customers on a regular basis. But during the Christmas season, broader reach media – an additional newspaper schedule and local television – may be added.

Geographic Considerations.

Geographic considerations are also important. As the saying goes, "location, location, and location."

Here are some examples of the questions you need to ask.

• Is a large, broad-audience medium needed for the job?

• Or can a small newspaper or other local publication that circulates in one area of the city or county do the job as well?

• Would a concentration of outdoor along a well-traveled route or within one neighborhood area be effective?

• How close is the audience to the business?

A small restaurant may draw from an entire city – but the surrounding neighborhood may be the prime target and return the most business for advertising dollars spent.

If that is the case, a truly local medium – like a zoned newspaper section, a neighborhood paper, direct mail within a local zip code (or, more targeted yet, to a specific customer database) – may be both less expensive and more effective.

The savvy retailer must think of cost per actual customer or cost per sale.

While a larger circulation medium may offer less cost per person or cost per thousand, much of the advertising dollar may be spent to reach people outside the primary audience.

For this reason, many advertisers consider this kind of buy to be a waste of their ad dollars.

Directing Traffic.
Direct mail within a zip-code zone can be both less expensive and more effective for a local business like a restaurant.

Same Location Different Markets.

Here's an example. Let's consider two local retailers right next to each other in the same small shopping strip.

DeLuxe Cleaners is a dry cleaner owned by Fred Brown.

Betters' Better Gourmet is owned by Sally and Bill Betters and is a gourmet take-out food store and deli primarily featuring pastas and sauces that come ready to heat or frozen.

The deli also offers salad greens and a selection of wines, sparkling waters, and fruit juice. All food is freshly made on the premises using only the finest quality. (Of course, the food is somewhat more expensive than pasta from the frozen food or deli section of a local grocery chain.)

They also offer special orders for large parties on a pick-up-and-go basis with a two-day advance order policy.

The two businesses share these things in common:

- **Same location**
- **Sufficient on-site parking**
- **Shopping center on a major commuting street**
- **New buildings with plenty of light and space**
- **Locally owned and managed**
- **Neighborhood identity**
- **New residential areas nearby**
- **Repeat business – ability to build loyalty**
- **Personalized, friendly service**
- **Lack of competition in immediate area**
- **A history of successful operations**

Continued on next page…

New Technologies – New Options.

As technology adds options for even the smallest businesses, new media opportunities will evolve.

The wide range of the Internet and the narrow range of local cable TV are just two examples.

It is important for both the retail marketer and the local media planner to be aware of all the opportunities available and their potential effectiveness in meeting the specific goals of the business.

Understanding all available media options is also a part of knowing how to develop the most advantageous media mix.

Local Map Exercise.

Review the example in the sidebar. You'll see that even businesses in virtually the same location may need to think about their media in very different ways.

One way to begin to think about how local retail markets are organized and the needs of different kinds of businesses is to choose one area of your own city and map out the kinds of businesses in that area.

Get a good-sized map and find a wall where you can hang it up for a while as you get a feel for the area.

- Use colored pencils, pins, or dots
- Have at least five retailer categories: clothing stores, supermarkets, family restaurants, fast food restaurants, etc.

Make a sheet that indicates the category code with the names of the retailers in the area in each category.

Note how many are in each category type (dry cleaners, grocery, shoe store, video store, etc.) and how close they are to one another. Which stores are most competitive with one another by both category and geography?

With your colored pencil, also note major routes nearby that would make it convenient for shoppers to reach these businesses on the way to and from work.

Think about the most effective media for each of these businesses. How often do you think they need to advertise?

A media planner might service clients for the entire shopping strip based upon geographic location, small business size, and local ownership factors.

And for these same reasons it might be tempting to recommend the same media plan for each of these clients.

But the needs and goals of these businesses are very different.

Let's think about them.

Business #1 – DeLuxe Cleaners.

Customers come to Fred's because of convenience and quality of service.

Fred's shop has already earned a reputation for good workmanship, pleasant service, and on-time work.

Many patrons drop off clothes on the way to work, so Fred opens the store at 7AM, and business is steady until 8:30 or 9AM. Customers also come in on their way home, so he stays open until 7PM.

Fred knows many of his customers by name. Most of them live within two miles of the business. He estimates only 10% of the customers live beyond his primary neighborhood area and use him because he's on their way to work.

Typically, these customers bring in bigger loads of shirts and come by once a week at most, on the way to or from work.

Fred thinks of DeLuxe as a largely neighborhood business.

He knows of two other dry cleaners within three miles, one of them on the same major thoroughfare.

Continued on next page…

Do they need media that would reach the whole city, or are they better served by a neighborhood medium?

Thinking about the individual businesses as needing to position themselves competitively and reach their target customers in the most cost efficient and effective way possible will make you better able to think about all the media choices they must make.

Getting a "bird's eye view" gives you a perspective you don't always get at the ground level.

Different Market Characteristics.

Now, let's try to look at an entire market.

First, we'll cover three examples, and then you'll need to develop a profile of your own market and the Media Mix.

There are similarities and differences in every local market. Let's look at three examples:

• **Market A – a large city**
• **Market B – a small city with a major university**
• **Market C – a tourist area**

Market A.

Chicago, for example, is a large city with many suburbs in the surrounding counties.

Market A.

Market A is a large city with many suburbs in the counties surrounding it.

Media Summary:

There is at least one major metropolitan daily in the main city.

Several smaller dailies serve the suburbs, and the metro daily publishes zoned tabloid editions targeted toward each of the suburban markets and inserts them into the larger papers delivered to these suburbs.

In addition, there are several weekly papers serving smaller areas and a monthly city magazine.

On the broadcast side, there are several local TV stations, including network affiliates and independent stations.

Two cable companies split this market.

There are over 40 radio stations, and every format imaginable is represented from all-news to religious.

Other media forms are also in great abundance:

• Two major outdoor companies and a company that sells signs on the sides of busses. A bus stop poster franchise has recently been awarded by the city.

• Numerous direct mail services are available, including Val-Pack. Mailers and inserts are also done by some of the weekly newspapers.

• There are two competing phone directories.

Major Challenges and Unique Opportunities.

Clearly, Market A offers options for nearly any kind of local and regional advertising package. The larger advertisers use a mix of mass reach media – newspapers and TV – and supplement with direct mail, radio, and outdoor.

Since special events, such as sports and concerts, bring people into the area on a regular basis, hotel magazines are popular with some retailers.

Specific neighborhoods may be targeted with any of the smaller media. Several larger advertisers – such as department stores at the large regional malls – regularly place full-page ads in the suburban dailies as Market A has a large retail trading zone that draws from a 50- to 70-mile range for regular shopping and from an even broader range for seasonal shopping.

Smaller advertisers find the metro paper expensive. Many feel the geographic reach is much more than they need.

Some place small ads on a weekly basis for fear of losing some potential customers. Others rely on the zoned neighborhood editions to concentrate on their own local area exclusively. Still others do not use the print media at all, but rely on a combination of radio and direct mail.

Many of these smaller advertisers have figured out their own markets and found media combinations to serve them in the most effective way they can afford.

Same Location – Different Markets (Cont.)

But the Betters' gourmet food business needs a geographically broader base medium as well. This non-routine business probably cannot survive – and is unlikely to thrive – with a strictly local clientele. This is just a shopping strip, not a major business center.

Bill and Sally would be missing potential customers if they fail to advertise more broadly. There are lots of people in other parts of town who might like to sample the gourmet pasta. Since much of it is sold frozen, a monthly trip to stock up is a definite possibility. And since supplying special orders for parties is another goal of this business, the more people who know about this service, the better.

Possible Plans...

One possible plan for Fred might include a local neighborhood paper (if available) and direct mail (zip code and customer database).

Sally and Bill can use some of the same, but their newspaper dollars might be better spent in a larger daily, particularly in the Wednesday food section and weekend editions.

They might also want to consider the local weekend entertainment section and a few "free" papers with an arts and entertainment focus.

Both businesses would want to have some kind of promotion targeted to newcomers to the area. They might do this through a Welcome Wagon promotion, through local realtors, or by direct mail to the newer areas.

Although every type and size of business has differing media needs, most of the smaller, truly neighborhood businesses find a combination of zoned editions, radio, occasional direct mail, and special promotions works well.

Cable TV is popular with some businesses, due to the relatively low cost, but many feel the reach is too great, since their cable systems reach far beyond the local trading area.

Some smaller businesses have an appeal beyond their own locality. They tend to rely on the metro paper and TV in a way similar to larger advertisers, although budgets are smaller.

Welcome to Ann Arbor

Market B.
Ann Arbor, Michigan – proud home to the University of Michigan Wolverines.

Market B.

Market B is a small city with a major state university.

Although the university is a dominant presence, the town also serves as a suburb for a larger metro area nearby.

Retailers and businesses in Market B distinguish between the college student market and the regular town market and tend to use different media to reach each contingent.

Media Summary:

For the college market, the college newspaper, three popular radio stations, flyers, posters, and word-of-mouth are the usual media choices.

Reaching the regular town market is more difficult. Print options are a small five-day-a-week local paper, a large daily from the nearby metro area, and a shopper.

Local cable is available, as is network affiliate television from the metro area. There are 14 radio stations.

Long-term local residents tend to use a lot of the media from the metro area, but many smaller businesses feel the rates are too high and the reach much more than needed for the kind of traffic they could generate.

The metro daily puts out a local insert three times a week, which is popular with advertisers.

Major Challenges and Unique Opportunities.

The general feeling is that it is harder to make media choices in this market than it would be in a city of similar size but without so much media coming in from the outside.

Local merchants feel the town is neither a real stand-alone city nor a real suburb. The usual media mix is the local paper, local inserts in the metro daily, cable, and radio.

For the college market, coupons in the college paper are quite effective for some local restaurants, but some managers feel they only bring in customers during the coupon discount time.

Market C.

Market C is a tourist area with several small towns strung along a beach.

Year-round population is around 30,000 and much greater during the heavy tourist season.

The nearest shopping mall is 20 miles away, though there is an outlet strip.

Market C is filled with small stores of all kinds to serve both year-round and tourist shoppers.

There are numerous restaurants, hotels, and condos throughout.

Media Summary:

Market C has one small daily newspaper, one semi-weekly, and 14 radio stations. While cable is available throughout the area, both it and all network affiliate television comes from a larger city 50 miles away.

A special weekly magazine is published during tourist season. An annual directory and tourist attraction magazine is published every year.

Major Challenges and Unique Opportunities.

Businesses in Market C rely heavily on radio.

Market C.

The Outer Banks of North Carolina is an Atlantic coast tourist area comprising several smaller beach communities.

For entertainment businesses, a special Friday section of the daily paper is important, as well.

There's not as much direct mail in Market C as in non-tourist markets of the same size since even regular year-round residents move in and out more often.

Virtually all businesses are listed in the directory, and many participate in a hotel package which offers listings and coupons. Outdoor is popular with restaurants and hotels, although there is a move to ban outdoor boards from the more scenic areas.

Market C businesses also advertise in the markets where tourists come from. Newspaper ads in Sunday travel editions in cities within driving range are judged quite effective.

The Media Mix Evolution.

Market A, Market B, and Market C are three very different markets with many possible choices and combinations in each.

Notice how media forms have developed to meet the needs of each market. Sometimes they are the result of large media companies modifying their products to meet local needs, and sometimes they are the result of an entrepreneur seeing an unfilled media niche in the marketplace.

This evolution is going on all the time.

It is simultaneously primitive and sophisticated – reps for local media make old-fashioned sales calls at the same time they use the latest computer technology to produce the paper.

This evolution simultaneously features success and failure. New media forms emerge, old ones go their way.

This is the way media evolves to meet the needs of business. As you look at your market, be sure to look for the evolutionary trends taking place.

The Local Market Profile.

You have to know your market.

You have to know the people in the market.

You have to know the media in the market.

You have to know how things work in your market.

Media planners are expected to be media and market experts.

That's just as true on the local level as it is nationally. Only locally, you have to rely on you own hard work – instead of expensive national media research.

Homework and Fieldwork.

A strong overall knowledge of your local market is the foundation of a successful career in local marketing, local market media planning, and even local market media sales.

Whichever career direction you choose, a good knowledge of the local market will be useful.

Even if you change markets, as often happens, knowing how to develop local market knowledge from scratch will be a foundation for building success in any new market.

The Local-Market Knowledge Base.

Researching your market is both a methodology and a way of thinking. And they work together.

It's a combination of state-of-the-art and "street smart." In this section, we'll cover the two dramatically different mind-sets you need for local media planning.

Getting to Know Your Market.

To really know your market, you have to be state of the art and street smart.

Sometimes you can use sophisticated marketing information to help an unsophisticated client make important marketing decisions.

And sometimes you have to go with your instincts.

Spotting a trend or opportunity and being the first to capitalize on it often means getting there before some market survey makes it obvious to everyone.

Sometimes you can use impressive amounts of data to identify the characteristics of an audience. And sometimes you need impressive amounts of insight and empathy. Sometimes understanding what's important to a client and that client's customers is as important as a demographic profile.

Market Knowledge = Added Value.

To function as a marketing partner, you must know your market in all its dimensions. For you are delivering market knowledge and market opportunity.

That's the added value that today's successful media person brings to every interaction. That's the extra dimension of effectiveness added to every successful program.

It pays off in a better match of marketers to a media's audience and a better developed message for that audience.

And it pays off in a faster, more effective response to opportunities in the local marketplace.

Existing Knowledge + New Information = Opportunity.

What would you tell someone if you were pitching them to locate a new business in your market?

- **Is the market growing?**
- **What is the media of the market?**
- **What kind of businesses are already there?**
- **Are some businesses moving out?**
- **Are new shopping centers coming in?**
- **Who competes and where? What's going on?**

Whichever you choose to emphasize, all of these factors depend on local market knowledge.

When a new question arises, you develop answers (or hypotheses) by integrating new information with an existing (and expanding) knowledge base.

That's why it's worth saying again – to plan successfully, you have to know your local market. So, let's get started.

An Overall Approach.

First, you have to know what to look for.

Differences and Commonalities.

Every market is different. Each city and town has strong points – and they are sometimes quite unique.

Comparing seasonal sales curves would show that Destin, Florida, a Gulf of Mexico beach and fishing community is quite different from Nantucket, Massachusetts, an Atlantic Ocean beach community.

Demographic analysis would show that Tucson, Arizona, is quite different from Fort Wayne, Indiana.

Yet, they all have some things in common. Destin and Nantucket have very similar types of tourist-based industries, and both the high-tech market of Tucson and the "Rust Belt" city of Fort Wayne have a very diverse and dynamic industrial base with some surprising similarities.

More Diversity – More Similarity.

Nationally (and internationally), every market is becoming more diverse and, at the same time, every market is becoming more similar.

What does this mean?

Once, small markets were fairly homogenous – even though there were income differences, people were very much like each other, went to similar churches, held similar beliefs, had similar (and narrower) purchasing and eating habits, and they even had fairly similar media habits.

After all, there were fewer choices.

Today, virtually every market is more diverse – within each market are people with a broader range of interests, consumption patterns, and lifestyles.

Across all of those markets, there are more and more niche markets that have a lot in common with each other.

Understanding these complex relationships and how they apply to your local market is an important part of a media sales person's intellectual capital.

State of the Art & Street Smart.

As we said before, you need both methodology and instinct. State-of-the-art methodology and street-smart instinct.

You will have a wide range of marketing research tools at your disposal. In the world of local media, sometimes you can base your decisions on state-of-the-art research and sometimes you have to operate on street smarts.

It's more than intellect. The best media planners are the ones who can sense when something is going on – and come up with ten ways to make that something work to their advantage. It's almost instinctive.

It's understanding how a new shopping mall on one side of town may have an impact on businesses all over town.

And it means knowing about a change in your market as soon as possible – before it shows up in a research report.

That's why getting to know – and understand – your own local market is one of the most productive things you can do for yourself.

To accomplish this, you need to work on two areas:

• Learn as much as you can about your market – through all kinds of sources and research resources

• Develop contacts – meet the people who are in touch with what's going on in your market

"Learning" Your Market.

Developing a feel for your local market is both high-tech and "high-touch."

Information can come from sources as diverse as: Chamber of Commerce reports, secondary and primary data sources, local publications, and industry studies.

It also comes from making friends with your dry cleaner, a few real estate agents, and becoming a regular reader of all the local business news you can get your hands on.

The good part is you get to know everyone and develop resources that become more valuable over time.

The bad part… you're never really off the job.

James Webb Young deals with this in his wonderful book *A Technique for Producing Ideas*. He talks about the need for two kinds of reading:

1. **General Reading** – to develop a broader background
2. **Specific Reading** – to become more expert on the subject at hand

Your task will be very similar in "learning" your market.

You will be developing general background on the market and then doing specific research on a client industry.

Market Background & Market Changes.

Everything you can learn about your local market gives you a little more of the background you need.

With this background, you will then be able to figure out what every change means to the market and to you.

Sometimes these are big changes, sometimes the changes are more subtle.

You have to look for clues and put it all in context.

A Marketing Approach.

In this part of the book, we want you to think about planning media on a local level by understanding local markets.

When you understand the dynamics of a local market, you'll be able to identify opportunities based on any market definition and you'll be able to plan more effectively based on the marketing needs of your client.

Using this marketing approach, you are creating the basic planning template for any client within your market.

Do not think of an individual client while doing this plan, think of the entire market.

This will give you a "jump start" on others, no matter what your job in advertising may be.

The Importance of Comparisons over Time.

Remember what you learned in Chapter Four about creative media analysis.

Figures as of one date are of little importance even if you are comparing local/regional markets at one time.

In order to understand the changes in a market (which are important to advertisers), you need to make comparisons over time. How does this number compare to last year at the same time? Whether these numbers are going up or down is critical to understanding the dynamics of the market.

It is also important to compare local markets to the state as a whole, to regions within the state and to national figures.

Be certain to account for inflation and report in real dollars.

When you're ready to get started, check out our Web site, www.adbuzz.com. There you will find a worksheet form for a local market profile, including the following sections: market population; market employment trends; specific geography and traffic patterns; demographic details like education and income; retail sales and tax trends; and, finally, specific media in the area.

Once you start thinking about your Local Market Profile you'll begin to see the specific research you'll need to help pull something like this together.

Research on a Local Level.

Media planners need media research. So do media sales people. This is true on every level – national, regional, local, big market, small market, broad target, or niche.

Many of the national syndicated research companies provide their data broken out into smaller markets.

For example, Nielsen Media Research will provide day-part and program ratings information by specific audience segments for each of 212 individual local markets throughout the country. Arbitron will do the same for every major radio market in the U.S.

For printed publications like newspapers and magazines, media planners can use circulation data reported by services such as the Audit Bureau of Circulation.

But what do you do for other media? Where do you go for information on media not covered by the bigger research services? You need another set of tools for this.

Local Market Research Tools.

These are the tools that will help you "fill in the blanks."

Knowledge Is Power.

The more you know, the higher your credibility with your clients and the better you'll be at your job.

To build that knowledge, you need the right tools.

Primary and Secondary Research.

First, you will need to get information from **Secondary Research** – material that is already available.

There is a lot of it – we'll show you where to look and what to look for.

Then, you may need to do **Primary Research** – where you generate the information yourself.

You'll be doing some of this informally with your store visits and interviews, but we're going to show you more comprehensive techniques, as well.

Secondary Research tends to be inexpensive – it's often free for the asking. Primary Research can be expensive – even when you do it yourself, it may take a lot of time to do it right.

Secondary Research is usually done first.

Secondary Research Sources.

Here are some of the main sources of Secondary Research.

Within these sources, you will find much of the information you need for your Local Market Profile.

Chamber of Commerce Reports.

Cities and towns of all sizes have their own reports.

These are both informational and promotional, ranging from flyers to complete packages – even books. Some are updated yearly.

Chamber reports give a good overview and are likely to include some area history, list major employers, industries, churches and schools, provide a demographic overview of the population, give phone numbers for local service agencies, and show a map with areas of major interest highlighted.

Survey of Buying Power.

This book, published and regularly updated by *Sales and Marketing Management* magazine, gives a breakdown of both population and retail spending in all counties in the U.S.

It lists major industries and payroll information as well.

The breakdowns are for all states and counties and for major cities as well.

Franklin's (Cont.)

New advertising and media ideas are always greeted cordially, but the Franklin's management team has their own inflexible ideas about advertising based on what has been done before. Old Mr. Franklin reads his local newspaper from cover to cover every Sunday morning.

Franklin's has not changed over the years, but the town has. The store is doing well enough, but it is missing many opportunities – leaving itself open to another, more savvy retailer to come in.

What Are Your Clues?

First, Franklin's is a typical case of a well-established retailer in a market that has changed.

Your clues are that the market has changed and Franklin's is maintaining a policy that resists change.

Your next task is to find market information that helps Franklin's management sell themselves on the need for change.

Use secondary data showing population, age, and growth trends over the years – help Franklin's see the opportunities that can come from expanding their target market to new audiences.

Show them the potential new business out there.

Although you'll have to be tactful, suggesting additional audiences and media may help Franklin's to see that they must update and expand their approach to keep their market share and protect themselves.

Play to both generations of Franklin's management by giving them useful information about "all generations" of new business in their market.

Donnelly Demographics.

Donnelly provides census data in a number of demographic categories and also contains some trend estimates of its own.

U.S. Census Data.

The census is updated every ten years.

It provides population, income, growth, employment, education, and other demographic data which can be extremely useful in both understanding your own market area and comparing it to others.

You can access census data online at www.census.gov. There are also other ways to get this data.

Larger newspapers and broadcast stations may have census data in either printed form or online. If that is not available, a state library or research institute will have it. There are also many sources that print certain facts from the census data – such as Donnelly (mentioned above).

U.S. Government Studies and Booklets.

The Government Printing Office publishes information and study summaries in a wide variety of categories.

This is one inexpensive (sometimes free!) source for both basic and detailed information about industries which may be important to your clients – and therefore to you.

U.S. Statistical Abstract.

This book, published yearly by the U.S. government, gives vital statistics for the country by state and specific categories such as health, sales, population, government structure, growth charts for gross product, manufacturing, and mining.

It is a valuable source for understanding trends.

Regional Studies.

There is a wealth of information available from state government sources.

In addition, many state universities have urban study centers which produce specific regional reports. Particularly valuable are reports in such areas as growth and planning.

Vital Statistics.
The Statistical Abstract of the United States *is a great annual source for following trends in the U.S.*

Industry Publications.

Every business has its own set of trade publications, and you should be familiar with those of interest to your clients.

Your clients read these publications on a regular basis. They range from automotive publications to hardware, home-building, food, and sports – every area you can imagine.

You should at least be familiar with these kinds of publications and keep up with the major trends. This shows the client that you have a sincere interest in his or her business.

Specialized Reports.

Just as with trade publications, your clients receive reports and newsletters.

Many businesses have associations of their own which publish newsletters and other publications of interest to those in that business. Again, you should be at least familiar with the major sources.

"Instant Backgrounders."

The Radio Advertising Bureau, and other media sales groups, often provide category profiles that can be useful. The *RAB Factbook* provides a wealth of information designed to help local radio sales people. Find out more at www.rab.com.

Such resources can provide you with summaries of the specific product category and other helpful marketing information.

Local Newspapers and Magazines.

The local news and business sections of local publications are full of news you can use in media planning.

Every change in the market – from promotions to store additions to road plans – can mean opportunity for you. Reading regularly also means you can discuss local events of importance with your clients.

Many papers have a special business section (sometimes it's in tabloid format), and some markets even have a free-standing business magazine. All have listings of new additions and promotions of people in various local businesses.

The Business.
Local business magazines are a terrific source of information from who's who to what's what in communicty business matters.

Awards, speeches, committee actions, and other activities often appear in the business section. If these mention the name of a possible contact, that's even better.

To get the most use out of the media news, start making a file of news and people who may be important in your territory.

For example, if you work on a bank account, you want to keep names of bankers in the news, clippings about special services, and announcements. And you want to keep information not only about your clients, but also about their competition.

Remember, ads in other media (not your own) are also a source of information.

National Newspapers and Magazines.

The important ones for you are the industry and trade magazines mentioned previously as well as *Business Week, The Wall Street Journal, Time* and *Newsweek,* and major newspapers such as *The New York Times* and *USA Today.*

What you want to look for here are the charts, graphs, and information pieces that give you some details about trends that affect your clients and business in general.

American Demographics is published monthly and can be a valuable source for tracking changes in customer habits, including leisure and shopping trends and growth and change in certain demographic categories.

Advertising Journals and Papers.

Many people might think these national advertising trade publications are not much use for local media sales.

But *Advertising Age* is important, particularly if you work with big clients or have a regional territory. They also feature regular articles and special sections covering various industry groups, which can be helpful.

There's also *AdWeek,* which also features good regional coverage of the advertising business, *Media and Marketing, Editor and Publisher, Radio Ink, Presstime,* and the *Journal of Broadcasting.*

You'll want to look into these on a fairly regular basis to keep up with trends in your own industry.

Advertising Journals.
MediaWeek *is one of many trade magazines focused on the advertising business, in particular the media part of the business.*

Radio Ink, for example, covers the activities of radio stations with emphasis on local sales and promotion.

If you want to know about other media to compare to your own, there's *Editor and Publisher Yearbook*, *Broadcasting/Cablecasting Yearbook*, *Standard Rate and Data Service,* and other similar publications.

These include basic information about markets and about rate charges and services provided.

Finally, if a client mentions some source as particularly useful for him or quotes from a source, ask about that source. Restaurateurs, for example, often read *Nation's Restaurant News*. Asking will make you seem interested (not uninformed), particularly if the source is one only those truly inside that business would be likely to know about.

CD-ROM Databases.

Some of the newest sources of information are the many databases available online and to CD-ROM users.

With these sources, you can locate almost any kind of published or catalogued information, read it on the screen and print pages right in your office.

The only limitations are access and expense.

ABI/Inform provides database information from business journals in all areas. This is a valuable source for information about businesses, market trends, new products, financial news, and economic indicators about business.

You can also retrieve information from trade magazines in many retail and small business categories.

Other databases provide governmental information – publications from the Government Printing Office, U.S. Census data, bibliographic information, and many others. A visit to your own library will tell you what is available locally.

If you are working in sales, your own business is likely to have access to a variety of pertinent database programs.

Here's a quick example of using secondary data to build a sales program.

ABI_INFORM

Interactive Data Catalogs.
Online databases like ABI Inform and LexisNexis can be a valuable source of information about business trends and economic indicators.

Mini-case #2: GreenStuff Nursery.

Media Survey Finds a Problem

GreenStuff Nursery (GS) is a three-year-old business run by a husband and wife team (Arlene and Ed) who are both botanists.

A combination nursery and yard store, GS is a year-round business with three distinct seasonal selling peaks: spring for vegetable and flower gardens, fall for trees and yard clean-up, and Christmas for decorations.

The remainder of the year, customers will buy house plants and herbs. Plants and trees are of the highest quality and are guaranteed.

Prices are somewhat higher than the grocery store and chain garden centers to reflect the quality.

The advertising plan has been to use local newspaper and radio at a reminder level much of the year, with additional ads at peak times.

Last year, the nursery placed a quarter-page in a gardening tabloid run in the local paper using a coupon for 10% off any purchase of $25 or more or a discount on tree planting.

These special offers brought some additional business. But, despite what GS feels is a good ad schedule, their business isn't growing, and customers brought in with special discount offers don't seem to come back on a regular basis.

There's strong competition from the chain store garden centers in both price and convenience.

Continued on next page…

An Example:

Suppose you've just read about a new regulation concerning lawn mower safety, and the publication says that a new safety feature will be required in 18 months. One of your clients is a hardware store that sells lawn equipment.

You visit that client soon after this information comes out.

You are now in a position to ask him about what he has heard from the manufacturers who supply him about their timetable for getting this new feature on the market.

He volunteers that he'll have a piece to retrofit mowers bought within the last two years – and that he'll have it well before the mowing season begins.

Now you have accomplished two things:

1.) Your client thinks you are not only interested in his business and his customers, but that you're really up on regulations that affect him, and

2.) You have the basis for a pre-season ad campaign to tell past and potential customers that this special equipment is available and positions your client as concerned about safety. (A family-friendly store.)

And your new ads (with extra space or time purchased) are just the way to get that across. You've made the sale by functioning as a marketing partner – and it's all based on knowing the market.

Look for first-rate sales opportunities in secondary data.

Primary Research Sources.

Though you'll always be using your own "primary research" of store visits and interviews, there are two basic areas for more formal primary research that can be used for local media planning or selling:

• Store or Customer Research

• Media Research

Sometimes these are separate studies, but many times a local medium will find out information about both areas in the same study, which may be a survey, or a focus group, or some other method – such as a mall intercept study.

GreenStuff (Cont.)

Although the ads seem to attract some new customers – particularly at peak seasonal times – the average spending level is disappointing, with most shoppers spending less than $15 per visit. A typical purchase would be a couple of herbs that the local groceries didn't carry, a tomato variety that was scarce, or a house plant for a gift.

Ed complained to his ad agency, "Our ads aren't doing us any good – or at least there is no gain we can measure over any kind of time. Ads should be an investment – but ours don't seem to bring any long-term return.

"People seem to think of us as a supplementary place, but not as the place to buy plants for the whole yard on any kind of regular basis."

The folks at the ad agency had a big meeting.

Worried that the GreenStuff account was in trouble, they brainstormed some ideas to find out how they might do a better job for Ed and Arlene, and fast.

The agency team decided that they needed to do some research, but there wasn't any money in the budget. The media planner suggested that they contact the local newspaper. She knew that the newspaper periodically ran a survey of its readers and, since GreenStuff was a regular advertiser, she knew they could participate in the survey at no cost.

The newspaper agreed and included GreenStuff as one of the nurseries in the next general survey. Responses showed that GS was regarded as a place to buy specialty items but not as a general plant source.

Continued on next page...

Stores use scanner data and databases of customers to find out detailed information.

The media also use databases of their users as well as of their advertisers.

Newspapers and broadcast stations may do research about the market and their users on a regular basis.

Primary research is expensive, but it can provide very specific information about the media product, user and non-user perceptions, and use patterns and importance of the media product for providing advertising information.

Information about the importance of the media product and its advertising messages to users can be very valuable.

Primary research can enable a newspaper, radio, or TV station to compile a profile of readers, listeners, or viewers – this can help sell advertisers on the value of the medium as an advertising vehicle.

Here are some of the things that primary research can help you learn:

Store or Customer Research:

This will usually cover the following categories:

- Awareness level of different stores
- Shopping habits
- Attributes customers find important
- How much customers spend on each store visit
- How customers feel about/use the competition
- Store traffic and patterns of use
- How customers use local ads
- Where customers get shopping information
- Problems: location, prices, image, or parking
- Major goods bought by customers in past year
- Plans to buy major goods
- Where customers/prospects work
- Where customers/prospects shop
- Which stores customers/prospects pass on the way home from work
- Which stores have the best values for certain products

GreenStuff (Cont.)

This confirmed what Ed and Arlene had thought.

But another important clue emerged. The survey showed that 73% of customers for all nurseries were afraid the plants they purchased would die or not produce well – so they hesitated to spend top dollar for vegetable plants or for small trees they could get at low prices.

Here was a clue that helped the ad agency develop a more persuasive message. The agency developed a new ad campaign to stress that the owners were botanists who grew their own plants from seed and would give professional advice about planting conditions and requirements for all sales – big and small.

The ads also contained tips for different kinds of plants, positioning GreenStuff as a reliable and knowledgeable source.

By inference, the ads showed the value in buying from local experts as opposed to mass-produced flats of vegetables and other plants found at chain stores.

Sales grew and Ed and Arlene were once again happy with their ad agency.

In this case, the media planner's knowledge of her market together with the survey results and owner insights were the critical combination that led to developing a more effective message and a stronger long-term position in the market.

That's the key to being a successful marketing partner.

- Which stores have the best customer service
- Restaurant use
- Bank and other service use

Media Research:

This will usually cover the following categories:

- Media use habits
- What attributes customers find useful/important
- How much/how often read, viewed, or listened to
- Time of day read, listen, or view
- Which medium provides best news
- Media features: personalities, subject matter, articles
- Use of different sections in local newspapers
- Reliance upon local media by differing demographics
- How customers read or use ads
- Coupon clipping/availability
- Level of coupon clipping and use

Primary Research Techniques.

These are the most common techniques used for local primary research:

Surveys.

Surveys are a means of obtaining specific information – such as shopping habits, attitudes about specific stores, media use, use of competitors, frequency of visiting certain shopping areas or stores, average dollars spent per visit, and demographic data for users as well as non-users.

A survey is a tool that can be tailored for specific needs and, with good questions and respondents who are representative of the group you want to know about, a survey can yield very useful answers to help both media and retailers plan advertising plans and ads for businesses.

Media such as newspapers or radio stations often do readership or listenership surveys for their own products.

The purpose of these surveys is to get a profile of the reader or audience, including how often they read or listen to the medium (and to competitors) and how much time they spend reading or listening every day.

Some surveys, such as those about shopping habits, include store preference, frequency, location, dollars spent, use of local advertising in making shopping decisions, and other shopping information.

Demographic data is gathered as well: age, income, housing, employment, number of children at home, length of time lived in the area, and other similar facts.

With this kind of information, the medium can talk to advertisers about specific buying habits of readers or listeners and use the survey facts to show that buying advertising in their medium is a good investment.

Questions should generally move from the general to the specific. In order to generate the most honest answers, the respondent should not know who the survey is for.

Focus Groups.

Focus groups are small groups people gathered together to talk and share opinions about a specific topic.

Although focus groups are small, the participants may bring up points that might not be included in a survey. Because of the face-to-face discussion, the moderator can follow up on points and explain difficult areas.

Often times this kind of group is used to get information and understand issues before writing survey questions. It can also be used just to find out more about the product use.

Asking about advertising use can also be a part of it.

Focus groups can even be used to find out more about advertisers and their perceptions of the medium itself.

Focus groups produce qualitative data in a setting that encourages many different ideas to emerge.

Though the results are open to subjective interpretation, they are easier and less expensive to implement than more formal studies.

Mall Intercept Research.

Another method of finding out information about consumers is a mall intercept study. Although this kind of study is not statistically significant, it does give a retailer or a medium some kinds of information about people who are actually in the mall or other shopping location.

Typical questions concern frequency of shopping, favorite stores, reasons for choosing the particular shopping area and opinions about differing kinds of products.

Sometimes people are taken to a research area, and asked to test products or fill out questionnaires.

Although this kind of study does not give you information from the broad range of customers in your retail trading area, it can give you some very specific information about people who are actually shopping or browsing on a given day.

One-on-One Interviews.

Sometimes, just talking to consumers can be helpful. If you can find a few "heavy users" of a store or product category – those with a lot of real-world consumer knowledge – you can find out a lot very quickly.

They can be a rich source of information – and you can do it on your own. One-on-one interviews can be a good way to do some primary research for almost any client.

"Di-ads" and "tri-ads" are similar to one-on-ones, only they use two or three respondents instead of one. (Note: You can find out more about these techniques in *Hitting the Sweet Spot* by Lisa Fortini-Campbell and *Advertising Campaign Planning* by Jim Avery – also published by The Copy Workshop.)

Evaluating Research Results.

It's not enough to just gather research. Just as we showed you in Chapter 4, you'll need to be creative about evaluating and interpreting the research results.

You have to do more than collect data – you have to convert it into usable information and actionable insights. Often, this means looking for "clues."

The sequence Lisa Fortini-Campbell describes in *Hitting the Sweet Spot,* is…

Data>Information>Insight>Inspiration.

Lisa talks about becoming a "consumer detective."

Insights.

Smart marketing and smart media planning is all about better insight. This book, by Lisa Fortini-Campbell, provides instruction in discovering insights.

You want to "unravel" all the data and then tie important pieces together into information that helps you understand the business.

And remember, you want early insights.

After a market opportunity has been developed, the potential is clear to everyone. You want to find the winners early on.

Finding a situation as it's just developing is the kind of opportunity-laden situation that can result not only in sales, but in being part of helping an exciting new business grow.

Discovering Insights.

Generally, two pieces of information will tie together to create an insight. As James Webb Young reminds us, "an idea is a new combination of two previously existing elements."

In this case, that idea, that new combination, is your insight. Using that insight, you can build a better media plan.

Research at Work.

Now let's consider some real-life examples that can help you use research.

We also need to talk about some real-life habits that can help you expand your market knowledge and discover new opportunities.

As we said before, local market planning often requires a combination of using sophisticated data and street smarts.

As you become a media person, you'll discover that even when you're just going about your everyday life – watching TV, reading a newspaper, or driving to the store – your antennae will be extended and you'll see new media opportunities.

The two mini cases (Franklin's & GreenStuff) presented earlier in this chapter serve to show you where insights can be generated by the media planner doing some detective work. The result can be a successful media plan and overall advertising program.

The exercises at the end of this chapter will give you a chance to see if you can unravel the data from an actual local business and tie it together into an insight.

Digging for Information.

Whether it's a garden shop, a pizza place, or someone who's never advertised before, you should be looking for information that is "advertisable."

"Find the problem the advertising must solve." You're a detective, a "problem-finder." You're looking for the insight that will be the key to unlocking those problems.

Research = The Right Start.

Whatever the problem, whatever the solution, it starts with the right information to help you develop the right focus and the right direction.

That means knowing how to do the right research.

That means:

- The right mind-set – state of the art and street smart
- The right research tools:
  - Secondary Research
  - Primary Research
- Looking for clues and opportunities
- Identifying the marketing problem
- Putting them all together into a program that solves that problem and builds long-term growth

It's a big job.

The right research will help you get the right start.

Summary.

So, we covered a lot of ground in this chapter, and we did it very fast.

You can see here that media planning on a local level is both the same as and different from media planning for a national business.

Many of the principles are the same, and certainly the process is the same.

But, the limitations are vastly different.

Planning on a local level requires some special agility and deftness in working with information. In fact, a lot of times, the media planner on the local level also needs to act as a media researcher.

On the local level, you need to know a lot *and* you need to know how to go out and learn more.

As we've said many times now, the best place to start is by knowing your own market.

Ruby Anik took a traditional path through her career. She started as an entry-level Media Estimator and worked her way up on the agency side before moving on to the client side. From her place now, at the top of all Best Buy advertising, Ruby sees a fascinating future for media and media professionals.

Career Capsule:

Ruby Anik, Vice President of Advertising, Best Buy.

Ruby Anik is Vice President of Advertising for Best Buy, a Fortune 100 company and North America's largest specialty retailer of consumer electronics, computers, software, and major appliances. Ruby holds an undergraduate degree in English Literature and a graduate degree in Marketing Management from the University of Bombay, India.

An In-House Ad Agency.

In her current position, Ruby leads all advertising activities through Best Buy Advertising, the in-house advertising agency for the Best Buy enterprise. Her staff of 110 employees is responsible for account strategy, creative development, commercial production, media planning and buying, and commercial trafficking for all Best Buy advertising spending. Ruby also manages Best Buy's outside agency partnerships.

Make no mistake, Best Buy advertising is a big deal. We're talking here about everything from national network television advertising to local level in-store signage. This includes viral marketing, interactive television, cinema advertising, radio, and locally specific newspaper advertising. All geared to drive name recognition, foot traffic, and sales volume on a store-by-store basis.

A major position like this, on a major retail business like this, is do-or-die every week and every month, year in and year out.

A Traditional Career Path.

Ruby started her media career as a Media Estimator with N.W. Ayer. She had been hired as an administrative assistant, and from there she says she pressured the Media Director to give her a chance in media planning.

She worked her way up and across agencies to positions as Media Director for Y&R and Group Media Director, Senior Partner at Tatham, Euro RSCG. While on the agency side, Ruby handled media research, planning, and buying for numerous brands in many different product categories including Brach Candies, Jenn-Air Appliances, Adidas Sportswear, Royal Canadian Mints, and several major Procter and Gamble brands.

Then she moved over to the client side. Ruby served as director of advertising for The Pillsbury Company, where she had strategic control over the media budget and responsibility for all media research, strategy, planning, and execution. She also served as part of Diageo's (Pillsbury's parent company) Global Media Team, a corporate level "think tank" focused on industry trends, agency performance, and approaches for improving media effectiveness for all Diageo companies worldwide.

From Pillsbury and Diageo, Ruby moved on to Best Buy as VP, Media before her current position leading all advertising. Ruby says her favorite thing about this work is producing great work and great results. Whether it's new technology for media planning and buying or great new advertising creative, she finds it all interesting and exciting.

Advice for the Future.

Ruby says that she never dreamed she would make it this far. She feels that what got her to where she is today is a lot of hard work and good dose of curiosity. Her advice for newcomers is *"Be curious and stay curious. Media is a fascinating world of change."* Students today need to be curious about and willing to explore new media and try out new ideas.

Ruby sees the emergence of new, alternative media as one of the more important developments in media today. New media applications like viral marketing via the Internet and interactive television via personal video recorders are changing the way that marketers like Best Buy do business. Even today, Best Buy is already looking for new media savvy as a particular skill among prospective new employees.

Discussion Questions.

1. Matching Media with Markets.

Why is it important to know your market overall?

When we are talking about just one city, what do we mean by "geographic considerations" within the city?

Should two stores in one location have the same media plan? Why or why not?

2. Local Market Profile.

What are the components of a local market profile?

What are some ways you might get to know more about your market?

Why is it important to compare data over time?

3. Research on a Local Level.

What is the difference between Primary and Secondary Research?

What are some good sources for Secondary Research?

Name and explain ten different sources.

4. Overall.

How is media planning on a local level different from media planning for a national business?

How is it similar?

Exercises.

1. Map Work.

Make or buy a map of your own city and map out the kinds of businesses in the area (if you live in a large city you might want to look at just one neighborhood). Use colored pencils, pins, or dots to identify locations for at least five different stores in each of five different retailer categories.

     a. Think about the competition for each location

     b. Think about the major streets in each area

     c. Think about the media in the area

Prepare a short presentation (5-10 min.) to share your map and your thoughts with the class.

2. Paperwork.

Visit the Chamber of Commerce for your home city and research the characteristics of the city. Write a short paper (1-2 pages) profiling your hometown. Be sure to include information on the demographics and the economic makeup of the city. Also include basic information about the local media an advertiser might want to use.

3. Brain Work.

Choose a local business and prepare a local media plan for that business. Think about the examples of Better's Better Gourmet and Deluxe Cleaners. Be specific about the business problems and needs, and be specific about the media you'll recommend and how each media will address the problems of the business. Be prepared to present your recommendations and rationale to the class.

9 Niche & Specialty Media Markets

BY NOW, YOU'VE LEARNED about media planning terminologies and techniques and various media vehicles. We've looked at media on a national, regional, and local market basis.

Understanding Niche Media Markets.

Niche media markets do not really differ in the way a planner must work.

They employ the same basic techniques and parameters.

The difference lies in the more refined (some say complicated) target market definition.

When we have to go beyond broad demographic and geographic classifications, we consequently need to use different media alternatives and strategies. After all, it's narrower lifestyle information and media exposure opportunities that makes these media choices niche.

These days, more and more marketers find themselves fighting for market position within a narrow market niche – or within a more narrowly defined niche of a larger market.

As categories have matured and product options exploded, one of the important possible strategies for many marketers is to find and exploit a niche market.

Micro marketing and Narrowcasting.

The idea of niche media planning is in fact closely tied to

305

the concept of "micro marketing." Micro marketing is a strategy that conveys an advertising message to a selected small group and eliminates mass-market exposure altogether.

Also known as "narrowcasting," niche advertising removes waste coverage by focusing solely on market segments that will likely become actual customers of the advertised brand.

Niche markets can be very profitable and are sometimes the sole revenue source for certain businesses. Think of collector's items (dolls, coins) or specialty supplies (parts for drag-racing cars, luxury accessories). Niches can exist:

- In industry and corporate arenas (textbooks, medical equipment)
- In lifestyles and interests (fan clubs, hobby groups)
- In geographic locales (Caribbean scuba adventure, Colorado ski country)
- In demographics (NASCAR dads, soccer moms)
- In ethnic groups (Latinos, Korean-American, etc.)
- In attitudes and behaviors (pro-environmentalist, Yuppies, evangelicals)

How we define a niche and a niche medium can get confusing sometimes. Dependent on the planner's subjective definition of a niche, it can get pretty big (e.g., are kids a niche market?). In many cases, media professionals can find a mainstream mass medium and use it as an appropriate vehicle to cover a niche market. The dual purpose of television as a mass medium (primetime shows on NBC) and a niche medium (pay-per-inquiry infomercial on special content cable channels) would be an example.

Chapter Organization.

We will discuss three things:

- **Niche Media**
- **Niche Segments**
- **Niche Media Planning.**

Here it is in slightly more detail.

Niche Media:

We'll start with a review of known media types and how they can be used as niche vehicles and a brief introduction of specialized media, often known as nontraditional media.

The latter are used almost exclusively to target audiences that cannot sufficiently be reached with mainstream media.

Niche Segments:

Following this, we will explain the process of media research for niche markets along some specific examples. The four most common niche segments are trade or professional segments, ethnic or cultural segments, attitudinal segments, and lifestyle or lifecycle segments.

- **Trade segments**: The typical situation when faced with a trade segment is when an advertiser sells something that is of exclusive interest to another business and not a private consumer. Business-to-business marketing has a long history and its own dynamics for advertising.

- **Ethnic segments**: The growth of minority groups and mixed-race families has caused advertising to evaluate the importance of culture-specific vs. standardized approaches. To date, there are hundreds of media servicing exclusively the many cultures in this country.

- **Attitudinal segments**: This portion will explore the issues surrounding small groups that share a common belief or conviction. This involves, among others, so-called "green" products targeted at environmentalists as well as advocacy messages targeted at activists.

- **Lifestyle segments**: This final segment deals with groups that engage in exclusive hobbies or select standards of living. Examples of this kind would be large-mouth bass fisherman or private day-trading investors.

Niche Planning:

Concluding this chapter, we will look at a case study in which an agency had to develop a niche media plan for a client. This plan had to work in a very short time and use only a limited budget.

Niche Media.

In previous chapters, we've introduced the major traditional media categories – print, broadcast, and the large group we called "other." We identified many different media types within each category.

In this chapter, you'll notice that some of the same media types also fit the categorization of "niche medium," due to their versatility in how they can be used. As we mentioned before, television was originally a broad-based medium, but with the advent of cable and satellite TV it has become much more of a niche medium besides remaining an important medium for mass appeal.

True niche media are more nontraditional; i.e., they might not be immediately recognized as an advertising medium. In fact, almost anything that can carry an advertising message could function as a medium. Since they can follow specific consumer segments into their everyday life or activity pattern, they use a very stealth-like approach to communicate. Moreover, they do not appear as overbearing and uninvited as most mass-media advertising, and they might even generate an emotional connection to a target audience. Niche media operate on the fringe of advertising and other IMC activities (such as promotions, merchandising, direct selling, publicity) and for the most part would be clustered in the vast out-of-home category. The other growing segment of niche media are part of interactive media which will be discussed in Part IV of this book.

Niche ←——————————————→ Mass

Media Spectrum.
Think about this as a continuum of media from mass to niche based on the size of the audience.

Mass Media as Niche Media.
Radio Today: From Mass Media to Niche Media.

Today, radio is viewed as a niche media by many.

But it didn't start out that way. Remember that radio started as a mass media. There was a time not all that long ago when 88 million Americans tuned in every week to listen to the hit radio program *The Lone Ranger*.

Formats for All.
Every station format attracts a uniquely different audience segment.

Cable Niches.
Many cable networks have small but dedicated niche audience appeal.

Then along came television, and radio's days as a mass media were numbered. But today radio not only survives, it thrives. Today, it's a niche media – primarily serving local retailers.

However, here is a good example of the duality at work.

A mass marketer, focusing on drive time for the whole market can, indeed, view his radio buy as a mass media investment.

Meanwhile, the concert promoter, focusing on one key station where listener's love a certain kind of music, can treat radio as almost a narrowcasting direct medium.

And liking a certain kind of music can be viewed as one example of a behavior or interest group.

Virtually every local radio station across the country programs its content according to one of about 30 different formats. From Country & Western to All News to Hip Hop to Contemporary Christian, each format attracts a different kind of audience. That's about 30 different audience segments you can target with radio.

Some are quite large and some quite small.

Cable Television as a Niche Media.

There are so many different cable networks, you wouldn't really want to count them all. And, counting wouldn't do you much good anyway – because the number of networks offered differs from one cable system operator to another, all across the country.

While some cable networks have a more general market audience, most have very small, but dedicated audiences.

This can make cable television a great media choice for niche marketing efforts.

For example, if the product is for kids, advertise on *Nickelodeon* or *Disney* or *Cartoon Network*.

If the product is for the home improvement market, then you might advertise on *House & Garden Television* (HGTV).

If it's a women's fashion product, try advertising on the *Style Network*.

If the product is for people who like to travel, advertise on the *Travel Channel*.

If the product is golf clubs, tee it up on the *Golf Network*.

You get the idea, right? Cherry-pick your niche – there's probably a cable TV network that will fit your market just fine.

Consumer Magazines Are Niche Media.

Some magazines have a very large audience. One of the biggest is the *AARP Bulletin*.

For Even the Smallest Niche.
Specialty magazines like this are a true niche media, with a small but loyal audience.

Ironically, the *AARP Bulletin* started as a niche publication for retired American senior citizens. As the U.S. population has aged significantly, and as many Americans are now retiring at an earlier age, this once-niche publication has built a near mass audience.

Aside from the *AARP Bulletin,* though, most other magazines have considerably less circulation. Most magazines deliver focused content to a small, committed, and loyal audience. And, this is a continuing trend as new specialty magazines are launched almost every day.

Trade Magazines Are Niche Media.

Trade magazines are business publications.

These magazines are written exclusively for people in business. And the advertisers in such magazines are almost exclusively business-to-business marketers.

Supermarket News.
If your business is groceries, then this is your trade magazine.

There are literally thousands of trade magazine titles published on a regular basis in the U.S. Each different title addresses the unique issues of one of almost every U.S. standard industry classification.

Some of these magazines may be very thin on content, but that's OK in this business. In fact, thinness can be a good thing. If the magazine content is meaningful and truly focused, and the audience is valid and loyal, then advertisers might even see thinness as a low-clutter advantage.

The Internet as a Niche Media.

For all of its mass audience penetration, the Internet is only as mass as its most popular website. Even today, that still isn't very mass.

The vast majority of the Internet is still very niche-oriented. And, the beauty is that, even as it grows, it will stay that way.

Even as individual sites, with some common affinity, link themselves to affiliate networks, the Internet is still accessed by consumers on a site-by-site basis that changes almost every day.

Internet search engines are great news for marketers who use the Internet as a niche media. Just as a search engine helps consumers to find information they are seeking, it can also help marketers find the consumers they are seeking.

If you are looking for an audience with a potential affinity for your product, just type in a couple of keywords and you'll have a whole list of places to go look.

Newsletters and Blogs Are Niche Media.

Newsletters and blogs are very popular right now and getting even more popular with advertisers.

Each is, by definition, very focused on a specific topic of interest to an audience.

They are also, right now, a very uncluttered media environment. Advertisers are taking note in the amount of $3,000 to $5,000 per month for the most popular blogs. And marketers can blog too. Nike, for one, has hired a big name in the business, Nick Denton (Gawker Media), to creat a Nike blog as part of a new marketing campaign.

Exclusive Niche Media.

Products as Niche Media.

Almost every product – within reason – can be used for advertising. If you currently wear a T-shirt or baseball cap that reads "Hardrock Café" or "Just do it" you know what we're talking about.

www.Niche.
The vast majority of the Internet is still very niche-oriented, like this website for media planners and buyers.

Product as Media.
In this case, even a cup of coffee can carry a latté of advertising.

Advertising to Go.

"Walking Billboards."

What are some other places for advertising?

Coffee drinkers might have encountered coffee cup or coffee sleeve advertising, handed to them when they purchase a latté or mocha. Since people often drink coffee at work or on the go, the advertising is both an indoor and outdoor vehicle.

Similarly, advertising on a pizza box and Chinese take-out box can deliver a message when the food is delivered to the home or picked up by the customer. Since leftovers are often kept in the original container, exposure to the ad message works over several days.

Shopping bags are another effective medium that creates a "walking billboard" when shoppers carry their bags around town. To obtain the rights to advertise on the bag of a retail outlet usually requires good negotiation skills and some benefits to the retailer.

Hotel key advertising places the ad directly into the hands of business or leisure travelers. Since the message is placed on the magnetic key card, guests will not only see the advertisement, but they keep it around for as long as they stay in their hotel room (excellent for frequency campaigns).

This is just a select sample of possibilities to advertise on everyday items that particular groups come in contact with. Others would include items such as food carts, food wrapper, grocery cart handle, back-of-ticket, gas pump – the possibilities are near endless for creative planners. What others can you think of? What niche targets would get the most exposure to these "media?" Can you construct a campaign with these media?

Locations as Niche Media.

You have heard throughout this book that creative media planning is about surrounding a prospect with the advertising message during opportune times. These should be moments where prospects are most receptive to what you have to say. Unfortunately it is difficult to reach many groups (e.g., Generation Y teens, business travelers) with traditional mass media. Not only is their time of exposure to many mass media limited, but some have also become quite jaded when it comes to mass media advertising. An alternative strategy is to be where these groups are, and be attractive enough to be noticed and accepted.

If you live in a major market and have been to your student union, health club, or record store lately, you might have noticed a wall rack with colorful postcards. In the last couple of years, two competing companies, m@xracks and GoCard, have created a national network of postcard display locations for advertising postcards. Targeting primarily young, educated, urban, affluent consumers, displays can be found wherever this group spends time (restaurants, coffee bars, campus gathering spots, health clubs, music and book stores). Since the postcards are intentionally designed like art work, they are voluntarily picked up to collect or send to friends (after all, they are postcards). A barcode tracking technology captures the quantity and date of card taken out of the rack. If you want to know more about them, visit the two companies' websites at www.maxracks.com and www.gocard.com.

Rip-away posters (24" x 36") work in a similar fashion, encouraging passers-by to rip down a poster from the pad. These posters are primarily used for brands whose advertising can be converted into poster art. The approach does not only actively involve the prospect (you voluntarily take the ad), but it also creates a shelf life for the campaign in that the poster is usually taken home and pinned on the wall.

Outdoor video and spotlight wall projections place the image or message of a brand on outdoor structures. These are mostly event-driven media and hence used in conjunction with promotional activities, such as street teams (groups of two, usually young, people chatting up people and handing out merchandise), urban event marketing, or nightlife entertainment concepts. The "hip" character of these activities suggests a teen or young adult "party crowd" target, exactly the kind of consumer who is hard to reach with mass media.

Rip-away Posters.
A new kind of voluntary ad selection for those brands with advertising like poster art.

Under the Radar.
Graffiti murals can be advertising.

Spokesdoll.
Recent advertising for Lee Dungarees has featured the adventures of Buddy Lee.

Remember that the key to a successful campaign sometimes was not the introduction of product benefits but the creation of buzz? Well, how can you create positive buzz? How should it appear, so that it grows like a snowball rolling down the hill? And who should be seen as the originator of that buzz? These are the questions that "under-the-radar" media address. Graffiti murals, guerilla programs (wild postings on construction sites, lamp post flyers, static clings, sidewalk decals) and word-of-mouth trendsetter concepts (magazine writers, DJs, restaurant staff, musicians, and night-club owners as opinion leaders) all work off the premise that cool, hip, avant-garde, unexpected executions will create a trickle-down effect. Moreover, they don't use the "sledgehammer" method of advertising, but – as said – fly in under the advertising-defense radar.

When the advertising agency Fallon McElligott reintroduced Lee Dungaree Jeans to young women, they launched the campaign with "odd" biography episodes of the Lee spokesdoll, Buddy Lee, on MTV during overnight hours and wild postings that did not reveal the brand name until enough buzz had been created about the campaign itself.

Online Activities as Niche Media.

With separate chapters on interactive media planning to come, we will just introduce an incomplete list of other niche activities that can be used on the Internet.

- Online video clip seeding is an activity where branded video content (e.g., TV commercials) are placed on websites, blogs, and online newsletters.
- Viral marketing uses the equivalent of street teams to engage members of chat rooms and message boards on brand-focused conversations and provide links to further product information. The overall name stems from the way a biological virus works, "infecting" a small group and then being transmitted to others. In that sense, online viral marketing uses word-of-mouth as a multiplier of the message.

- Online product placement (also an offline activity) places brands close to features, events, or celebrities to provide authenticity and awareness.

Niche Segmentation.

A few years ago, two books – *The One-to-One Future* by Peppers & Rogers and *Permission Marketing* by Godin – proposed a rethinking of consumer marketing. They argued that instead of maximizing the number of new customers through mass media appeals, the focus of marketers should be on keeping a smaller niche segment longer and over time obtaining more revenue from them.

Given that a niche approach is built on the target audience's permission to be engaged in a "relationship," a key consideration is the environment in which the advertising will appear. Similar to a personal relationship, relationship marketing requires both the right words and right atmosphere for the relationship to grow and intensify. The proper media are usually those that not only reach a target where they live, work, and play, but also provide the frame in which the advertising message fits the mood of the media consumer at the moment of exposure.

To that effect, niche media's purpose is oftentimes different from selling the product. Planning niche media campaigns requires a good understanding of the niche audience and how they would prefer to learn about a product or service. It could be as simple as asking for permission to send more information through another medium. For instance, a tourism resort might advertise on a travel TV channel that more information is available in a special brochure, which prospects can order on a website.

Having covered a variety of niche media, let's look at some applied examples of different niche audience segmentations and campaign plans.

Trade Segmentation.

The business-to-business advertising discipline is probably the least glamorous in the eyes of the typical advertising student educated on Nike and Coca-Cola. Yet, it is big business in the U.S. Overall, "b-to-b" (also seen as "B2B") advertising spending was $12.7 billion in 2002. The biggest of the big spenders in B2B are the telecommunication companies. The three largest advertisers in 2002 were Verizon Communication, Sprint Corporation, and SBC Communication, with AT&T Wireless Services rounding out the top five. Together, these four companies spent more than $1 billion in B2B media.

In the last few years, the idea of psychographic targeting has entered B2B advertising. Just as consumers became defined by attitudes and values rather than demographic profiles, business buyers are now viewed as human beings with likes and dislikes rather than decision-making machines. While it is still common practice to appeal on facts and logic, emotional appeals to business buyers are on the rise. AT&T, for instance, has advertised its business service with a campaign showing managers mourning the decision to switch companies. This campaign played as much on the very rational values of reliability as it did on the emotion of fear.

Knowing the target segment has become as important as it has for consumer advertising in order to plan the right media. Let's look at two examples:

Drilling for Customers – ExxonMobil Exploration.

Born out of the merger of Exxon Inc. and Mobil Oil & Gas, ExxonMobil is a huge company with total revenue of $246.7 billion in 2003. Many of us only know this company as a brand of gasoline when we fill up the car at the gas station. Yet only a fraction of ExxonMobil's revenue comes from selling gasoline to people like us. The typical oil and gas company is organized along the entire supply channel; i.e., there is a so-called "upstream" division (in charge of the exploration and refinery supply of crude oil and natural gas), there is a "downstream" division (oil refining and gasoline and lube marketing), and there is a chemicals division (production and supply of petrochemicals and catalysts). Besides these three main tasks, the company is also involved in research and development of oil- and gas-related technologies (drill heads, offshore platforms, and refineries).

The clients for the majority of these activities are businesses, such as independent refineries, oil drilling companies, airport fuel depots, and gas deliverers. An agency, hired by ExxonMobil's Upstream Division, has to become intricately familiar with the "players" in the market that this division caters to.

Since speed is a big issue in this fiercely competitive market, keeping up with the latest technologies and worldwide developments is an important proficiency of managers working in the customer market for ExxonMobil Exploration. Oil traders eagerly read their specialized and highly focused magazines (*Oil& Gas World*, *Offshore*, *World Oil*, to name a few) and attend exhibits and luncheons whenever time allows. Since the magazines are skimmed mostly for key nuggets of new information, good positioning of the advertisement is crucial. Furthermore, direct-marketing activities (in particular, relationship-building events) connect well with these high-strung, no-nonsense individuals.

Advertising to the Advertisers – *Time* Magazine

Who doesn't know *Time* magazine? Every week, *Time* reaches 22 million readers, capturing 44% of the lucrative news-magazine market. However, what if your job is to sell *Time* magazine to advertisers; i.e., *Time* is no longer a media vehicle to choose for your plan but for your client who needs a plan of her own. The target market for this media plan is again a B2B market, in this case, for the most part, the advertising industry itself. Or, more precisely, media planners and buyers in an agency.

Selling Time.
Sales reps for Time *are responsible for selling space in the magazine to advertising clients.*

How does one advertise a magazine to advertisers? If you have looked carefully at the SRDS entry for *Time*, you might have noticed that *Time* actually offers targeted editions. These are extra editorials to qualified subscribers based on specific criteria. For example, *Time Business* goes to business managers, *Time Gold* goes to affluent subscribers over the age of 50, and *Time Luxury* goes to households in high-income zip codes. Targeted editions afford advertisers an opportunity to place their brand adjacent to a compatible editorial. They can become important strategies for media planners, but planners might not know about them.

If you happen to be a media planner that has to create a campaign targeting media planners, the job can become quite self-reflexive. Understanding the typical planner, one must grasp the way she works, what resources she consults for information, and what convinces her to take a closer look at a medium. Like any other industry, advertising has its trade journals as well in *Advertising Age* and *Adweek*. If you've ever looked at one, you might have noticed that media vehicles do indeed advertise in them. All of these journals also have Internet sites which have become stand-alone operations. On average, the usual media planner can be described as young, hip, time-pressed, educated, and always looking for the one breakthrough idea.

2002 US Population Estimates by Race and Ethnicity

	2002 Census Estimate	2001 Census Estimate	Percent Change
White	191.2	190.6	.03%
Hispanic	37.9	36.2	4.7%
African American	33.2	32.6	1.8%
Asian	11.1	10.5	5.7%
Other	7.1	7.1	0.0%
Total	273.4	269.9	1.3%

Ethnic Segmentation.

More and more advertisers today want and need to target the various cultural segments of the U.S. with separate campaigns. The largest cultural groups are shown in the table to the left. Oftentimes, advertisers hire ethnic agencies to work on campaigns directed at their peers.

Many believe that ethnic advertising might soon leave the area of niche targeting given that, according to forecasts, a clear majority will cease to exist toward the middle of the 21st century. Hispanic-Americans, followed by Asian-Americans and African Americans, are fast-growing population segments in this country. Only just a few years ago, ethnic or culturally specialized campaigns weren't the norm. As a matter of fact, in the early days of advertising, agencies adhered strictly to the "melting pot" concept and typically prepared only one campaign. The current momentum toward fragmentized campaigns is closely tied to the realization that other cultures do not as readily assimilate to the mainstream market as had been assumed in the past.

Paired with a rapid increase in buying power, ethnic markets have become important consumer targets for many brands. As a result, marketing and advertising had to become artifacts of the cultural milieu as much as business propositions. That is, campaigns and media choices have to build upon the common interests of ethnic groups with which consumers identify. As such, media vehicles that ethnic segments consume need to reflect distinctive aspects of their lifestyles and speak their "language."

The Case of Hispanic Media.

For example, Spanish-language TV is big and getting bigger. The biggest players in Spanish-language TV are *Univision* and *Telemundo*.

Univision reportedly has an overall audience equal to about 70% of the Hispanic market.

Some of the new players on the block are getting bigger. For example, *MTV*, with its two entries, *MTV Espanol* and *VHUno*. Other new ventures are coming down the road.

Telemundo recently relaunched *Mun2* as a younger, *MTV*-like network. *Univision* launched its new network *Telefutura* in January 2004, and still to come is the completely new venture *Si TV*.

The most popular program form on Spanish-language television is still the novela, a combination drama/soap opera format. However, other formats are also doing well.

Protagonistas.
This is hot new reality programming for Spanish-language TV.

Hispanic Outdoor.
This is a great example of Hispanic advertising via the outdoor media. Such boards are typically located in predominantly Hispanic neighborhoods.

Even reality TV has hit in Spanish-language TV. Last spring *Telemundo* launched its first reality show, *Protagonistas de Novela*, searching for the next major novela star. They plan to follow-up this year with *Protagonistas de la Musica*.

Sports programming is also popular with Hispanics.

In this area, *Telemundo* just landed a three-year deal with the NBA to air basketball games as well as complementary programming.

Print is also a popular media for the Hispanic market.

According to a recent study, more than 60% of Hispanic adults read magazines (Spanish- and English-language). New titles are coming – like *Thalia,* named for a popular Mexican singer – and current titles are booming, like *Latina. Latina* announced a 45% increase in guaranteed rate base for 2004.

Radio can be a good way to reach Hispanics, particularly in larger markets.

Outdoor also works in larger markets where advertisers can post messages in predominantly Hispanic neighborhoods.

However, you might expect this to change in the future. As the Hispanic market overall grows in size and personal wealth, we might expect to see shifts in the population and likely fewer of the predominantly Hispanic neighborhoods.

The Pepsi Story: the African American Cola.

Forecasts predict that the current African American population of 35 million will increase by about 51% to 54 million by 2050. African Americans have become increasingly upwardly mobile with a growing disposable income. However, close to 55% still live in urban areas, predominantly in the inner city. Contrary to the "poor ghetto" stereotype though, inner-city shoppers have a combined spending power of $85 billion and represent 7% of all retail shoppers.

As a culture, African Americans tend to follow a long tradition of respect for oral communication – talk with family and friends about products is well pronounced – and there

Multicultural Pioneers.
Early ads for Pepsi featured African Americans in key roles.

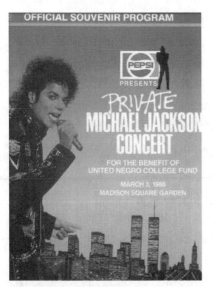

Concert Campaign.
In the '80s Pepsi sponsored concert tours for major-name performers like Michael Jackson and Tina Turner.

is a great reliance on in-store displays and sales people. Other than that, African Americans heavily use broadcast TV and radio (although they watch and listen to different programming), and they subscribe to premium cable channels at higher levels. Middle- and upper-class African American women are also heavy readers of African American magazines like *Ebony*, *Essence*, and *Jet*. Overall, there appears to be a growing demand for an "African-centered" perspective, which includes authenticity, resilience, and "telling it like it is."

Pepsi-Cola's story is as synonymous with ethnic marketing, multicultural management, and corporate citizenship as it gets. When a young pharmacist named Caleb Bradham invented the drink in 1898, his assistant, a young African American by the name of James Henry King, was the first to try the new beverage. Pepsi-Cola has been tied to the African American community ever since.

By the 1940s, Pepsi was the first company to employ college-educated African Americans. It was the only soft drink available to African American soldiers as a result of segregated regiments and a push from Pepsi to make the drink available to them. It was also the first company to engage in target marketing toward African Americans, and early on it featured African Americans in its advertising. Beginning with the 1950s, Pepsi signed major advertising contracts with Black-owned print media (*Ebony*, newspapers), and started underwriting record and film series documenting African American achievement on PBS.

In the 1970s, Pepsi-Cola was again among the first companies to get involved with community marketing events such as Black History Month and Martin Luther King Jr. Birthday celebrations. Its campaigns – such as the 1980s campaign "Pepsi Generation" – kept prominently featuring African Americans, while the company embarked on its own event sponsorships with the underwriting of concert tours by singers, such as Tina Turner and Michael Jackson.

Diet Pepsi and Ray Charles in 1990.

Pepsi and Beyoncé.
Just the latest in a long corporate history of Pepsi's multiethnic operations.

In 1990, the company launches its Diet Pepsi commercial, starring Ray Charles and the "Uh-Huh Girls," while the regular Pepsi spot featured Shaquille O'Neill.

By the year 2000, Pepsi capped six decades of multiethnic operations in a website titled "Diversity @ work." In 2003, Pepsi-Cola North America named Spike DDB, the joint venture between world-renowned film director Spike Lee and DDB Worldwide, as its multicultural agency of record. Their first mutual work launched soon thereafter – a TV commercial starring African American singer and actress Beyoncé Knowles.

Pepsi-Cola is a company that has, since its inception, understood the "African-centered" perspective of authenticity or "being real." If you read the company history (at www.pepsico.com/citizenship), you'll learn quickly that Pepsi does not only feature African Americans in their ads, but that the company is totally committed to the community in all that it does. The Pepsi case teaches a valuable lesson in ethnic niche planning. Brand advertising (and, for that matter, corporate hiring and management styles) needs to show a true interest, understanding, and commitment to an ethnic market to be successful. This oftentimes involves activities that have little to do with traditional media efforts.

Not surprisingly, Pepsi was named in 2004 by Diversity Inc. among the "Top 10 Companies for African Americans." It also remains the most popular soft drink among African American soda drinkers.

Attitudinal Segmentation.

People that hold certain attitudes about issues (abortion, gun control, environmental protection, safety belt use, and so on) are not all that different in terms of their demographic or psychographic profiles. They can be young or old, wealthy or poor, live in the city or country, or be extrovert or introvert. What makes them different is the intensity and direction with which they hold an attitude toward a specific issue. An easy way to understand attitudinal (and usually behavioral) segments is a look toward issue advocacy campaigns (e.g., "Only you can prevent forest fires," "Don't drink and drive"). What makes this segmentation particularly interesting is the range of sub-segments within the broader definition of the term. Let's look at household waste recycling groups as an example.

Why would people recycle garbage? After all, one has to continually stop and think what can be recycled and then actually separate the trash out. Research – primarily commissioned by city waste collection departments – has found some interesting differences in people's motivations to recycle. There are the "activist recyclers" (those that feel the need and duty to save the planet and tell others to do the same), the "compensation recyclers" (those that recycle for refunds only, the tit-for-tat crowd), the "convenience recyclers" (those that recycle if it does not disturb their daily lives; i.e., they would do curbside recycling, but not collection site drop-off recycling), and the "social pressure recyclers" (those that recycle because the whole neighborhood or apartment complex does it).

How do you talk to these four groups? Where do you reach them? Which one is the easiest to reach through reinforcement or conversion messages? It seems that whatever recycling group one falls into, it has implications for an overall "green" attitude.

Key for attitudinal segmentation and planning is locating the best (which means easiest to reach) sub-segment, learn everything possible about them, and draw on messages and message environments that speak to that group emotionally. This group is usually the most likely to support the idea of the campaign on their own later on. If we look back at the recycling example, we might uncover some important truths here. Whereas it seems that quite a few people do not recycle if the conditions they claim to need are not existent, no research has ever found anybody saying that he wants to voluntarily pollute or contribute to the waste problem. Similarly, no one plans to get into a car crash while driving drunk or set a forest ablaze (well, at least a vast majority doesn't).

The main issue seems to be that an advocated issue is not perceived as a problem by many, neither personally nor societally. Correspondingly, a change in behavior toward the advertised one seems too much trouble compared to potential rewards when running a pro-con analysis in one's head. Economists understand this as the "prisoner's dilemma" phenomenon. Given the chronic low budgets of advocacy groups, media planners need to be especially creative to place the right message to the right target at the right time.

"TRUTH" – Florida's Youth Antismoking Campaign.

On August 25, 1997, Florida won its "landmark" case worth $11.3 billion against the tobacco industry. Subsequently, the state initiated a multi-component tobacco pilot program targeting youth aged 12-17. The program's mission was to prevent and reduce youth tobacco use by implementing an innovative and effective education, marketing, prevention, and enforcement campaign that empowers youth to live tobacco-free.

After evaluating the experiences of other states, program executives in Florida concluded that it would be vital for the program's success to involve key players who would have a genuine stake in its outcome. From the start, the Florida policy stressed that youth would play a leading role in the development of a substantial marketing effort.

In early 1998, a tobacco-free partnership was established in all 67 Florida counties. Bylaws stipulated that at least 25% of the partnerships' members would be youth less than 18 years old. To attract youth to the partnership and to elicit input, the Miami-based advertising agency hired for the campaign convened a Teen Tobacco Summit in Spring 1998. The major aim of the Summit was empowerment. During the Summit, 500 teens from across the state created a youth ad-

Truthful Tone.

The non-preachy tone of the Truth campaign was an important part of its success.

Outdoor Truth.
This outdoor board shows the campaign focus: "Their brand is lies. Our brand is Truth."

vocacy group (Students Working Against Tobacco, or SWAT) and developed the major advertising theme to be used throughout the campaign. On the final day, the teens presented their ideas to the governor. Two weeks later, the $25 million annual advertising campaign was launched. The slogan the teens chose for the campaign was "Their brand is lies. Our brand is Truth."

Awareness of the targeted television, radio, and print campaign reached 92% among youth aged 12 to 17 in May 1999. More importantly, by the end of the first year, Florida youth had stronger anti-tobacco attitudes and different behavior patterns than a national comparison population. After further reflection, marketing experts with the advertising agency listed seven specific key elements that made this campaign successful: real money, youth involvement, a youth marketing approach, the tone of the message, an anti-manipulation strategy, branding of the "product," and focus.

Florida was the first state where young people have driven all facets of a campaign from the onset. Not only did they come up with the theme, but they also co-determined the tone of the message. Moreover, they starred in the television spots and ads. Unlike standard anti-smoking ads, the "Truth" ads did not preach about what to do or excessively warn about the dangers of smoking. Teen participants in the campaign insisted that most young people know the lethal health risks of smoking. Thus, the campaign's focus on the real reasons for youth using tobacco (emotional rather than rational) was to a large extent the result of youth involvement in the creation of the message. In addition, they organized and executed a myriad of activities and outreach programs throughout the state that ran alongside the media campaign. The campaign's winning formula rested in a modern marketing approach to a social message paired with the inclusion of important stakeholders like state administrators and young people in all aspects of the campaign.

Lifestyle Segmentation.

Targeting by lifestyles (such as hobbies and passions) has become a standard technique in advertising and media campaigns in an increasingly competitive landscape. Lifestyles provide an important segmentation tool for media planning, allowing planners to place an advertising message in compatible environments and thus reduce the chance to be overlooked, tuned-out, or avoided.

Research that indicates that calorie-reduced beer drinkers enjoy reading trend magazines (*Esquire*, *Maxxim*, *Vogue*, etc.) and spend very little time watching network TV would give planners important cues where to go. So would findings revealing that frequent business air travelers have an extremely light media diet, skimming a few pages in business magazines and newspapers as well as Internet sites, but consuming little else.

Many companies carry products that are of interest to only a very select lifestyle group. Think of brands such as Spyder fishing lines (anglers), Gaiam mattresses (yoga enthusiasts), e-trade (direct investors), Tag-Heuer watches (the upscale style-conscious), and – for the most part – Ace Hardware (do-it-yourselfers).

While these groups are admittedly rather small, they are epitomized by greater product familiarity, loyalty to a proven brand, and inexhaustible enthusiasm for this lifestyle. This passion often leads to an active search for information and – unlike typical casual shoppers – high involvement with the purchase decision. For those reasons, advertising is best placed in informational media that actively connect with the particular lifestyle (e.g., fishing magazines, cooking shows, as well as the niche media described earlier).

Since many special interest segments get a great sense of accomplishment from locating information and deals themselves ("thrill of the hunt," being first, trendsetting), plans can be strategically placed with one medium pointing to another one for more information.

Viking Range Corporation.
Selling appliances for a gourmet lifestyle.

Upscale Cooking – Viking Kitchen Appliances.

In Spring 2004, the Viking Range Corporation of Greenwood, Mississippi, launched a $4 million campaign to introduce premium-priced, commercial-style cooking products for the home. Viking argued at the time that it is not selling utilitarian appliances, but a gourmet lifestyle.

With retail rates for their kitchen ranges and ovens well above average, the target market not only had to enjoy a lifestyle of entertaining in the kitchen, but also the disposable income to trade up to their product line. Accordingly, Viking and its agency combined a consumer trend of refocusing toward the home (known as cocooning) with a passion for gourmet cooking among upscale socialites. The result was a campaign composed of cable TV spots on the *Fine Living Channel* and *The Food Network*, complemented by a print campaign in upscale magazines such as *Bon Appetit*, *Cigar Aficionado*, *Departures*, *Gourmet*, *House & Home*, *Saveur*, and *Wine Spectator*.

Power on the Lake – Mercury Outboard Motors.

Mercury Marine of Fond du Lac, Wisconsin, is the world's leading manufacturer of marine propulsion systems – i.e., boat motors and propellers. A specialist in its field, Mercury Marine competes with Johnson-Evinrude Corp. (another boat motor specialist) and a host of Japanese manufacturers, more known for their motorcycles and cars (Yamaha, Honda, Suzuki).

Not Created Equal.
People use boats for different purposes; Mercury Marine builds motors based on different uses.

Apart from the competition in this product category, there are also distinct differences in the kind of motors and accessories required for the boating hobby. In a way, this requires again the sub-segmentation we've encountered before. While one can readily eliminate everybody who is not into boating and water sports, it must still be determined which particular water sport enthusiast one is targeting given a specific boat motor (say, the Mercury 200 OptiMax vs. the Mercury Saltwater V-6 EFI).

Boating Magazines.
The boating magazine category is very deep, with several competitive titles for each major target sub-segment.

Since we have to be aware of the fact that each particular product belongs to a particular hobby, and that each hobbyist is very familiar with his or her hobby and knowledgeable about suitable equipment, it is of importance to grasp the nuances of product differences. In general, water sports enthusiasts fall into four broad categories: pleasure boaters (yachting, house boating, day cruising, etc.), speed boaters (race boating, jet skiing), freshwater anglers (bass fishermen, walleye fisherman, etc.), and saltwater anglers (deep sea fishermen, big game fishermen, off-shore/near-shore anglers). These hobbies each require different boats, which in turn require different engines. In addition, different aspects of the product come into play (e.g., durability for saltwater fishing, performance for speed boating).

Finally, different media exist for the various water sports hobbies. The boating magazine category alone is very deep and requires media planning and buying skills from the planner in charge of this buy. Content fit is almost more important than impressions and CPM figures. For example, *Yachting* magazine has a miserable CPM rate, as there aren't that many people owning a yacht. On a CPM basis, *Yachting* is not as good a buy as, say, *Boating World*. However, if the advertised brand is a big yacht (!) motor with lots of horsepower, this magazine is certainly a better buy. In addition, non-traditional media (product advertising, word-of-mouth, or events) offered by the media vehicle as a bonus, are an important consideration when planning the buy.

For target segments that appreciate expertise and straight talk, anything that insinuates these criteria in the advertising effort has a good chance to be well received. For any segment that is as far away from mainstream as lifestyle segments are, planners need to leave the comfortable world of audience and efficiency measurements and draw from their creative and detective skills.

The Niche Media Plan – An Example.

Up to this point, we have encountered the two important components for niche planning: niche media and niche segments. Let's use an example to illustrate the steps in building a plan and maintaining a budget when faced with a niche situation.

Imagine the following situation: in the mid 1990s, Qualcomm Cellular, a telecom client of the Minneapolis-based advertising agency Fallon McElligott, had invented one of the first dual-band (analog/digital) cell phones, and wanted to make a splash in announcing this to dealers, resellers, the trade media, and other important stakeholders and related opinion leaders. They planned to make this announcement at a major upcoming trade show in New Orleans. They asked the agency to support the announcement with any possible form of advertising, so that the new phone could not be missed. The budget was sufficient for a trade show, but small when compared to an annual media buy.

"Day-in-the-Life" of the Target Segment.

Since Qualcomm had made it pretty clear that they wanted favorite press coverage and sales support from dealer groups (business-to-business) as a result of the "blitz" campaign, and since the trade show lasted only a week, there wasn't much time to promote the phone. Fallon's media team, which has had good experiences with concentrating on media encounters rather than media audience compositions, started planning by asking how this week might look for the visiting dealers and media representatives from the moment they arrive at the airport – and, consequently, what "media" (this term was left wide open) they might come across. Here's what they came up with:

Upon arrival, typical conference visitors pick up their luggage, hail a cab or a shuttle, and commute to their hotel. After unpacking, they might go for a drink or dinner. The following few days, they will spend most of their time in the conference center, either manning a booth, or prowling the aisles to make connections. In-between, they will socialize with business acquaintances and "old friends." They will most likely set aside a few hours or a day to sightsee, and will fly back home after a few days.

Media Encounters.

Let's start with the airport: after exiting the plane, visitors will be exposed to terminal dioramas, luggage carousel boards, and luggage cart handles. If using a taxi cab, visitors will see taxi tops, taxi trunk boards, back of receipt, and dashboard posters. In the hotel, there is the key card, complementary newspaper wraps or special sections, and welcome signage for attendees (if this is the official conference hotel). On the street, there are hot dog vendor carts (incl. umbrellas), horse buggies, and event support for the official social meetings of this exhibit. Finally, in or near the conference center, there are opportunities to use product-based media (coffee cups, conference brochure sleeves, info desk tabletop tents, closed-circuit TV program loops, etc.)

Execution.

The "day-in-the-life" technique was particularly useful since time and money were of the essence and the niche target was unlikely to consume the standard mass media during the time of the exhibit.

After collecting all possible choices, Fallon's media team settled on choices that were subtle and elegant enough to not appear too blatantly as advertising, raised the already positive high-tech image of Qualcomm, and could be executed quickly and in a flexible manner. The team chose airport coverage, taxi coverage, and conference arena coverage combined with a sleeve wrapper on *USA Today* editions delivered to the two biggest conference hotels on the most important days of the conference. The plan called for advertising until the day before the conference ends except for the taxis and airports, which ran until the day after. In addition, after some research into where most visitors can be expected to come from, additional airport advertising was purchased in the home airports, which visitors would see upon arrival back from the conference as a last reminder.

Results.

Qualcomm received very positive press coverage in many related trade and consumer magazines and also got a number of early order calls immediately following the conference.

Over 80% of conference goers remembered having seen the Qualcomm ads somewhere, while nobody perceived them as intrusive. Having understood the niche market and its habits, and strategically combining niche media into a fast-paced campaign, worked extremely well.

Summary.

This chapter has covered some pretty broad ground.

Under the general heading of "niche" marketing we have touched on

- niche media,
- niche applications of major media, and
- media planning related to some of the more common niche target definitions.

Niche Media.

You noticed, no doubt, that what we called niche media here was in fact regular media with the ability to more precisely target smaller groupings of audience segments. Niche media, as we showed you, can be product delivered or location specific.

Among media companies, this special targeting ability results from a strong focus on media content. Niche marketers just need to know how to take advantage of such focus in the media environment.

Mass Media Can Be Niche Media.

Even looking at some of the more general and broadly targeted media, like network television, we talked here about carefully selecting special programs that enjoy smaller, loyal audiences. We saw that certain widely distributed network TV programs can be and are used to target certain niche market segments.

Target Segments.

We talked about several different ways to segment a target audience. We covered lifestyle segmentation, ethnic segmentation, attitudinal segmentation, and even commercial segmentation.

In each area we reviewed specific case examples. We discussed the media issues and the media planning considerations relevant for each segment example.

And we noted that even in narrow niches, you often have use of the full range of IMC possibilities, including:

- Direct Marketing
- Event Marketing
- Public Relations and Publicity

From this discussion overall, we hope that we have captured your interest. When it comes time for a job, this might capture your interest as well.

Niche media is booming as a specialty media field. If you haven't thought about this possibility yet, we hope you will now; you might want to check out a couple of niches looking for your ideal job. We said it before and it's more true than ever, you'll find riches in niches!

Lisa Weidman is an example of how you can build an exciting career with a specialty magazine. From a not-very-successful career as a stringer on a small paper, to a stint brewing coffee, to an executive job with an exciting niche publication – THRASHER, a magazine specializing in skateboards and related extreme sports activities.

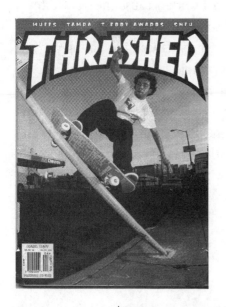

Career Capsule:

Lisa Weidman, Ad Manager, THRASHER .

Lisa majored in English at the University of California at Davis. She worked for the college newspaper in her junior year, covering campus news and arts and entertainment.

A First Job in Journalism.

The local Davis newspaper, the *Daily Democrat* (circulation 30,000), noticed Lisa's writing and hired her as a stringer in her senior year. She reviewed music, modern art, contemporary theater, and performance art events; wrote features on artists and musicians; composed editorials; and put together the weekly event calendar, getting paid $7 per review, $15 for a feature, and $19 for the calendar.

Such is life as a stringer at a small paper.

Lisa ended up having to supplement her income with 32 hours a week at a coffee house. (Thanks a latté!)

She was afraid of getting stuck in her college town. So when her lease came up, she packed up and headed off to Berkeley.

Lisa worked at a clothing store in Berkeley for a year while trying to find a job in publishing. No luck. So she left for San Francisco. Her luck changed as soon as she arrived.

She landed an interview with a relatively new magazine called *THRASHER*.

THRASHER – All Aboard!

THRASHER is a skateboarding publication read by 350,000 teenage boys. They are devoted readers who pass along the magazine to an average of seven friends. They tend to read the magazine in a group.

THRASHER also covers music and snowboarding.

Lisa's background in alternative music and pop culture seemed like a good fit for the magazine. She was hired as Advertising Manager.

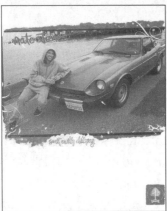

Some sample ads from THRASHER.

THRASHER was a hot magazine when Lisa came on board. As a matter of fact, there was a waiting list of advertisers who wanted to buy space and advertise in it. (WOW!)

Lisa started with a one-inch thick binder filled with signed advertising contracts.

These companies all wanted to jump on board the skateboard craze.

Smart Preparation. Dumb Luck.

Lisa admits that the job was a complete fluke, but as you will see throughout this book, many careers are a combination of smart preparation (Lisa's writing skills) and dumb luck (showing up at *THRASHER*).

Lisa wanted editorial, not advertising. She wanted a job where she could write. She took the Ad Manager position because *THRASHER* was a magazine she had read.

The publishers also convinced her that the magazine would be around for a while. Lisa saw this job offer as her "big break" – her foot in the door.

Small Company. Big Responsibility.

Working for a small magazine with a staff of just 25 allowed Lisa to do more than one job.

She was Ad Manager for six years and a copy editor for four. She did the additional work because she wanted to.

The magazine needed someone to pick up the slack – and Lisa was that someone. Her job is far from boring because she is involved in so many projects

This a typical example of how new media can grow rapidly if and when they connect with a new and rapidly growing activity. The manufacturers of specialized equipment and consumers interested in that equipment provide the framework for a profitable new media enterprise.

Discussion Questions.

1. Niche Media.

What is the difference between mass and niche media?

How can our conventional mass media be used as niche media?

What are some of the exclusively niche media we covered here?

What niche media do you see around you on a regular basis?

How large or small should a media audience be?

2. Niche Segments.

What are some of the most commonly identified niche segments?

Every person in America is part of some niche segment, including you. To which niche segment might you belong? How does this make you feel?

Why do marketers want to target messages to certain niche segments?

3. Niche Planning.

How is niche planning different from traditional media planning?

Exercises.

1. Think about cable TV. Study your local cable TV guide and study the programming offered on different cable networks in your city. **For each niche target segment listed below, make a list of 3-5 cable networks you think might fit the niche.** Be specific and explain your choices.

   - Teen girls aged 15-19
   - Early retirement adults aged 50-64
   - African American adults aged 18-24
   - CPAs and tax accountants

2. Go to a specialty store. Go to the place where they sell specialty magazines – for example, a pet store like PetSmart, an auto parts store like Trak Auto, or a hobby or computer or crafts store. **Buy a specialty magazine and study it. Take note of all the products you see advertised and consider the editorial content covered by the magazine.** Write a short report about the people and products that fit the publication's niche.

3. Choose one of the following products or services:
   - American Orient Express – deluxe rail journeys
   - Rogan Corporation – custom knobs and levers
   - Sparrow Sound Design – specialty jazz record label

   Imagine that you are the media planner working on this client's business and recommend a niche media plan for the client. Identify the niche segment you will target. Consider and identify the media you will recommend for use in delivering the client's message to the target segment. Write this up as a 2-3 page report.

IV New & Interactive Media Planning

THIS SECTION WILL COVER the venue of new media, the technology that created it, how this technology is being manifested, and how to buy and sell advertising in this new realm.

Welcome to Cyberspace.

It's a new world – a world full of new kinds of hardware and software and possibilities that science-fiction writers only dreamed of. And it's changing every minute.

Inside of that world, a real business is growing. In advertising alone, it's already over $8 billion, according to the Interactive Ad Burea. As an ad media, it's bigger than outdoor.

How This Section is Organized.

Part IV will introduce you to new media in three chapters:
• **Chapter Ten** will survey media's changing world.
And you'll learn about the forces driving that change.
• **Chapter Eleven** will dive into new media technology.
You'll learn about all the different new media options.
• **Chapter Twelve** will connect us with media in cyberspace.
You'll learn about how new media is bought and sold.

A True Story.

In 1997, I attended a professional seminar about direct marketing strategies and tactics.

The seminar had nearly two hundred different class break-out sessions on myriad topics ranging from creative treatments to list procurement. With all of these courses, there were only two focusing on new media (or as they euphemistically called it: electronic marketing).

I attended these two courses. Both of them were more focused on minimizing and degrading the media than actually offering anything constructive on how to capitalize on the growing trend.

I will never forget one of the more outrageous quotes from one of the seminar facilitators. He said, in very stentorian and practiced tones *"Chase, if you will, the electronic butterfly of this new media, but do not be surprised when it leads you off a cliff. A cliff to your professional doom and demise."*

Many of my fellow attendees scribbled their notebooks furiously, hungrily absorbing every word the facilitator uttered. Others of us rolled our eyes and began doodling in the margins of our PowerPoint printouts.

The facilitator had obviously lost those of us whom were evidently committed electronic butterfly chasers.

Then, I received the brochure for that same conference just one year later. I noticed two very interesting things.

First, the agenda of classes now featured two hundred and fifty break-out sessions – *half of them* were about new media.

Secondly, the facilitator who warned us about new media the previous year was nowhere to be found.

Maybe those butterflies pushed *him* off the cliff.

Such is the nature of new media. It is a very powerful force, capable of changing the way people see things and conduct business, and of doing so very rapidly.

But what is "new media?" An online search will provide dozens of pages of definitions for the term ranging from the academic to the obscene.

Electronic Butterfly.
Chase if you will…but don't forget that MSN already owns it.

Our Definition.

For the purpose of advertisers and communicators, here is our definition: **New media** is probably best defined as *the use of **digital technology** to **communicate** with a target audience.*

Please note that this definition says nothing specifically about the Internet. New media requires computer technology, but it does not necessarily require the World Wide Web.

Digitization and Interactivity.

The most important facets of new media are these: digitization and interactivity.

Digitization is the technological wonder that makes new media possible. It translates all kinds of information (data, text, graphics, and sound) into bits and bytes – into a binary language. This allows information to be manipulated and transmitted quickly, easily, and securely.

All new media, to some extent, depend on digital technology. One other unique result of this is often a degree of **interactivity** unrivaled by traditional media.

The transmitter is able to receive feedback from the recipient and establish a dialogue.

Computer hardware and software, in all shapes, sizes, and configurations (think beyond your PC or Mac), are the vehicles on and between which new media travels.

New media is a convenient term to describe a wide range of options now available to communicators.

Many examples of "new" media are basically upgrades (albeit high-tech upgrades) of familiar, more traditional arrows in a communicator's quiver.

But some of the resultant media are legitimately new and novel. They implement methods that were, a decade ago, thought more at home in the milieu of science fiction than in the hands of consumers. The old *Star Trek* communicators brandished by Kirk and Spock are nearly indistinguishable from today's new cell-phones with nationwide walkie-talkie features … right down to the chirping beep.

Digitization. Dig It!

Digitization is the technological wonder that makes new media possible.

It means you can translate all kinds of information, including your favorite music, into a binary language.

This allows information to be manipulated quickly, easily, and securely. And it means an iPod can fit in your pocket or purse.

The New Media Difference.
You don't just plan it and buy it.
In many cases, you design it as well.
That means lots of opportunities for smart
cookies.

One Big Difference

There is one big difference between new media and the traditional media of print and broadcast.

With new media, you don't just plan it and buy it. In many cases, you design it as well.

Or, at the very least, have significant input and impact on the design and implementation of your new media program.

The fact that you can participate in its creation makes new media one of the most exciting areas of the world of media.

10 Media's Changing World

TECHNOLOGY IS THE DRIVING FORCE that is changing the media world. It always has been: from Gutenberg's 15th century perfection of printing with moveable type, to the 20th century inventions of broadcast and telecommunications, to the 21st century developments now coming into our lives.

The Constant is Change.

It will always be this way.

While media professionals don't necessarily have to be techno-savvy, they do need to be technologically literate.

That's what this chapter is all about.

Chapter Organization

In this chapter, we will:

- Examine The Digital Revolution and its role in the creation of new media;
- Discuss Moore's Law;
- Identify and examine the benefits of digital marketing:
  - Customer Interaction – here, we'll help you understand what new technology does and doesn't do for communicators and media managers as they work to design their programs.

341

- Digital Environment – help you to recognize how new technology changes or enhances your existing communication options; and
- Examine the concept of convergence.

The Digital Revolution.

Defined as *the translation of textual, graphic, or audio information into a transmittable binary language understandable to computers*, **digitization** is one of the most important technological advances in decades.

It is similar in magnitude to Gutenberg's perfection of the printing press in that it made more information more approachable and available to more people than ever before.

And there was revolution. Have no doubt.

The Reformation, and even our own American Revolution, powered in many ways by the printing press was a media-driven revolution. And there's a another one going on.

Whereas Gutenberg made the mass production of books, pamphlets, and newspaper possible, digitization has made the production and distribution of word, sight, and sound possible to everyone with access to a computer.

Digitization is the means for the spread of the Internet; satellite communications; compact discs; DVDs; digital photography; and hundreds of other innovations we now take for granted.

Is revolution too drastic a word? Hardly.

The Internet and satellite communications have allowed us access to immediate and unfiltered news, ideas, and information globally.

Governments have fallen, people have been liberated, borders have faded, and fortunes have been made (and lost) – all under the influence of digital technology.

As Larry Grossman, former president of NBC News noted. *"Printing made us all readers. Xeroxing made us all publishers. Television made us all viewers. Digitization makes us all broadcasters."* Think about that. It really is a revolution.

Binary Digits.

Bits are the basis of the binary language of computer code. A bit is either a "1" or a "0."

A Bit of Background.

To understand this big thing, you'll have to understand a small thing. All of this change and innovation is owed to something as simple as a **bit**.

A bit, short for **bi**nary dig**it**, is the basis of the binary language of computer code.

Quite simply, it is either a "1" or a "0." These two numbers, or digits, are toggles. Think of them as light switches that tell a computer to do either: this or that, on or off, black or white. Interesting, but pretty basic and limited.

It's when you start putting more and more of these bits together that you begin to realize the power of digitization.

A string of eight bits creates a **byte**. Bytes are where the magic begins to be created.

A single byte has 256 unique permutations of 1s and 0s, beginning with 00000000 and ending with 11111111.

Remember that number, 256, as you will see it comes up quite often in new media technology.

Depending on the programming, a single byte can represent a letter, a word, a color, a sound, a movement, or an action.

Bits and Graphics.

For example, graphics are described by the number of bits used to represent each dot or pixel (picture element).

- A 1-bit image is monochromatic (a bit representing either black or white).
- An 8-bit image supports 256 (2 to the 8th power) colors or variations of gray (grayscales).
- 16-bit graphics represent the ability to show roughly 65,000 colors.
- 24- or 32-bit graphics support what is more or less true color (millions of possible colors).

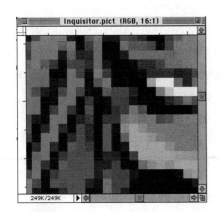

Inquisitor.pict (RGB, 16:1)

249K/249K

Pixel This.

Graphics are described by the number of bits used to represent each dot or pixel.

Combinations.

When bytes are used in combination to create sounds and images, for example, they work together to form things like the latest music CD or DVD, computer program, website, or video game. When they're used in combination to create words and graphics they can create something like this textbook.

Result – Multimedia.

The beauty of bits is that, while that digital information may represent different things (text, music, colors, etc.), they combine effortlessly making multimedia possible.

Multimedia is the complete digital technology package, combining the computational data, text, graphics, and sound into one easy-to-create and easy-to-distribute package.

This packaging of sight, sound, and information is one of the hallmarks of new media.

Distribution.

Distribution is made possible by sending that multimedia digital information over the airwaves or wires from a transmitting unit to a receiving unit.

The complexity and amount of digital data transmitted is limited only by something called bandwidth. **Bandwidth** is the number of **bits per second** (bps) that can be transmitted and received through a given channel.

To ensure the full digital experience is received, the bandwidth needs to be matched to the type of data transmitted. Here are some example of the bandwidth you need to get digital information in "real time":

- Simple text = 14,400 bps
- Graphics = 28,000 bps
- Voice = 64,000 bps
- Stereo audio = 1.2 million bps
- Video = 45 million bps

What's Your Bandwidth?
Bandwidth is the number of bits per second that can be transmitted and received through a given channel.

The Need for Bandwidth.

If you do not match the bandwidth, you risk losing the customer because they will be unable to access your material in a timely fashion. So, determining the bandwidth available to your target will be a key factor in determining what new media you want to use and how you want to use it. If you are using online or wireless transmission to send your message, you are limited by the type of connection your target has. You will need to understand that.

Types of Connections.

As the first edition of this book is written, most Americans still have dial-up modems, which limit the type of digital traffic they can receive – they simply do not have the bandwidth to receive more bit-intensive data. The various types of connections available and the capabilities and limitations of each are:

- Dial-up Modem – 56.6K most common, though some people still have slower
- Cable Modem Broadband – 20x faster than dial up – 1.2 Mbps (megabits per second) download speed / 128 Kbps upload
- DSL Broadband (Digital Subscriber Line) – still faster (depending on subscription) – 384 Kbps to 7.1 Mbps download / 384 Kbps to 768 Kbps upload
- Satellite Broadband - Available to anyone - 400Kbps download / 50 to 80 Kbps upload
- Fixed Wireless - Just like digital telephone service; roughly as fast as DSL, but prone to weather issues

To Each According to Their Ability...

Target your medium to the abilities of your target market.

Most businesses and universities have access to the high-speed, broadband connections, while most home computers are still tied to the phone-line modems.

But that does not mean that you are precluded from reaching the at-home audience.

For example, other new media, such as CDs or DVDs, bypass bandwidth constraints by offering users direct access in lieu of transmitted messages.

So you can still get the message across in all of its multimedia glory to a target with limited bandwidth.

Remember... new media is not just the Internet.

Moore's Law.

New technology is usually very expensive – at least in the beginning. So, how has computer technology become so ubiquitous and relatively *inexpensive*?

It's because of something called Moore's Law.

Moore's Law is named for Gordon Moore, the co-founder of Intel, who observed something in 1965. And then made a prediction. He saw that computing power seemed to double every 18 months.

It was a simple observation based initially upon the ability to place a greater number of transistors on integrated circuits. Since more transistors could be placed, more power and speed would result.

It was a simple engineering observation, but it had powerful implications. In fact, it's the basis of a high percentage of the technological change we are all experiencing.

Moore's Law.

Named for Gordon Moore, a co-founder of Intel, his prescient observation (it's not really a law) is an explanation of the speed at which technology is reinventing itself.

Powerful Implications.

Moore's engineering observation had powerful economic and operational implications.

As computational power increased, the price for computers and their derivatives fell and use became more widespread.

A computer was no longer the sole domain of advanced research organizations, corporations, and universities.

The practical effect of Moore's Law is that as the computing and storage capacities increased, the cost of doing so decreased. As this decrease was realized, the complexity and acceptance of programming not only increased, but it also multiplied the places in which computerized and digital technology was found.

Moore's Law at Work.

Here's an example.

The price for a hard drive in 1970 was roughly $50 per megabyte. In 1999, the price was 10¢ per megabyte.

As Moore's law went to work, businesses were able to substitute cheaper, computerized features for other, more expensive features.

Think of a digital watch. Suddenly you have fewer moving parts and more capabilities.

As costs kept going down and capabilities kept going up, computers could be found in more and more places. This availability of cheap, powerful computing power is the genesis of new media.

Everyday items that have been around for decades now function like little computers. Your car, digital watch, television, and toaster all have computing power. That personal digital assistant (PDA) or your MP3 player have more computing power than the first NASA space flights.

Some New Problems.

But for every new wonder there is also a new worry.

Computers were not just replacing mechanical functions, but were also replacing human jobs.

Digitally controlled telephone answering services and automated teller machines were cheaper to operate and made businesses more efficient and profitable, but they also forced people out of work.

Moore's Law is often cited, quite deservedly, as the reason that "new" computer you bought six months ago is slower than the "new" computers at the store this month and almost obsolete a year after it's brought home. But that's also the explanation behind the rise of the digital age and new media marketing.

Digital Marketing.

As we have seen, digital technology is the cornerstone of new media. It allows not only the distribution of marketing information and material, but also the immediate and interactive exchange of information.

The impact of this on marketers and communicators can be resounding. It allows you to create digital environments in which you can communicate and conduct business.

You can create digital environments that are **logical**, **responsive**, and **comprehensive**; all of which contribute to allowing you to:

- Serve and anticipate the needs of your customers by using databases to track preferences and patterns, even suggesting alternatives or new offerings based on their past purchases or actions
- Become a truly global organization, regardless of your company's size, location, or resources
- Communicate quickly and effectively with customers around the world faster and more easily via e-mail, wireless and satellite communications, and the Internet
- Garner and develop sales leads more effectively using interactive kiosks; toll free numbers; and/or Internet registration

Let's take a deeper look into these digital environments.

Digital Environments Are Logical.

Digital technology has long been used as a business support tool based on its logic-based procedure.

Not only that, but they can remember a lot and find it for you fast.

Databases Are the Brains of the Computer.

Databases store *data* and provide *information*. Data are the raw facts and figures about whatever a business decides to collect: inventory; prices; colors; optional features; warehouse location; or interoperability with other products.

The list of what a database can store is virtually endless. It can even store other databases.

And the list keeps growing. Because the more data collected the more powerful and flexible the database.

Information Please...

Information is the result of querying the treasure-trove of data stored in the database. It is the answer to your question. You use information to make your decision.

Database-driven information has, for years, been used for inventory, accounting, shipping, and myriad other logistical functions. But, it has only recently begun to be used as a marketing and communications tool.

From the Backroom to the Showroom.

As computers became more ubiquitous, people became more comfortable with them. And as computing power increased, computers could become more "user friendly."

WYSIWYG and GUI

The advent of WYSIWYG (What You See Is What You Get) and GUI (Graphical User Interface) programming like Windows has further expedited the acceptance and usage of computers for more functions. By the way, that's pronounced "wizzywig" and "gooey." This "user-friendliness" has made it easier for everyone.

The Internet was originally designed for the military and academics to communicate and share ideas and information.

What it has become is, in effect, the democratization of digital technology. It has taken the power of this tremendous computational and logistical engine from the behind-the-scenes world of the engineers, accountants, and warehouses and thrust it forward to the showroom and the desktop.

The intuitive interface, coupled with widespread, easy, and secure access to a company's database allows businesses and customers to communicate and operate directly with each other, thereby letting them do things like:

- Research product specifications
- Order product
- Schedule service calls
- Check available inventories
- Check shipping progress
- Inquire about payments
- Request more information
- Ask questions and troubleshoot problems

These functions have been digitized for decades, but now, since the customer is also a part of the digital world, the need for the middleman is gone, allowing for a more efficient and cost effective business relationship.

What we're seeing emerge is something new and powerful – interactivity. The communication is now going both ways.

Cookies and Registrations.

Here are two examples of this interactivity.

The database can be used to enrich an ongoing customer relationship as well. The database can help your business to "remember" certain aspects of a particular customer's relationship with your business, and help to tailor the interface with them whenever they digitally visit you.

Cookies.

One way of accomplishing this is with cookies.

A *cookie* is a line of text that is written to a text file and placed on the user's hard drive when visiting a website.

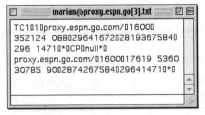

A Tasty Treat?

No. An Internet cookie is a simple line of text placed by a website onto a computer hard drive.

Contrary to what many believe, a cookie cannot worm its way through the user's hard drive looking to loot and pillage your files and share all of your secrets with the entire web world. Cookies don't do that.

Only the server (i.e., the site) that placed a cookie can access that cookie. It is not an open door for the entire Internet.

Furthermore, a cookie knows nothing about the user that it isn't given by the user. It does not surreptitiously sneak around your files looking for your address, phone number, and credit card number.

If it does have this information, it's only because you provided it on a previous visit – in a "shopping cart," for example.

The cookie remembers this information, and it makes your subsequent visits more fluid and enjoyable. Hopefully.

It remembers your personal information so you do not have to retype it during your next visit.

It can also remember things about your editorial or product preferences, what pages you visited last time, what items you left in your shopping cart, and so on.

Registration.

Another way of remembering you and using this memory to enhance your visit is via site registration.

Registrations are often nothing more than a simple means for a site to discover who visits and how often they return. But many sites use site registrations to do a lot more.

They will survey new registrants for data that they will use to "learn" about the visitor.

Ask Your Registrants Questions about Themselves.

As long as the questions are pertinent to their visit and your Internet visitors know they will get something of value in return, they will answer and do it honestly.

Questions You Should Ask in Your Registration Survey:
- Name
- Title
- Job responsibilities

- Company
- Kind of business that company does
- E-mail address (whenever you ask for a visitor's e-mail address, be sure tell them why you are asking for it and include either a synopsis of your e-mail privacy policy or a link to the entire policy. If you do not have a privacy policy, you had better develop one ... FAST!)
- Visitor's input for user ID and password

Some additional questions you may ask, depending on the nature of the site and your business:

- Decision-making influence of the visitor
- Areas of interest on your site
- Website for visitor or their business
- Language preference of visitor
- How the visitor discovered your site

Log-ins and Passwords.

With a log-in and password, the visitor is no longer a stranger. It's their admission into the site and database.

Depending on the sophistication of the business and the degree of "learning" the site is capable of, the log-in can trigger instantaneous changes to the site designed to suit their particular needs and wants:

- Feature products and services that meet the stated or demonstrated needs of the customer
- Offer automatic price adjustments based on account activity (loyalty point or quantity discounts) or previously demonstrated buying triggers (if a customer reacts more favorably to a on-the-spot discount or free shipping offer)
- Dynamic inventory adjustments (eliminate back-order problems and give real-time delivery estimates) can help customers plan purchases and shipments to meet their schedules
- Suggestions for complimentary products or services based on their purchase or browsing habits

- Automatic reminder of need to purchase replacement components that may be required for a current or previous purchase

All of these are driven by the interaction of new media with database technology.

Make Use of the Databases You Already Have.

By the way, sometimes you may have powerful tools for new media already at your disposal. For example, if your accounting, shipping, inventory, marketing, and sales-lead-management databases are not tied into your online business, you are missing a golden opportunity.

What New Media Should Do.

New media should not be an intimidating, difficult-to-use encounter for your customers.

For many businesses, an online encounter may be the first and only impression the customer has with them.

If it is a negative, they are gone. It takes less energy to click the mouse and jump to another site than it does to get in a car and drive to the next strip mall.

New Media Makes It Easy.

Fortunately, new media makes it very easy to ensure the customer is treated well and enjoys their experience.

As of 2004, most people in the developed world are familiar with computers.

Therefore, half the battle is already won. To be in line to win the war, you must remember a few basic tenets:

- Ease of use is of paramount importance.
- Simple and consistent interaction with customer.
- Make the customer want to interact; dialogue and information makes the sale.

Ease of Use Is of Paramount Importance.

Digital technology allows some very powerful, very cool things to be done on a computer screen. Because these things can be done does not mean they must be done.

Your new media venture is created to communicate your message to your audience, not wow your IT (Information Technology) team or win your ad agency an award.

You need to always make sure your customer can receive, use and understand whatever you create.

Remember Your Audience.

Are you a business-to-business operation that deals with customers who visit you from their office Internet account?

Or is your audience more likely to be consumers visiting you from their home?

The answer to this question can mean the difference between success and failure if you do not take bandwidth into consideration.

Remember, most office accounts have high-speed, high bandwidth connections while homes are still more likely to be accessing the web via dial-up modems.

A website designed for a home-access consumer clientele must therefore avoid large file, multimedia intensive creative or risk losing their customers.

On the other hand, a business-to-business site can get away with more bandwidth-hogging files.

Other Factors Affecting Ease of Use.

Ease of use is not restricted to memory and bandwidth

• Be sure your copy is understandable to your audience

• Avoid jargon unless the audience all know what it means

• Do not fall victim to a beautiful, but un-navigable design

• Make the site as easy-to-follow and intuitive as possible

Customers will not resent you for having a simple, clean, staid (dare I say, boring) design if they can follow the navigation, find what they want, buy it, and leave.

However, even if you have the coolest graphics, most intense animations, and wildest music out there … if they can't figure out where the order form is, you're toast.

The Key – Simple and Consistent Interaction.

What does your online customer expect when they visit your site? Do they know their way around?

Or does every visit feel like their first time?

Have you ever noticed how the big retailers' stores look the same in Decatur, Georgia, as they do in Decatur, Illinois.

As soon as their customers walk through the door, they know (more or less) where everything is.

This comfort zone is conducive to loyal, repeat business. They do not reinvent themselves with every new store they open. They understand the importance of consistency.

It's the same with new media.

The Importance of Consistency.

Your online presence, your kiosks, your e-mail campaigns, your wireless messaging – everything – must be consistent if you want to enjoy maximum impact with your customer. While it is in keeping with the tenets of Integrated Marketing Communications, we are talking about more than issues of look and feel, colors and logos.

It goes beyond that into understanding basic consumer behavior. With each visit to a site, you are conditioning your customers to respond in a certain way.

You are providing them certain stimuli and cues on how to navigate your site to research, shop, and buy.

Each visit to your site should be consistent. Think before you change the design and operation of your website.

Again, just because you *can* redesign frequently does not mean you should.

Once your customers are comfortable with doing business with you, you should be reluctant to make changes so drastic as they do not recognize you from one visit to the next.

Sometimes Change Is Necessary.

However, sometimes it cannot be avoided.

If you find that because of technological or operational issues, you need to implement a wholesale redesign, try to make the changes as smoothly and intuitively as possible.

Do not just spring the change on your customers.

Use new and traditional media to advertise and hype the changes. Tell your customers why the new design is being implemented and the benefits they will enjoy when they visit.

The Optimum – Make the Transition Seamless.

The best surprise is no surprise.

Ensure that existing shopping carts and cookies from the previous site design link and work with the new design.

Try to keep the key components of your site in the same location from one site to the next. Offer an automated guided tour of the new site, or even offer a link to use the previous design for a transitional period of time.

Make the Customer Want to Interact.

Remember that new media allows you to interact.

Digital interaction can serve as your customer service representatives, your technical assistance, even your sales force. But whereas sales people (*usually*) understand what it means to *be friendly to customers*, computers must be told.

To do so successfully does not mean programming a sunny personality or disposition into your site.

Doing so means helping your customers understand how to talk back to you and know what to expect when they do.

Remember you are trying to create a dialogue, so be conversational. Ask questions. Answer questions. Provide information.

Comfort Is Key.

When you succeed in making your customer comfortable enough to interact, you are on your way to establishing a relationship, and that is the ultimate goal.

A relationship allows you customize your messaging, your media selection, and even your product.

Digital Enhancement.

Digital environments have the ability to store, maintain, and access incredible amounts of data, and with a few strokes of the keyboard – information.

An Information Warehouse.

This inexpensive and comprehensive information warehousing allows you to maintain and instantaneously access encyclopedic records and documentation of such important features as your inventory, specifications, troubleshooting assistance, and customer relationship tidbits gleaned from things such as surveys, previous purchases, or simply from sales and customer service conversations and correspondence.

Such detail allows you to tailor your communications to a specific audience. You can highlight products or features that are of particular interest to segments of your market that you could not feasibly or economically address before.

Special-Interest Communications.

You can create special-interest newsletters or other direct marketing efforts that are of interest to niches within your overall customer base that previously were either unknown or simply too expensive to try to reach before.

Your product development teams can use this type of information to determine if product modifications are warranted to be able to reach untapped, smaller markets.

Your media buys (both traditional and new media) will be enhanced by illuminating facets and segments of your market that may be better served by employing more targeted communications vehicles.

Creating New Business Models.

Some companies have translated their ability to gather, catalogue, and query database information into profitable consumer businesses in their own right. Amazon.com catalogued every book, CD, and DVD and made them available online.

Amazon did not actually stock the items, they established a medium for accessing the information and the infrastructure for procuring them in an easy and efficient way.

Doing so would have been cumbersome, if not impossible, without a digital environment in which to operate.

As you can see, in new media, it's relatively easy to bring new ideas into reality.

Virtual Warehousing.
A new media kind of new "product" idea.

The Power of Convergence.

New media has given rise to **convergence** – the combining of disparate technologies or media and their related industries into new (and sometimes competitive) products and services.

For example, the ability to fax documents was an example of a technological convergence where the technology of telecommunications and optical scanning and printing industries collided.

Fax machines were being incorporated, produced, and marketed by manufacturers that had previously specialized in making phones, copiers, scanners, or printers.

Not only product offerings but entire industries are now experiencing convergence.

Companies that had previously carved their own niches out of the consumer and business worlds are now, thanks to the technological advances brought about by new media, forced to venture into other venues to expand and survive.

Convergence and Choice.

Consumers already deal with the choices convergence represents. Another example – a decade ago, homeowners had separate phone, long-distance, and cable-television services.

Now, consumers can obtain these services (and more) from the same company. Wireless phone services can either compete with traditional phone services or can converge and offer their customers hybrid services.

Convergence has companies scrambling to meet the needs and expectations of customers, as well as to simply survive.

How does a long-distance provider survive when its customers can speak to anyone they want to across the planet using their local dial-up Internet access?

How will the Postal Service continue when everyone has e-mail and online bill paying capabilities?

What new services should banks incorporate into ATMs to ensure customer service and loyalty is maintained?

And how will traditional media evolve when your newspaper, your favorite radio station, and even video enter your house through your computer?

These are all real-world questions that face companies in general and marketers in particular. How they are answered will determine their ultimate success or failure.

The Challenge of Convergence.

From a marketing and communications perspective, convergence represents a number of challenges. For example – message integration.

As the methods available for transmitting our messages increase, we must simultaneously make sure that the message is consistent across the various platforms; while also doing our best to make the best use of the various media's capabilities and the fact that different niches may be interested in different messages.

Convergence reflects the merging of industries, technologies, and content that used to be considered separate:

- Computer hardware, software, and services
  - Microsoft was initially a software company, but is now involved in myriad other related ventures from gaming hardware (Xbox) to entertainment networks (MSNBC) to online portals and information providers (MSN).
- Telephone, cable, satellite, wireless
  - Your cable or satellite TV company is now also probably your telephone service provider; which also offers digital and cellular telephone service.
- Entertainment, publishing, and information
  - AOL/Time Warner anyone?

Convergence and Media Planning.

As a communicator and media planner, you must be cognizant of the changes taking place due to convergence.

And, with Moore's Law still in force, the speed of that change can be truly breathtaking.

The phenomena can open up broader and more lucrative media arrangements for you by allowing you to negotiate with a single source for broader exposure on more diverse vehicles.

However, it can also represent challenges if a preferred medium, with which you have an established relationship, is suddenly absorbed into another, competitive entity.

Either way, you must recognize the synergies converged companies enjoy and do your best to capitalize on the opportunities they represent.

Summary.

This chapter provided a glimpse of what makes new media possible and realistically *new*.

New media is the outcome of the digital revolution and the ability to translate what were, heretofore, divergent media options into one, easy to use, highly transportable multimedia package.

We reviewed the basics of digital technology and how it has created an exciting and increasingly ubiquitous digital environment, allowing the storage, transfer, and manipulation of incredible amounts of data.

We discussed how this data, when made understandable and usable, becomes information.

We discussed Moore's Law and illustrated how, while originally developed as a technological phenomena, it has also made the rise of digital technology felt in everything from computers to cars to toaster ovens.

We examined the power and characteristics of the digital environment and how it is so well suited to the marketing and business world. Creating the ability to build relationships and solve customer issues with the stroke of key or click of a mouse.

And we discussed convergence and the challenges and opportunities it represents for both businesses and communicators.

Discussion Questions.

1. The Digital Revolution.

What does the word "bit" stand for? What is a bit?

What is bandwidth? Why should media planners know this?

2. Moore's Law.

What is Moore's Law and what does it imply about new-media development?

What are some of the problems or issues that we might explain by citing Moore's Law?

3. Digital Technology and Marketing.

What are three distinct advantages of marketing in a digital environment?

What is a "cookie?" Is a "cookie" a good or bad thing?

What can you do to ensure a good first impression among customers experiencing your company in a digital environment?

4. The Power of Convergence.

What does "convergence" mean in the world of media?

Is convergence a good thing?

What does convergence mean for people who want a career in media or media planning?

Exercises.

1. **Write a short report on cookies and registrations.** Explain each in your own words. Then, from a consumer's perspective, consider the advantages and disadvantages of each. From the consumer's point of view, do you think cookies and registrations are a good thing? Your final report should be 1-2 pages in length.

2. Consider your university's website. study the site and critique it according to the three major criteria discussed here:

- ease of use,
- simple and consistent interaction, and
- level of interactivity and dialog.

What improvements would you recommend?

11 New Media Technology

THE FOLLOWING MEMO WAS WRITTEN in 1876 by Western Union executives.

"This "telephone" has too many shortcomings to be seriously considered as a means of communication. The device is inherently of no value to us."

An Instructive Example...

An electronics store was faced with an all-too-common retailing dilemma.

Sales of a once-hot product were declining.

Demand seemed to have fizzled out.

The brick and mortar storefront was unable to eliminate product or obtain RA (return approval) to return unused product to the vendor.

They needed to sell the overstocked items, but they also needed to do so with minimal advertising expense.

Their solution was to use the Internet.

SEO = Search Engine Optimization

In particular, they used a strategy called **SEO** (**search engine optimization**). SEO is a strategy for increasing the number of visitors to a website by ranking high in the search results of a search engine.

The higher a website ranks in the results of a search, the greater the chance that that site will be visited by a user.

Internet users don't usually click through many pages of search results, so where a site ranks in a search is essential for directing more traffic toward the site.

SEO helps to ensure that a site is accessible to a search engine and improves the chances that the site will be found by the search engine.

Via their in-store research, this retailer realized that the product had high brand awareness and was being requested (and therefore purchased) by name.

This information helped their SEO efforts by allowing them to concentrate their key word strategy on the brand name.

Further, they focused their efforts on a text-driven search engine. This engine did not show the graphics and distracting banners that other search engines feature.

The rationale for this approach was that their offering would cut through the visual clutter by being text only and appeal more directly to serious shoppers for the product, rather than the more casual browser for whom graphics and product pictures would be more appealing.

But they didn't stop there. They knew there would still be competition – even for the serious shopper's eye.

To attract more attention, the retailer bought a prominent sponsorship position for the keywords and tailored an attractive offer that was communicated in crisp, succinct copy. Ten words.

The results? The retailer's brick and mortar sold 14 units in the month the SEO campaign was run.

Online sales were 144 units – ten times the volume.

The product was no longer overstocked.

In fact, it was back-ordered.

This is a meaningful demonstration of the power of a well targeted and coordinated new media campaign.

What Kind of New Media Are out There?

There are many new venues for marketing messages.

Each offers challenges quite different from traditional marketing vehicles. Each also offers new opportunities to interact with your customers and build stronger and more robust relationships as well.

How do bits and bytes translate into dollars and cents?

Can new media transform the staid, traditional world of brick and mortar retailing into click and ship e-commerce?

Or is it simply a complimentary, new means of getting your message out to the public?

In some ways, the answer is "yes" for every business that wants to survive in the 21st century.

Ultimately, the purpose of the digital revolution, as far as business is concerned, is to improve the bottom line – to survive and prosper in a changing world.

Throughout this chapter, we will address the core question. Simple but complex. Basic but profound.

How do you do that?

How do you get to "yes"?

Chapter Organization.

In this chapter, we will:

- Discuss the common goals of new media marketing
- Explore the basic communication characteristics of digital marketing
- Identify the myriad forms of new media available

For the purposes of this discussion, there are five primary areas of new media:

1. **The Internet;**
2. **The Intranet;**
3. **Wireless;**
4. **General business applications;** and
5. **Home/personal entertainment.**

Let's take them one at a time.

The Internet.

The Internet is the most visible and easily recognized of the new media. In less than a decade, it has gone from high-tech plaything to ubiquitous business and lifestyle tool.

It has become the means for business to expand its reach, message, and ultimately its client base.

The reach of the Internet is indeed global. As of September 2002, there were an estimated 605.6 million Internet users worldwide.

The majority of these users are now in Europe, followed by Pacific Rim and Asia, with North America a close third.

With the audience of web users spread throughout the world, virtually every business is now international.

The local, family-run sporting goods store in Huntley, Illinois, is, thanks to their web presence, now able to attract and conduct transactions with customers in Huntly, Scotland.

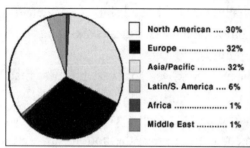

☐	North American 30%
■	Europe 32%
☐	Asia/Pacific 32%
▨	Latin/S. America 6%
■	Africa 1%
▨	Middle East 1%

Going Global.
The majority of Internet users are in Europe, closely followed by Asia and North America.

Four Types of Internet Sites.

There are four basic types of Internet sites, each with their own, distinct goals. We'll define these types of sites as:

- **Channel Churners**
- **Matchmakers**
- **Digital Destinations**
- **E-Bazaars**

Let's take these one by one.

Channel Churners.

The primary goal of a Channel Churner site is to attract attention, or in the online vernacular: build traffic.

This type of site wants to attract and maintain as many visitors as possible. And then capitalize on the traffic.

This type of new media venture is most often found on the Internet. Online portals are the best example of sites that have this goal. Sites such as Yahoo!, Google, Juno, or AOL fit in this category.

Channel Churners.
Google is an online portal and search engine, a very successful example of a channel-churner type of Internet site.

Their revenue is derived primarily from selling their visitors, or more accurately, selling the *prospect* of their visitors' attention in the form of advertising space.

The more Channel Churners learn about their visitors, the more lucrative their visitors become. At least, potentially.

Good Channel Churner sites require registrations for enhanced benefits, conduct frequent surveys, and analyze visitors usage patterns to derive information about them that will enable the sites to segment visitor likes and interests, ultimately helping them predict visitor behavior.

If they can accomplish that, they can then charge higher advertising rates based on their ability to more accurately target a particular niche within their overall market.

Matchmakers.

The goal of a Matchmaker site is to generate interest.

This interest is measured in terms of leads.

Leads can be either formal or informal. **Formal leads** are the more easily measured of the two varieties.

They are interactively obtained via online registrations, questionnaires, contests, or other request mechanisms such as downloads, trials, or contests.

The information garnered from formal leads is then qualified and passed on for further action, such as a sales call.

Informal leads are akin to traditional advertising and are more difficult to measure. Informal leads are those that result from a communication resonating with the target and developing enough interest that the target continues along the AIDA (Attention, Interest, Desire, and Action) model and develops desire and/or action.

Informal leads are rarely measured directly, but are rather inferred by resulting increased traffic or sales.

Matchmakers are not exclusively ventures of the Internet.

Though, as you will see, most of the new media vehicles we will discuss lend themselves readily and effectively to this goal.

MORTGAGE LOCATORS

Matchmakers.
MortgageLocators.com is an example of a matchmaker site, focused on developing leads for sale to advertisers.

American Girl®

Digital Destination.

AmericanGirl.com is a good example of a branded online destination, offering information, entertainment, and editorial about the brand and related products.

Gameplay.

Many times you will see branded destination sites offering games as a way to attract daily visitors, like this game at www.nabiscoworld.com.

monster®
today's the day™

Monster Branding.

Monster.com is an example of a digital destination more dependent on advertising to build its brand awareness.

Digital Destinations.

Digital Destinations are websites that exist to create or enhance brand awareness and desire.

This knowledge of the brand is what makes these Digital Destinations, particularly online. Their Internet address is directly tied to their recognized brand persona: Tide.com, Nabisco.com, ESPN.com, AmericanGirl.com.

Digital Destination sites offer information, entertainment, and editorial about the brand and related (often co-branded) products or topics. Internal resources, advertising or e-commerce (combining facets of other digital goal categories) funds them, but the primary focus remains the brand.

Tide.com is an excellent example of a Digital Destination. Tide laundry detergent is not typically an item that people will purchase online. Rather, the goal of the site is to enhance the Tide brand.

As such, it offers articles on fabric care, provides an interactive Stain Detective where users can determine how to get a particular stain out of a particular fabric … often using a treatment involving Tide or a related P&G product.

Tide.com is not heavily advertised as an Internet address, but is, nonetheless, a Digital Destination because of its pre-existing brand cache. Brands that immediately come to mind with a "www" thrown in front of them and "dot com" at the end are easy. But what about developing brands?

These sites are more dependent on advertising to help develop the initial brand awareness. Monster.com is a good example of this route.

Monster.com is a Digital Destination, albeit one with burgeoning Channel Churning tendencies. Initially, they placed advertising almost exclusively online to build the brand and bring visitors to the site.

Now Monster.com is one of the most recognized (and successful) Digital Destinations in new media.

E-Bazaars.
Sites like ebay and fogdog.com are representative examples of e-Bazaars, where product sales is the primary goal.

E-Bazaars.

These ventures have a rather straightforward goal: sales.

These ventures are the proverbial click-and-ship operations that run as the online arms of traditional retailers like Sears' Lands End at <u>landsend.com</u> or Barnes and Noble Books at <u>barnesandnoble.com</u>, or as pure click and mortar e-tailers such as amazon.com or fogdog.com.

Aside from their wares, these sites are selling two other key factors: convenience and selection.

Their convenience is immeasurable: 24/7 availability, easy shipping, potential tax savings on their purchases, no travel to and from the retailer, etc.

Selection is enhanced because e-Bazaar ventures do not have to worry about things like shelf and display space.

As discussed in the pervious chapter, digital environments are encyclopedic and allow for virtually unlimited inventory. If a book was published, a CD recorded, or a dress sewn – regardless of size or color – it can easily be catalogued and accessed through an e-Bazaar site, whereas a traditional retailer might not have the space or inclination to stock it.

This is fundamentally the success of such sites as ebay. If you want something, anything, old or new, you can find it on ebay.

It's the Content, Stupid.

How do websites achieve these goals?

One common denominator goal for each of the four types is that they provide **information**.

We tell website writers and designers that when they are writing copy, they must: "Think PR, not Advertising." Granted, like a good magazine or television ad, the home page of the site must engage the surfer. It has to have some sizzle and eye-catching WOW effect.

But once the visitor gets past the home page, the most important factor a site has toward accomplishing its goal is the CONTENT.

"Think PR, Not Advertising."

The "Think PR, not Advertising" war cry comes from the approach a communicator should take toward writing a solid press release versus a piece of ad copy.

Ad copywriters are looking for punchy, catchy ways of stressing the unique selling position.

PR writers also have their eyes on the ultimate prize, but they take a more straightforward and informative approach. They look for a story the media wants to run.

This differing approach is owed to the dictates of the media in which they are working. Ad copywriters are constrained by a set word count or amount of broadcast airtime.

They do not have the luxury of being able to provide reams of information. Moreover, since they're paying for the time or space, they can pretty much say anything they want.

PR writers have different constraints. They can provide the necessary information for communicating their message in its entirety.

They have the ability to give background specifications, answer questions, and provide follow-up information vital to their audience.

Critical to a successful PR campaign is the need for a story that the media wants to run. However, new media changes this dynamic in an important way. New media has almost infinite capacity to post information – so you can do more on the Internet with a PR mindset.

This is the philosophy I instill in my online team.

As we saw in the last chapter, space is not a rare commodity in the digital world. Visitors are looking for information of some degree, shape, or form... give it to them.

Think. What kind of information can your Internet presence offer? Of course, it depends on your business, but on the Internet, the possibilities are limitless.

Many sites offer information like:

- Multimedia or virtual reality demonstrations of your product or service
- White papers or newsletters
- Catalogues and inventory
- Customer service and troubleshooting assistance
- Product specifications
- Replacement parts and component listings
- Upgrade notices and downloads
- PR archives
- FAQs

Remember, the people visiting are interested in learning more. Tell it well.

Regardless of the goals discussed earlier, providing a consistent depth and breadth of robust and helpful information is what will drive your site toward success.

Intranets.

An intranet is a company's internal network of information and communication. It is often one of the most overlooked components of a company's new media plan.

It is frequently looked at as nothing more than a repository of basic company information: downloadable forms, phone numbers, and other mundane corporate information that used to take up an entire bookcase of binders. But it can be more than that.

Currently, most corporations make use of their intranet to provide information like:

- Internal announcements and information
- Industrial news and PR
- Company stock performance indicators
- HR policies and forms
- Sales directives and product specification information
- Training schedules and opportunities
- Accounting and expense report forms and/or processing

- Travel arrangement procedures
- Routine office supply orders
- Lunchroom menus

This type of information is important. Providing employees with ready access is an excellent use of an intranet.

But, as we said, it can be so much more.

More than a Bulletin Board.

If a company just uses their intranet for simple, mundane, or esoteric functions, it is failing to take advantage of it its full capabilities as a communications tool.

Often, the intranet is a tool of either the HR department or Corporate Communications. As such, it is rarely considered as a marketing or sales-communications tool.

Think what can happen if a company's intranet occasionally breaks the bonds of these more inward looking corporate functions.

For example, the Marketing Communications team needs to look to this tool as an integral part of their IMC arsenal.

Internally, it is vital for ensuring that a company's message is consistently and accurately delivered to its employees.

Have you ever spoken to someone from a company and asked them about a promotion, ad campaign, or press release and received a blank expression or shrug of the shoulders?

Unfortunately, the last people communicators tell about the latest campaign or media placement are often co-workers.

The intranet can be an excellent vehicle for internal marketing.

Intranet as a Profit Center?

An intranet might also be a venue to consider for your external communication goals.

Depending on the size and corporate demographics of the company, this could be an opportunity for your message to be seen regularly (and exclusively) by an important and captive audience.

Intranets are often a low priority on corporate budgets and operated on a shoestring. Some companies may even entertain sponsorships or advertising on their intranets as a means of maintaining the site.

Don't overlook the opportunity to reach a key target for your marketing message for minimal expense and effort.

Wireless.

Wireless technology is a complex and booming field.

In some manifestations, it is the realm of digital traffic beamed across the horizon, bouncing off satellites miles above the reaches of the Earth's atmosphere at the speed of light.

Other times it's not so grandiose, merely a special grouping of tables at the neighborhood fast food restaurant or café.

Wireless networks can stretch across continents or merely extend a few feet from a transmitter to a receiver.

Either way, it is the ability to send and receive digital traffic without the cumbersome tether of being physically plugged into a wired network.

Telecommunications.

The most common wireless component of the modern world is telecommunications.

Wireless digital telephones have become so ubiquitous that, in some cases, traditional wired telephone companies are scrambling to remain relevant (recall our discussion of convergence in the previous chapter).

But the wireless revolution extends beyond the freedom and mobility afforded consumers by their wireless phones.

It also offers the opportunity for highly targeted multi- and unidirectional communications that a media professional might consider as part of their new media plan.

Phone, PDA, Handheld, and More.

The new generation of digital telephones is no longer content to simply send and receive calls.

They're hybrids – combining the strength and features of telephones with Internet and e-mail access of a computer

XHTML MP & WAP CSS

XHTML MP: Short for *Extensible Hypertext Markup Language*, a hybrid between HTML and XML specifically designed for Net device displays. When applied to Net devices, XHTML must go through a modularization process. This enables XHTML pages to be read by many different platforms.

WAP CSS: Short for *Wireless Application Protocol Cascading Style Sheet*, a secure specification that allows users to access information instantly via handheld wireless devices such as mobile phones, pagers, two-way radios, smartphones, and communicators.

Although WAP supports HTML and XML, the WML language (an XML application) is specifically devised for small screens and one-hand navigation without a keyboard.

Source: www.pcwebopedia.com

Wireless Technology.
New systems, like this PDA from Blackberry, function on XHTML and WAP.

with the archival programming and time management assets of a PDA (personal digital assistant).

Do you have the ability to proactively communicate with customers or prospects using these hybrid devices?

Forward-thinking businesses are doing so right now.

Airlines are sending passengers alerts to changes in their itinerary or reservation; e-commerce sites send their customers delivery notices; or an online auction sends a bidder a notice that someone else has just outbid them.

In the future, media planners and communicators will need to know how to leverage the power of these devices.

A Bit of Alphabet Soup.

While these little computers have the ability to log on to the Internet, because of their graphics limitations not all sites can be accessed. If your Internet goals lend themselves to being available to wireless customers, are you ready and able to be reached by them?

These new systems use a different form of HTML called XHTML MP and WAP CSS.

This alphabet soup is not important to you as a media buyer, but it is something you need to discuss with your developers to ensure you develop a site capable of working with wireless handheld technology.

These systems are growing in popularity, as the hardware that accepts them is becoming more widespread.

However, the number of different hardware systems in the market is also the root cause of the major issue facing them right now – a lack of common standards.

With each phone, PDA, and other system on the market having different screen sizes, color configurations, and interface requirements, there is still a glaring lack of agreed-upon development standards.

But this will probably change. Right now, it is merely a blip on the growing popularity of the medium.

Wireless Drive Time.

Computers have helped operate and control the modern automobile for decades. Recently, computers have moved from under the hood to inside the dashboard.

The GPS (global positioning system) triangulates the exact location of the equipped vehicle using satellites, making it possible to know where any given car or truck is located at all times. If you know where the vehicle is, you can communicate with them, too.

General Motors has capitalized on this with OnStar.

Generally marketed as a safety tool, OnStar can automatically recognize if the vehicle was in an accident with air bag deployment. It can contact the vehicle and, if necessary, dispatch authorities to the exact location of the accident.

OnStar can also communicate with the vehicle to do things like unlock the doors or provide a lost motorist with directions to the nearest gas station or hospital.

OnStar also offers subscribers digital phone service and a host of other subscription enhancements, recognizing the power of wireless and digital technology in a novel and potentially lucrative way.

Wireless Radio Reborn.

Listing radio programming as a wireless wonder seems a bit dated ... by about 80 years.

But again, owing to satellite and digital technology, radio is experiencing a bit of a rebirth. Satellite radio allows subscribers to listen to uninterrupted radio service without the constraints of traditional radio (analog) signals.

Traditional radio is analog, meaning that the signal is transmitted in directional waves, requiring line of site to the transmitter signal.

If you moved too far from the transmitter (FM), or something got between you and the transmitter (AM), the signal was lost.

Onboard Communications.
General Motors' OnStar computer system is a leading-edge example of applied wireless communications.

Digital Radio.
Satellite radio uses digital signals that deliver additional information along with the song.

Satellite radio makes such issues a thing of the past.

The height of the satellites relative to the receivers (outer space versus the tops of skyscrapers) coupled with the digital nature of the signal makes such issues moot.

A subscriber can tune into a station in Los Angeles on a cross-country trip and be listening to the same station in Bangor, Maine. The digital signal also includes information like the artist, name of the song, and whatever other information the transmitter chooses to include.

Currently, such service does not feature advertising and operates instead on a subscription basis.

However, this does not preclude an advertiser from participating via avenues such as sponsorships.

It is also not unforeseeable that the technology, in order to reach a wider audience, will abandon all or portions of the subscription model in favor of advertising supported programming, making this an appealing *new* new media venue to consider.

General Business Applications.

Digital technology has opened up a number of new media marketing and business venues, such as:

- **Computer-based Training**
- **Kiosks**
- **Web-based seminars and conferences**
- **Ad screens**

Each of these applications offers unique challenges and opportunities to marketers today and tomorrow.

Computer-based Training.

Computer-based training, or CBT, is a growing medium for both marketers and educators.

CBT in Education.

Today's school age society has never known life without computers, so using them as a means of learning is an elementary leap for them.

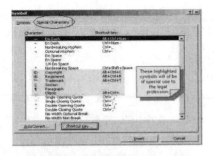

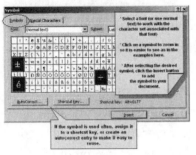

Training.

The computer tutorial is one of the most common examples of computer based training.

Similarly, as the majority of the American public is fairly computer savvy, using the tool as a means for training and educating customers and prospects is a similarly likely expectation for today's businesses.

The most common example of computer based training is the computer program **tutorial**, a short, self-guided tour of a program wherein the user can learn to operate the system and try the features of a piece of new software or hardware.

The tutorial is hands-on, allowing the user to see some function or feature performed and then given the opportunity to try to replicate what they have just seen.

A more complex form of CBT is to actually present educational material to a student and, using quizzes and exams, adjudicate the student's progress through a computer-based curriculum. These programs are often housed on the Internet, intranet, or on a designated terminal's hard drive.

Some universities are using CBT to conduct coursework both on campus and across the country. It provides students the opportunity to take a class at their own pace; provides 24/7 access to the lectures and materials, and provides real-time feedback and grading for their exercises.

CBT in Marketing.

For a marketer, CBT offers opportunities in the form of enhanced customer service and product training for employees and customers.

It can help tech writers fine-tune their instruction manuals; product managers develop new features or uses for their products; and companies to up-sell or cross-sell by demonstrating a product's interoperability with other "fine ACME products or upgrades."

The principle behind using CBT as a marketing tool is basically that of a test-drive.

Show a company's product in use, allow the user to play with it (even virtually), and put it through its paces.

After the demonstration, you are much more likely to have gained a customer.

Interactive Selling.
Point-of-purchase displays such as this are popular applications of computer-based kiosk technology.

Kiosks.

The technology and software logic used for CBT, is also easily translatable to computer kiosks.

Kiosks are free-standing computer terminals, usually equipped with touch-screen technology, that provide consumers with information about a product or service.

Most of us have seen kiosks as high-tech point-of-purchase (POP) displays, often located in supermarkets, malls, office buildings, or other high pedestrian traffic areas.

Supermarket kiosks provide information like dietary facts, recipes, product shelf locations, and the like.

Often, such kiosks will have small printers that print the information from the screen for easy use.

It can also print in-store coupons for the queried product (or a featured replacement; i.e., competitive product).

Consumers use kiosks when they provide solid, useable information. However, kiosks can also be used to gather information from the consumers.

Kiosks can be used to conduct surveys or questionnaires and track the services about which consumers are asking.

Kiosks can also provide other advertising opportunities by way of sponsorships or by running ads while the kiosk is not in use. The kiosk monitor at this point becomes a television screen, so these ads, when designed with wit, color, and motion can and do attract attention.

Often, it's these advertisements which initally alert consumers to the kiosks.

Kiosks are placed by networks or by the retailers themselves. However, individual manufacturers can also place them, leasing the hardware and negotiating for floor space allotments for the placements.

Webinars.

Internet companies like Web-ex provide the conference call connections that allow all participants to simultaneously view and interact with the demonstration.

Web-based Seminars and Conferences.

Another example of using digital-based demonstration and education as a sales and marketing tool is the increased use of web-based seminars and conferences.

Introducing the "Webinar."

Recognizing the scaling back of corporate travel budgets, marketers have begun to organize "webinars" to attract interest in their products and services or to demonstrate the expertise of their personnel and solutions.

Webinars allow customers to participate in real-time demonstrations and presentations.

All the "comforts" of the customer's office or cubicle without the distractions inherent with the resort settings of a traditional conference. Using an Internet connection (via a company like Webex) and a conference call line, all participants see the demonstration simultaneously, and can ask questions of the presenter, demonstrator, or even each other.

Marketers use web-based conferences and demonstrations to get the right message to the right people.

Participants are self-selected. They have an interest in hearing the message or they would not have logged in.

Webinars also provide the marketer with the opportunity to employ the right resources for the presentation.

Many times, companies have a key researcher or subject matter expert that the market is interested in hearing.

This format allows this "market star" to present to everyone at the same time.

Media planners need to work with their marketing, marketing communications, and event planning teams to ensure the webinar is scheduled, advertised and produced.

It's usually a good idea to capture the presentation as well, recording the demonstration as well as the audio and any of the attendee's questions.

Webinars can then be archived and made available after the fact either online or in CD-ROM format for future use. Reruns work well for the TV networks, why not for you?

Digital Ad Screens.
Ad screens play advertising on small, flat, digital-technology screens often found in confined places, like elevators, with captive audiences.

Ad Screens.

It's human nature to want something to do when there is nothing to do. Sounds silly, but think about how many two-year-old issues of magazines you've looked at while waiting in the dentist's office.

Advertisers take advantage of this whenever and wherever they can. And new media has a new player in this field – digital ad screens.

Ad screens are ads – either static images or video clips – that are played on small, flat digital-technology screens. These screens are often in confined places with captive audiences that have little alternative but to look at the screens.

Two venues where this technology seems to be flourishing are elevators and taxicabs. National and local advertisers both use these media to good effect.

Elevator screens often advertise for tenants or businesses in neighboring buildings; while taxicab screens will offer suggestions for eateries, hotels, or entertainment spots.

The media is sometimes interactive, using touchscreen technology. Riders can touch categories and be guided through the participating advertisers until they find a fit for their search … or their ride ends.

Ad screens are purchased in local or national network buys in the case of taxis, limousines, and busses. Elevators can be purchased through network placements or directly from larger building management companies.

Home / Personal Entertainment.

Digital technology and new media have had a tremendous impact on consumers' home and personal entertainment.

While viewership of traditional media has plummeted in the last decade, new media alternatives have grown. In fact, they've been a major contributor to this decline in traditional media.

Apart from the obvious usage of the Internet as an alternative information and entertainment source, other digital media are also available to the public, and they offer opportunities to new-media-savvy media buyers.

Digital Music and Video.

Digital technology allows for the compression and encryption of multimedia material such as music and video.

The most popular ways of packaging the results are on CD-ROM (Compact Disc – Read Only Memory) or DVD (Digital Video Disc) technology.

These discs are read with an optical laser, translating the digital information into sights and sounds.

CD and DVD players are very common and are now relatively inexpensive (thank you, Moore's Law). Today, consumers often own multiple devices capable of playing and even recording these new media.

These digital services have numerous advantages over their ancestors (audio- and videotape), most notably quality of the sounds/image; portability; ease of navigation within material on the media; and space available for content.

The amount of space on these discs is tremendous.

Because content is digitized, the required memory is minimal and the amount of material that can be included on a disc is increased exponentially.

Extra scenes, games, and documentaries are now appearing in the special feature sections of DVDs.

Entire seasons of television programming are now available on multiple DVD sets – dozens of viewing hours, all commercial free. It's enough to keep marketers and media buyers up at night.

But the amount of space on these discs also leaves room for additional new media opportunities, and marketers are beginning to capitalize on them. The producers of these discs are beginning to make advertising space available within the packaging of the DVD and CDs, as well as within the content of the discs.

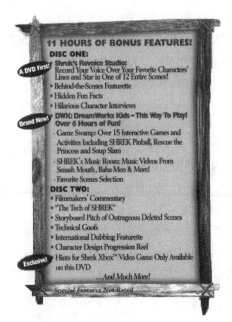

Special Features.

Extra scenes, games, documentaries, trailers, music videos – tons of extra features digitally compressed on a DVD.

SPECIAL FEATURES
* PEDAL TO THE METAL:
  THE MAKING OF *THE ITALIAN JOB*
* PUTTING THE WORDS ON THE PAGE
  FOR *THE ITALIAN JOB*
* *THE ITALIAN JOB*-DRIVING SCHOOL
* THE MIGHTY MINIS OF *THE ITALIAN JOB*
* HIGH OCTANE: STUNTS FROM *THE ITALIAN JOB*
* 6 DELETED SCENES
* THEATRICAL TRAILER
* WIDESCREEN VERSION ENHANCED FOR 16:9 TVs
* DOLBY DIGITAL
  - ENGLISH 5.1 SURROUND
  - ENGLISH DOLBY SURROUND
  - FRENCH 5.1 SURROUND
* ENGLISH SUBTITLES
  SPECIAL FEATURES NOT RATED

Mighty Minis.
The Italian Job *DVD sold with a special feature segment promoting the mighty Mini Cooper cars used in the movie.*

Marketers are producing commercials for inclusion on DVDs – usually as part of the promotional features. In keeping with the vehicles onto which they are hitching their commercials, some of these ads are usually more edgy or cinematic than the marketers' usual television or radio fare.

Negotiations for such placements are conducted with the releasing studio, network, producer, or recording label.

Such placements are expensive, but can be very effective and worth the expense if involved with the project.

They have exclusivity and a shelf life of decades.

Summary.

This chapter examined some of the vehicles available to marketers in the realm of new media. As you have seen, digital media is, in many ways, very similar to traditional media.

It still adheres to the traditional **AIDA** model of advertising and advertising's effect on the audience.

We must attract the consumer's **Attention**, generate **Interest**, foster **Desire**, and spur them to **Action**.

Whether the canvas is bits and bytes or ink and paper, we must still develop persuasive copy and engaging graphics and place them in the most beneficial vehicle possible for reaching our target market.

We discussed the common goals of new media marketing, examining those new media ventures that are Channel Churners, Matchmakers, Digital Destinations, and e-Bazaars.

We looked at the importance of content as the most basic communication characteristic of digital marketing and new media. After all, whatever the media form, consumers are interested in content.

Finally, we reviewed the myriad forms of new media available, grouped by medium:
* The Internet
* Intranets
* Wireless

- General Business Applications
- Home/Personal Entertainment

Discussion Questions.

1. Internet.

What are the four types of Internet sites?

Name an example of each type.

What is the difference between a formal lead and an informal lead?

How would you classify a functional site like Expedia.com? Explain your answer.

What is the common goal of all four types of Internet sites?

2. Intranet.

What is an intranet?

Why would an advertiser want to place ads on another company's intranet?

3. Wireless.

What are the advantages and disadvantages of advertising via the new wireless media (cell phones, PDAs, and handheld computers)?

Can you imagine a time when General Motors might sell advertising placements via OnStar as a media?

What kind of advertisers might be interested in such a placement?

4. Other Marketing/Business Implications.

What are the other new media marketing and business venues?

We talked about computer kiosks in supermarkets.

Name at least ten other locations where you might find a computer kiosk.

5. Home and Personal Entertainment.

Do you think consumers will accept advertising on music CDs? How about DVDs?

Exercises.

1. **Consider the four types of Internet sites.** Explain the advertising application of each type and name a different advertiser for each type. Describe how you imagine the advertiser would use each type of site.

2. Most universities these days have an exclusive intranet site for the faculty, staff, and students of the university. Think about your university and check out the intranet site. **If you were trying to sell advertising space on your university's intranet site, which advertisers would you contact?** Make a list of five different advertisers who you think might be interested. How would you convince each advertiser to buy a commercial placement on the university's intranet?

3. Get out there and do some research. Think about the people who shop for DVDs. **Prepare a survey to find out who they are and what they think of special features that come with the DVDs.**
   - Do special features make any difference in their purchase decisions?
   - How do they feel about commercials on DVDs? Would they ever watch them?

   Prepare and present a report on the findings of your research.

12 Media in Cyberspace

I REMEMBER THE VERY FIRST new media ad that I placed. It was 1996. I was a veteran of countless traditional media placements, and I ventured into the new media world confident of my abilities – full of swagger and arrogance.

My Wake Up Call...

I was quickly humbled.

I had to relearn all of the basics; color management, graphics resolution, even copywriting. And that re-education was not restricted to design and development.

I also rediscovered the nuances of niche targeting, reporting, traffic, and evaluation in a world without audits. There was a whole new vocabulary to learn – often with familiar words that now had strange new meanings.

It was an interesting couple of years as the online advertising world shook out.

Progress...

I am happy to report that things are now (slightly) more settled. New media advertising ventures have established media kits. The audit bureaus have discovered the Internet and are beginning to place their seals of approval (and disapproval) on sites.

Still, for a beginner in the world of new media purchases, the vocabulary and specifications can be confusing.

385

Chapter Organization.

This chapter is designed to assist you in better understanding these factors. We will discuss the steps you need to follow when venturing into the cyber world to either buy or sell advertising space. We will discuss the following:

- **New Media advertising techniques**
- **Site selection**
- **Billing models**
- **Selling ads and analyzing what you have to sell**
- **Online media kits and how to decipher them**

New Media Ad Techniques.

The first discussion necessary in this section is to briefly address the types of advertisements available online. The most common new media advertising techniques are as follows:

- **Site as the Ad**
- **Banners**
- **Buttons**
- **Text links**
- **Sponsorships**
- **Advertorials**
- **Push ads**
- **Interstitials**
- **Pop-unders / pop-intos**
- **Search engine optimization**
- **Meta-tags**

Site as the Ad.

These were among the very first sites on the web. Sometimes called **brochureware**, these are sites that often do little more than recreate existing print ads or collateral, but they reside in the digital world. They may or may not have e-commerce abilities. Most have little interactivity, beyond the ability to download spec sheets, provide a link for an e-mail inquiry, or provide contact phone numbers.

Site as the Ad.
This is the home page for OC Management Consulting, a good example of a Web site serving as the ad itself.

This ad model is relatively inexpensive. It requires little expenditure save the price of registering the domain name, developing the site, procuring web hosting, and keeping the content relatively current.

The success of such sites is dependent on what your goals are. Most often, such sites do not have terribly lofty goals in the first place. They are often Matchmakers, looking to generate leads or provide basic customer service. As such, they can be relatively successful.

To meet goals, such sites must be well integrated into your other marketing communications vehicles and/or be the benefactor of your company or product's overall brand equity or recognition. If you have great brand recognition and the URL is intuitively tied to this recognition, your site can succeed at attracting visitors and reinforcing your brand experience.

Banners.

The most popular and common form of online advertising is the banner ad. It's the billboard of the information super highway. It is typically placed on the content provider's website either above, below, or to the side of the site's primary content. Clicking the banner will link you to the advertiser's site.

There are three types of banner ads:

- **Static banners**
- **Animated banners**
- **Rich media banners**

Let's click through them one by one.

Static Banners.

Static banners are graphics and/or copy alone – no motion, music, or other bells and whistles. They are minimally effective in terms of their **click-through rate** – the number of times an ad is clicked on as compared to the number of times the banner is viewed. Static ads are inexpensive to create and field and are accepted regardless of the computer platform.

Animated Banners

These utilize motion (via rudimentary animated GIF files) to attract attention and thereby entice viewers to act. The click-through rate is moderately better than static ads. Basic animated ads are also easy and inexpensive to create and are accepted across computer platforms (PC, Mac, Unix) without requiring plug-in programs.

Rich Media Banners

These are often animated as well, however, their primary claim to advertising fame is that they also permit full-scale interaction – play games, input data, even allow visitors to place orders and transact business.

These banners are developed with HTML or other proprietary codes like Flash and Fireworks.

Plug-ins Light up Click-Through.

The proprietary codes, such as Flash, are widely accepted across platforms, but most require **plug-ins** – small, free, downloadable programs that enable the banners to function. Plug-ins are more and more common and included in many versions of the most popular Internet browsers.

Development of these banners is a bit more expensive, but the click-through rate is higher than its two less technologically complex siblings. Placement requires more memory and bigger files, but many content providers make concessions for, and even encourage, such ads.

More Space Means More Message.

There is a new generation of rich media banners that is developed and placed by third party vendors. One such company called Point.Roll (www.pointroll.com) has a family of expandable banners (FatBoy, TowelBoy, and BadBoy) that provide advertisers with a luxury they have always been lacking – space. The banner begins within the basic parameters dictated by the content provider, but when moused over, the ad expands and provides up to 300% more space for messaging and interaction.

Top Rich Media Advertisers		
Fourth Quarter 2002		
Rank	Advertiser	Impressions (Millions)
1	Hewlett Packard Company	3,116
2	SBC Communications, Inc.	1,557
3	Microsoft Corporation	653
4	Cassava Enterprises (Casino-On-Net)	574
5	Harris Investor Services LLC	550
6	Sony Corporation	470
7	AT&T Wireless Services, Inc.	292
8	NBA	290
9	Toyota Motor Corporation	270
10	USA Interactive	259
Source: Nielsen//NetRatings, January 2003		

The Click of a Mouse.
This is a short list of some of the biggest rich-media advertisers as measured by total impressions.

Click-through Rate

This is a new media response measurement. It's a percentage comparing the number of times an ad is clicked to the number of times that banner is viewed. Here's how to compute it, step by step.

Step-by-Step Math

Click-through Rate

1) Banner A is viewed by 1,000,000 adults online during the month of June.

2) In the same month, 200,000 adults actually click through Banner A to check out the offer.

3) The Click-through Rate for Banner A is:

$$200,000 \div 1,000,000$$
$$= 20\%$$

Bigger Is Better.

The Point.Roll family of expandable banners; each ad expands to as much as 300% of its original size when the viewer rolls a cursor over the base banner.

Development of these banners is extremely easy as the vendor performs the development, testing, and placement.

The service can even be included with your advertising package with some content providers, negating the development expense.

Banners are easily the most prevalent and versatile of the new media advertising venues. When well-targeted and placed in the right locations, they can be very effective at attracting attention and bringing visitors to your site.

Some, however, have begun to point to the reduction in click-through rates as an indication that perhaps banners have run their course.

However, we caution against this interpretation.

Remember to think of them as billboards. Even if they do not cause immediate visits, when they are seen cumulatively, they do help you in the serious and necessary business of building your brand.

Buttons.

Buttons are essentially miniature banners.

They are rarely anything more than a logo or brief, recognizable slogan that serves to link to the advertiser's site.

Development expense is non-existent and placement is inexpensive, dependent on the traffic and audience of the content provider.

Click-through rates vary. They are comparable to static banners or text links if the logo or slogan is well recognized.

Text Links.

Extremely easy and inexpensive to develop, text links are company names, brand names, or segments of copy programmed to link to your website when clicked.

Text links can reside within editorial of a content provider's site or even an e-mailed newsletter. But they will more often reside in an isolated "advertiser" section of the site.

Text links are popular on sites that do not feature heavy graphics for reasons of design or desire for faster uploads.

Expense for development is non-existent – just write the copy within the parameters of the character limitations presented by the content provider. Cost for placement is dependent on traffic and audience of the content provider site.

Sponsorships.

A sponsorship is an advertisement by association.

You pay a new media content provider to sponsor a page, feature, or event. It can be a highly effective method of advertising, provided that you ensure there is integration with the subject you are sponsoring.

It must make sense that you are sponsoring what is being discussed. Remember that your ad is trying to reach and influence a particular audience. If your sponsorship is not germane to the audience, you're wasting your time and money.

This ad model is very easy, often requiring little more than a logo and a link. The content provider will do everything else. The cost is dependent on the traffic, subject matter, and desirability of the targeted audience to other advertisers.

Often, online sponsorships can be negotiated as value-adds to other media buys, especially with network radio and television. It never hurts to ask.

Advertorials.

Like its traditional media sibling, advertorials are advertisements disguised as content.

They are especially prevalent in the direct-to-consumer pharmaceutical and nutritional supplement sites.

They can be quite effective, again, provided they are germane to the subject matter being discussed on the site and they provide some real value – i.e., information – along with the copy pitch.

More often, these are in the forms of white papers or protocol reports that conveniently link or are accompanied by banner advertisements to the contributing author, product, or service's site.

Park City Chamber
The Park City Chambers goal is to promote the ski resorts, lodging, and tertiary businesses located in Park City. We developed an Advertorial that showcased Park City, and then integrated it into OnTheSnow.com.

click to enlarge

Advertorials.

Advertorials are ads disguised as content. Mountain News is a web-design service that specializes in web advertorials. Check out this and other advertorial examples at www.mountainnews.com/html/ots_advertorials.html.

These are inexpensive to produce and relatively cheap to place. But you must be aware of a possible ethical backlash if your content is either too overt or, conversely, too subtle. The site accepting advertorials will usually be very thorough in their review and vetting of what you place. It's their reputation at stake, as well. Check their site thoroughly and examine the content of other advertorials they may accept.

Interstitials / Intermercials.

There are different variants of interstitials (euphemistically called intermercials) in use today.

Users of ISPs like Juno or Net Zero today know the most common version. They are full screen advertisements that appear before the ISP connects to the Internet.

These ads are actually placed when the user is logging out of their previous foray onto the web. The recipient can either accept the offer and, upon entering the web, go to the advertising site or click on the "No thanks" link and launch to the user's established home page.

This variant is inexpensive to create, as it is little more than a static page with copy and a link.

The expense to place such ads are negotiable, but can be expensive depending on the targeting you require.

The chief benefit of such placements is exclusivity. There is no competition for the viewer's attention, save their desire to get onto the web. The downsides are that the ad's success is negligible and it is sometimes viewed as an annoyance.

However, the original interstitial has become the epitome of new media annoyance advertising and has become known under a different, more infamous name: pop-ups.

Pop-Ups.

In the early days of the Internet, lower-speed modems made surfing the web painfully slow. In those days of the "World Wide Wait," some sites would solicit advertising that would load quickly and thereby give visitors something to read or do while the content laboriously loaded on screen.

Internet Limbo.
Interstitials are Internet ads placed on your desktop, usually as you log off your ISP connection.

Selling Pop-Ups.

This pop-up is made possible by the GAIN Network, a company specializing in online-advertising software.

Blocking Pop-Ups.

Many Internet service providers today have built-in pop-up blocking filters to minimize the annoyance of pop-up ads. But for a small fee, you can buy and install your own software to do the job.

This was the original online interstitial ad.

However, as modem speeds increased and websites loaded more rapidly, these interstitials no longer served as intermediary reading material, but simultaneously appeared with the content – popping up on screen, often to the detriment to the viewer's experience.

What was originally designed as a means of keeping visitors interested while waiting for the site's content became a competitive distraction.

The future of pop-ups is murky, at best. When the message is well written and the offer well targeted, the ads can still be quite effective. However, fewer and fewer people are actually seeing them. Pop-ups have become so unpopular that many ISPs now offer built-in pop-up blocking filters to stop them from even appearing on your screen.

These filters can be toggled on or off, and while most visitors seem to prefer them to actively block pop-ups, many still sneak through.

Purchasing placement of pop-ups is dependent on the content provider. Development expense for the ads is low. In its simplest form, a pop-up is a static page with a link.

More elaborate pop-ups are roughly 400 x 250 pixel, one-page HTML ads.

As stated earlier, pop-ups can be successful. They do get visitors' attention, and that is a major part of the battle.

But their reputation is currently just below pit bull terriers, so they may not be the best answer for all products or services.

Many sites have stopped accepting them as an advertising model both because of the backlash against sites with the ads, as well as the uncertainty of whether the ads will be viewed.

Pop-Unders.

A less intrusive, though no less controversial, version of the pop-up ad is the pop-under. These ads are identical to pop-ups except that they do not interrupt the content provider screen, instead popping behind it to be discovered upon exiting the web. These ads are also filtered by pop-up blocking software and are becoming more and more difficult to purchase and place.

Search Engine Optimization.

As discussed in the introduction to Chapter 11, search engine optimization (SEO) is the process of increasing the amount of visitors to a website by optimizing your positioning in the search results of a given search engine.

The primary tool of SEO is the keyword. **Keywords** are words or phrases that describe the subject matter of a site or web page. Search engines match these words to those submitted by searchers to find and prioritize the websites and pages that successfully match the search.

Search engines, like Yahoo!, display their results based on two criteria: keyword matching and the percentage of "match" to the requested query and payment for keyword placement.

The first result is more or less free, but is dependent on the quirks and foibles of the technology searching and matching the websites' and queries' keywords.

Paying for keyword placement allows advertisers to ensure that their site and a brief description of their product or service is prominently displayed, often in special sections at the top of the page.

Purchasing keyword placement is either done directly through the search engine (such as Yahoo!) or through services representing multiple online search engines (such as Overture).

Payment for keywords is accomplished via negotiation and bidding, sometimes on a daily basis – depending on the competition for the keywords. The most difficult aspect is the development and cataloguing of the correct keywords.

Keywords Advertising.

Services like FindWhat.com and Overture broker keyword advertising for search engine optimization. Keyword ownership can be a good way to drive traffic to your website.

Keywords and phrases should include the obvious – names and descriptions of your product, service, or company – but you must also be creative, including misspellings, uses (and mis-uses) for your offering, etc.

Some firms are very aggressive and bid on competitor's brand names. This is a touchy and questionably unethical area, and you must be careful not to infringe on service and trademarks.

Also, be careful to ensure you are not bidding against yourself for keyword placements. Distributors and retailers of your products are often bidding for the same words you are to help you sell your product.

Depending on your goals and expectations, it is sometimes best to simply bow out of the bidding and allow your channel partners to pursue the search engine placement.

Meta Tags.

Meta tags are special HTML insertions, often a list of keywords, which provide information about a web page.

Unlike normal HTML tags, meta tags do not affect how the page is displayed.

Instead, they provide information such as who created the page, how often it is updated, what the page is about, and which keywords represent the page's content.

Many search engines, in their search for keywords, use those found in meta tags to build their results.

Meta tags are easy and inexpensive. Utilize the keywords you developed for search engine optimization and add them to your site during site development.

It is important to note, however, that one of the most popular search engines these days, Google, is now using Boolean search criteria instead of meta tags. Boolean is almost exclusively a popularity contest. The website with the most hits will get the highest Boolean search placement.

Site Selection.

As we discussed in Chapter 11, there are four different types of Internet sites, each with their own, distinct goals: Channel Churners, Matchmakers, Digital Destinations, and e-Bazaars. These four have different appealing and repellent qualities to advertisers.

As a new media purchaser, you must decide if the site's goals and audience align with the goals of your client, the advertiser.

Even if, and maybe even especially if, your client is a website, you must decide if the client goal as a Channel Churner, desiring maximum traffic to your site, is best achieved by advertising on another Channel Churner site.

Strategic Questions.

This is not a simple yes or no answer.

The pros and cons must be evaluated on a case by case (or in this case, site by site) basis.

Sometimes, a business that has the goal of traffic building will get lost on another highly trafficked site and should instead concentrate on advertising on other sites, perhaps e-Bazaars or Digital Destination sites.

Just as in traditional media, you must know and understand the audience if the client message is to resonate and successfully be received.

In the world of new media, there are myriad choices for audiences to find the information they're searching for. Niches have niches, which in turn have even more narrow niches. You must find and purchase space in the places where you can reach the most (or at least the most profitable) target prospects as possible.

The beauty of online advertising is the ability to test inexpensively, easily, and quickly.

Before you launch a new campaign in traditional media, ensure that your audience and messaging is on target by honing it online first.

Run trials for your offers, graphics, slogans, or targeting for pennies on the dollar when compared to traditional media. And the flexibility the digital environment offers is light years beyond what is available in print or mass communications.

Once you have analyzed your goals and know your target audience, it's time to start looking for a place to reach them.

Key Considerations.

When investigating sites for purchasing ad space, it is important to remember several key things:

- **Audience coverage**
- **Target selectivity**
- **Reporting**
- **Flexibility**
- **Size and placement**
- **Inventory available**
- **Performance guarantees**
- **Technology**

Audience Coverage.

How does the site's audience correspond to your identified target? Ask the content provider for visitor demographics and other user information.

If they register their visitors, they should have a wealth of information to share. Look at the other advertisers on the site. Are they familiar companies from your other media selections?

Think about other niches. Don't be afraid to venture beyond just your general target. This could be your chance to cultivate more business from previously under-delivered niche segments of the client's target audience.

There are dozens of quality sites available to try. Remember that this is an opportunity to try and cultivate an entirely new market for your product or service for a fraction of the price of other media.

Target Selectivity.

You want to ensure that your target visits your site, but maybe you want to further refine your selection.

If your audience is that all-important 18- to 30-year-old male, there are countless sites you can investigate.

For example, let's say that upon reflection and research, you notice a particular connection with college sports aficionados. You could place your ad on ESPN.com, but you might further refine your placement. You might want to be on their NCAA basketball and football pages.

Many sites will offer this degree of specificity in your placements… for a premium, of course.

Reporting.

A content provider's information on their audience, visitors, traffic, and business is only as good as the data they are able to gather. This data is available via server analysis and is done regularly (usually each night), if not constantly with real-time analysis.

As an advertiser, you need to know and trust the reporting information the content provider gives you.

Many of the payment models we will discuss later in the chapter are based on this information.

At a minimum, you need to know how many visitors – total number of cumulative viewers that visit a given site – are exposed to your ad each month.

Ideally, you will also know how many unique visitors – individual visitors who visit the site at least once during a given month.

A content provider should be able to tell you:

- The number of repeat visitors
- Average length of time on the site
- The most frequently visited/requested pages
- Average number of click-throughs from their site
- From what other site(s) their site is most often visited
- How often your ad was/will be on screen
- The browser and platform visitors most often use

Aside from ensuring your billing is accurate, this depth of reporting information will help you in your ad development, page selection, and setting your goals and expectations.

Flexibility.

Have you ever opened a magazine and noticed an error in your ad and tried to change it? What about running an ad for a product that was recalled right after the ad hit the street?

Such disasters are easily resolved in the online world.

Ads can be pulled or changed with the stroke of a mouse. Flexibility is one of the hallmarks of online advertising, so make sure your content provider is prepared to offer it.

What kind of lead time does the site need to drop or change an ad? Many sites use ad management software which accept multiple ads and queues them so they rotate.

This way, a repeat visitor does not see the same advertisement twice in a row.

A nice benefit of such flexibility is that it provides the ability to test and tweak ads, offers, and messages.

Try the same ad with three different price points on three different sites, find the one that resonates the most, and adjust the others accordingly. Or... save yourself from a potentially devastating or embarrassing error in advertising judgment or editing.

Ads can usually be replaced overnight, but many sites can do it immediately upon receiving a phone call or e-mail requesting it.

However, do not make a habit of the last minute, emergency changes. It causes a bit of lost leverage at the next rate negotiation.

Size and Placement.

One of the most frustrating issues of designing online ads is the lack of standardization in banner size specifications.

Granted, the differences are often minor, but an adjustment of ten pixels here or there is pretty substantial when designing in what are already pretty tight size restraints.

Internet Ads.
On this page, an example of each of the three most common online ad formats.

The most common formats for ads are:
- skyscraper,
- banner, and
- box.

The format also gives you an idea as to placement. A skyscraper is a vertically proportioned ad and most often appears on the right or left side of the screen.

A banner is horizontally proportioned and resides at the top or bottom, though they may occasionally be offered in the middle as a section break (especially in e-mail newsletters).

An ad box is square and is often offered anywhere the content provider can squeeze them.

Negotiating placement is important. Many pricing options are based on "run-of-site" positioning. This is similar to "run-of-publication" in print. It speaks of where an ad will run relative to the home page. However, it does not specify placement relative to the page itself.

Again borrowing from the print world, the best place for an ad to be on the page is "above the fold" – any place above 600 pixels, or the bottom of the screen on the base 800 x 600 pixel screen resolution.

You do not want to depend on a viewer scrolling down a screen to see your ad. "Above-the-fold" placement is negotiable when you sign your add insertion.

Inventory Available.

Depending on the site, the amount of available inventory may or may not be an issue. You do not want to be on a site with too much advertising space on screen as it will be too difficult to try and compete for the visitor's attention.

If the site has limited space available, but a hefty stable of ads in its ad management software queue, your ads may not appear as often as you would like. There is a middle ground upon which only you can decide.

This is also a time to decide if there are any exclusivity issues that need to be addressed.

For example: Are you averse to appearing on the same site or page as a competitor?

Can you arrange for an exclusive advertiser premium?

Often, this can be done if you sponsor a page or feature. It can be very important to investigate such options.

Performance Guarantees.

If a content provider is so confident that their visitors are ready to click-through and buy at a substantially higher rate than other sites on the web, find out if they will put their money where their mouse is. Examples of such guarantees are:

- Negotiating lower price-per-viewer rates up front and offering a bounty for click-throughs
- Paying a commission based on a percentage of any sale you make via a click-through from their site
- Accepting a make-good on any shortfall of expected visitors during a given time period

Most sites are quite amenable to such guarantees, provided your client's business model results in a good percentage of closing the visitors who actually click-through.

Technology.

If your ad is a rich-media spectacle of sight, sound, and animation, you'll need to ensure that the site on which you bought advertising space has the technological wherewithal to host it.

That's why it is always wise to create a low-tech, static (and even a text-link) version of all your high-tech ads, just in case.

New media advertising is driven by technology, but that is not necessarily true of new media advertising providers. The advantage of flexibility and reporting can be lost (or at least slowed considerably) depending on how they handle the server technology on which their site is hosted.

It is not a case of whether they outsource the web hosting or manage it in-house, but rather how expertly whichever arrangement they enjoy is performed.

In many cases, a full-time, professional web administrator on staff can handle changes and reports more expeditiously. That is not to say that you must steer away from sites without such staff professionals, it is simply a suggestion that you keep your expectations in line with the logistics and infrastructure they have.

After all, an ad will not be changed overnight if the site only makes site edits once a month.

Billing Models.

There are several different models of payment for online advertising space, including:

- **CPM** – Cost per thousand with a minimum number of impressions guaranteed
- **CPC** - Cost per click/click-through
- **PPS** - Pay per sale
- **PPP** - Pay per purchase
- **Flat fee** – your ad appears for a set fee for an agreed period of time regardless of traffic or clicks
- **Hybrid** – Usually a lower CPM or flat rate with a percentage of any sales made from click-throughs/referrals.
- **Affiliate agreements/networks** – advertising is placed free on the content provider's site, and payment comes strictly as a commission for sales made from click-throughs/referrals.

There is no commonly accepted standard billing model, allowing sites and advertisers flexibility to negotiate the best price and system for the two parties. The model used and the price charged will reflect such logistical factors as:

- The reporting infrastructure in place

- The amount of traffic visiting the site
- The number of unique visitors to the site
- The historical buying history of the site's visitors
- The specificity of the targeting of the site
- The placement of the ads on the site

Affiliate Arrangements.

A payment model that deserves special consideration is affiliates. This system can be an outstanding way of increasing your company presence on the Internet at minimal cost. It is effectively the establishment of an online commission-based advertising network.

Web sites across the country (and even around the world) will feature your banners, buttons, and text links on their site for free, expecting a commission payment only when the ad attracts an agreed upon action, such as:

- **Successful click-through**
- **Qualified lead generation**
- **Completed sale**
- **Percent of sales**

Some affiliate sites will aggressively market your product, even going so far as to create special URLs (website addresses) which ultimately link to your site, or initiating aggressive search engine optimization campaigns.

These arrangements can be quite lucrative, helping you get the word out there and offering customers another avenue for reaching you and your product line.

However, as is often the case, if not handled carefully, this blessing can quickly become a curse.

While affiliates are encouraged to use the banners and ads your MARCOM department or agency has developed, the aggressive affiliates may go above and beyond in their marketing efforts, sometimes straining the branding efforts and identity standards you have in place.

As affiliate arrangements are often handled by the sales department, their attitude toward such things can be a bit more lax than yours may be.

You must make a concerted effort to keep track of affiliates and their efforts to ensure that they are not being too aggressive and taking liberties with your logos, slogans, and messaging. Be especially wary of unsubstantiated claims or infringing on competitive trademarks and copyrights.

When this happens, the competition comes after you, not the affiliate. Ultimately, this is your responsibility.

Also, make sure that your affiliates maintain a current stable of banners and buttons for their use. It is embarrassing, but all too common, to stumble across a site that is proudly proclaiming their affiliation to you with a banner from five campaigns ago, maybe even with a price or offer that is similarly stale and out-of-date.

Most importantly, you must remember that not all online sites are reputable, and you must take every precaution to ensure you are not associated with a company or site that may bring you headaches and bad PR along with a few leads and sales.

Affiliate Networks.

One way of handling some of these issues is to use a good affiliate network.

These networks will maintain your stable of ads, announce the fees and percentages you are offering, and will even help you keep track of the affiliates advertising your site. There are several such networks available.

ClicksLink is a good online source of multiple affiliate networks.

Selling Online Space.

Depending on the type of website you manage and your goals, you may find yourself on a new side of the media purchasing transaction. Maybe you're the one looking to sell some on-screen real estate.

Are You Ready?

If you find yourself in this position, there are several basic questions you must ask yourself before hanging out a space-available sign:

- Does your site stand out from the crowd?
- Do you have the time and staff to sell the space?
- Do you have the flexibility to offer the service and attention an advertiser expects?
- Can you add value through quality reporting or other marketing/positioning arrangements?
- What online inventory are you willing to offer?

Let's review each of these critical factors to website success.

Stand out from the Crowd.

Is your site well trafficked by either a wide spectrum of unique visitors each month or a unique but loyal audience base? If the answer is yes to either of these questions, then you have the potential to attract attention from advertisers.

Advertisers want to put their message in front of as many eyes or as many interested eyes as possible. If you qualify, spread the word that you are interested, and you may soon have a new online revenue stream.

Time and Staff.

Who is going to sell the ad space you have available? Chances are, you have a sales force, but they are out selling your product or service already. Can they afford a portion of their time to sell online real estate, too? In-house sales is not a realistic option for all firms.

But don't allow this to stop you from selling ad space on your site – there are other sales strategies available, namely:

- **Site representation (rep firm)**
- **Ad networks**
- **Barter networks**
- **Auctions**
- **Affiliate networks**

Rep Firms.

Rep firms are basically hired guns – sales people for hire that will represent your site, as well as others, in their online real estate portfolio. They will pitch your site to their established book of advertisers and/or develop new contacts within businesses that will find your site and customers attractive.

Rep firms can be highly specialized, concentrating on specific industries, demographic, or geographic areas. This can be attractive for niche sites or those sites with a highly developed and selective target audience.

The key benefit for hiring rep firms is freedom from the issues of developing your own sales force. One drawback is the requirement that most rep firms will insist upon exclusivity as a representative of your site. This can translate into a lack of service and attention for smaller sites

Ad Networks.

Similar to the traditional television network system, websites can become members of online networks. Once membership is established, you dedicate a standardized size and location on your site, and the network does the rest.

They will sell the real estate and even manage the rotation, placement, and tracking of the ads they sell.

There are several benefits for the content provider.

You can either substitute or augment any in-house sales force they have in place. You do not have to buy ad management software. And it is an easy way to ensure you sell any remnant or leftover inventory.

Advertisers benefit as well. They enjoy a standardized ad size and specification profile, consistent ad delivery, a single rep for multiple sites, competitive pricing, and exposure to multiple target opportunities.

Barter Networks.

Barter networks are an option that is often attractive to smaller sites. Barter networks are a cooperative network of sites, often within the same industry, which agree to exchange ad placements.

There is usually no payment associated with these placements, though commissions are not unheard of for sales or leads being generated by bartered ad placements.

Auctions.

Again, taking a page from the traditional mass media playbook, online ad auctions will help you sell available remnant or discounted inventory ad space to the highest bidder.

This can be a good way to sell off last-minute inventory.

Service and Attention.

When you are offering space for advertisements, you must be prepared to provide the flexibility you expect when you are buying space.

Can you make immediate or overnight changes to an advertisement, or do you only edit your site once a month?

Reporting and Marketing Arrangements.

Can you offer insight about your customer base that will help your advertisers better serve or understand their target audience? Do you have opportunities in other new or traditional media venues to offer your advertisers? Opportunities like participation in tradeshows or customer expos, inclusion in your product packaging, or statement stuffers?

Anything that will assist your clients in integrating their messaging and association with you and your customers will make the sale of a few hundred square pixels that much more attractive – and profitable.

Giving up the Space.

This is often the most difficult question to answer because it requires more than a band of white space at the bottom or side of your home page to qualify as inventory. Some questions you need to consider when deciding on available inventory: What do you have to sell? And is your site ready?

What do you have to sell?

- **What ad formats are you prepared to accept?**
  Banners? Buttons? Text Links? Sponsorships?

- **What tech specs can you support?**

  Can you handle Firework or Flash ads?

- **What on-screen locations do you offer?**

  Do you have a uniform portion of screen that can be dedicated to ads? Is the location desirable (above the fold)? Is a redesign necessary?

Is your site ready?

- **What monitoring and measurement steps are in place?**

  How thorough is your website log analysis? Do you have the measurement mechanisms in place to track transactions, referring URLs, and traffic tracking to the page level?

- **What is your ad payment model?**

  Are you offering a set price per thousand visitors or are you looking for a piece of the action?

- **How will you handle ad management?**

  Are you going to invest in ad management software or place and swap ads manually (if at all)?

- **Is your site audited?**

  Hey guys, welcome to the other side of the table. You ask this question of everyone else, it's only fair to expect it back at you.

There is some serious consideration that must go into determining the inventory you have available for sale.

If you are comfortable with the answers, good luck and good selling.

Setting Your Price.

So you have decided that you do have the space – and the desire to sell it. The next big question is – What do you charge? Answering this requires a careful review of:

- **Size and diversity** of ad inventory available: supply and demand come into play here. Fewer ads mean more attention to the ads present – and that can translate into a premium price.

- **Revenue needs:** is advertising your bread and butter or simply a little gravy on the side? This will help dictate the price you seek and what you are willing to accept.
- **Competition:** If you are going to charge premium prices, you had better have and offer premium value and service when you are being compared to the competition.
- **Size of site audience and content:** If you have a unique and valuable visitor base, you can charge unique and valuable rates.
- **Site's reach and interaction:** a brochureware site that targets llama farmers in the Pacific Northwest is not going to be a big rate earner.
- **Ad placement:** Ads below the fold or only on back pages are not going to generate a lot of interest or revenue. Remember the old real estate adage: location, location, location.
- **Day parts:** Yes, there is an online prime time for many sites. You may be able to demand and receive top dollar if your site enjoys higher target traffic at particular times of the day (or night).

Online Media Kits.
The online media kit is an important part of buying and selling in cyberspace.

Media Kit.

Whether you are buying or selling new media advertising, the online media kit is an important feature to understand. It is, in many ways, similar to the media kits from traditional media, but the headings bear some discussion to uncover some of their digitized meanings.

Site Overview and Features.

This section of the media kit will contain an explanation of the site's goals and purpose. It will contain information such as an editorial calendar, site map, opportunities for sponsorships and partnerships, multimedia offerings, related sites or media, privacy policy, etc. It is a good first stop to investigate the site and determine if it is one worth further research.

Contact Info.

Who you need to contact if interested in pursuing advertising opportunities on the site.

This will often link directly to an e-mail form that will ask you many of the pertinent qualifying questions up front, saving you and the site's sales force time.

Advertising and Sponsorship Programs.

This section will provide a point-by-point discussion of all of the advertising options a site may have available.

Some may be brief, others extensive, depending on the sophistication and inventory available for sale.

Rate Card.

Bear in mind, like those of the traditional media world, the rates stated are starting points for negotitation and discussion. The rate card will contain pricing detail for ads by size, shape, and placement on screen.

Site Traffic.

An analysis of who visits the site: how many visitors, how many unique visitors, how many registered members, etc.

Some analyses are more in-depth than others. The best will go so far as to detail visitors by page within the site.

Use this as a clue to the sophistication of their reporting and analysis prowess.

Audience Demographics.

This section offers a description of the site's customers and visitors. This information is usually only available for sites that profile, register, or survey their customers.

Ask to see an example of the questionnaires from which this information is gleaned and ask if any premiums were given in exchange for providing the answers.

Information garnered from online surveys is notoriously suspect when the participants receive premiums, unless the premiums are directly related to the subject matter of the site and its target audience.

Production Specs.

This section outlines the sizes, memory limits, resolution, and format requirements accepted for online ads. Here, the site will indicate its technological limitations (if any).

Delivery Specs.

This section will inform advertisers of the acceptable ways to receive ads: e-mail, FTP transfer, disk, etc. This section will likely also provide details of timing for delivery. Specifically, when new material is needed in order to keep the update schedule.

Reporting.

This section indicates the depth and breadth of information that will be provided for measurement and tracking. Who is tracking what? How discrepancies are reconciled, etc.

Summary

Buying media placements is a bit different when you are purchasing pixels. The terminology may be similar, but the meanings are not.

This chapter highlighted some of these differences and explained how you should approach and analyze your new media purchasing decisions.

We reviewed what advertising techniques are most common in the new media. In particular, we concentrated on the online medium, and looked at the most prevalent forms of ad buys on the web.

We looked at where to buy advertising online. What kind of targeting and reporting you should expect and what kind of questions to ask.

We looked at new media's most popular billing models and what negotiations you could expect.

We also looked at new media sales. We examined the possibilities of being on the other side of the negotiations and what to look at if you're interested in selling new media advertising and analyzing what you have to sell.

And lastly, you were introduced to online media kits and deciphering their components.

New media is a burgeoning field and one that this section has only touched upon. But like the technology that has fostered and facilitated its growth, it is ever changing.

Stay on top of these changes and you will find a competitive advantage for you and your company for years to come.

Discussion Questions.

1. New Media Advertising Techniques.

What are the new media advertising techniques?

In your opinion, which three are the best of the new media ad techniques?

Do you think banner ads have "run their course?"

Do text links make good, effective advertising?

What are the possible ethical issues associated with web advertorials?

2. What to Look for in a Location.

What are the factors to consider in deciding on a web location for an advertisement?

What does "above the fold" mean in web ad placement?

3. Billing Models.

What are the different billing models for online advertising?

What is an affiliate arrangement in web advertising?

4. Selling Online Space.

What are the important issues to consider before you start selling your cyberspace?

5. The Online Media Kit.

What are the components of an online media kit?

How do online media kits differ from traditional media kits?

Exercises.

1. **Consider the advantages and disadvantages of advertising through an affiliate network arrangement.** Write a short report discussing both advantages and disadvantages. If it were your company to decide, would you use an affiliate arrangement to advertise your site?

2. **Use whatever resources you may have available to find a copy of a traditional media kit for a magazine that also has an online presence.** Also find a copy of the same magazine's online media kit. Compare the two media kits. What are the similarities? What are the differences? Is the online audience the same as the publication audience? If they are different, how?

V Media Applications in IMC

UP TO THIS POINT IN THE BOOK we've covered the more traditional advertising media perspectives and the exciting new, digital media applications. In this last section, we'll open the aperture to explore the wider world of media in Integrated Marketing Communications (IMC).

A Booming Growth Area.

This is a booming growth area of media.

Part of this boom is driven by media mergers – the companies themselves are becoming more "IMC." And part of it is simply the continuing evolution of media in a media age.

Today, opportunities abound for jobs among product/service companies, agencies of all kinds and sizes, and even individual consultant/practitioners in highly specialized fields.

These last two chapters will give you a sneak peek into this exciting, future world of media.

Chapter 13 will explore the unique aspects and applications of the other media of IMC elements. We'll look at the media related to the more common IMC tools: Public Relations, Consumer Promotions, and Direct Response.

We'll also cover specialty areas like Relationship Marketing, Sports Marketing, and even Product Placement.

Then, in **Chapter 14**, we'll show you what it's like trying to put an IMC cross-platform, multi-media deal together.

Here we'll define the concepts of multimedia and cross-platform media integration.

We'll outline a process for planning to achieve corporate objectives.

Then, we'll consider the key players in this area and the motivations of each.

Through these last two chapters we hope to give you a sense of the wide range of possibilities and opportunities available in the multi-media IMC world.

We expect that many of you reading this today will be working tomorrow in this cross-platform IMC world.

As we see the continued growth and the continuing mergers, opportunities might possibly be growing here even more so than in traditional advertising media.

Here we go…

13 Media Across IMC

T HIS CHAPTER WILL PROVIDE A BASIC background for some of the other media tools that can be considered in the IMC arena. That's a pretty big world. By no means do we expect this chapter to be all-encompassing.

Media Objectives Meet Marketing Objectives.

As a media planner or buyer you will be faced with media plan decisions that are affected by the marketing objectives that call for the use of IMC elements.

These effects may shape your plan objectives or they may impact the dollars available for your media plan.

As a planner, your responsibility to your brand is to identify the vehicles that will best meet your brands' objectives, whatever these vehicles may be.

Chapter Organization.

We'll cover material in this chapter in two big sections.

First, we'll identify and discuss the media channels for each of the most common IMC tools.

- For the media of Direct Response Marketing, we'll cover broadcast and print, mail marketing, and telemarketing.
- For Promotional Marketing, we'll cover the media of consumer promotions and in-store marketing.

- We'll cover the media of Marketing Public Relations (MPR).

In the next section, we'll move on to specific media issues and applications in specialized IMC practices:

- Business-to-Business Marketing
- Customer Relationship Marketing
- Sports Marketing
- Entertainment Marketing

This chapter is meant to give you a sense of the many possible media applications in the multi-media, IMC world. Each area covered in this chapter represents another promising field for development of new media and new media jobs.

Media among IMC Tools.
The Media of Direct Response Marketing.

Direct response marketing is marketing communication designed to prompt the prospect to take a desired response action. The direct response message can be delivered via mass media or delivered directly to the individual customer but will always carry a method for the prospect to respond directly to the advertiser.

Direct response media can include virtually any media vehicle where the message delivered to the reader, viewer, or listener is designed to solicit a response directly to the advertiser. This includes the use of many of the conventional media in unique ways and customized programs delivered directly to the consumer.

Conventional broadcast and print media can be used as direct response vehicles by creating communications that prompt the prospects to take a desired action. These messages must be designed to be more "attention grabbing" and provide sufficient information for the prospect to respond. They must also provide a relatively easy method to respond.

Thirty-second TV commercial units may be the standard commercial message length for most advertisers, but this length is not often used by direct response marketers.

With only 30 seconds of information, these messages usually don't provide the prospect enough information to result in a response.

For many years, the additional time available in 60-second TV commercial units was the standard unit length for direct marketers. These units provided greater opportunity to present a response generating message.

Broadcast "Infomercials."

It Really, Really Works.

The men of the Popeil family were early pioneers of direct response informercials with products like the Veg-o-matic and the Pocket Fisherman.

As more media outlets became available and the advertising environment became more cluttered, direct response marketers turned to longer-form TV units. Although there is no "standard" advertising unit for direct response advertising, most direct marketers utilize longer form units to better communicate their messages. These longer forms provide the information necessary to sell items that cost hundreds of dollars direct to consumers. These longer units range from 60-second commercials on up to "infomercials" that are 30 minutes or more in length.

The most common response mechanism for direct response TV messages is the toll-free telephone number. This offers the prospect a simple and convenient method to respond. To maximize the response generated by these investments, marketers track the responses they receive from each commercial or program unit and measure efficacy and efficiency. This monitoring occurs throughout a schedule and may prompt the buyer to change the commercial purchases to improve response. Working with the stations or networks who are broadcasting these long-form commercials, the buyer reviews results and moves units into programs that are expected to generate greater response.

Longer-form infomercials may also be found on radio. However, this is not common.

Print Techniques.

With the longer lead times needed to place print advertising and the longer audience build associated with most print media, the ability to make immediate changes in schedules is

First Response.

Catalog offers like this are commonly used to generate a first response from interested consumers.

RESERVATION APPLICATION

The Danbury Mint
47 Richards Avenue
Norwalk, CT 06857

Send
no money
now

The Diamond Kiss Ring

YES! Reserve *The Diamond Kiss Ring* for me as described in the accompanying announcement.

Name _____
Please print clearly.

Address _____

City _____ State _____ Zip _____

Signature _____
Orders subject to acceptance. Allow 4 to 8 weeks after initial payment for shipment.

DKR7F11(

Bingo Cards.

Business reply cards (BRCs), like this one from the Danbury Mint, are another common print response mechanism..

an issue making print a lesser factor. However, print media are used as direct response vehicles. Generally though, the first response generated from a print advertisement will not be a sale. Often advertisers are trying to generate an initial inquiry that leads to a longer-term relationship with the prospect.

Print media can be used in many forms. As with broadcast, the objective of the advertising is to grab the attention of the prospect and provide enough information that they respond.

"Advertorials."

Just as broadcast response marketers use longer-form infomercials, so too do print response marketers use longer-form ads. In print this is called an "advertorial." An advertorial is a custom-written blend of advertising and editorial content. Often generated completely by the marketer, the advertorial is meant to engage customer interest more completely by providing more detailed information.

Response Mechanisms.

Print response marketers will use a variety of response mechanisms depending on the media vehicle. Whether an advertorial or simply an ad page, the marketer may use a toll free number or an on-page coupon to generate response.

Another commonly used response mechanism is the business reply card, or BRC. The BRC is particularly valuable if the response desired does not need to be immediate, like a request for a catalog or product information brochure. The BRC, or bingo card, can also be used to attract additional attention to the ad because these cards tend to stand up as the page is opened in the print vehicle.

Personal Media Channels.

More "personalized" media can also be used to solicit response. This would include any advertising material distributed to prospects by name and address by way of mail, e-mail, house-to-house delivery, etc.

A Personal Invitation.
Individually addressed direct-response mailings come through like personal invitations.

You've Got Mail.

Direct mail solicitations delivered to the home of the prospect are common methods of generating a direct response. Such mailings can be addressed directly to the intended recipient or to the "occupant" of the home. The addresses can be compiled using a proprietary database or via a purchased mailing list. As you can likely attest from your own mail, an envelope addressed specifically to the recipient rather than the more impersonal "occupant" will draw greater opportunity for response.

In designing a program using the more personalized media, a direct response marketer must consider the cost associated with each step of the process.

The first step is developing or purchasing a mailing list. Marketers communicating with current known customers will be able to use their own proprietary database for names and addresses.

If the purpose of the effort is to generate response from prospects who may not be current consumers, the marketer will need to purchase a mailing list from a list provider. The price of such lists is a factor of the quality of the information available. For example, at a relatively low cost, marketers can purchase lists of addresses with little or no other information.

On the other end of the spectrum, lists that have been pre-qualified based on selected factors will be more costly. For example, the business-to-business media collect a depth of information about their subscribers. As a result, they are able to provide lists that might be sufficiently focused to reach only individuals who are purchase decision makers in a specific industry.

The method of delivering the "personalized" mail message will also impact the cost of the program. For example: if a marketer sends a product sample or a premium to key prospects, the costs associated will include the production of the mailing materials, the cost of the list, and the added postage or shipping charges.

Follows is our monthly "Your Source" update. Download a PDF version (for better printing or viewing) at www.swid.com/pdf/source0704.pdf

You've Got Spam.

At present, the main downside of e-mail marketing is spam.

E-mail marketing provides a popular method to deliver a visual message to prospects. With many of the same attributes as direct mail, e-mail can deliver a message in a very efficient manner. An e-mail program will still include the development and list costs, but without many of the costs associated with production of a mailing piece and postal charges. As a result, e-mail programs can be very efficient.

An added advantage of e-mail programs is that you can (and should) incorporate an immediate, interactive response mechanism.

Telemarketing.

Another form of direct response communications is telephone solicitation. This method of pursuing prospective consumers has been used commonly and efficiently by marketers and charitable organizations. The costs associated with this type of program will include the list costs, copy (script) development, and the costs associated with the outgoing telephone calls and operators.

This method can be efficient in generating a positive reaction and will be useful in creating immediate response. The success of telephone solicitation has come with a price; the enactment of federal legislation created the "Do Not Call" list. This list provides an opportunity for consumers to be removed from telephone solicitation lists with significant penalties for marketers who continue to call. Even so, we expect telemarketing will continue and thrive as a valid and powerful direct marketing medium.

The Media of Promotional Marketing.

As an element of IMC, promotional marketing covers a broad range of activities including consumer promotions and in-store marketing. Here we'll cover the unique media vehicles of each.

Consumer Promotion Media.

The objective of consumer promotion is to provide an incentive for consumer purchase of the brand. Many tactics can be used to address different brand needs in this regard. How you use the media of consumer promotions will depend upon the brands' marketing objectives and its situation in the marketplace.

Consumer Promotion Objectives.

For established brands, one objective of consumer promotion may be to increase the purchase rate of the brand. This can be done by providing an incentive to buy more of the product or visit the retailer more often. The incentives can include a coupon providing a specified discount or rebate that returns part of the purchase price to the consumer. Special offerings such as a special advertised price or limited time product or package availability also serve the same purposes.

Another objective is to increase the frequency with which consumers purchase the brand. The goal is to decrease the time between purchases. For example, this might be done to reward consumer loyalty through the use of membership clubs or cards. These ultimately offer a frequent purchase award such as future discounts or premiums.

Consumer promotions can also be used to buffer competitive threats by encouraging "pantry loading" or stocking up on the product. When consumers have stocked up on your product, there's less chance for them to be enticed to buy a competitive product. This can be done by timing the promotion so it is in market immediately prior to a high sales or consumption period. With more product in the home, it is often used more regularly which increases total consumption.

Consumer promotion is also an important tool for introducing a product. For example, the use of a coupon, sample, or a "trial size" package will encourage potential users to try the new product at a lower level of risk.

These same tools can also be used successfully for established products by generating trial among a broader base of new users and retaining consumers who might be attracted to a competitive product.

Buy More Product.

One goal for consumer promotions is to get the shopper to buy a higher quantity of the product. The theory is buy more, eat more.

Added Value, Lower Risk.

Marketers will often use promotions to add value as a way of lowering the consumer's risk in commitment to a product or service.

Buy and Win.
Sweepstakes are commonly announced via print where more detailed information may be presented clearly.

Bundle of Savings.
SmartSource is one of the biggest players in coupon distribution.

Delivering Consumer Promotion Messages.

Preceding has been just a short list of consumer promotion objectives and the tactics employed to accomplish each. Certainly there are more consumer promotion tactics, but this is not a consumer promotion textbook. So, let's get back to media. From a media perspective, the vehicles that are used for consumer promotion activities would include anywhere the desired message can be effectively communicated. We can use conventional media to deliver such messages.

For example, the announcement of a sweepstakes could be communicated using many media vehicles. Television might be used to quickly raise awareness of the sweepstakes and communicate the desired excitement and immediacy of such an event. In addition, a sweepstakes may need to be supported using print media to communicate the necessary details. The Monopoly games at McDonald's use this combination of support. Television is used to raise consumer awareness of the game and pique excitement by announcing big prize winners throughout the promotion. Radio is used to supplement the television message. Sweepstakes details, rules, and a game board are delivered to consumers through print media.

Delivery of a coupon has historically been executed through print media where the prospective consumers will cut out the coupon to bring to point of purchase and redeem it for the designated value. More recently, we've seen development of the online coupon. With current technology, consumers can visit a website to request a coupon that they can print using their own printer, and redeem in the same manner they redeem other coupons. Or, they might simply input a code and redeem coupons online while e-shopping.

One of the most commonly used coupon distribution vehicles is called a Free Standing Insert, or FSI. You see these inserts in your Sunday newspaper every week. Each insert is composed of multiple companies and products, anywhere from ten to 30 pages of ads with coupons.

There are two major companies that dominate the channel for FSI coupon distribution. One is Smartsource, a division of News America Marketing, and the other is Valassis. Marketers book their coupon placement with each company and the company then handles printing and distribution to the newspapers, which are then distributed to the consumer's home. Because this medium is delivered by newspaper, we tend to measure it by total circulation.

In-Store Promotional Media.

Increasingly, we are seeing promotional marketing efforts deployed at the point of purchase, actually in the store where the product is sold. A growing body of research suggests that more and more consumers make their product purchase decision at the store. This trend has led to an explosion of new in-store media options.

In-Store Ads.

Increasingly so, grocery stores are a distribution point for advertising and promotions.

When you consider the wide range of retail store offerings out there, you'll see that this can get very complex and confusing very fast. So, for simplicity sake, let's consider just the average grocery store.

Just walk into a grocery store and you'll see promotional marketing everywhere: video ads, ads on aisle markers, ads on the shopping carts, ads on the shelf, ads on the windows, ads on the floors! You'll also see coupons everywhere: coupons on the shelf, coupon kiosks, and coupons at the cash register when you check out.

Check Out These Savings.

A common in-store promotion, checkout coupon distribution is tied to the cash register.

There are a lot of companies that, together, offer a blanket of promotional coverage for the average grocery store. For example, Catalina Marketing offers a number of in-store media channels. One of the biggest products is the "Check-out Coupon" machine. This is the machine that is connected to the cash register. It prints out store-specific coupons directly related to the groceries purchased.

Two other major players in store are Smartsource and Valassis, again. You can check out all they offer at their websites: www.smartsource.com and www.valassis.com. You'll be amazed.

In-store promotional media is measured a couple of different ways. At a simple level, you can get a count of the total number of coupons distributed. This would be roughly equivalent to circulation. Then you can use coupon codes to track coupon redemption, the number of coupons actually redeemed by consumers who bought the product. This is particularly easy at grocery stores where everything is scanned by UPC codes.

All Commodity Volume.

The other thing you have to consider in measuring grocery store promotional marketing is coverage. In grocery store promotions, the word "coverage" refers to a specific measure of audience unique to retail marketing. This is important because not every grocery store has the same media available. For this reason we track the unique measure we call All Commodity Volume, or ACV.

ACV is an industry standard measure of the average percent of product sales volume done by a given store in a given market.

As a media person, any time you place a buy for a grocery store promotional media like the check-out coupon machine, you'll be buying a certain percent ACV. Depending on the company and the market, you may find that you have to supplement the buy with other media in order to get better coverage (that is to say, higher percent ACV) of the market

The Media of MPR.

Marketing Public Relations (MPR) is an IMC tool intended to create goodwill for a person or an organization. The main goals of MPR are to build positive relationships with an organization's various communities through positive publicity, to build up a corporate image, and to offset unflattering rumors, gossip, and negative events. Some of the tools used in MPR include the following: news releases (including written, audiovisual, or corporate identity materials) speeches, special events, public service activities, and websites.

The media vehicles of MPR tactics are of course the conventional media we've already covered. However, the applications are vastly different.

Consider, for example, news releases. With advertising messages we go to the conventional media and buy time or space from the Ad Sales department and then we run the ad that says what we want to say, how we want to say it.

In public relations we write a news release and we send it to the editorial staff of the media. Editorial is the content side of the media. We're not actually paying for this media attention. Instead, we are hoping the media will produce a story featuring our product and message as we explain it in our news release.

Building a Media List.

As a media person in public relations, it's all about the list – to whom will we send our news release. Our goal is to find and buy, or create ourselves, a list of the media most likely to pick up our story and run it the way we hope. Whether we're sending out a news release, holding a press conference, or staging a special event, our media list is how we make a difference. We can build the list a couple of different ways.

In a very general way, we can use the PR Newswire to get our story idea out. But this isn't very selective. The PR Newswire is a national service that distributes marketer press releases directly to media newsrooms (broadcast and print) nationwide.

Another way to do it is to build a proprietary list of known media contacts in a specific industry area. For example, if our client is marketing a tool for the home improvement market, we might assemble a list of the key editor (by name) for each newspaper that writes specific home or hardware features on a regular basis.

PR firms do this for their major clients. They have a staff that tracks down the appropriate media contacts and maintains an up-to-date record. Such agencies may even compete for clients on the basis of who they know in the media.

Top 10 PR Firms	
	(in millions)
1. Fleishman-Hillard	$342.8
2. Weber Shandwick	334.9
3. Hill & Knowlton	306.3
4. Burson-Marsteller	303.9
5. Citigate/Incepta	243.9
6. Edelman PR	238.0
7. Porter Novelli Int'l	208.2
8. BSMG Worldwide	192.2
9. Ogilvy PR WW	169.5
10. Ketchum	168.3

Costly Relations.

Top 10 PR firms ranked by billings in 2002.

Measuring Media Effect.

Another important media responsibility in public relations is measuring the media effect of a PR effort. To do this effectively, we have to track the media that actually carries our story and then add up the total audience exposed to this media.

PR firms hire special clipping services to help with tracking of a client's story. These services report the media that carry the story and typically indicate some measure of the story. Common story measures will include things like the size of the story (column inches for print or minutes for broadcast), the quality of the story (run with visual or not, prominence of the story), and character of the story (positive, neutral, or negative).

With this information as input, together with conventional media audience research, the PR media person will report total press mentions and total audience count. Then, in certain cases, the PR media person might go on to adjust the measurement based on quality or character of the story.

A Highly Specialized Practice.

The job responsibility for a media person in PR is highly specialized. PR agencies can build and lose their reputation on basis of their media staff and media practices. If you are interested in media and have some specific training in PR, this might be a great place to start your career.

Media by IMC Practice.

In this section we'll consider media across specialized fields of IMC practice. We'll do this by covering some of the unique audience and media issues and applications in each practice.

Here we'll cover Business-to-Business Marketing, Customer Relationship Marketing, Sports and Event Marketing, and, finally, Product Placement and Entertainment Marketing. These are just a few of the many specialized IMC practices we could cover. We've chosen these few to demonstrate specific IMC media applications.

Media in B2B Marketing.

Business-to-Business Marketing falls into two primary categories: promotion of consumer goods to the middlemen of their respective industries and promotion of goods and services to businesses for the manufacturing of products, or as the end consumer of the goods and services. Both are often referred to as "trade" marketing due to their focus on the businesses involved – the industry or "trade" targeted.

We covered the B2B market in Chapter 9 as an example of a "niche" market application. We are covering it again here for two reasons. To focus on the specific media of B2B marketing and also to empahsize the importance of this growing field of marketing practice.

The B2B Buying Decision.

The business buyers targeted by B2B efforts make decisions based on the key needs of the business. The business-buying decision process is very different from the typical consumer-buying decision process.

For example, business buyers tend to have deeper knowledge about what they buy. This includes a greater knowledge of the products being considered and the competitive alternatives available. As a result of this pre-existing base of knowledge, business buyers tend to be looking for specific information and detail to help them make and justify their decisions.

Business buyers also follow a more systematic method of selecting products to recommend and purchase. For large purchases like capital investments in machinery or technology, determining a long-term supplier for manufacturing supplies, etc., this process usually begins with an initial investigation and a deep comparative analysis into the product choices available. For these large purchases this step may be meant to simply reduce the number of potential suppliers or products to a more manageable list of candidates for further consideration. Often, the objective of business-to-business marketing is to get your product on this "short list" of products who will be asked to submit a formal proposal.

Top 5 B2B Agencies

Agency	Location	2003 Est. Billings ($millions)
Digitas	Boston MA	$42.0
Sullivan Higdon & Sink	Wichita KS	$15.3
Bader Rutter & Associates	Brookfield WI	$14.0
Sanna Mattson MacLeod	Smithtown NY	$12.8
Schubert Communications	Downington PA	$12.4

B2B on the Rise.

Among the agencies that report billings, these are the top five business-to-business agencies nationwide.

B2B Magazines.

Business-to-business marketing communications tend to be focused into a limited number of very targeted vehicles. Most industry categories are supported by a narrow list of respected news and information publications dedicated to the industry or a more focused specialty within the industry. Many of these trade publications are "must-reads" necessary to keep abreast of the industry. Advertising in these publications is often viewed as a source for additional product information and, to a degree, can augment editorial coverage of the product and competitors.

Subscriber information for these publications is often very detailed as reported by BPA Worldwide and the Audit Bureau of Circulation (ABC). Choosing the publications that meet your needs would require an analysis of these circulation audits relative to your objectives and a review of the editorial reputation and quality of the publication within their industry. Selecting the most trusted publication in the category will often be more valuable than selecting the most target efficient.

BPA Worldwide.
BPA and the Audit Bureau of Circulation (ABC) are good sources for audience measurement of business publications.

B2B Newsletters.

Many of the publishing companies responsible for the production of these industry "bibles" have expanded their capabilities to provide their constituents with extended or more-timely information via opt-in newsletter services delivered by mail, fax, or e-mail. These capabilities also pay dividends to marketers by offering focused delivery of their messages using delivery devises for direct communications. These subscriber lists offer a highly qualified audience.

Measurement, if any, of B2B newsletters is commonly handled by the newsletter publisher. Media people need to use caution in this area. Remember that measurement isn't everything, but you will need to have some way to assess the effect of the media relative to its expense.

Conventional Media as B2B.

Occasionally marketers of business-oriented products that have been broadly adopted might be faced with the opportunity and need to communicate to a broader audience. In these occasions, selected broad-focused media vehicles may play a greater part in the communication with brand prospects. This becomes an option as these marketers need to attract a broader base of prospects to their brands.

The computer industry is a good example of how marketers capitalize on the broader audience. Most computer manufacturers use selected television shows, magazines, and newspapers to reach their potential audiences in addition to very targeted industry publications aimed at the technical decision makers and managers in targeted industries. This broad targeting works to raise awareness and confidence in these brands to alleviate the uncertainty that is associated with the purchase of new technology.

Media in Relationship Marketing

Customer Relationship Marketing, or Customer Retention Marketing, is a tactical marketing practice based on customer behavior. The concept of CRM relies on the belief that if a business is able to retain its positive relationship with its customers, it will prosper. The goal of Relationship Marketing is to align the goals of a company with those of its customers.

The premise here is that it is more important to retain the customers you have than to try to acquire new ones. From this perspective, customer relationship marketing is profit oriented. It is more efficient and profitable to capitalize on existing customer relationships than to attempt to develop new ones.

Research has placed this value at different levels for various situations. The value of existing customers has been estimated to be as high as seven times more profitable relative to new customers.

Many businesses use CRM to develop and maintain customer satisfaction and retain loyal customers. Often the right

Mileage Plus Update
Enhanced service through Washington, D.C.

A STAR ALLIANCE MEMBER

CRM Mileage.
Airlines know the value of their best customers by tracking mileage through membership programs.

CRM solution for one company or one customer definition doesn't work for another. The solution must fit the marketer's abilities and the needs of their customers. Relationship marketing has applications across both business-to-business and consumer marketing. The principles of both are similar, but the scope and basis of the relationship is inherently different.

In order to create the appropriate relationship with customers, marketers must take steps to "meet" and "know" their customers. First, marketers need to define who their key customers are demographically and psychographically, learning their behaviors, and then segmenting these behaviors. Next, they need to learn more about these customers based on research into their needs and the marketer's ability to communicate with them. The research should be designed to help determine current customer satisfaction levels and areas that need improvement and help determine the anticipated effectiveness of various methods to communicate with them. Ideally, this review will also help determine the profit value of the customer.

Know the Customer.

Interviewing customers enables the business to improve their products, services, and customer relationship processes. There are critics of the customer interview method. They argue that the interview may fall short on statistical reliability.

Ultimately, CRM marketers need to realize the importance of their customers and address their needs through properly thought-out strategies and tactics. It is important to continuously monitor the results of any CRM program to ensure that timely adjustments are made immediately to reinforce the relationship with the customer and capitalize on any changes in their behavior.

Know How to Reach the Customer.

Many organizations keep a database on their customers and use it to their advantage. Important to a successful CRM program is the development and maintenance of an appropriate database. The collection and maintenance of the information needed to populate this database can be expensive and difficult to execute. These hurdles must be overcome because this is the foundation of any CRM program. Organizations have spent hundreds of millions of dollars on technology to develop and maintain a database.

A Response-Driven IMC Practice.

The use of CRM is largely practiced as a direct response field. This makes sense because the objective of direct response programs is to elicit an initial response from the prospective customer. With the fulfillment of the initial offer or purchase, the relationship with this customer is established and future communications can be modeled.

Though it might be response driven, CRM is clearly an IMC practice, often involving multiple IMC tools including advertising, promotions, and PR along with direct response.

For example, let's take a look at how this might work for a consumer marketing relationship. First, the initial communication might be accomplished with an advertisement carrying a response device through which the consumer requests a specified catalog. Next, based on the data collected from previous requests from other consumers, the marketer might project that the prospective consumer is more likely to make an initial purchase with the inclusion of a discount certificate or coupon promotional offer. If, as expected, the consumer makes the initial purchase and potential subsequent purchases, the marketer uses direct response tools to collect information on the purchase behavior and send selected communications to the consumer featuring items that are similar to prior purchases or complement those previously purchased items. See? In this simple example we covered three major IMC tools.

The Media Role in CRM.

How are media used to facilitate CRM? Look again at the example above. You'll see that advertising media is used to

Banking on CRM.

Banks are among the leading companies in the practice of CRM. This is a promotional offer from a bank, delivered by mail to a customer the bank knows to be a home owner.

431

communicate with potential customers to generate the initial contact. And as we discussed in reviewing Direct Response vehicles, nearly all media can be used to generate this initial response. Once the first response is a reality, the relationship with the customer has begun. How media are used from this point will be directly impacted by the needs of the customer and what previous modeling suggests they will respond to.

In our consumer relationship example, the marketer may communicate the appropriate product and promotional offers to the customer via mail or e-mail. The collection of consumer information to populate a database can come from responses to advertising via toll free numbers or business reply cards or from opt-in registration to mailing lists available on most brand websites.

Abercrombie & Fitch, for example, offers visitors to its site the chance to opt-in to a mailing list. Other marketers like the Gap, L.L. Bean, and Spiegel offer similar opt-in opportunities.

Following registration, the marketer will add the customer to selected e-mailings based on modeled and actual behavior. The customer continues to allow the messages to be delivered as long as they are provided with relevant product offerings and the marketer will maintain the customer on their e-mail list until they appear to have become inactive.

Sports Marketing.

Sports Marketing is the place where the sports world collides with the marketing world. It is the place where corporations are able to use their relationships with athletes, teams, and leagues to help communicate with customer prospects. It is also the place where the athletes, teams, and leagues are paid substantial sums of money.

These payments are often disparaged as being excessive relative to the contribution made. Excessive or not, teams use these funds to help support the huge payrolls or scholarships they must carry to compete. Leagues use these funds to

Opt-in Opps.
This is the opt-in screen greeting visitors at www.gap.com. *Notice the e-mail opt-in along the bottom of the image.*

Little Leaguers.
Sports marketing can be effective at any level, no matter how small.

Baseball Cards.
One of the earliest examples of modern-day sports marketing.

support the advancement of their organization in the fight for a share of the viewing public's heart.

Sports marketing is not limited to major sports leagues or college athletic programs. In the fight to maintain quality youth programs, smaller organizations too will turn to marketers for support. In this sense, little Jimmy's tee ball team can be as important to the neighborhood dry cleaner as the Los Angeles Lakers are to Staples.

Marketers continue to push for a competitive advantage and the sports athletes are happy to receive the money offered. Every level of sports from peewee leagues to the pros has been affected by the sports marketing trend.

The Origins of Sports Marketing.

The birth of Sports Marketing may have come as early as the 1870s when tobacco companies packaged baseball cards with packs of cigarettes. As with any premium, companies did this to increase sales and brand loyalty. The tobacco industry today continues to have a huge impact on sports marketing. These cards were probably the first example of promotion of the sports industry for another industry's benefit. The use of baseball cards evolved into bubble gum cards and ultimately has grown into an industry of its own; even without the gum.

Adidas may be able to claim the first use of named athletes to promote products. In the 1936 Berlin Olympics, Jesse Owens received free Adidas shoes. His success in winning four gold medals in Nazi Germany was important on many levels. It is difficult to determine if this relationship between athlete and marketer was a success. As the exposure of athletes became larger throughout the remainder of the 20th century, the opportunities for athletes in sports marketing increased significantly.

The Evolution of Sports Marketing.

In the '50s and '60s, sports marketing became a lightning rod for social revolution. When Jackie Robinson became the first player to integrate baseball, in 1957, sports became a symbol of social change. Robinson was still faced with the effects of segregation, but his experience set an important precedent later followed by other sports. By including African American athletes in "big league" sports, the market for sports in general advanced. Culture started to change and sports marketers could reach blacks and whites through integrated sporting events. Robinson's entrance was important in respect to the civil rights movement, societal change, and the advance of marketing through sports.

Also in the 1950s, television created a great medium for sports personalities by offering the visual action of sports. With the availability of broadcast coverage of sports and the advertising opportunities they presented, marketers, for the first time, could reach large audiences with messages that were relevant to the sports listener or viewer. As the audience was able to see sports figures in action, people began to emulate them on and off the field. This included interest in the equipment used, styles worn, and brands consumed.

Strange Bedfellows.
Tobacco company sponsorship of sports was a big new idea but poorly conceived.

When advertising of cigarettes was no longer allowed on television, the funds previously used to support these efforts became available. Tobacco companies were in search of new venues to promote these products. Sports teams and personalities were major beneficiaries of this change. Notable sponsorships like Winston Cup Racing of NASCAR and the Virginia Slims Tennis Circuit were born as a result of this forced change in marketing direction.

The Revolution of Sports Marketing.

During the 1970s the prominence and visibility of athletes surfaced as a trend which was quickly capitalized on by marketers. Although sports personalities had previously endorsed products, the increased visibility of marquee athletes made their endorsement more valuable. For example, early in the '70s New York Jets quarterback Joe Namath was branded as a sex symbol and used to sell pantyhose. Late in this decade

Popular Partnership.

The advertising partnership of Coca-Cola and "Mean" Joe Green led to one of the most popular TV ads of all time.

Pittsburgh Steelers defensive tackle "Mean" Joe Green starred in a Coke commercial, one of the best known ads ever.

Also in the '70s, even the fashion industry came to be influenced by sports. Athletic shoes were no longer worn only by competitive athletes. A number of key brands were lifted up via endorsement of athletes who, in turn, began to market their on-field performance and off-field personality to secure lucrative sponsorship deals.

ESPN was launched as the first all-sports network, and would grow as sports continued to grow. The first corporate sponsored stadium was named in Buffalo for Rich Foods, Inc. Teams seemed to develop their unique personalities and the public began to develop stronger connections to their favorite teams. Teams grew in national prominence and popularity as television brought teams from across the country into the spotlight.

Not Just a Guy Thing.

Although Title IX was implemented in the 1970s the real impact would not be felt fully until decades later. Entitled to the same rights and opportunities as males in college athletics, women athletes would quickly become a powerful and influential market and spawn many successful endorsements.

As society continued to change, sports became a greater part of our daily lives. As baby boomers began to reach their '20s and '30s, individual participation in sports began to rise, further fueling the growth of the sporting goods and athletic shoe industries.

In the 1980s particular athletes caught the attention and affection of the entire nation. Michael Jordan, Larry Bird, Magic Johnson, Bo Jackson, and Joe Montana all rose to great fame. Everyone wanted to "be like Mike." Closing the decade, the Olympics in L.A. turned an even hotter spotlight on sports and brought the sports and entertainment worlds even closer together.

With the onset of free agency, salaries increased dramatically. As a result, the money from television contracts became an important contributor to a team's bottom line and its ability to pay top players.

The Media in Sports Marketing.

The 1990s continued the growth trend for sports marketing and sports. Leagues took advantage of this continued growth by expanding into additional markets hungry for their own home team. Television money available from even more broadcast and cable outlets continued to support college and pro leagues.

Most professional teams earn the majority of their income from TV deals negotiated by the league. Revenue sharing and salary caps have helped teams continue to compete in most sports. Baseball does not have these protections and, as a result, teams in Atlanta, New York, Los Angeles, and Chicago benefit from TV contracts that teams like Montreal, Pittsburgh, and Milwaukee cannot attain.

Stadium signage and naming rights have changed the environment the games are played in, and luxury boxes have funded much of the construction costs associated with new facilities.

Sports marketing is also mined with significant risk if you don't select the right partner. Issues today arise from incidents of racist or sexist remarks, violence toward coaches or spouses, disloyalty to community, and sometimes unfair labor practices. Before entering into a sports marketing partnership, marketers must familiarize themselves with the po-

Stadium Make-Overs.
Stadium naming rights are another way that large corporations cash in on sports marketing. Sometimes, however, as in the case of the Houston Astros, problems with a corporate sponsor can necessitate a quick name change for the ballpark.

tential partner and secure their interests with behavior clauses in contracts.

Recognize that not all partners will turn into the next Michael Jordan, and some could turn into a disaster like Kobe Bryant in 2004.

Media Clutter in Sports.

Many teams and stadiums have taken steps to minimize message clutter, but, in most cases the opposite is occurring. NASCAR racing includes so many logos and sponsors that they are almost impossible to count.

Unique to sports, the Masters golf tournament has run commercial free the last couple of years. Even before this, there were only three sponsors, and CBS could only run advertising from approved sponsors.

It is unlikely that the teams and stadiums who limit advertising will find themselves in the majority soon. With pressures to field winning teams and the demand for stadiums that offer amenities to attract more fans, only the elite organizations will be able to reject the offer of marketing funds. Such marketing partnerships help these organizations stay profitable, or at least minimize financial losses.

Consumers will ultimately have the power to influence how the sports industry views marketing partnerships in the future. If these relationships with marketers continue to positively influence consumer behavior they will undoubtedly continue to grow and sports organizations will continue to reap the benefit of this growth. If consumers don't respond to brands as a result of their investments in sports, the investments will move to other marketing activities.

Fans too will have the power to determine the future of sports marketing. Two conflicting interests create a Catch-22 for fans. They demand performance from their teams. They demand comfort and convenience at their stadium. Do they understand that there is a price attached? Local and state municipalities no longer willingly fund new stadiums with-

Uniquely Uncluttered.
By design, the Masters golf tournament airs with little to no advertising.

out significant political backlash. Broadcast audiences are not rising at the level that might justify the increased broadcast rights fee increases demanded by major sports. Ticket prices continue to rise, making it impossible for families to attend these events.

Delivering Sports Marketing Messages.

From a media perspective, Sports Marketing isn't so much a story of how you might use the available tools. Instead, it is a story of how Sports Marketing has created some of the major media brands that are today a part of our culture. The popularity of sports and the marketing of sports have made the multitude of dedicated TV sports networks, radio networks, magazines, newspapers, and websites a phenomenon.

Where sports was once an area that marketers would use only to reach men, these media alternatives and the enormous popularity of sports in the United States today provides marketers a wealth of opportunities to reach many targeted audiences.

The interrelationship of media with sports will continue. And marketers will still capitalize on these connections.

Ultimately, each media planning or buying decision will need to compare the choices available. In any case, the plan objectives must be met and the costs to meet the objectives in sports must be compared to other relevant choices. For many marketers, the use of sports is a given. Either the brand is so tied to sports, like Nike, or the competition is so visible in sports, like beer, that they have no choice but to include sports in their plans.

Sports Marketing as IMC Practice.

To this point in this section we've discussed the roles of advertising and promotional sponsorships as IMC tools in sports marketing applications.

Another very common IMC tool in sports marketing is public relations. The most common link here is a charitable cause. Virtually every professional sports league and most pro teams support a charitable cause. Many marketers will try to ride

Sponsored Causes.

A joint partnership between Major League Baseball and the National Prostate Cancer Coalition was sponsored by Gillette, Sanofi, and CBS Television in conjunction with Father's Day.

along with a popular team by sponsoring the cause. One of the more recent relationsihps of this nature is "Take a Swing Against Prostate Cancer." This partnership between Major League Baseball and the National Prostate Cancer Coalition spawned special events, which were jointly sponsored by Gillette, Sanofi, and CBS Television. While prostate cancer awareness is an ongoing campaign throughout Major League Baseball, sponsored screenings like this one were scheduled city-by-city nationwide.

Entertainment Marketing.

Entertainment Marketing is a large and growing field of IMC. Loosely defined, Entertainment Marketing includes all advertising and promotional activities in which a product or service partners in some way with an entertainment property. The perfume brand sponsorship of a rock band concert tour; the beer company presentation of open-mic night at local bars; the ice cream retailer featuring special, movie-themed flavors; the toymaker marketing new toys based on cartoon characters; the car manufacturer promoting a limited edition, entertainer-inspired options and detailing package – these are all examples of Entertainment Marketing today. And this is by no means an exhaustive list. The possibilities are endless.

The interrelationship between product and property can be accomplished in many different ways. Some of the most common are partnerships, sponsorships, licensing agreements, and product placements.

In a partnership, both the product and the property agree to promote each other in a mutually beneficial way. In a sponsorship, the product is generally paying for the privilege of association with a hot (or hopefully hot) property. Licensing agreements involve product payment for the rights to use some particular component of a hot property. And product placement is an arrangement whereby the entertainment property agrees to use the product in some negotiated entertainment application.

439

However the association is arranged, the goal of the product-property association is simple – shared equity. Someone, either the product or the property or both, will gain stature and value as a result of the relationship.

The Media of Entertainment Marketing.

In addition to all the conventional media, entertainment marketing also counts both the product and the property among the media channels available. The product itself can become the media in a couple of different ways.

Product as Media.

First, the actual product itself becomes a promotional message for the property; for example, the *Shrek* ice cream feature flavor at Baskin-Robbins. Another example of this is the continuing relationship between the Nickelodeon Kids cable TV network and the Kraft Foods company. Among other things, this relationship has given us *Fairly Oddparents* brand Cheese Nips brand snack crackers and *Rugrats* brand pasta shapes for Kraft macaroni and cheese. The toy company character toys and the car company special-edition automobiles are also examples of product as media.

The product can also be a media channel by way of its packaging. The Kellogg's and Disney World partnership is a good example of this. At the time this book was written, Kellogg's was the official sponsor of breakfast at the Walt Disney World Resort in Florida. This relationship was heavily promoted with Disney World advertising and promotional offers on packages of Kellogg's breakfast products, like Kellogg's cereals and Eggo brand frozen waffles.

Package as Media.

Kellogg's made its breakfast product packages available for Disney advertising.

Package as Delivery Media.

In the breakfast cereal aisle, we see examples of entertainment premiums delivered via product packages.

The product can also be a media channel by delivering promotional material, coupons, or premiums in packages. Hot Wheels NASCAR replicas were distributed in packages of Cheerios. The entertainment-inspired toys in McDonald's Happy Meals would be another example of this.

Product Placement – The Property as Media.

Product Placement is the process of integrating an advertiser's product clearly and visibly into an entertainment property like a motion picture or TV show. It is an important part of the entertainment industry and offers the potential to reach millions of people in the context of the entertainment. In this sense, the entertainment property becomes the media for the product's message.

It used to be that every product in television and motion pictures was generic. In fact, often the logos would be brushed out or removed from any product being used in programs. The characters in the program or film might consume a soda or beer and the colors of the can might look a little bit like a Budweiser or Coke, but that was as close as you could get to identifying the product.

Today, branded products appear everywhere. In most cases, they play a supporting role and appear as they would in real life. For example, the cell phone that is being used might be identifiable as Nokia, the car that the police officers are driving is a Ford sedan, the beverage that the high school student is drinking is a Pepsi, or the pizza that is being delivered is from Domino's.

In other cases, the product is playing a very important role. Right out front. For example, for many years James Bond drove an Aston Martin, until he was given a BMW for *The World Is Not Enough*. To give the BMW more visibility, it was given special features and powers. Now try buying that Beemer out of the showroom! To make the placement in the movie even more visible, BMW created an entire campaign in conjunction with the motion picture, featuring scenes from the picture showing the car in action.

Product Placement.
If you're looking for an agency specializing in product placement, check out the Entertainment Marketing Association at www.emainc.org.

Integral Partners.
In the movie Castaway, *FedEx stood out more because it was integral to the story.*

In the *Italian Job*, the Mini Cooper was also given a very important role in the movie. There was no mistaking that the entire team was driving Mini Coopers. In every commercial for the movie and for the video, the car is featured.

How are these products cast in these important roles? They appear as a result of the efforts of specialized companies that bring marketers and entertainment companies together. These product placement specialists work as partners with both advertisers and entertainment representatives to secure visible placement for clients and provide products needed for production of the entertainment.

To be most effective, the product needs to be relevant to the story. In the movie *Castaway*, Tom Hanks survives a plane crash. Whose plane was he in? You can bet it was not a recognizable commercial airline. Imagine the negative impression that could create! It was a recognized brand – FedEx – that did not risk the negative reaction a commercial airline would face. Once the plane goes down, Hanks interacts regularly with additional FedEx packages and their contents washing ashore. Even after he is found and returns home, he is welcomed at a FedEx press conference starring FedEx CEO Fred Smith.

Occasionally, placements will have less relevance to the story and may be cut in the final version of the show or film. This was the case with the contentious relationship ultimately between Reebok and *Jerry McGuire*. In the movie, Cuba Gooding's character was the star in a Reebok commercial. The director opted to cut out the commercial in the final edit. As part of a settlement agreement, the Reebok commercial is part of the special features included with the DVD.

The cost to place a product in a production will be a function of many factors. For example, the anticipated audience of the production may dictate the cost associated with placement. Placing a product in a motion picture that does not include major talent will often cost the marketer less than a production with a proven cast. The inclusion of a major celebrity in a cast will likely increase the viewing potential and, therefore, the placement cost. But use caution.

Product partners for the movie *Gigli* might have expected a hit movie because of the cast – Ben Affleck and Jennifer Lopez. Imagine how disappointed they were!

Along this same line, placement in television or video productions will be influenced by the popularity of the series. The relevance of a product to the script will also influence cost. If the producer or director wants a specific product because it is relevant to the story, the placement of the brand may be accommodated at a more reasonable cost.

Entertainment Marketing as an IMC Practice.

Here we've talked about many IMC tools used in marketing a product-property relationship. Advertising is often shared. Premiums and other promotional offers are distributed. Press conferences are usually held to announce the relationship. You get the idea, right? Entertainment marketing works as an IMC practice on many levels.

Summary.

In this chapter we opened things up to consider the possibilities of media work in the new IMC world.

We covered the most frequently used tools of Integrated Marketing Communications including Direct Response Marketing, Promotional Marketing, and Marketing Public Relations. In each area we covered the common applications of conventional advertising media. And we introduced some of the unique media specific to the IMC tool.

Then we moved on to cover specific media issues and applications in some specialized IMC practices.

We covered Business-to-Business Marketing to show how a media career can be made in this field. We talked about media work in the practice of Customer Relationship Marketing. We discussed Sports Marketing and, finally, Entertainment Marketing.

In truth, this was a short list of IMC practices. We selected these particular practices to show how media plays a role. In the interest of space and time, we left out several other fields. If you are interested in any specialty practice of IMC, there are whole books published on each that we covered here as well as others.

The point here is that media plays a role through all of marketing and IMC. The possibilities are really endless.

Discussion Questions.

1. Direct Response Marketing.

What media tactics do we use to deliver direct response communications?

How do we use conventional media?

How do we use other media?

What are "personal" media channels?

2. Promotional Marketing.

What are the tactics of consumer promotions, and how do we use media to deliver each?

How do promotional objectives affect our media decisions?

What are the unique media of consumer promotions?

What are the unique media of in-store marketing?

3. Marketing Public Relations.

What is Marketing Public Relations?

What are the media of Marketing Public Relations?

How do public relations activities use conventional media?

And, how is this different from advertising use of the conventional media?

How do we measure the media effect of PR?

4. Business-to-Business Marketing.

How is the business buying decision different from the consumer buying decision?

What are the media of B2B marketing?

How is B2B marketing an IMC practice?

5. Customer Relationship Marketing.

What is the role of media in CRM?

What is a database and why is this important in CRM?

How is advertising used in CRM?

6. Sports Marketing.

What is Sports Marketing?

What is the role of media in sports marketing?

How has sports marketing impacted the media?

How is public relations a factor in sports marketing?

7. Entertainment Marketing.

How does a product become a media channel in entertainment marketing?

How might an entertainment property become a media channel?

Exercises.

1. Choose a familiar product or service. **How would you prepare a media plan for a direct response campaign for your chosen product or service?** Consider things like the media you would use, the list you would use, and your timing. How would you do this? What steps would you take? How would you find the informatoin you need about options and costs? Write a report on this and be prepared to present your report to the class.

2. **Imagine you are the agency media planner working on a well-known over-the-counter pain reliever.** One day you arrive at work and learn that packages of your client's product have been found to be laced with cyanide and people are dying. The police have caught the person responsible (not a company employee). What would you do? How will you spend the next hours,

days, weeks, months? What steps will you take to help your client through this? Remember you are the *media planner*. Write a 2-3 page report on this.

3. Choose a movie from some of the more popular films released on video/DVD over the last six months. **Get a copy of the movie and watch in carefully. Answer the following questions.**

   a. Name all of the products or services you see used in the movie.

   b. Sort the list of name-brand products/services according to level of integration with the plot of the movie:

   • Background placement as set dressing
   • Actual use or integration with movie characters
   • Fully integrated into the plot of the movie

   c. Identify a product placement opportunity that was *not* utilized in the movie.

   Prepare a presentation of your findings for the class.

14 Multi-Media & Cross-Platform Integration

IN THIS CHAPTER WE WILL REVIEW how consolidation of media resources into a limited number of multinational and global media companies has made it possible for advertisers to make single purchases across many media platforms, called multi-media and cross-platform purchases.

A New Playing Field.

This is a new field in the world of media.

The key players in this field are the media companies, the media agencies, the marketing companies, and even the U.S. government.

Each of these key players is faced virtually every day with decisions that will impact the development of this field.

Chapter Organization.

In this chapter we will discuss the development to date of this new field of practice. We'll do this in three sections.

First we'll try to define and explain the field. We'll give you a good working definition. Then we'll outline some of the important considerations and limitations of cross-platform deals. Also in this section we'll consider the motivations of buyers and sellers and we'll provide a brief historical perspective as background.

In the second section of this chapter we'll spend some time talking about the general industry trends and the specific company trends that have combined to make this field a reality. Included here you'll find a detailed history of each of the biggest media companies in the U.S. as well as a quick review of the biggest clients in this field so far.

Finally, we will briefly consider the future. It seems evident to many experts that this field is here to stay, but the truth is we really can't know for sure. Scale is a big factor, and scale in both media and marketers is something that changes every day. Here we will try to imagine the future in the hope that we might stir your imagination.

Multi-media and Cross-Platform.

Multi-media plans and buys are media plans or purchases that include more than one media vehicle. For example, a plan that includes television and magazines would be a multi-media plan or media mix. If we are able to buy both media from just one seller in a consolidated buy, we would call that a cross-platform buy.

Cross-platform Integration takes the multi-media buy to the next level by bringing these elements together within one media company.

"Cross-platform" applies for any multiple media combination. For example, a combination of television with magazines. And also within vehicle combinations like broadcast and cable television, or multiple magazine titles.

Cross-platform deals including multiple magazine titles are sold by the large publishing companies. These deals provide corporate volume incentives in addition to or in place of individual publication discounts available on rate cards or attained through individual publication negotiations.

Cross-platform deals that cross over television vehicles are sold by major broadcast companies who own a combination of television assets. These deals include various combinations of broadcast and cable TV elements. The most visible of these deals are developed with companies owning the major networks, but can also be structured to combine national and local assets through the television station groups of the broadcast companies.

Cross-platform deals that include multi-media elements like TV and magazines combine multiple media forms into a single purchase. These deals tend to be large and complex and often include other marketing elements, such as a promotional tie-in.

Considerations in Cross-Platform Planning.

We begin the development of multi-media, cross-platform plans in the same place we begin the development of all media plans – we review client objectives.

In the case of cross-platform planning and buying, we start with brand goals knowing that we are working towards a corporate goal. Often, cross-platform purchases will help achieve broader corporate goals that may not otherwise directly impact your media plan objectives. They tend to address the overall corporate objectives more so than individual brand goals.

Of course, the sum of all of the brand goals should combine to achieve corporate objectives. However, not all brands are created equal in large corporations. Sometimes a corporation may emphasize one brand more than others in the overall portfolio. This can be important in cross-platform planning and buying.

Clearly, any activity recommended should reach your brand's prospects effectively and must be appropriately targeted according to the plan objectives. ALL aspects of the plan, including elements secured through cross-platform buys, should be developed with the same target audience in mind. The only exception to this rule is if there are overriding corporate objectives involved.

Next, the media vehicles must be compatible with your advertising message. It is important to ensure that cross-platform deals are able to address any specific communication needs required by the brand's advertising message. First and foremost in these considerations is the availability of effective advertising to appear in each media vehicle included within the cross-platform purchase. Further, we must consider if there are specific brand attributes that need to be conveyed. If the cross-platform buy incorporates vehicles that will not effectively communicate these attributes, the deal won't work. These vehicles will need to be minimized or eliminated and replaced with others that are effective.

Then the cross-platform deal must be flexible to allow you to control the timing of your efforts so messages appear when and where you need them. You must be able to cover key dates and time periods. You might need to reconsider if the cross-platform deal culminates in an event or focuses efforts into only a fixed period of time. Particularly if that time is less valuable to your brand.

Geography is another limiting factor. As sellers and marketers include local assets in cross-platform deals, marketers must determine if they need any marketing activities that require support within the indicated geography. While most of the highly visible cross-platform deals have focused primarily on national vehicles, many sellers will try to focus their capabilities in a more localized fashion. This localized focus provides an opportunity for marketers who need greater local support or customized local marketing communications.

Cross-platform opportunities need to address your required communication levels. Deals can be structured to emphasize reach or frequency. As we have reviewed in earlier chapters, the use of multiple media can aid in broadening the reach achieved by your plan. This is true for the use of multiple television vehicles as well as the combined use of television with other media vehicles. For example, packaging multiple

Considerations in Cross-Platform Planning

1. Properly targeted to the right marketing audience
2. Compatible with the ad message strategy
3. Flexibility with regard to timing and geography
4. Effective communications delivery (reach and frequency)
5. Cost efficiency

cable television networks delivering similar audience demographics in different program types in one deal will aid in developing reach among the audience.

Conversely, if greater frequency is needed to deliver your brand's message effectively, cross-platform deals can be designed to focus exposures into vehicles that will provide duplicated exposure. For example, to provide greater frequency you might package cable television networks delivering similar programming and demographics like a combination of A&E and the Biography Network.

Cross-platform deals can help you create a media mix, but you should consider how they address your media mix needs. The basis for the selection of a media mix is a combination of the communication levels and the effectiveness of the message to the medium. These factors drive the media vehicle choices for the overall plan. In the development of cross-platform buys the same principles should be adhered to. This means limited or no use of undesirable media vehicles.

Finally, we should examine the cost structure of the cross-platform buy to ensure that it is cost effective against the objectives. Many cross-platform deals combine dollars planned for multiple platforms to increase buying leverage and net positive impact on target audience delivery for improved cost efficiency. But it's not only about costs. Dependent upon the objectives, you may be willing to pay a cost-efficiency premium to take advantage of the other synergies afforded to your brand or the immeasurable value of the package as it relates to your overall goals and corporate objectives.

Why are Marketers Buying?

From the marketer's perspective, there are many motivations to enter into cross-platform deals. As marketers have built their brand portfolios the opportunities to use multimedia or cross-platform programs have been more attainable. Large, multi-brand companies have the ability to spread the risk of major purchases across many brands.

Marketers expect lower pricing and improved cost efficiency when making these investments. Just as the larger and longer-term commitments made in the upfront television market typically provide marketers with cost efficiency advantages, most marketers expect and demand greater efficiencies and leverage from cross-platform deals. This potential for increased return on dollars invested is important.

Often advertisers pursue cross-platform purchases to support themed marketing efforts. In order to make this work, the vehicles of the cross-platform purchase must have the ability to fit a common theme or focus. This might be a theme that resonates with the brand or with a promotional approach of the marketer. The trick is finding a media company with multiple media holdings that will fit with the brand theme. For example, consider the case of a major sports product marketer. Which of the major, multi-media holding companies owns enough sports media to be able to package a cross-platform, sports-themed deal?

One obvious answer is Disney. Disney is the parent company for all ESPN media properties. This includes ESPN Radio, *ESPN Magazine*, and the several ESPN cable TV networks. It also includes ESPNZone amusement centers. And, of course, there are other Disney properties like ABC TV and its long heritage of sports programming.

Another good reason is that cross-platform purchases can help satisfy plan communications objectives. They help with reach requirements by covering additional prospects that might not be reached by any individual vehicle. And, as we mentioned earlier, cross-platform purchases can also be designed to build message frequency.

The large scale purchases that make up many of the most visible cross-platform plans have great public relations opportunities for marketers. As a result of this positive press, the news of these deals has a positive impact on the reputation of these companies. In this market-driven world, posi-

A Sporting Deal.
A marketer looking for a sports-themed cross-platform deal might want to consider the sports properties of Disney.

tive press can improve stock performance. This can be important to a large corporation.

What Are Sellers Selling?

As consolidation of the media companies has pulled more assets into fewer companies, major media players have been challenged to deliver synergy within their new companies. One of the greatest criticisms of the merger of Time Warner and AOL was management's inability to deliver on the synergies promised to the investment community. To gain the support of the financial and investment community, such companies project cost savings and opportunities for improved revenue as a result of the improved ability to sell in the cross-platform environment. But this can backfire if the company can't deliver.

Sellers can only offer their current menu of available assets. If the assets on hand are numerous, as we would find in the mammoth media companies, the flexibility available to them is great. The pressure to show significant gains in integrated deals is intense. In smaller media companies with fewer assets available, the potential is more focused but no less intense. Either of these situations can benefit brands if considered in light of their marketing objectives.

The assets available from a cross-platform seller will dictate how they try to address marketers' needs. If assets are focused in national broadcast, then sales efforts will be focused on national advertisers. If the seller's assets offer greater strengths across local markets, then the sales approach will be more local in focus. This might mean local advertisers, but it could also mean local emphasis for national advertisers.

Sellers might attempt to provide marketers with an editorially themed focus. As we previously noted, this is potentially important to marketers. If the cross-platform seller can offer programming across numerous assets of a particular affinity, they will be in good position to package the programming around a theme that could be relevant to marketers.

Events provide great opportunities for cross-platform selling. The popularity of sports and sports marketing has turned major sporting events into marketing vehicles. For example, the right to televise the Olympics has become so expensive that media companies must provide coverage across multiple broadcast venues to meet the financial objectives of the coverage. This coverage provides a rich, multi-media platform opportunity for both sellers and marketers.

Other sports coverage can offer the same opportunity for cross-platform sales. Where the coverage of the sport is shared between multiple venues, such opportunities can achieve the same scale as the Olympics. For example, chamionship series coverage can offer smaller scale opportunities over an extended period of time. Also, in the pursuit of programming that attracts a desirable audience, programmers may create events.

An example of a network-created event is the ESPN X-Games. The X-Games are an original Olympic style event created by ESPN in 1995. The event combined competition in "extreme" sports over a ten-day period. The original summer sports expanded to include the Winter X-Games. The combination of these two events provided ESPN with an opportunity to reach young, male viewers with programming specifically designed to attract them over extended periods twice each year. These events have grown into ESPN marquee programs and have spawned the creation of other themed events on ESPN like the "Great Outdoor Games."

Sellers, like ESPN, know that such events provide great opportunities for advertisers. Media companies like Disney can spread out the coverage and promotion of the event across multiple media properties including: broadcast network ABC; cable TV networks ESPN, ESPN2, ESPN News, and ESPN Classic; network radio ESPN Radio; and online at ESPN.com.

This is win-win marketing that builds brands for both marketers and media.

The media created March Madness as a major event built around the NCAA National Basketball Championships.

Creating a Themed Event.
The ESPN-created X-Games are an excellent cross-platform media opportunity for marketers.

It may seem that the only objective of the sellers is to increase sales revenue. Certainly this is one of the many objectives that media sales people must address on a day to day basis. Without increased sales, these companies cannot grow.

Sales revenue for cross-platform sales organizations is great, but what these companies really hope for is incremental advertising dollars that are over and above what media companies' individual sales units are able to generate.

The double-edged sword in this equation is the desire to realize incremental dollars without cannibalizing dollars already placed through these other entities. As advertisers hope for additional savings by consolidating purchases, the media companies can find themselves in a net negative position if they're not careful.

Here's how things might go wrong. Let's say a marketer has allocated $100 million to support a sports-themed campaign. Without considering cross-platform opportunities, the media planner/buyer might decide on her own to spend the money mostly on ESPN properties because that makes sense. If the ESPN sales team, sensing an opportunity, jumps in to offer a special package rate and added exposures, then ESPN might just be giving up more in exchange for the same dollars they might have gotten without the package.

It's true this is a risk, but most of the cross-platform sellers will tell you it's a risk worth taking. In today's very competitive media world, no one media vehicle or company can sit back and feel confident about getting any percent of a big buy – much less a majority of a big buy.

Often, the seller's objective is to get increased share of client dollars. This can result from shifts of existing expenditures moving from multiple sellers into a cross-platform buy or from spending being maintained with the seller in light of shrinking budgets. The latter is common in periods of decreasing spending within this industry.

The consolidation of marketers promises to bring the media greater operational efficiency. The financial and investment communities are expecting the delivery of these efficiencies and marketers are looking for efficiency in execution. Achieving greater efficiency in turn delivers better profit and positive stock performance. The performance of stock in the multi-media companies is also impacted by the positive press generated by the announcement of these large scale deals and the partnerships created with highly visible marketers. As is the case with marketers, sellers hope to appear to be innovative and in the front of creating new ideas in the marketplace. These deals aid in creating the look of an innovator.

Cross-platform buys can also protect sellers by helping them retain dollars in the event of budget cutbacks. These large deals tend to be longer term. If cutbacks occur, the long-term commitments from the marketer will protect the seller at least to a minimum level.

Some Background Perspective.

Cross-platform deals have become more commonplace as media companies have grown and acquired more assets.

Most of the early offerings tried to fit relevant assets into the plans of related marketers. For example, Time Warner's music company assets offered tie-in to youth oriented marketers. Assets were typically discussed as an outside element of a single-platform deal.

In the 1990s, many of these companies began to have a limited number of representatives responsible for the sale of multiple marketing elements. As the decade progressed, these representatives became more able to offer assets to marketers across a broader range. As these offerings took hold, many smaller scale deals, relative to what would come later, were concluded. Overall, the industry struggled with the model to develop and negotiate these deals. As a result, in the early days, they seemed to be achieved mostly by direct client involvement.

Blazing the Way.
P&G and Viacom broke new ground in 2001 with their announcement of a $300 million cross-platform deal, the first really major collaboration.

Agency Pooled Deal.
The first agency-driven deal was a one-year shot between OMD and Disney. OMD spread the major sports deal across several willing clients.

Cross-platform deals really hit the map in 2001 with the announcement of a deal between P&G and Viacom valued at $300 million. At the time, the announcement of this major deal was expected to open the door for other marketers and sellers doing similar deals for multi-media buys.

The P&G cross-platform deal was the largest of its kind up to that time. The deal represented about 20% of P&G's total advertising budget and about 30% of its television budget – an increase of 50% in P&G's spending with Viacom. The deal included advertising in Viacom's broadcast networks, cable networks, syndicated TV properties, and non-media, like promotions and sponsorships. It was also expected that it might include radio, outdoor, and involvement at Blockbuster video stores. This pioneering deal was surpassed in 2002 as P&G expanded its cross-platform deal, increasing spending to over $350 million. This represented a 17% increase in spending versus the first year and included even more Viacom businesses. The goal for the second year was to include additional cable channels and more integrated elements like product placements, promotional ties, and minority marketing programs.

Deals with the other media giants also naturally leaned toward their strongest assets. For example, Time Warner deals have a tendency toward print and online assets, including a $100 million deal with Unilever in 2002.

Also in 2002, the first major agency-driven cross-platform deal was developed. Media specialist agency OMD reached an agencywide integrated deal with Walt Disney Co. including all of its media divisions. This deal was estimated to be worth $1 billion! Major lures for OMD to do the billion-dollar deal included the Super Bowl, which ABC aired during the 2002-03 broadcast season and the NBA, which was starting a new TV contract with ESPN and ABC. This deal was innovative and expected to be the first of many, but it was not renewed in 2003 as OMD clients' needs were met in other venues for the 2003-04 TV season.

Leaders in Major Media Cross-Platform Sales

Viacom Plus	$600 million
ABC Unlimited	$500 million
Time Warner	
Global Marketing	$150 million
News Corp./Fox	$100 million

Today, deals of this magnitude are not found, and typical cross-platform agreements are struck with individual clients in the much smaller $10 million to $15 million range. One of the few exceptions to this trend is still the P&G / Viacom deal, still active at the $300 million level.

Viacom Plus and ABC Unlimited, the integrated sales groups for Viacom and Disney, are the industry leaders as it relates to cross-platform sales volume. Viacom Plus sales are estimated at approximately $600 million, with a major part of these sales from the P&G partnership. These sales revenues represent about 4% of the $16 billion net advertising revenues for all of Viacom. ABC Unlimited has accomplished deals estimated to be worth $500 to $550 million in annual sales including the marketing partnerships Disney entered before the creation of the ABC Unlimited sales group, which are now serviced by it. ABC Unlimited partners include McDonald's, Home Depot, and Nestle. These sales revenues represent about 6% of the $10 billion net advertising revenues for Disney.

Other integrated media sales groups are at lower sales levels. Time Warner's Global Marketing group is estimated to be in the $100 to $150 million range – less than 1% of total revenues. News Corp. is also estimated to be in the $100 million to $150 million a year range – approximately 2% of total revenues. Fox Broadcasting handles all integrated sales for News Corp.

Integrated sales groups incorporating multiple marketing elements aren't new. But their goals are more humble than the bigger media companies and they are willing to cut deals that are valued at more modest levels. For example, until recently, Discovery Networks had limited sales through its integrated partnership deals. It now has $225 million in annual deals. Significant to these sales is the P&G cross-platform deal struck in 2002 that combines Discovery's eight cable networks. Like the deals cut with the major media compa-

Smaller Scale.
Deals on a smaller scale can still be highly visible, like the partnership between Swiffer and Trading Spaces.

nies for larger sums the Discovery deal uses the cable TV assets of Discovery networks as the foundation of the buy and covers a variety of integrated marketing efforts, including, promotions and sweepstakes tied into Discovery.com, and the Discovery Channel stores. Also include in the deal was product placement in programming, including a partnership between Swiffer cleaning brand and *Trading Spaces*; a series that appears on Discovery network's TLC network, and Discovery Channel's *Surprise by Design*.

The Makers & Shakers of the Cross-platform World.

The cross-platform field is populated by many players on both sides of the buying and selling relationship. Although the larger players tend to get the greatest amount of attention because they make big deals, the opportunities to develop cross-platform relationships can be equally as valuable for the smaller buyers and sellers.

The most visible sellers are a who's who of the media giants. These corporations have aggressively developed and acquired many media assets. The foundation of this media practice is built upon marquee properties that were launched as far back as the 1920s. These giants could not have reached their current size and diversity without being important players and leaders within the consolidation trends of the advertising industry or without the explosion of media in the last 30 years.

The assets of these major companies tend to cover a broad spectrum of resources ranging across all media. The availability of these assets makes the creation of cross-platform deals possible. The top companies in terms of annual media revenues are the owners of major television, cable, and radio networks, numerous television and radio stations, large circulation magazines, and many other entertainment assets. Later in this section we will look at the five largest U.S. media companies in terms of net media revenues as reported by *AdAge* in its most recent report of the top media companies.

Important to the media marketplace is the combined power that these five companies hold. Together they represent over one-third of the net media revenue of the entire industry. That would be $80 billion! How can five sellers amass so much power in the marketplace?

Law Makers Pave the Way.

The consolidation of the industry and many of the earlier moves to break up companies have been affected by the U.S. federal government. As each FCC, FTC, or Justice Department decision is added to or alters the existing rules, regulations, and guidelines, doors are opened to control consolidation or to make integration easier. As with any laws, telecommunications law has evolved over time to address the situations of the day and preserve competition in the future. Current interpretation of these laws favors consolidation and the promotion of competition through deployment of technology to gain industry efficiencies.

Media Ownership by Studios.

The Paramount Decree of 1948 helped to define what was appropriate and fair for studios to own. In the early days of the movie industry Jack Warner at Warner Bros. and Louis Mayer at MGM Studios controlled all aspects of moviemaking. The practices of that day were considered to be anti-competitive. The Paramount Decree ruled that studios were not able to own certain assets throughout the movie industry such as theaters. As a result of these rules, the movie studios were required to sell parts of their companies.

Over time, the influence of the Paramount Decree diminished. The rules have been relaxed over the last few decades as the integration and consolidation of assets across many levels of the entertainment industry has become popular.

Program Ownership by Media.

An important rule was implemented by the FCC beginning in 1970 – the Financial Interest and Syndication Rule (Fin-Syn). It was designed to encourage diversity in televi-

Studio Power Reined In.
The Paramount Decree of 1948 limited studio ownership of certain assets, like movie theaters.

sion programming and has had a significant impact on the ownership of the many assets that are part of these major companies. Fin-Syn was designed to rein in the programming monopolies then held by the three major television networks: ABC, NBC, and CBS. Before Fin-Syn, independent producers were unable to gain access to the airwaves without giving up some financial interest in their shows to the networks. Before the ruling, the three networks had a financial interest in a very high percentage of the programs broadcast on their airwaves.

Enter Deregulation.

The Telecommunications Act of 1996 significantly deregulated the media industry. This landmark legislation opened the industry to a different definition of competition and allowed companies to significantly increase the amount of radio stations they could own. As a result, many companies were able to add or develop local broadcast strengths that they had previously not owned.

In addition to these actions, the federal government has taken a number of other steps to make consolidated ownership either easier or more difficult.

The 35% ownership cap limits networks from owning local stations when it would give them coverage of more than 35% of the national market. The spirit of this rule is to force ownership and the ensuing control of ideas to more companies rather than the few. For example, the premise here is that if a single news organization has control over a more substantial segment of the market, the free flow of ideas and opinions will be negatively affected in favor of the opinions held by these few owners. As rules require, the current ownership is spread over many companies that have the opportunity and obligation to report the news as they see fit. This rule is debated regularly, but has been reaffirmed at each of those occasions.

Rules controlling duopolies are also debated regularly. Duopolies are the ownership of two stations in a local market. As with the 35% rules, allowing duopolies is argued to be inhibiting by those opposed to allowing their existence. Broadcasters favor relaxed rules on duopolies to be able to take advantages of the efficiencies generated by combining some local operations. These combined operations might include the combination of news organizations which is feared to be limiting in the perspectives available.

Shakers Make the Game.

In Chapter 2 we talked about the media whirl. Remember? We used an analogy to the popular "merry-go-round" playground ride. We explained that the media owners today seek new media acquisitions as a way to maintain and gain weight, or grip, in the world of media.

Here we are going to talk about the biggest of the big media players. If you think back to that merry-go-round analogy, these are the players with the best seats on the ride!

Time Warner.

The largest of the U.S. media companies is Time Warner, with net media revenues of nearly $29 billion – 75% greater than the number-two media company. Time Warner has been successfully built into a company that owns assets across many media and in many of these areas holds the industry leader.

The Early Years of Time and Warner.

Time Warner's roots date back to the 1920s with the launch of *Time* magazine and the formation of Warner Brothers Pictures Inc. These two companies would later merge to form Time Warner.

In the 1930s, Time Inc. begins its long-term growth with the launch of *Fortune* magazine and *Life* magazine among others. In this period, Time Inc. also begins to develop capabilities in other media by producing newsreels.

Foundation of Time.
Magazines were the foundation of the Time media company.

Warner Early Years. *The Warner media company started in the studio business producing content.*

TIME in the 1970s.
In the '70s Time built success with new magazines, book publishing, and a new venture into pay-cable with HBO.

New Developments.
Also in the '70s Ted Turner started building his company with Turner Communications and the Atlanta super-station WTBS.

In the 1940s, Bugs Bunny first appears in a Warner Brothers cartoon and later Looney Tunes Studios was acquired by Warner Brothers.

In the 1950s, Time Inc. continues to expand its blue chip magazine stable by launching *Sports Illustrated* and makes its first investment in television by purchasing KOB TV in Albuquerque, New Mexico. Also during the 1950s, Warner Brothers launches Warner Music.

Expansion in the '60s.

In the 1960s, Time Inc. continues to expand its publishing capabilities by forming Time-Life Books and later acquiring Brown, Little, Forman. During this decade Warner Brothers goes through a tumultuous period. Warner closes Warner Animation Studios and buys Reprise Records and Atlantic Record. Before the end of this decade Warner Brothers is acquired twice and closes the 1960s known as Warner Communications.

In the 1970s both companies grow at an even more feverish pace. Time Inc. launches *Money* magazine and *People* magazine and makes their first move into cable television through the acquisition of Home Box Office. At the same time, Warner expands their music industry holdings by acquiring Elektra Records, acquires video game company Atari, and makes a move into cable television with the acquisition of cable system operator American Television & Communications.

As Time Inc. and Warner Communications grow and diversify, the foundation of a future component of Time Warner is laid. The outdoor company owned by Ted Turner which will later become Turner Communications is converted into a future broadcasting powerhouse with the purchase of WJRJ in Atlanta. This station becomes WTCG for Turner Communications Group and later WTBS for Turner Broadcasting Systems and is launched as the first "superstation" in 1976 – as it is beamed via satellite to cable homes across the country.

In the 1980s, Time Inc. continues growth through the launch of magazines and refines its publishing capabilities through the acquisition of Scott Foresman & Company book publishing unit and then the sale of this unit and Brown, Little, Forman. Ultimately, near the end of this decade, Time Inc. and Warner Communications merge to become Time Warner.

The cable television industry experienced explosive growth in this decade. Turner Communications was at the forefront of this growth with the launch of many of the household names in cable television. Turner launched the Cable News Network – CNN – in 1980 and CNN Headline News in 1982. Turner acquired the MGM library of films in 1986. The acquisition of this source of programming led, in part, to the launch of TNT in 1988.

The 1990s continued the explosive growth and change of the media landscape. This was a pivotal period in making Time Warner what they were to become. One of the most significant events in the history of Time Warner occurred when Gerald Levin took control of the company following the death of Steven J. Ross.

Time Warner continued to succeed in the magazine arena with the launch of *Entertainment Weekly* in 1990 and *In Style* magazine in 1994. Time Warner continued its expansion of cable TV holdings throughout the '90s. And it became known as an innovator with the adoption of new technologies.

In 1994, Time Warner became the world's largest music publisher after its Warner/Chappell Music unit acquires CPP/Belwin. In 1995, Time Warner becomes a major player in television with the launch of the fifth broadcast network, the WB, with the help of partners including the Tribune Companies, owners of the *Chicago Tribune* as well as powerful independent television stations in New York, Los Angeles, and Chicago.

Turner and Cable.

Turner expanded into cable television and acquisitions of movie production companies.

Concurrent with the Time Warner growth, Turner broadcasting is expanding to stay at the forefront of the cable television industry. In 1992, Turner Broadcasting launches its fifth cable network; The Cartoon Network and in 1994 Turner Classic Movies is launched. In this period, Turner also expands its program production and distribution capabilities through the merger with Castle Rock Entertainment and New Line Cinema.

Time Warner and Turner.

In 1996, these two media powerhouse companies combine as Time Warner acquires Turner Broadcasting System. This combination and others that will come later are made possible by the passage of the Telecommunications Act of 1996.

Also in the 1990s, AOL is born and grows into a leader in their field. In 1991 an Internet bulletin-board system called Quantum Computer Services changes its name to America Online. This company is founded by a group including future chairman Steve Case. That same year, the Tribune Company purchases a 9% share in AOL after making a $5 million investment in the company and one year later, America Online becomes a publicly traded company. AOL continues to grow at a rapid pace, reaching 1 million U.S. subscribers in 1994. In 1995, AOL expanded its services to Europe. Throughout the second half of this decade AOL acquires many of its smaller or struggling rivals including CompuServe and Netscape. At the close of the decade, as the Internet bubble is poised to explode, AOL finds itself in the position of being the leader in the industry

With the dawn of the new millennium, Time Warner appears to be building upon its past success and purchases the Times Mirror magazines from the Tribune Company, including *Golf, Ski, Skiing*, and *Field & Stream*.

AOL Time Warner.

AOL Time Warner became a reality in 2001 and later renamed to Time Warner.

AOL Time Warner.

In 2000, AOL and Time Warner stun the media world, announcing a $183 billion merger. The largest corporate merger in history is finalized in January of 2001. The company changes its name to AOL Time Warner and becomes the world's largest media and entertainment company. In 2001, AOL Time Warner returns to the path of past success and acquires the top magazine publisher in the United Kingdom, IPC Media. In 2002, AOL Time Warner buys out AT&T's stake in Time Warner Entertainment and creates its own cable operation. In 2003, after investors feel that the synergies promised by the combination of these two companies are not being realized and AOL Time Warner reports a $54.24 billion quarterly loss, Steve Case steps down as AOL Time Warner chairman and the company changes its name back to Time Warner.

As reported by *AdAge*, Time Warner is the largest of the U.S. media companies, with $28.6 billion in net media revenue. This revenue comes from an expansive portfolio of media brands. Time Warner owns a majority interest in the WB Network, currently the 5th ranked broadcast network; owns 3 of the top ten cable networks: TBS, TNT and CNN; operates the largest magazine company with titles that include, *Time, People* and *Sports Illustrated* among a lengthy list of titles; owns the second largest cable TV system operator; owns the largest Internet company, America Online.

Viacom.

Viacom is the number-two media company, with net media revenue of over $16 billion. Like Time Warner, Viacom holds assets across many media forms and is one of the most diversified media companies. The history of Viacom dates to the early 1900s.

In the Beginning.

The origin of Viacom dates to the founding of four companies in the 1910s and '20s who would later combine to be

Studio Developments.
Famous Players Films became Paramount Pictures, then Famous Players-Lasky Corp,. and then Paramount Pictures again.

A Broadcast Heritage.
CBS Radio and Television was built on its news heritage.

the nucleus of Viacom as it exists today. First, in 1912 the Famous Players Film Corp was founded then went through a series of name changes before it became Paramount Pictures then Famous Players-Lasky Corp in 1916. Around the same time, Westinghouse engineer Dr. Frank Conrad began experimental radio broadcasts from his home in Pittsburgh and on November 2, 1920, Westinghouse's KDKA in Pittsburgh began scheduled radio programming with the Harding-Cox Presidential election returns. Later in the '20s Simon & Schuster was created with the publication of a crossword puzzle book.

In the 1930s, Famous Players-Lasky Corp. becomes Paramount Pictures again after going through bankruptcy and reorganization. CBS Radio establishes their news reporting leadership heritage as Edward R. Murrow and William L. Shirer do a radio news program that eventually becomes *The CBS World News Roundup*. Near the end of the decade, CBS buys American Record Company, who owns the Columbia Phonograph label and renames the division Columbia Record Corp.

Growth and Expansion.

In the 1940s, CBS builds on its news reporting leadership with regular broadcasts by Murrow reporting from war-torn London. Broadcasts originating during and after blitzkrieg attacks become famous. Murrow broadcasts these reports throughout WW II and continues to influence CBS News and the news industry in general through the 1950s and early '60s until he retires in 1961.

While developing this heritage, CBS lays the foundation for the television industry with the first commercial, black and white television broadcast in 1941.

At the close of this decade, resulting from growing monopolies, the Department of Justice announces the Paramount Decree, which forces the film studios to sell off their movie theaters.

Government Intervention.
Viacom was formed after CBS spun off its television programming arm as a direct result of the FCC Fin-Syn Ruling.

Blockbuster Deal.
In 1994 Viacom acquires Paramount and Blockbuster Video.

National Amusements Inc. (NAI), a chain of movie theaters and later a major influence on Viacom, benefits significantly from this decree. Important to the future of Viacom, Sumner Redstone, the current Chairman of Viacom, took control of NAI in the mid-1950s. Also during the tumultuous 1960s, CBS teams with Sony, a Japanese company, to form CBS-Sony Records. And near the end of this decade, Paramount Pictures is purchased by diversified conglomerate, Gulf + Western.

In 1970, as the FCC Fin-Syn ruling limits the financial interest television networks can have in syndicated programming, Viacom is formed after CBS spins off its television programming arm. Although the implications of these rules had major impact on the entertainment industry in the 1970s, the impact has diminished over time.

As the industry entered the 1980s, we were about to begin an era of rapid change and growth. On August 1, 1981, MTV launched and later is purchased by Viacom. As we know, this unique network had and continues to have a major influence on broadcasting. In 1987, NAI buys a majority interest in Viacom, and Sumner Redstone becomes Chairman of the Board. In 1989, Gulf + Western changes its name to a more recognizable and relevant Paramount Communications. Around this same time, the first Blockbuster Video store opens in Dallas, and CBS gets out of publishing, selling its entire book publishing division.

Consolidation.

In the 1990s, each of these companies goes through dramatic change and the consolidation begins. First in these major combinations are the acquisitions by Viacom of Paramount Communication and Blockbuster Video in 1994. Shortly after these acquisitions, Viacom sells Madison Square Garden and its related properties to Cablevision and sells its cable systems to TCI. On January 16, 1995, the UPN network joins the television competition. In 1997, Viacom sells most of its publishing businesses except Simon & Schuster.

Important to this company in the 1990s, CBS is sold to the Westinghouse Corporation, buys the American Radio System then buys the Infinity Radio Broadcasting and Outdoor Advertising Group. These acquisitions are mainly a result of the Telecommunications Act of 1996. In a move that signals the importance of this growing media company, Westinghouse changes its name to CBS in 1997 and sells its hardware and manufacturing businesses. To close this decade, CBS buys King World Productions, a leading television program syndicator, and purchases the Outdoor Systems billboard group.

A Powerhouse Merger.

On September 7, 1999, Viacom and CBS announced their merger. The $50 billion combination immediately becomes the largest media merger ever. This merger is made possible, in part by, and comes one month after, the FCC gives approval to duopolies – the ownership of two television stations in the same market.

The combined Viacom/CBS owns 33 television stations and surpasses the FCC's 35% ownership cap we discussed earlier. Viacom challenges this limit to avoid the mandatory divestiture of the duplicated stations. In 2001, the District of Columbia Circuit of the United States Court of Appeals, gives Viacom temporary approval to exceed the 35% ownership cap.

In 2001, Viacom purchases BET Inc., and in 2002, Viacom purchases KCAL-TV in Los Angeles. The deal forms a Viacom duopoly in Los Angeles, raising the number of markets where it owns two broadcast stations to eight.

Today, Viacom is the second largest media company in the U.S. Viacom owns the number-two broadcast network – CBS – and two of the top ten cable TV networks – MTV and Nickelodeon. The Viacom Television Stations Group owns and operates 39 TV stations in 31 markets. Infinity Broadcasting is the second-largest radio station operator, owning and operating 185 radio stations in 40 markets, second only to Clear

A Media Powerhouse.

The CBS and Viacom merger was announced in 1999 with major holdings in television, radio, outdoor, publishing, movie production, video retailing, and movie theaters.

Channel Communications. Viacom Outdoor is the largest outdoor advertising group in North America. In addition, Viacom owns Paramount Pictures and Home Video.

Comcast.

The third largest of these companies is Comcast. Unique to this group, Comcast makes its way to the top of the rankings primarily because of their cable television system holdings. Comcast is the largest cable television system operator in the U.S. as a result of their merger with AT&T cable, completed in 2002. Revenue from these holdings alone is only slightly smaller than the total revenues of Viacom. Total net media revenues for Viacom are estimated to be around $16 billion.

A Cable System Start Up.

Relative to the other companies found in the upper level of the entertainment industry, Comcast is a newcomer. Comcast was founded in 1963 as American Cable Systems with the purchase of a small cable system with 1,200 subscribers in Mississippi. Over next 40 years, Comcast would build their subscriber base to a total of 21 million – about 30% of cable TV homes.

Through the investment in building their subscriber base, Comcast also invested in unique programming opportunities. These include diverse programming such as their founding of QVC (the largest electronic retailer) in 1988, and later acquisition of controlling interest in G4 (a network dedicated to entertainment, news, and information about video games and the interactive entertainment industry), TV One (cable television network serving African American viewers), Comcast-Spectacor (launched in 1996 as a sports venture owning and operating the Philadelphia Flyers, the Philadelphia 76ers), as well as a regional sports channel, Comcast Regional Sports Television that is continuing to roll out across more of Comcast's subscriber base. In addition, Comcast owns significant or controlling interest in E! Entertainment, the Golf Channel and the Outdoor Life Network.

A Different Kind of Media Company.
Comcast holdings include a couple of major league sports teams along with a large subscriber based cable television system bringing in a lot of direct-from-consumer income.

While Comcast was building their cable television system holdings, the company was also investing and growing a significant mobile telephone business. This business was ultimately sold to SBC Communications in 1999.

A Different Business Model.

As the largest operator of cable television systems, Comcast has the capability to reach millions of homes representing a significant portion of the U.S. population, but does not have much to reach them with. Comcast program assets include relatively small cable television networks and an expanding network of regional sports media assets.

This relative lack of programming capabilities was a motivating factor behind Comcast's unsuccessful hostile takeover bid for the Disney Company. The combination of these companies would have provided Comcast the capabilities they need for further growth. The overtures toward Disney have been rejected, for now. Comcast will likely continue to search for an acquisition to provide them the programming they need to offer their cable subscribers. As Comcast currently exists, they are relatively singularly focused in a subscriber-based model.

The Walt Disney Company.

As we see with each of the previously described companies, Disney holds many assets and is one of the most diversified media companies. The Walt Disney Company is the fourth-largest of the U.S. media companies, with estimated net media revenues of almost $10 billion.

Animated Origins.

The Walt Disney Company began in the 1920s based on the popularity of Mickey Mouse and other cartoons produced by Walt Disney Productions including Steamboat Willie and Snow White and the Seven Dwarfs. Snow White was Disney's first full length animated film released in 1937. Walt Disney Productions made their first public offering of stock in 1940 to help lower debt.

The American Broadcast Company network is formed after the FCC rules in 1943 that NBC must sell one of its two radio networks. Later, the ABC Company is bought in 1951 by United Paramount Theaters. Buena Vista Distribution Company is formed in 1953 to act as Disney film distributor.

The long-term relationship between Disney and ABC begins in 1954 as *Disneyland*, the first weekly television series from Disney studios debuts on ABC. In addition, Disneyland opens three years later in Anaheim, California, with the ABC television network as an investor, and the *Mickey Mouse Club* debuts on ABC. These companies continue to grow throughout the coming decades but make no real notable acquisitions. Disney opens Walt Disney World in 1971 and Tokyo Disneyland opens in 1983.

Expansion into Cable TV.

As the foundation is set for the growth of cable television in the 1980s, sports network ESPN is launched in 1979 by Getty Oil, and the Disney Channel is launched in 1983. Five years after the launch of ESPN, ABC acquires this network and two years later Capital Cities Communication, a large broadcasting group, acquires the ABC television network. In 1987, ESPN is awarded the NFL's first cable broadcasting agreement. The opportunity to broadcast one of the leading sports in the U.S. brings greater legitimacy to ESPN as a significant force in sports television.

Mergers and Acquisitions.

The 1990s are significant years for the Disney Company as its assets begin to take the shape of what they will become. In 1993, Disney acquires Miramax Films, and in 1995 Disney announces its intent to purchase Capital Cities/ABC. The deal is the largest media merger to this point and one of the largest mergers ever in the U.S. Notably, Disney expanded their media diversification through the launch of ESPN Radio in 1992, Disney.com and Radio Disney in 1996, *ESPN: The Magazine* in 1998, and the acquisition of Fox Family Worldwide, which later becomes known as ABC Family.

ABC Disney.

The Walt Disney Company is the fourth largest U.S. media company with estimated net revenues of almost $10 billion.

Today, The Walt Disney Company is the fourth-ranked U.S. media company, with estimated net media revenues of $9.8 billion. Disney owns a vastly diversified portfolio of media assets including the third broadcast network – ABC – the leading cable TV network franchise – ESPN – and substantial local broadcast holdings with 10 TV stations in 10 markets and 64 radio stations in 38 markets.

National Broadcasting Company.

NBC Television is a subsidiary company of the diversified General Electric Company. As a result of the recently completed acquisition of Universal, NBC is expected to move into the number four position with over $15 billion in net media revenues.

The National Broadcasting Corporation (NBC) was formed in 1926 as a result of the combined investments of RCA, GE, and Westinghouse. NBC acquired WEAF in New York City and WJZ in Newark and launched them as the flagship stations for the new NBC Radio network. These stations were known as NBC's "Red" and "Blue" networks respectively.

A Media Pioneer.

NBC was a pioneer company in the broadcasting industry, credited with many firsts. In 1927, NBC Radio broadcast the Rose Bowl to the first nationwide audience. At the 1939 World's Fair in New York City, NBC was the first to introduce television to the world. Later, in 1941, NBC received the first license for a commercial television station. In 1954, NBC telecasts the first color broadcast of the Rose Bowl parade to a small audience – since very few people had color sets in use.

RCA began to diversify their related holdings in 1929 with the purchase of the Victor Talking Machine Company and began manufacturing radios and phonographs.

In 1932, GE and Westinghouse sell off their investments in RCA due to concerns of a growing monopoly. Although this move was not directly prompted by public FCC action, the move was clearly a result of the rising influence of NBC.

In 1941, the Federal Communications Commission (FCC) releases its "Report on Chain Broadcasting" which is critical of the growth of broadcast networks and demands that NBC sell off one of its two networks. To protect their assets, NBC challenges this ruling and fights the FCC, but loses the fight in 1943. To satisfy the ruling, RCA sells off the NBC Blue Network, and it eventually becomes ABC.

Fast Forward to the '80s.

In 1985, NBC is acquired by GE as part of a deal for the purchase of RCA.

In 1989, NBC enters the cable television marketplace through the launch of cable news and financial network – CNBC. In 1996, NBC expands its investment in cable TV with the launch of MSNBC. This cable news network is a joint partnership between GE and Microsoft. In addition to these investments in cable TV network launches, GE / NBC continue to invest in other television assets. Notably, in 1999 GE purchased a 32% stake in Paxson Communications and its PAX TV network and in 2002 GE acquires the Telemundo Communications Group and later acquires the Bravo Network.

The All-New NBC Universal.

Most recently, in 2003, GE and Vivendi Universal announce the deal to create NBC Universal. In the deal, GE acquires Vivendi Universal's entertainment holdings which include theme parks, production studios, and three cable channels, including the eighth ranked USA Network.

NBC Universal, with expected revenue of $15 billion for 2005, will trail Time Warner, Viacom, and Comcast. NBC Universal includes the leading broadcast network (NBC), the number two Spanish-language network (Telemundo), the eighth ranked cable network (USA Network), a film studio (Universal Pictures), TV production studios (Universal Television and NBC Studios), a television station group of 29 NBC and Telemundo stations, and interests in theme parks, including Universal Studios Hollywood and Universal Orlando.

More Than Friends.

NBC Universal holdings include television and movie production companies, theme parks, broadcast and cable television networks and stations, and radio properties throughout the U.S.

Overview of Assets Owned by the Top 5 U.S. Media Companies

	Time Warner	Viacom	Comcast	Disney	NBC
Television Networks	X	X	-	X	X
Cable TV Networks	X	X	X	X	X
Radio Networks	-	X	-	X	-
Television Stations	-	X	-	X	X
Radio Stations	-	X	-	X	-
Cable TV Systems	X	-	X	-	-
TV Program Syndication	-	X	-	-	X
Consumer Magazines	X	-	-	X	X
Outdoor	-	X	-	-	-
Online Service	X	-	-	-	-
Publishing (Books)	X	X	-	X	-
Movie & TV Production	X	X	-	X	X
Music	X	-	-	X	X
Entertainment Venues	X	X	-	X	X
Retail Outlets	X	X	-	X	-
Sports Franchises	-	-	X	X	-

With the media landscape constantly changing and consolidating, the *Columbia Journalism Review* includes a regularly updated listing on their website (cjr.org) of "Who Owns What" for forty-five major media companies.

The chart above presents a visual summary of assets owned by these mega companies.

Marketers Play for Scale.

As with the sellers, the most visible buyers have the size and funding necessary to drive mega-deals. Typically, these companies have many brands that can share the assets purchased through multi-media, cross-platform deals. This opportunity to share the buys with many brands limits the risks in these large purchases and increases the opportunity of greater rewards.

Procter & Gamble.

Procter & Gamble is perhaps the greatest example of how companies can take advantage of these cross-platform deals. Procter & Gamble ranks at or near the top among all U.S. advertisers and supports 83 brands. Most of these brands are widely used consumer products that might be found in any home in America. This kind of scale allows P&G the ability to consider opportunities that other marketers cannot. They bring size and target flexibility into the consideration of these opportunities. P&G has negotiated several visible cross-platform deals including the $300 million dollar deal with Viacom we mentioned earlier.

Kraft.

Kraft is another company with scale and a portfolio of leading consumer brands. Kraft has also taken advantage of numerous cross-platform opportunities including deals with both of the top media companies – Time Warner and Viacom. As a leading food brand marketer, Kraft brand alignment offers great opportunities to incorporate products under the umbrella brand names of Kraft – Jacobs, Philadelphia, Maxwell House, Nabisco, Oscar Mayer, and Post. This affords Kraft the opportunity to also look at unique approaches like product integration into programming.

Unilever.

As the world's largest advertiser, Unilever is also a visible player in the cross-platform arena including a multi-million dollar, multi-year deal with Time Warner that included pri-

Media Specialists.
Some of the largest media specialist agencies are changing the industry.

marily U.S. assets, but left the door open to include European assets in the future.

Many other advertisers have quietly reached deals with cross-platform sellers, and we can expect more to be developed in the future.

As marketers have consolidated and grown they have demanded that their ad agencies be prepared to handle their business on a global basis. They have also demanded that their agencies operate with scale and authority in the media marketplace. Large agency holding companies bought agencies to complement and enhance their U.S. and global capabilities. An outgrowth of this consolidation was the birth of the large media specialist companies owned by these agency holding companies.

These media specialist companies are changing the industry by pursuing consolidated media planning and buying assignments from major clients. As a result of these consolidated assignments, these specialists are more involved in the decisions being made for an advertisers' entire list of brands. These media specialist companies command vast budgets and create opportunities to make enormous buys. They are required by their clients to push the buying paradigm and uncover new, effective and efficient ways to support their brands.

The Future of Cross-platform Integration

Cross-platform integration has the potential to shake up the current media buying industry. Although experts disagree as to the extent of impact, such deals could easily have an impact on the annual network upfront season, when most of the coming year's TV ad dollars are bought and sold.

Today there are separate upfront negotiations for each network TV daypart, cable, syndicated TV, and kids TV. An increase in cross-platform deals could have the effect of combining the individual upfronts into one cross-platform selling season. At a panel discussion at the annual media conference of the American Association of Advertising Agencies in 2001, executives from some of the world's biggest media agencies said cross-platform deals might make up as much as 40% of marketers' spending by 2006.

It is unlikely that these deals will eliminate the upfront season. There will probably be a place for cross-platform deals alongside the current upfront season. As we currently have the scatter market to meet the needs of advertisers who are unable to participate in the upfront, there will likely continue to be multiple market levels to accommodate the varying needs of marketers. If the advantages are sufficient to pull more dollars into cross-platform deals, they will continue to increase. If the advantages are minimal, the potentially lost flexibility of these deals might push dollars back toward a traditional single medium approach.

Summary.

In this chapter we have considered this developing field of cross-platform media integration.

We defined cross-platform media integration in a particular way. We showed you that cross-platform integration is the packaging of multiple media assets completely within one media company. By this very definition you can see that here we are talking about some of the very biggest of big deals in the world of media.

We discussed some of the most important considerations and motivations driving the use of cross-platform integration. The important considerations were issues of corporate, brand, and then media objectives. This includes communication goals, target audience focus, media mix needs, schedule timing, and geographic emphasis.

Marketers are buying cross-platform packages because they seem to offer more media impact for the cost invested. Media comapnies are selling cross-platform packages in order to gain an increased share of the marketer's budget. Of course there

are risks, but ultimately such deals can be mutually beneficial as long as everyone stays focused on the objectives.

Another big section of this chapter considered each of the
biggest name players in this field. We started with the U.S.
government, reviewing some of the key laws and rulings that
affected development of the big media companies. Then we
reviewed the development history of the five largest media
companies in America – Time Warner, Viacom, Comcast,
Disney, and NBC. And, finally, we talked about the big client
companies and the brand portfolio scale that it takes to make
cross-platform integration viable.

In truth, the future of this specialized piece of the media
world depends on a lot of things. Government will continue
to play a role in media company ownership rules. And agencies will play a role in shaping client interest in such deals.
You too could someday play a role.

As we have seen with any other media decisions, cross-
platform deals need to provide solutions to your brands' marketing needs. Satisfying client needs through cross-platform
purchases will not work for every marketer. A critical mass of
spending is needed to provide a sufficient plan level to support these efforts. Rather, the issue is to avoid fragmenting
dollars into too many venues to be effective in any one of
them. There are opportunities on every scale and at every
budget to develop cross-platform deals.

Brad Simmons is a lifetime learner. Every career move he's made has given him a chance to try something new and learn from the experience. Brad feels it is this kind of attitude that will best serve the media professionals of the future. He sees a future where change is a constant, and media people need to be change agents.

Career Capsule:

Brad Simmons, VP Media Services, Unilever U.S., Inc.

Brad Simmons sent out a lot of résumés, went on a lot of interviews, and finally landed his first job as a Media Analyst for Campbell-Mithun in Minneapolis, Minnesota. He feels that it was hard work, patience, and the work he did as an undergraduate student at the University of Wisconsin – studying advertising, selling ad space for the school newspaper, and participating in the student ad club ad competitions – that helped him get the job.

Top of the Game.

Rising from his entry level starting point, Brad is now at the top of the media game. In his current position Brad and his staff are responsible for all U.S. media planning and buying activities on all Unilever-advertised brands, with a total budget recently estimated at more than $500 million annually. In just the last couple of years Brad has been named to the *AdWeek* magazine list of 25 people to watch, and the *Advertising Age* list of 50 Industry Power Players.

Getting There Took Energy.

After more than six years at Campbell-Mithun, Brad felt it was time to explore the corporate side of the media business. He did a short stint at Miller Brewing Company, where he worked with ad agencies to negotiate deals for advertising and sponsorships with local sports franchises. Then he moved to the Pillsbury Company, where he had oversight responsibility for television advertising negotiations. Brad says that this was one big reason why he moved to the client side, so that he could have responsibility for both the strategic planning and buying negotiations.

From Pillsbury, Brad moved to Helene Curtis, where he progressed to the level of Director of Media and Advertising Services. Then one day Helene Curtis became part of the consumer goods giant Unilever. Just like that, Brad thought he would be out of a job.

Instead, he found himself promoted within Unilever and now responsible for consumer promotions and public relations as well as media and advertising services. At the same time he took on responsibility for internal and external communications reporting directly to the President and CEO. He feels that his learning curve here was at its steepest, *"but, it was also the most stimulating part of the new job."*

From there Brad made just one more move, to the corporate position of Vice President, Media Services, for all of Unilever U.S. This was not an easy move to make. It meant relocating his family and refocusing his career on media. But, in the end he feels this last move was a great decision.

Learning Is Growing.

For Brad, every job move was about trying something different and learning something new. In his last move, refocusing on media might have been different, but he made it work.

In his new job Brad found opportunities to participate in high-level discussions on significant industry issues. Brad sits on the Board of Directors for the Association of National Advertisers (ANA) and for the Ad Council of America. Brad is Chair of the ANA Financial Management Committee, Co-Chair of the Family Friendly Forum, and now Chair of the Enhanced TV Initiative – studying the advertising effect of emerging technologies like digital TV, Video on Demand, and DVR/TiVo.

Advice for Students.

Brad feels there has never been a more exciting time to enter the field of media. From the marketer's perspective, he feels new technologies *"will fundamentally change the business model for commercially supported free television."* He also foresees the coming challenge of reaching tomorrow's consumers.

Students who want to pursue a media career should be prepared to embrace change as a constant. Brad suggests, *"Explore job opportunities that allow you to develop a greater breadth of media knowledge. See for yourself how learning in one area can be applied in another."* This is the knowledge that will get you through challenge of change.

Discussion Questions.

1. Cross-Platform Integration.

What is cross-platform integration and how is this different from multi-media buying?

What are the important considerations in cross-platform integration? And, how do these considerations reflect conventional media planning?

Why do marketers want to buy into cross-platform deals? What are some of the main reasons for marketer interest?

Why do media companies want to sell package cross-platform deals?

What are the risks for marketers and media companies?

What were some of the first cross-platform deals? Who was the marketer? Which media company?

2. Players in the Cross-Platform World.

How has the U.S. government hindered and promoted the development of cross-platform opportunities?

What are the five largets media companies in the U.S.? How did they get to be what they are today? Was it luck or planning?

The major companies today (Time Warner, Viacom, Disney, NBC Universal) own both TV media assets and motion picture production companies. Why is this significant?

Aside from the handful of big client companies mentioned in this chapter, can you think of some other companies who might benefit from cross-platform integration?

3. The Future of Cross-Platform Integration.

How will cross-platform deals change the media marketplace in the future?

Exercises.

1. Choose one of the top five media companies we mentioned in this chapter. Research the company to identify each of its many media assets. From what you know about each media asset, **recommend 3 possible themed packages that might be sold to client marketers.**

   For example, in the text we talked about the ESPN and ABC sports property assets of the Disney company – you can't use this example.

   Prepare a report for the class, presenting your three favorite themed package ideas.

2. Read through the industry trade press including *Advertising Age*, *AdWeek*, and *Variety*. **Find an example of a cross-platform deal like we've discussed in this chapter.** Find out everything you can about the deal. What do you think of the deal? How is this deal mutually beneficial to the client and the media company? Write a 2-3 page review of the deal. Be sure to explain the details of the deal and how you expect it might or might not be effective in the marketplace.

3. **We've been talking large scale, but now we want you to think smaller scale.** Choose one of the following products:
   - Welch's brand grape jelly
   - Murphy's Oil Soap household cleaner
   - Jackson Hewitt Income Tax and Financial Services

   Imagine you are the media planner for this client product. How would you approach a recommendation for a cross-platform media deal? What media company could you approach and which media assets would you want to use? How would you convince the media company to sell you this package? Prepare a presentation for the class. Assume that the class is the management team for the media company and you need to convince them to do this deal for your client.

Appendix 1: Example Media Plans

Presented in this appendix are three examples of media plans. Each plan was written by one of the authors of this book, based on his or her professional experience as a media planner.

These plans are completely fictionalized with numbers, details and circumstances made up specifically to demonstrate some of the key concepts of this book. To emphasize the fictional nature of this material, we've used fictional brand and product names as well.

Although the brand and product names may seem real, they are not. We've chosen these names to seem most obviously fake in order to further emphasize our point that these plans are made up and NOT REAL. Get it?

Now that we've got that settled, you need to know that each plan is significantly different from the others in several ways. This too, we've done purposefully. Our hope is to illustrate the full range of possibilities and decision-making necessary in media planning.

First, we've chosen three very different product categories and three different approaches for each of three different planning situations. The resulting look, feel, and flow of each plan demonstrates three effective media plan styles. Any one of these three should help guide you effectively through any media planning exercise your teacher may assign.

Then, within each plan you'll see applications of some important concepts from earlier in the book. Following is a short summary of each plan for the approach taken and the concepts demonstrated.

National Traveler luggage and accessories

This is a conventional media plan in many ways. This plan is national in scope and annual in its scheduling with heavy-up emphasis at certain key periods of the year. The media used are traditional and fairly easily and consistently measured so that audience impact can be assessed in terms of Reach, Frequency, and TRPs. The method used here for budget analysis is the Share of Voice competitive spending method and the recommended budget is mid-range by today's standards.

This plan includes several analyses including a competitive spending analysis, a budget analysis, a seasonality analysis, and a simple geographic analysis. Further, this plan incorporates a selection of well-written, quantitative media plan objectives as they relate to marketing and advertising objectives for the fictional client.

This plan style and approach can be easily adapted to incorporate newer or non-traditional media. This kind of plan would be appropriate for application to most consumer goods products or services.

Premium Telecommunications, Inc. PreTel phones and service

This is a low budget very targeted niche media plan in which a company with significant new product news is attempting to make a splash at an important convention. This plan uses a unique "day-in-the-life-of" approach to identify all possible message exposure opportunities available for the reach of convention attendees. Based on this approach, this plan shows how a product on a very small budget can effectively assemble local media in a way that leaves an impression of sponsorship without incurring the cost.

This plan style and approach would be appropriate for use with most business-to-business or business sales marketing efforts.

Orange, Inc. Digi-PAS personal audio system handheld

This plan is written specifically to demonstrate how a product's media plan might be designed in consideration of cross-platform, multi-media deals. In this plan the product message is targeted to teens and young adults, both notoriously hard to reach with mass media. The plan itself shows the use of both quantitative and qualitative objectives building toward a selection of designated media packages from two of the largest US media companies.

This plan style and approach is unique and applicable mostly to cross-platform media planning situations. Some might see this as putting the tactics of media buying before the strategies of media planning. Quite the opposite, this particular write-up shows how to effectively make multi-media buying decisions in the proper context of plan strategies.

So, here we go one last time. The three plans presented here are completely fictionalized. Any resemblance, real or imagined, to any existing brand or product media plan is purely coincidence and unintentional.

National Traveler Luggage and Accessories
Recommended Media Plan

Purpose:

The purpose of this document is to present a calendar year media plan recommendation for National Traveler brand travel luggage and accessories.

Agenda:

I. Executive Summary

II. Background and Analysis

    a. Marketing and Advertising Objectives

    b. Budget Summary

    c. Competitive Analysis

III. Media Plan Objective and Strategies

    a. Media Objective and Rationale

        i. Media Target

        ii. Communication Goals

        iii. Budget Analysis and Recommendation

    b. Media Strategies and Rationale

        i. Seasonality and Scheduling

        ii. Geographic Coverage and Emphasis

        iii. Media Mix

IV. Recommended Media Scheduling and Flowchart

I. Executive Summary

- This year's recommended media plan is significantly more aggressive than previous years.
- In accordance with the brand's goal of share growth, and given an advertising objective of doubling awareness, this plan recommends a 100% increase in media spending. Recommended budget of $6 million in working media.
- In order to achieve a 25% increase in market share the advertising plan calls for a 100% increase in brand awareness to 80%. In order to achieve 80% brand awareness, this media plan delivers a very high reach goal of 90% with an average frequency of 8.1 exposures every six months.
- To accomplish an aggressive reach goal of 90%, this plan utilizes a rich mix of media including national network television, cable television, consumer magazines, and Internet banner advertising.
- Media this year is scheduled to deliver continuity throughout the year building to two key peak points to address the biggest luggage sales seasons of Spring and Fall.

II. Background and Analysis

Marketing Objective

- Within one calendar year, increase the National Traveler brand share of the travel luggage category by 5 percentage points from 20% to 25%.

Advertising Objective

- Double top-of-mind awareness of National Traveler brand luggage to 80% by the end of the year building awareness in increments throughout the travel and gift season as follows:

  From Base Awareness 40%

  To Spring Gift and Summer Travel at 60%

  To Fall Gift and Holiday Travel at 80%

Budget Summary

- The client allocated budget for the calendar year is $6,000,000 total.

  Working Media $5,500,000

  Advertising Production $ 500,000

- This is an investment budget intended by the client to drive incremental sales volume.

Competitive Analysis

- Focus competitors in this category are Samsonite, Hartmann, Louis Vuitton, and specialty brand Eddie Bauer.

Market Share

- National Traveler brand luggage is the #2 brand in the category and Samsonite is the category share leader.

	Previous Year Percent of Sales
Samsonite	35%
National Traveler	20%
Hartmann	13%
Louis Vuitton	8%
Eddie Bauer	5%
Other brands	19%

Competitive Media Spending

- Media spending for the travel luggage category peaked at a total of almost $18,000,000 largely driven by investment spending behind Louis Vuitton and the Eddie Bauer brand launch.
- After a sharp decline, spending recently has rebounded to $15 million and industry projections suggest further increases in the coming year.

- Samsonite is the leading advertiser with a budget of $6 million each year for the past several years.

Past Three Years' Total Advertising Spending By Brand ($000)

	Year 1	Year 2	Year 3
Samsonite	$5,828	$5,975	$6,031
Nat'l Trav	2,500	1,799	3,000
Hartmann	1,200	1,378	1,425
L Vuitton	3,513	1,775	1,239
E Bauer	3,781	2,012	1,953
Others	1,109	998	1,302
Total	$17,931	$13,937	$14,950

Industry Spending by Advertising Medium

- Magazines and Network Television are the primary media of the travel luggage category.

Past Three Years' Consolidated Category Spending By Medium

Magazines	32%
Network Television	29%
Cable Television	13%
Spot Television	11%
Newspapers	9%
Radio	6%
Total	100%

Industry Spending by Calendar Quarter

- Category advertising is for the most part concentrated in the spring and fall; these two quarters are big gift and travel planning seasons leading up to annual travel peaks in the summer and over the Holidays.

Past Three Years' Consolidated Category Spending By Quarter

Jan thru Mar	9%
Apr thru Jun	44%
Jul thru Sep	7%
Oct thru Dec	40%
Total	100%

III. Media Plan Objective and Strategies

Media Objectives

Primary Objective: Reach cumulative 90% of US adult travelers an average of 8 times each six months of the year.

Secondary Objective: Maintain a minimum base level of 40% reach with a monthly frequency of 2 or better among US adult travelers during the off-peak months of January, February, July and August.

Rationale:

- A high primary reach goal is appropriate given the aggressive advertising objective of 80% awareness, double the current level.
- Seasonal emphasis is appropriate and consistent with industry sales and spending trends.
- The recommended planning target audience of Adult Travelers represents a total audience of approximately 100 million adults.

Travelers are:

Equally male/female	(48/52)
Aged 25 – 54	60% (Index of 110)
College educated	45% (Index of 129)
Above average Income	48% (Index of 125)

- The measurement target for media analysis and buying purposes will be Adults 25 – 54.

Budget Analysis and Recommendation

- The National Traveler brand marketing goal for the year is a five-point growth in share representing a 25% real gain in market share versus the competition.
- To accomplish this marketing goal, the advertising objective calls for a 100% increase in top-of-mind brand awareness.
- Appropriately, this media plan recommends a 100% increase in media spending, from $3,000,000 last year to $6,000,000 this year.
- This requires an increase of $500,000 compared to the client's allocated budget; effectively the cost of production.

	Client Allocation	Agency Recommendation
Working Media	$5,500,000	$6,000,000
Production	$ 500,000	$ 500,000
Total Budget	$6,000,000	$6,500,000

Media Strategies

Seasonality and Scheduling

- Schedule media for continuous coverage in each of the primary months (Mar-Jun and Sep-Dec) building throughout each season to heavy-up coverage in the most peak months

  Nov/Dec combined 32% of luggage sales

  May/Jun combined 19% of luggage sales

- Schedule media for lower coverage in the off-season, secondary months (Jan/Feb and Jul/Aug).

Rationale:

- Overall sales volume by month skews heavily to November and December followed next by May and June.

Total Luggage Category

	Percent Sales	Index
Jan	4%	48
Feb	5	60
Mar	5	60
Apr	5	60
May	9	108
Jun	10	120
Jul	5	60
Aug	9	108
Sep	8	96
Oct	8	96
Nov	11	132
Dec	21	252
Total	100%	100

Geographic Coverage and Emphasis

- Schedule media for national coverage with no regional emphasis.

Rationale:

- Virtually no regional skew to the sales of the luggage category in general.

Total Luggage Category

	Percent Sales	Index
New England	4.5%	87
Mid-Atlantic	17.4%	101
East Central	13.1%	102
West Central	15.0%	99
South East	20.5%	101
South West	10.8%	95
Pacific	18.7%	105
Total	100.0%	100

Media Mix

- Use a rich mix of national network and cable television together with consumer magazines and Internet to achieve the high reach goals of the plan.

    Network television will be used to emphasize reach only during most peak months of May/Jun and Nov/Dec

    Cable television will be used to lay a base of quality reach television coverage throughout the primary seasons March-June and September-December.

    Consumer magazines and Internet will be used to provide a base level of continuity throughout the year

- Utilize a daypart mix for Network Television to provide high reach among the target audience segments

    Use Morning News and Late Fringe in combination (50/50)

    Networks and programs selected to deliver a balance of both male and female travelers

- Utilize a core mix of cable networks to balance reach and ensure frequency throughout the peak seasons

    Select cable TV networks specifically to compliment the Network Television schedule

    Schedule for high frequency on the core cable network list

- Exclusively utilize 15-second television units to extend the budget for optimal reach delivery

- Utilize a broad mix of consumer magazines to build reach and frequency with the target market

    Select titles to deliver a balance of male and female travelers

    Schedule a minimum of 6 insertions per year for monthlies, 12 insertions per year for weekly magazines

- Schedule a 12-month continuous rotation of Internet banner ad placements on the major travel service websites.

IV. Recommended Media Plan and Flowchart

Plan Budget by Medium

Media	Budget
Network TV	$1,546,526
Cable TV	$2,477,500
Magazines	$1,710,640
Internet	$ 250,000
Total	$5,984,666

Plan Delivery Relative to Goals

Calendar Period	R/F Goal	R/F Delivery	Index to Goal
Off-Peak Months	40/2.0	41/1.8	94
Six Month Cume	90/8.0	90/8.1	102

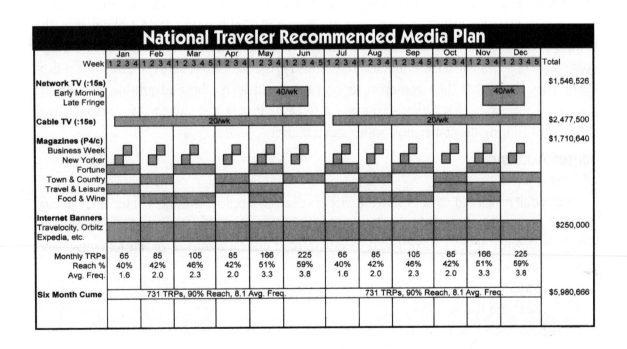

Premium Telecommunications, Inc. – PreTel Media Plan

Media Plan Overview

The awareness blitz campaign for PreTel during the CTIA Wireless Convention (Feb. 8-10) in New Orleans calls for thorough message encounter saturation of the target group of business attendees of this convention at all possible times during their stay.

To account for their hectic schedules and subsequently lack of traditional media advertising opportunities, a niche media campaign, encompassing media encounters during all phases of the typical attendees' routines (airport arrival, expo presence, after-hours happy hours in town), is recommended. The proposed media budget reflects the objectives set for this campaign, which can be summarized as turning the CTIA convention into a PreTel convention.

Situation Analysis

Premium Telecommunications Inc., the wireless service and accessories company out of San Diego, CA, invented a combination cell phone-PDA device, named "pdQ Phone," and improved the technology with which cell phone calls are transmitted (enhanced CDMA technology). The company is planning to announce/unveil these developments during the next annual wireless convention (the Cellular Telecommunications Industry Association (CTIA) Wireless Expo) in February. They have asked their agency to support this event with a blitz advertising effort in the convention's host city, New Orleans. The goal is to create instant and ongoing buzz among major stakeholders during the conference, with a small budget.

Target Audience

Objective:

Reach adult males and females who are wireless dealers, resellers, members of the trade media, or other important cellular and electronics stakeholders and opinion leaders that either are affected by the new inventions or could otherwise have critical influence on PreTel's image and business success.

Demographics:

Adult males and females, 18+

Household income of $30,000+

Influential in wireless industry: shareholders, government officials, business executives, retail management executives, media representatives, dealers and suppliers

Residents of United States (secondary: any other country)

Psychographics:

Skeptical about traditional advertising and PR

Knowledgeable about PreTel and competitors' products

Time-pressed and bottom-line oriented

Rationale:

Generating instant word-of-mouth publicity and goodwill among an audience that can be considered in a gate-keeping role for both brand and company image, makes this the key trade target to reach during the few days of the conference.

Strategy:

The biggest challenge will be to get them to pay attention to the messages. Given their compressed schedules, it is essential to generate unavoidable media encounters in order to create buzz among members of this group. Since it is unlikely that they will consume traditional media during their conference days, non-traditional (surprise) media vehicles will be used.

Geography/ Reach & Frequency

Objective:

Expose conference attendees to PreTel's message at any possible venue they frequent in New Orleans (work-hours and after-hours) from the moment they arrive at the airport to the moment they leave. This includes airport area, transit to hotels, convention arena, French Quarter, and related entertainment districts.

Although R/F are hard to measure for this campaign, the targeted goal is maximum reach (80-90) with sufficient encounter repetition (3-5) over the course of five days.

Rationale:

The above objective is based on a "day-in-the-life-of" research approach that meticulously considers the movement of target audience members from their first day to last day during their stay, and overlays possible media encounter opportunities around town. Reach and frequency objectives are derived from the marketing goal (instant exposure, blanketing of the "market," recall effects, word-of-mouth snowball-style buzz).

Strategy:

Critical encounter venues are the airport (New Orleans International Airport), the various fleets of taxicab companies (e.g. Yellow Cab, Medallion Cab), the CTIA-recommended conference hotels (Holiday Inn, Hilton, Wyndham), the conference center (Ernest N. Morial Convention Center), and the entertainment district (French Quarter, downtown, Mississippi River boardwalk).

Media Mix

Airport:

Standard-sized, back illuminated displays distributed throughout the main terminal arrival and departure areas will provide an early exposure to attendees. Furthermore, acting as moving billboards, baggage carts that circulate throughout all areas of an airport, will be used to support the goal of high reach and frequency.

Transit:

Because taxis go where people go, taxi media offer high frequency via daily exposure. Their 24-hour presence on freeways, in downtown areas, airports and business communities guarantees complete market penetration and maximum exposure. Taxi top and back advertisements deliver eye-level impact directly to consumers. The illuminated two-sided taxi tops reach suburban commuters, tourists, and pedestrians on both sides of the street and infiltrate the French Quarter and conference area at every corner.

The additional use of taxi receipt advertising provides additional punch to the program as most conference goers keep their receipts to submit them for expense reimbursements after the conference.

Hotel:

The chosen conference hotels customarily offer a complimentary copy of *USA Today* to their guests in the morning via drop at the room door. Research has shown that between 60-80% of business travelers read their complimentary morning paper within 2-4 hours of picking it up. A sleeve wrap (roughly 5 inches), holding the folded paper, will provide a daily reminder during the time that attendees prepare for their conference day.

Convention Center:

Hot dog/snack food stands on the plaza in front of the main entrance to the convention arena as well as in the rotunda (perimeter walkway inside the expo space) are convenient and inexpensive locations for refreshments without leaving the conference vicinity. These hot dog stands are highly visible due to their colorful umbrellas and signage. PreTel's name will appear on these umbrellas and cart signs during conference days.

In addition, small announcements and placement of the company logo in the daily conference program – handed out at the badge checkpoint into the expo space – will provide additional exposure opportunities in a vehicle that many attendees consume to get updates on the day's events.

Tourism:

Royal Carriages of New Orleans' fleet of mule-drawn carriages offers transport to and from hotels, meetings and restaurants as well as service to the Riverwalk, New Orleans Convention Center and the Superdome. Their sightseeing tours of the sights and sounds of the French Quarter are a popular tourist activity. Their advertising program allows placement of a logo and message on their carriages throughout the duration of a convention. This non-traditional medium will supply a huge impact for the overall plan.

Moreover, directly across from the Morial Convention Center is a popular restaurant/bar venue that allows advertisers to hang a gigantic banner (so-called building wrap) on its structure. Having PreTel's name prominently displayed this way reveals its true impact when attendees exit the conference center at night and can't help but face the building across the street.

Rationale:

All chosen media do not only work hard in their function as surprising encounter vehicles, but they are in their own rights creative enough to connect the PreTel name with innovativeness. Using these media in combination will guarantee recognition and awareness without appearing intrusive or like a traditional advertisement.

Scheduling

Objective:

As the attached media flowchart illustrates, the campaign will begin two days prior to the conference start day (February 6) in media that will be encountered early during the conference. In the subsequent days, more media will be added selectively. Transit and airport media will run until the day after the conference to reach late check-out segments of the target audience.

Rationale:

Traditionally, some conference goers arrive at the conference site early to have a few days to themselves for preparations and relaxation. In addition, those segments of the conference attendees who have to work late on the last day of the conference (expo booth take-downs, business negotiations, etc.) will not check out until the day after the conference has finished.

Budget

Objective:

To achieve maximum exposure and recall effects within a budget of $10,000.

Rationale:

This budget was set using an objective/task method. That is, the cost to purchase the above-mentioned media delivery determined the budget.

Awareness results will be measured post-conference to guage the effectiveness of the plan.

Premium Telecommunications, Inc. - Niche Media Plan
CTIA Wireless Expo, New Orleans

Advertising Medium	Feb														
	1	2	3	4	5	6	7	8	9	10	11	12	13	14	15
Airport															
Diorama															
Baggage Cart															
Transit/Taxi															
Tops, Backs															
Receipt															
Tourism															
Carriage back															
Banner (House wrap)															
Convention Center															
Hot dog stands															
Info brochure															
Hotels															
Newspaper sleeve															
TOTAL															
Conference Days															

Orange, Inc. – Digi-PAS Media Plan and Execution

Marketing Overview

- Orange, Inc. was the first brand to enter the digital music category with its Digi-PAS personal audio system handheld.
- As the first product in this market, Orange, Inc. is the category leader still holding a share of approximately 60%.
- Digi-PAS product penetration is approximately 40% and aiming to grow another 10% annually in the coming fiscal year (July – June).
- Current brand awareness for Orange is in the 90% plus range with individual product awareness ranging from a high of 75% to a low of 10%.
    - The Digi-PAS product currently enjoys awareness levels of 75%
- As a rule, Orange product sales are skewed toward major metropolitan areas.
- Orange, Inc. has achieved significant market growth via on-going partnerships with key retailers.

Marketing and Advertising Objectives

- Reinforce Orange, Inc. leadership
    - Strengthen #1 brand position
- Increase Orange, Inc. corporate volume + 12.3%
- Achieve Orange brand and Digi-PAS product awareness levels of 90% among targeted consumers.
- Achieve advertising awareness and message recognition of 70% among targeted consumers
- Strengthen partnership with key retail accounts.
- Build on momentum generated by recent targeted promotional efforts.
- Capitalize on the musical equities of the product and the current advertising campaign

Media Objectives & Strategies

- Overall Media Plan Objective; Capitalize on the musical equities of the product and the current advertising campaign to achieve marketing objectives
- Target –
    - Objectives; Reach current consumer base to increase awareness and Digi-PAS purchase penetration
    - Strategies: Provide advertising support to reach People 12-34 – expected to be critical in generating incremental volume.

- Geography -
    - Objectives; Focus advertising in key markets to build on the brand's strengths and the product's opportunities
    - Strategies: Support national business to maintain Orange brand awareness and increase local support in important retailers' markets and high volume markets
- Seasonality and Scheduling
    - Objectives; Deliver on-going continuity and capitalize on periods of higher interest and seasonal sales variance.
    - Strategies: Maximize brand presence throughout the year with increased emphasis preceding the anticipated higher sales periods around the beginning and end of the school year and the holiday gift giving period.
- Communication Levels
    - Objectives; Generate high levels of awareness among prospective purchasers to motivate purchase. Utilize appropriate marketing environments to support the Digi-PAS product message.
    - Strategies: Generate high levels of plan reach with significant levels of frequency to increase awareness.
        - Primary Target — Heaviest advertising in priority top ten volume markets with promotional level support in key retail markets and base level support in high opportunity markets, as afforded
            - National Base Plan: 95% reach / 85% reach at the 3 or more frequency level / 19 time average frequency / 1,800 TRPs
            - Key Market incremental Plan: 95% reach / 90% reach at the 3 or more frequency level / 27 time average frequency / 2,600 TRPs

Buy Overview

- Corporate-wide, Orange brand media requirements were achieved through a consolidated media purchase with the Brand's specific needs achieved through multi-year, cross-platform deals with two key sellers:
    - Time Warner
        - The foundation of the Time Warner deal is a promotional tie in with Time Warner Music Group which provides free music downloads for purchasers of this product.
    - Viacom
        - The foundation of the Viacom deal is the placement of this product in many Teen and Young Adult targeted "Reality" programs and music programs on each of Viacom's music networks.

Plan Components

Time Warner

- WB Television Network
  - Significant Primetime Television schedules throughout the Teen and Young Adult oriented WB Television network Primetime schedule.
  - Single sponsor programs custom produced to air on The WB Network.
- Warner Brothers Film and Television Production
  - Custom produced Music events / programs to appear on the WB Network in July, November and March as single sponsor programs.
  - Product placement in selected Television Programs and Motion Pictures.
- Time Warner Cable Television
  - Local Cable TV advertising schedules in selected key retailer markets.
- Time Warner Music Group
  - Sponsorship and on-venue involvement in concert tours of selected artists. Sponsorships to tie into custom produced Network TV programs noted above.
  - Access to the library of Time Warner Music companies like Atlantic, Elektra, Reprise and Warner Brothers Records available as downloadable online premiums for promotional purposes.
- AOL Online Services
  - On-going presence at high level on America Online (AOL) used to promote the brand and its association with the artists above, including the free download promotion.
- Time Warner Magazines
  - Advertising schedules in selected Teen and Young Adult oriented magazine titles like, Sports Illustrated, SI for Kids, People, Teen People, Entertainment Weekly and In Style used to reach audiences in relevant editorial environments including adjacencies to reviews of new music and musical performers.

Viacom

- CBS Television Network
  - Significant Primetime Television schedules throughout selected Teen and Young Adult oriented CBS Television network Primetime, Late Night and Sports programming.
  - Sponsor involvement in marquee CBS Sports programs (2007 Superbowl) and special events
  - Single sponsor programs custom produced to air on The CBS Television Network.
- CBS (Television) Stations
  - Significant local (spot) TV schedules in key retailer markets designed to provide on-going continuity in network programming used above.

- Cable Television
  - Significant schedules on selected Viacom cable TV networks including; music oriented networks, MTV, VH1, and CMT and entertainment networks BET, Spike, and Comedy Central.
  - Sponsorship involvement with selected major events like the MTV Music Awards and Nickelodeon Teen Choice Awards.
- Infinity Radio Stations
  - On-going continuity schedules in key retailer markets promoting the product and the free download promotion secured as part of the Time Warner deal.
  - Access to local on-air personalities for product promotion including; on-air live promotions, local promotions (in addition to national promotions) and personal appearances.
- Westwood 1 Radio Networks
  - On-going continuity schedules on selected Westwood 1 radio networks.
  - Title sponsorship of live broadcasts of major concert series.
- Paramount Pictures
  - Product placement in selected Teen and Young Adult Television Programs and Motion Pictures.

Glossary:

Here are media terms you should know.

35% Ownership Cap – A government enforced limit on the extent of media ownership within a market.

Above-the-line – All expenditures appropriated to advertising media.

Accountability – To be held responsible for recommendations and show that these actions help contribute to the overall marketing communications goals.

ADI (Area of Dominant Influence) – Arbitron's mutually exclusive TV marketing areas defined by counties where the majority of total TV viewing occurs.

Adjacencies – In print, the editorial content next to the print ad. In broadcast, the programs next to a TV or radio commercial.

Advertorial – Long-form print advertisement delivering a custom-written blend of advertising and editorial content.

Afternoon drive – Weekday commuting hours from 4:00 to 7:00 p.m. when radio usage increases dramatically.

All Commodity Volume (ACV) – A grocery industry standard measure of the percent of product sales volume achieved by a given store within a given market.

Alternative newspapers – Weeklies that present non-mainstream ideas, lifestyles, and viewpoints – usually in a tabloid format.

Arbitron – A national audience measurement service that provides ratings for radio and television stations.

Audience – the number of subjects, people or households, exposed to a medium.

Audience Composition – Description of a media vehicle's total audience in terms of demographic classification of individuals.

Audience Profile – Description of characteristics, physical, psychosocial or behavioral, of a medium's audience.

Bandwidth – Digital transmission capacity, the number of bits per second (bps) that can be transmitted or received through a given channel.

Barter – The practice of selling advertising time and space in exchange for goods or services, not money.

Below-the-line – All promotional expenditures which are not allocated to paid media advertising.

Best Food Day – Designated day of the week (usually Thursday or Wednesday) when newspapers feature food product or supermarket advertising and coupons, frequently with related articles on health, recipes, etc.

Billboards – Large outdoor structures posted with advertising messages, erected in strategically chosen areas to reach the maximum number of passersby per day.

Bit – Short for binary digit, the basis of the binary language of computer code. Simply a "1" or "0".

Bleed – a print media term used to describe an advertisement that runs larger than the usual margins of space. Bleed ads are commonly charged at a premium price.

Blinkering – One of four types of ad schedules that is characterized with short in-and-out bursts of advertising throughout the ad campaign period. Hiatuses are approximately the same length and are brief.

Boolean Search – Internet search strategy using words and combinations fo words in logical (mathematical) operations – AND, OR, NOT, etc.

Brand contact points – An IMC concept referring to every instance in which a consumer interacts with a brand – from seeing the package on the shelf, the logo at a sporting event, a mention in an article, or an ad. Each of these is a brand contact point.

Brand Development Index (BDI) – Standardized measure indicating the strengths and weaknesses of a brand's business. Commonly applied geographically but also applicable in any situation where data can be distinguished into discretely defined cells (see Seasonal Development Index).

Broadcast – To transmit a radio or TV program to a mass audience.

Bulletin – The largest standard billboard structure, measuring 14 x 48 (672 square) feet, generally erected in or near high-density traffic areas.

Business-to-business advertising media - Media which specialize in business-based communication, primarily trade magazines.

Byte – A string of 8 bits with a total of 256 possible unique permutations of 1s and 0s.

Cable Television – Signals received through either coaxial cable or satellite dish, as opposed to those sent via airwave and received through antennae.

Circulation – The total number of copies of a newspaper or magazine distributed by subscription, newsstand, and/or bulk.

Click-through Rate – A percentage comparing the number of times an ad is clicked to the total number of times the ad is viewed.

Clutter – Quantity of messages which compete for attention within a media vehicle, a medium, or in the media environment overall.

Commercial Break – Used in broadcast media to mean the period of time, representing an interruption of the programming, during which advertisements are broadcast.

Consultative Selling – "marketing driven" sales approach used by media sales representatives who approach media sales as marketing consultants.

Continuity – Refers to a continuous ad schedule where media weight is scheduled constantly throughout the year with no variation in the amount of advertising and no hiatus.

Controlled Circulation – Publications distributed to select audience members and generally free of charge.

Convergence – The combination of disparate technologies or media into new products and services.

Cookie – A line of text written into an computer text file and placed on a computer user's hard drive.

Co-Op (Cooperative Advertising) – Retail advertising that is partly or fully funded by a manufacturer.

Cost Efficiency – A calculated relationship between the cost of a media vehicle or a media schedule relative to the audience delivery of the vehicle or schedule. This calculation is done for purposes of comparison between and among options being considered.

Cost per point (CPP) – Used in cases where rating points are used to represent the audience delivery of a media vehicle or a media schedule

Cost per Thousand (CPM) – Method of comparison whereby the cost of an advertising vehicle is multiplied by a thousand and divided into the vehicle's total audience. The CPM shows how much it costs to reach a thou-sand audience members, and thus it can be used to compare which advertising vehicles are most cost efficient.

Coverage – A measure of a medium's audience potential, commonly expressed as a percentage of the total possible audience. Depending on the media, coverage may be used in reference to a geographic audience or some other audience population – people or households.

Cross-Platform – Multiple media activities executed within one media company.

Customer Relationship Marketing (CRM) – A tactical marketing practice based exclusively on customer behavior and the relationship between customer and marketer.

Daily impressions – Billboards that reach members of a market's population in one given day.

Database – Storage location of business data and information.

Daypart – A particular period of time within a day. Applicable to broadcast media. Standardized daypart definitions are used to separate the broader media day into more homogeneous sub-segments.

Demographics – Term used to refer to the physical characteristics of people. The most commonly used demographic variables are age and gender.

Designated Market Area (DMI) – Nielsen's mutually exclusive TV marketing areas defined by counties based on the dominant TV station viewership in the county.

Diary – Audience measurement technique where participants are asked to record in writing all their listening, viewing, or reading activities.

Digitization – The translation of any kind of information – data, text, graphics, sound – into a binary transmittable language.

Direct Response Marketing – Any marketing communication designed to prompt an immediate response action from the consumer or prospect.

Double Truck – A two-page newspaper spread where the editorial content or advertising runs across the gutter.

Drive Time – Morning and afternoon time spent by commuters listening to their car radios.

Duopolies – Same-company media ownership of two stations in one local market.

Duplication – Measure of audience members who are counted more than one time in an audience measurement. Refers to duplication of audience within the same medium or across multiple media.

Entertainment Brand – A media property that stands out from its competition because it has a distinct personality, trademark, name, identity, or visual appeal.

Entertainment Marketing – Any of a number of marketing activities resulting from a relationship between a marketer and an entertainment property of any kind.

Exclusivity – A guarantee of freedom from competitive advertising messages within a particular medium. Advertisers will typically pay a higher price or commit a heavier schedule in order to secure such a guarantee and lock-out of the competition.

Exposure – A measure of likely contact with an advertisement. The measurement is based on the number of people who say that they have read or looked at a given magazine, watched a given television program, or listened to a particular radio station.

Flighting – One of four types of ad schedules which includes periodic waves of advertising followed by long periods of total inactivity.

Financial Interest and Syndication Rule (Fin-Syn) (1970) – A ruling by the Federal Communications Commission (FCC) that limited media company ownership and financial interest in the production of television programming content.

Flowchart – Graphic representation of a media schedule. Features specific details of the media plan including media vehicles, schedule timing, weight levels, and budget.

Free-Standing Insert (FSI) – A newspaper-distributed media vehicle used to deliver promotional messages and coupons for multiple marketers.

Frequency – The number of times an individual or household is exposed to an advertising message over a certain period of time.

GRP (Gross Rating Points) – The summation of rating points. A duplicated figure that shows how much weight a particular media buy is delivering.

High-involvement – Refers to a product that requires considerable thought and consideration from consumers when it comes to purchase – a computer, for example.

HTML – Hyper Text Markup Language – universally accepted internet text language system allowing virtually any computer anywhere to be able to read the content of a Web page.

HUT (Households Using Television) – A Nielsen term which refers to the percentage of households that is tuning into television at a given time.

Impressions – A measure of the total audience of a media schedule. A raw-number sum of the duplicated audiences of all media vehicles combined in media schedule.

In-bound Telemarketing – Consumers use their telephones to initiate a call for more product information or to purchase a product. The consumer calls in to the call center.

Index – a standardized ratio of numbers most often relating a percentage to a particular base for purposes of identifying above or below average magnitude.

Infomercial – Long-form broadcast advertisement that provides detailed product information and/or demonstrations. May run as long as 30 minutes or even more.

Interactivity – The degree to which any communication may proceed back and forth between sender and receiver.

Intermedia Comparison – A comparison among different media. For example, radio compared to television.

Interstitials – Full-screen advertisements that appear before ISP connection or avter ISP logout from the Internet.

Intramedia Comparison – A comparison of media vehicles within a given media class. For example, daytime television compared to primetime television.

Keywords – Words or phrases that describe the subject matter of a Web site or Web page.

Kiosks – Free-standing computer displays typically found in airports, rail terminals, malls, and stores, usually equipped with touch-screen technology

Lifestyle Variables – Term used to refer to the measurable physical or psychosocial characteristics of a population. Some of the commonly used measures include, education, occupation, household income, and presence of children in the household.

Local Advertising – Term used to refer to the advertisements placed by local retailers.

Local Media – Any media whose coverage is limited to its particular geographic market of origin.

Low-involvement – Refers to a product that requires little thought and consideration from consumers when it comes to purchase - a package of gum, for example.

Mailing List – A consolidated collection of names and mailing addresses.

Market – Specific geographic area. Can range in size from a small city or town to the full size of the United States.

Market Profile – Used two ways. 1) a description of a specific geographic area. This description will included definitions of the people and the economy of the market. 2) a description of the people or households who buy or may buy a particular product.

Market share – Measure of the percentage of a given market dominated by a particular product. For example, Budweiser beer holds a 16% share of the beer sales market.

Media – Plural term used to refer to all means that can be used to speak on behalf of a brand. Traditional media include newspapers, magazines, radio, television, outdoor and Yellow Pages. Nontraditional media can be far-reaching, from fruit stickers to T-shirts.

Media Fragmentation – The splintering of mass media audiences into small, specific groups.

Media List – A PR term meaning a list of key media contacts (names and addresses) usually maintained by the PR firm.

Media Objectives – These are the goals of the media plan that specifically state what the course of action will be to help achieve the marketing goals.

Media Plan – Written course of action that tells how media will be used to help achieve marketing objectives.

Media Rep (representative) – Person employed by a media company that sells either time or space to advertisers.

Media Strategy – These are statements that specifically outline how the media will be used to help achieve the marketing goals. They flow directly out of the media objectives.

Medium – One of the forms of communications that can be used to deliver advertising messages to consumers (e.g., magazine is a medium; newspaper is a medium).

Metropolitan Statistical Area (MSA) – A specific geographic area defined by the Federal government according to certain criteria including population, metropolitan character and culture, and economic and social integration with surrounding communities.

Moore's Law – Named for Gordon Moore of Intel, it is the observation of the general engineering principle that computing power essentially doubles every 18 months.

Morning Drive – Weekday commuting hours fom 6 to 10 AM when radio usage increases dramatically.

MRI (Mediamark Research, Inc.) – A national company that supplies syndicated information on media audiences' demographic characteristics, audience media exposure, and product/brand usage profile data.

Multimedia – The combination of computational data, text, graphics, and sound into one package.

Multi-Media – Media planning and/or buying activities involving the use of more than one media vehicle.

Narrowcast – Specialized electronic programming or any other specific medium that is geared toward a specific target audience, thus delivering a narrow portion of the total media audience.

Newsletter – A type of publication that deals with the special interests of a particular group.

Newspaper – A publication that is issued for use by the general public at frequent and regular time periods.

Niche Media – Specialized types of media geared toward distinct groups of viewers, listeners, and readers.

Nielsen (A.C. Nielsen Co.) – 1. A national company that measures both local and national audience television viewing as well as other marketing research. 2. TV ratings from Nielsen.

Nontraditional Media – Media that are often driven by technology and can be any new media form that allows for commercial expression.

O&O (Owned and operated station) – A station that is owned and operated by a network.

On Target – A media recommendation that has succeeded in reaching its specified target audience members.

Out-bound Telemarketing – When a telemarketing firm initiates the telephone call to contact consumers about its product or service. The call center calls out to the target consumer.

Outdoor – Billboard advertising that comes in three formats: bulletins, 30-sheets, and 8-sheets.

Out-of-home advertising – Forms of advertising located outside of the home, which include traditional and place-based media. Includes: aerial/inflatables, bus shelters, telephone kiosks, bus benches, outdoor (billboards), transit, and taxi advertising.

Paramount Decree (1948) – A major government ruling that forced large studio companies to sell off ownership of certain other assets, such as movie theaters.

Pass-along Readership – Magazine that gets read by a person other than the subscriber or the purchaser of the magazine. Pass-along readers are those who get the magazine secondhand, patients waiting in a doctor's reception room, for example.

Pixel – One picture element of a graphic image.

Place-based Media – Advertising that occurs at places where consumers intersect with brand messages. This can include airport and in-store advertising opportunities.

Plug-ins – Small, free, downloadable programs that enable rich media banners to function.

Pop-unders – A less intrusive version of a pop-up. A pop-under appears behind the onscreen web content and is only discovered when the main screen is closed or minimized.

Pop-ups – Unsolicited advertisements of varying sizes that appear onscreen in front of Website content.

PR Newswire – The company name of a national service that distributes marketer press releases directly to media newsrooms via wire service machines.

Precision Marketing – Marketing aimed at a specific segment or even individuals.

Price/item Advertising – Also known as display advertising – a form of local display newspaper advertising where a variety of merchandise is displayed in the ad with a description and a price.

Product as Media – A term used here to describe a marketer's use of product to deliver a marketing message. Includes the use of the product itself as well as the product package.

Product Placement – The specific practice of integrating a branded marketer's product clearly and visibly into an entertainment property.

Proprietary Database – A consolidated collection of consumer/customer information owned and maintained by a marketer for its own proprietary use.

Prospects – Individuals identified as those most predisposed to buying a company's product or service.

Psychographic – A term used to describe the psychological characteristics of a group of people – often based on the expressed attitudes or beliefs of the group.

Pulsing – One of four types of ad schedules which combines continuity and flighting. Pulsing includes a continuous base of advertising that is reinforced by periodic bursts of heavier media action.

PUT (Person Using Television) – A Nielsen term that refers to the percentage of individuals who tune into television during a given time period. It reports the total persons tuned into TV, not to specific programs.

Rate Card – A listing published by print and broadcast media that show advertising costs, mechanical requirements, issue dates, closing dates, and circulation information.

Ratings – A figure that reports the number of different individuals who tuned into the electronic media or read the print media over a specific time period.

Rating Points – The percentage of individuals who tune into a particular program for a specific time.

Reach – The number or percentage of different individuals who tune in, listen to, read, or interact with the media over a specific time period.

Readership – A term used to refer to a publication's audience which tells the total number of different persons reading an average copy of a magazine.

Representative – Also known as a "Rep." This is a term used to describe sales people who act or work as agents representing specific media vehicles. A representative firm may handle several media vehicles within a particular media class. (See Media Rep)

ROP (Run of the press, or run of paper) – A newspaper ad insertion that runs anywhere in that paper. Position not specified.

Rotary Bulletins – Billboard or other outdoor that can be moved from one location to another for maximize exposure in different locales.

Search Engine Optimization (SEO) – A strategy for increasing the number of visitors to a web site by ranking high in the search results of a search engine.

Seasonal Development Index – Standardized measure indicating the seasonal strengths and weaknesses of a brand's business. This characteristic is also referred to as "seasonality."

Sheets – Poster panels printed with advertisements and affixed to billboards to display an ad message.

Showings – A collection of poster panels or bulletins that cover a specific market. Usually referred to as 100, 50, or 25 showing (100%, 50%, or 25% of the market).

SMRB (Simmons Market Research Bureau) - National research company that provides syndicated information on media audiences' demographic characteristics, audience media exposure, and product/brand usage profile data.

Space Rep – "Rep" is slang for representative. A space rep is someone who sells print media.

Sports Marketing – Any of a number of marketing activities resulting specifically from a relationship between a marketer and a sports property (person, equipment, team, league, stadium, and/or media coverage).

Spot TV/Spot Radio – Purchasing television or radio on a market-by-market basis.

Standard Rate and Data Service (SRDS) – Service that publishes advertising rates, discount structures, mechanical requirements, closing dates, production capabilites, and other important media information.

Superstation – Local independent television stations that uplink their signals onto a communication satellite, giving them national exposure.

Syndication – Television programs that are sold, licensed, and distributed to stations by independent firms.

Syndicated Research – Data that is sold to companies by independent research firms.

Target market – A group of individuals that has been identified as having real sales potential for the brand and can be defined in concrete terms that can include demographics, psychographics, product usage, etc.

Target Profile – For media planning purposes, the target audience is quantified and defined in terms of demographics, psychographics, product usage, and media usage.

Telecommunications Act (1996) – The act of congressional legislation that deregulated the media industry, negating some of the previous ownership limitations established with the Paramount Decree and the fin-syn ruling.

Telemarketing – Any of a number of marketing communications activities involving the use of a telephone.

Themed Marketing – Marketing activities developed around a common theme or focus that resonates with the brand or with its promotional approach.

Time Shifting – process where in TV viewers videotape a show and then watch it at a different time that is more convenient to them.

Trade Marketing – A term used to describe any of a number of marketing tactics focused on the intermediaries or business customers of a marketer.

Traditional Media – These include newspapers, magazine, television, radio, outdoor advertising, and Yellow Pages – media that are established and have been in the marketplace for a long time.

Tutorial – A short, self-guided tour of a computer program wherein the user learns how to use a piece of new software or hardware.

Unit Cost – The amount of money charged for a specific unit of time or space in the media.

URL – Universal Resource Locator – a fancy name for a Website address.

Zapping – Switching commercials off.

Zipping – Fast-forwarding through commercials.

Index:

Website Index: